A glimpse into
MELBOURN's
past

The Melbourn Village History Group
Sponsored by The Local Heritage *initiative*

Published by The Melbourn Village History Group,
Melbourn Village, Cambridgeshire.

Published 2005

© Melbourn Village History Group 2005

Concept, design and production Peter & Jan Simmonett

Text researched and compiled by Ann Dekkers, Peter Dekkers,
Mavis Howard, Eric Johnston, Colin Limming, Terry Rolt,
Jan Simmonett, Peter Simmonett and Sally Wright.

Illustrations, maps and layout by Peter & Jan Simmonett
except illustrations *pp.24–25* ©Albion Archaeology

Acknowledgements

The Melbourn Village History Group would like to thank the following for
their help and contribution to the History Project: *The Antiquarian Society*;
Barbara Birch; Daphne Black; Holly Duncan, *Albion Archaeology*; Ray Ellis;
Tim Hallett; Charmian Hawkins, *Historic Buildings, South Cambs District Council*;
Chris Jakes, *Cambridgeshire Collection*; Brenda Meliniotis; Dr. Dennis Mills; Craig
Peacock; *Peterhouse College Library, Cambridge*; Sarah Poppy, *Cambridge County
Council Archaeology Department*; Sovati Smith, *The British Museum*; Anne Taylor,
University of Cambridge Museum of Archaeology and Anthropology; Mary Woodcock.

Copyright Photographs

We are grateful to the following and permission to reproduce their photographs.
Albion Archaeology, back cover, *pp.*18, 19, 20, 21, 22, 23; *The British Museum*,
back cover, *p.*16 (Flagons 1853,0627 11/12 & Samian ware 26/27); *University
of Cambridge Museum of Archaeology and Anthropology*, *p.*7 (rim sherds 1953.223),
*p.*9 (Bronze Age pots 1948.344-347), *p.*12 (2 pieces of antler Z.21748A/B),
*p.*14 (pottery sherds 1953.314/5), *pp.*18-19 (Anglo-Saxon material 1953.187/190),
*p.*20 and back cover (beads 1953.187); *University of Cambridge Unit for Landscape
Modelling*, *pp.*6, 11 (RC8-CK137), *p.*10 (NG30), *p.*12 (BLQ31), *p.*15 (BLQ17);
Fitzwilliam Museum, (Anglo Saxon coins) *p.*8 1984.019, 2003.0197, 2003.0198

Printed by Cambridge Printing Park, Milton, Cambridge. CB4 6AZ

ISBN 0-9549120-1-2

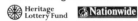

Local Heritage *initiative*

Heritage Lottery Fund Nationwide The Countryside Agency

Contents

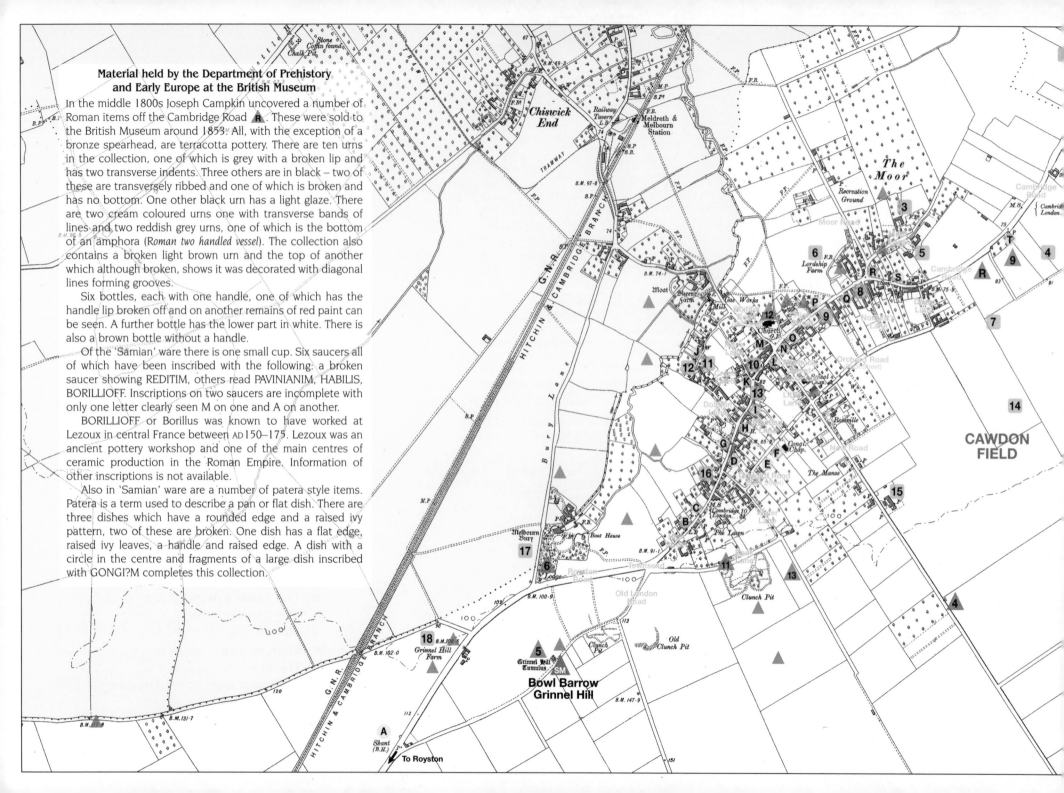

Material held by the Department of Prehistory and Early Europe at the British Museum

In the middle 1800s Joseph Campkin uncovered a number of Roman items off the Cambridge Road ℝ. These were sold to the British Museum around 1853. All, with the exception of a bronze spearhead, are terracotta pottery. There are ten urns in the collection, one of which is grey with a broken lip and has two transverse indents. Three others are in black – two of these are transversely ribbed and one of which is broken and has no bottom. One other black urn has a light glaze. There are two cream coloured urns one with transverse bands of lines and two reddish grey urns, one of which is the bottom of an amphora (*Roman two handled vessel*). The collection also contains a broken light brown urn and the top of another which although broken, shows it was decorated with diagonal lines forming grooves.

Six bottles, each with one handle, one of which has the handle lip broken off and on another remains of red paint can be seen. A further bottle has the lower part in white. There is also a brown bottle without a handle.

Of the 'Samian' ware there is one small cup. Six saucers all of which have been inscribed with the following: a broken saucer showing REDITIM, others read PAVINIANIM, HABILIS, BORILLIOFF. Inscriptions on two saucers are incomplete with only one letter clearly seen M on one and A on another.

BORILLIOFF or Borillus was known to have worked at Lezoux in central France between AD150–175. Lezoux was an ancient pottery workshop and one of the main centres of ceramic production in the Roman Empire. Information of other inscriptions is not available.

Also in 'Samian' ware are a number of patera style items. Patera is a term used to describe a pan or flat dish. There are three dishes which have a rounded edge and a raised ivy pattern, two of these are broken. One dish has a flat edge, raised ivy leaves, a handle and raised edge. A dish with a circle in the centre and fragments of a large dish inscribed with GONGI?M completes this collection.

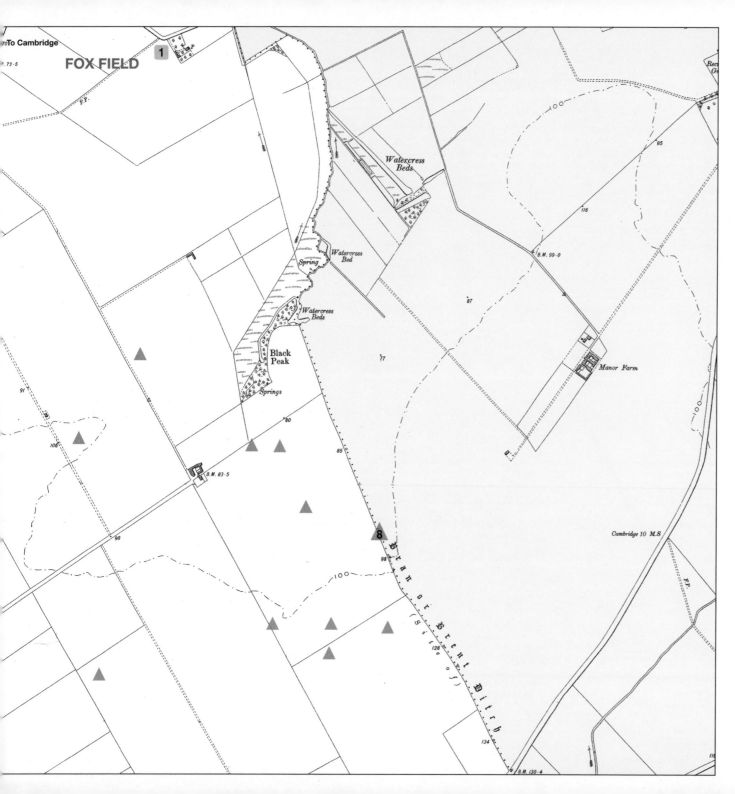

Melbourn

Archaeology

This map shows excavations and Scheduled Monuments around Melbourn

SM Scheduled Monuments (SMR)

▲ Position of finds discovered at Melbourn

Sites in order as they appear in the archaeology section

1. **Five Hill Field/Heath Farm**
2. **Goffers Knoll**
3. **Summerhouse**
4. **New Road**
5. **Grinnel Hill**
6. **Lodge cottage**
7. **New Farm**
8. **Brand Ditch**
9. **Portway**
10. **Flint Cross**
11. **Back Lane**
12. **All Saints' Church**
13. **Water Lane**

Taverns, inns and alehouses

A. **The Shant**, Royston Road
B. **The Oak Tree**, High Street
C. **The Locomotive**, High Street
D. **The White Horse**, High Street
E. **The Black Horse**, Orchard Road
F. **The Beech House**, Orchard Road
G. **The Red Cow**, High Street
H. **The Dolphin**, High Street
I. **The Hoops**, High Street
J. **The Carrier's Arms**, Dolphin Lane
K. **The Rose**, High Street
L. **The White Lion**, The Cross
M. **The Tailor's Arms**, Station Road
N. **The Old Elm Tree**, High Street
O. **The Anchor**, High Street
P. **Spotted Dog**, High Street
Q. **The Star**, High Street
R. **The Royal Oak**, The Moor corner
S. **The Red Lion**, High Street
T. **The Bull's Head**, Cambridge Road
U. **The Coach and Horses**, Newmarket Road

FOX FIELD

To Cambridge

Watercress Beds

Watercress Bed

Spring

Watercress Beds

Black Peak

Springs

Manor Farm

B.M. 99.0

Drain of Brent Ditch (Site of)

Cambridge 10 M.S

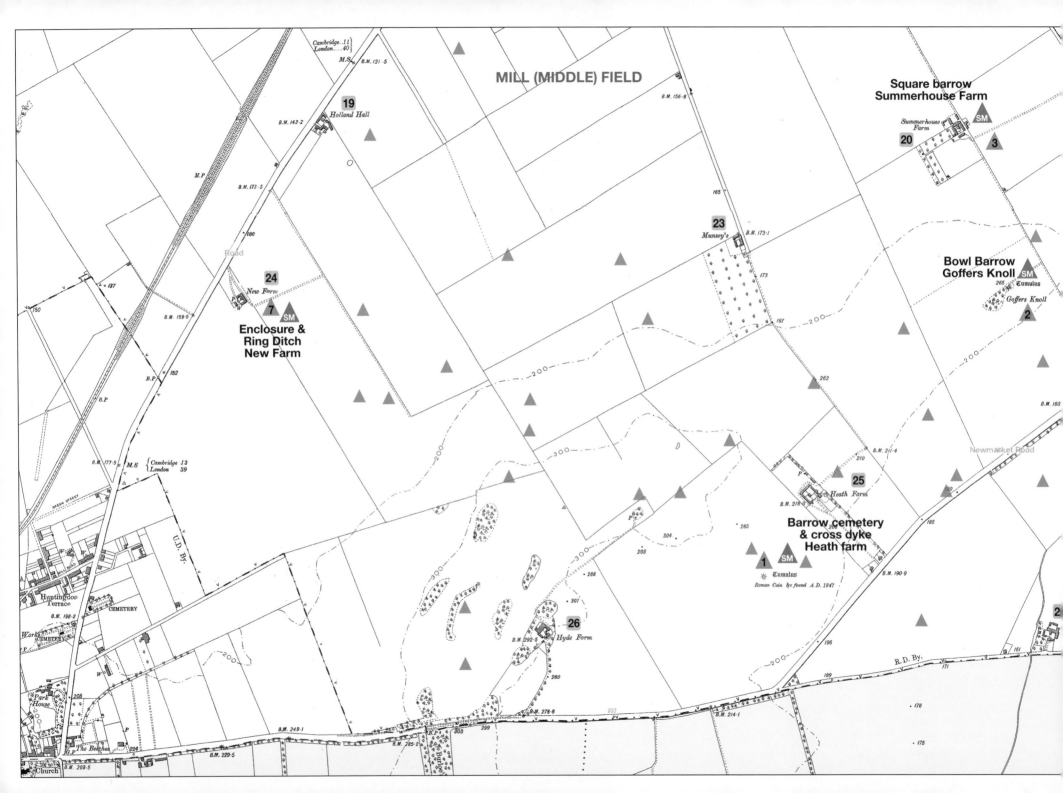

MILL (MIDDLE) FIELD

Square barrow
Summerhouse Farm

Bowl Barrow
Goffers Knoll

Enclosure &
Ring Ditch
New Farm

Barrow cemetery
& cross dyke
Heath farm

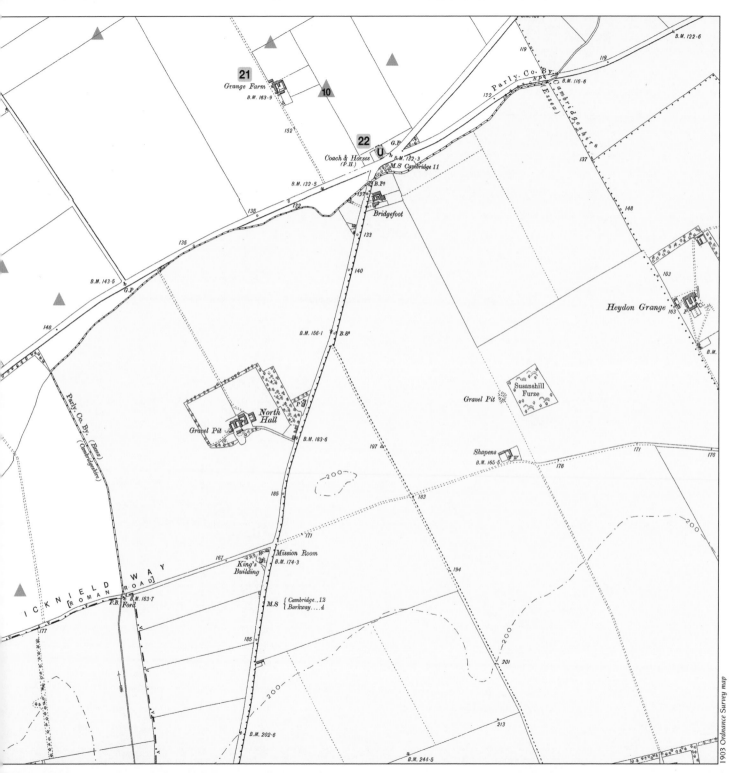

Farms of Melbourn

1. **Foxfields** (STANFORD), Cambridge Road
2. **White House** (BICHENO), Cambridge Road
3. **Moor Farm** (NEWLING, WHITING), Moat Lane
4. **Solway Farm***, Cambridge Road
5. **Moat House Farm**, Moat Lane
6. **Lordship** (ARGENTINES), High Street
7. **Tostock***, Cambridge Road
8. **White House**, Norgett's Lane
9. **Wood's Farm** (BROWNING), High Street
10. **Vine's**, High Street
11. **Clear's**, Dolphin Lane
12. **Wedd's Farm**, Dolphin Lane
13. **Stockbridge Farm**, High Street
14. **East Farm**, Cambridge Road
15. **Grange Farm** (SPARROWS), New Road
16. **Old Farm** (IVY VILLA - STOCKBRIDGE), High Street
17. **Melbourn Bury**, Royston Road
18. **Grinnel Hill Farm**, Royston Road
19. **Holland Hall Farm**, Royston Road
20. **Summerhouse Farm**, New Road
21. **Grange Farm**, Newmarket Road
22. **Black Peak Farm**, Newmarket Road
23. **Muncey's Farm**, Old London Road
24. **New Farm**, Royston Road
25. **Heath Farm**, Newmarket Road
26. **Hyde Farm**, Newmarket Road
27. **Noon's Folly**, Newmarket Road

Note: Road names marked on the above list are for reference and show the entrance to the Farm.

Farms have changed owners and names, and land has been bought and sold. Farms marked as being inside the village mainly refer to the farmhouse and yard only. Noon's (possibly Nun's) Folly is the only farm believed to exist outside the village prior to the Enclosures Act of 1839. Many of the public houses and businesses also farmed small amounts of land, or kept pigs or chickens; these are not marked.

*15&16 are council owned, top of Portway

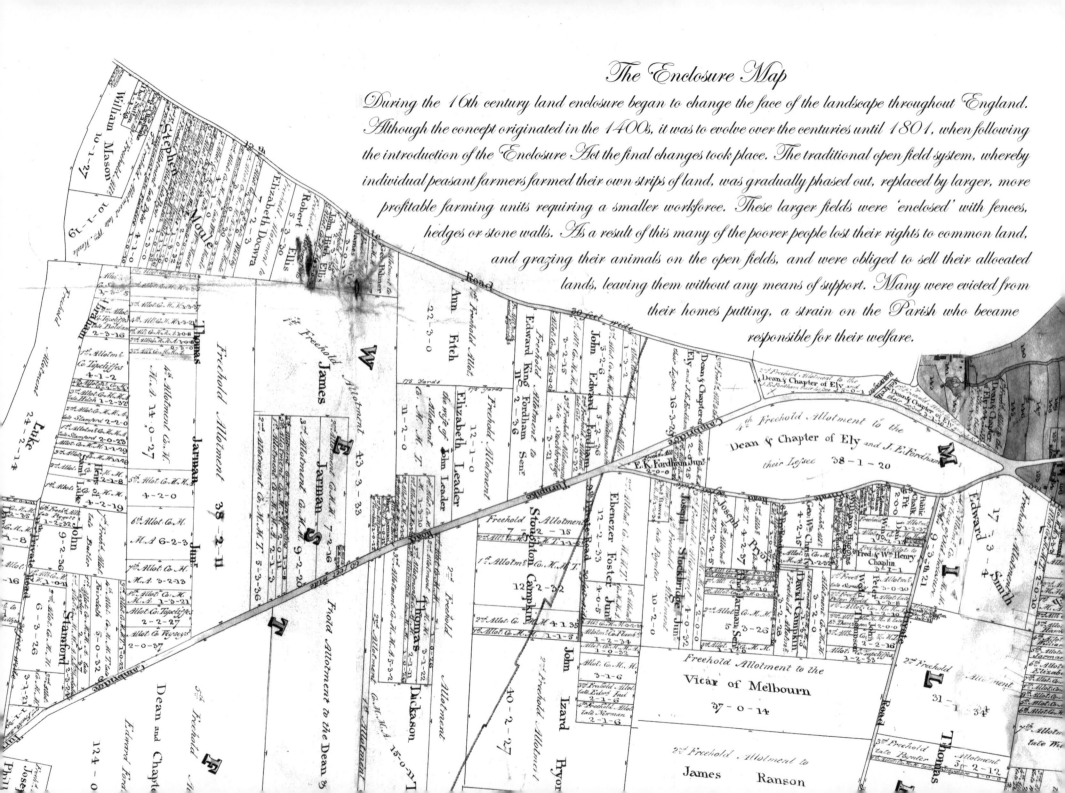

The Enclosure Map

During the 16th century land enclosure began to change the face of the landscape throughout England. Although the concept originated in the 1400s, it was to evolve over the centuries until 1801, when following the introduction of the Enclosure Act the final changes took place. The traditional open field system, whereby individual peasant farmers farmed their own strips of land, was gradually phased out, replaced by larger, more profitable farming units requiring a smaller workforce. These larger fields were 'enclosed' with fences, hedges or stone walls. As a result of this many of the poorer people lost their rights to common land, and grazing their animals on the open fields, and were obliged to sell their allocated lands, leaving them without any means of support. Many were evicted from their homes putting, a strain on the Parish who became responsible for their welfare.

PLAN
OF THE PARISH OF
MELBOURN
in the
County of Cambridge

As allotted and awarded by the Commissioners appointed
to Inclose the same pursuant to an Act of Parliament passed
A.D. 1839.

This map was produced in 1839 and shows the distribution of land in Melbourn after the Enclosure Act

Enclosure map from
Cambridge Archive Service, Castle Hill, Cambridge

Introduction

*This book is dedicated to all
the residents of Melbourn
past, present and future*

The concept of A *glimpse into Melbourn's past* came after a conversation one morning between an elderly resident of the village and two people out for a walk. The gentleman was reminiscing over old times and his knowledge of local history was vast.

Following this conversation, the Melbourn Village History Group was formed, to research and record information, such as that of the elderly resident, to make it available to everyone and to preserve it for future generations.

A wealth of information on the history of our village is stored in local archives including the Cambridge Collection and County Archives, with newspaper reports dating back to the 18th century and old photographs. A number of interesting books have been written by local residents and historians such as Nina Campkin, Jan McNiece, Dr. Dennis Mills and Dr. William Palmer. It is from these sources, together with artefacts, memorabilia, photos, and information supplied from local residents, that this publication was produced.

Over three years was spent in preparation.

During this time, over 1000 photographs of Melbourn were collected. An enthusiastic photographer and local resident, Percy (Peep-Bo) Salmon, took a great number of these in the early 1900s.

The photographs came to us in varying states; some were in excellent condition, others faded with time or damaged, but by using modern technology, we have been able to restore them and in some cases reveal areas which were previously difficult to see.

In light of the initial conversation that sparked the idea of the project, two 'tea parties' were held, where local residents chatted over tea and cakes, and their conversations recorded. These can be heard on the accompanying DVD together with a 'slideshow' ~ *Memories from days gone by*.

This book has been compiled and researched by volunteers and hopefully, we have produced an enjoyable and entertaining book, as well as preserving some of the history of Melbourn for the future, and that you are taken back in time, to the days before piped water, electricity and gas and transport was by horse and cart or Shanks' Pony.

Thank you to all those who have contributed to this book through information they gave, stories told and the many photographs loaned. Also to the residents who came to the village tea parties and gave us some wonderful tales of their childhood days.

The Melbourn Village History Group

General background information has been included to help understanding of historical events, and also where no specific local facts were available. The spelling of surnames is as researched or supplied, and in some cases, no forenames were available. Spellings throughout newspaper accounts have been transcribed verbatim. It is inevitable that there will be errors and omissions in the book.

The book covers historical events up to the mid-1950s. However, the archaeological digs that took place after this date have been included, as the finds originate from a much earlier period.

Imperial measurements have been used throughout the book and we have not attempted to convert values into today's terms. A conversion chart can be found at the back of the book.

From Stone Age to modern times

... the Romans invaded England around AD 43 and occupied it for nearly 400 years. However, there is little evidence to show their occupation of Melbourn

Melbourn may have seen visitors from as far back as the Old Stone Age *c*.500,000–10,000 BC. There is no evidence of their way of life before the Middle Stone Age *c*.10,000–4000 BC, but after this time those coming to this area were nomadic hunter-gatherers. By *c*.3000 BC a settlement was beginning to develop and these early farmers constructed their buildings (often rectangular) of timber.

The area around Melbourn was mostly woodland with oak, ash, elm and beech trees. Small areas of growth began to appear with edible plants such as blackberries, barberries, sloes, crab-apples, haws and hazelnuts. Certain weeds could also be eaten. Wildlife included deer, wild cattle known as auroch, elk, wild boar, badgers, hedgehogs, a variety of wild cats and smaller animals such as shrews. The river contained a rich diet of fish. The only domesticated animal was the dog, used for hunting.

The early settlers used polished stone axes, pottery and new flint-knapping technology. They raised animals and grew crops. This shift to farming enabled a change in lifestyle ~ families had a greater chance, too, of raising more than one child, for example. The Neolithic landscape was also changing dramatically as trees were felled for buildings and fuel. Reeds, grass and clay were also invaluable commodities.

Nothing was wasted ~ animal skins were used for clothing, bedding and containers, and bones were transformed into useful tools, some as fine as needles. Weapons were also fashioned from these materials as well as from stone.

Religious monuments were also being constructed containing burials or cremations. However, the style of tombs varied from region to region. In Melbourn round and square barrow burial mounds have been found, surrounded or enclosed by ditches and banks.

The Bronze and Iron Ages

By *c*.2300 BC bronze, copper and gold had been introduced. The use of metal for weapons, agricultural tools and jewellry appeared alongside a new style of pottery, the finely made and decorated Beaker pots. Beakers are found in settlements as well as buried with the dead, leaving a distinctive archaeological 'hallmark'.

The discoveries of flint tools, arrowheads, knives and buckets, etc. together with remains of woven cloth and ornaments, show the beginnings of an early industry in Melbourn, developing alongside farming. With the invention of the wheel during the Bronze Age, a cart or wagon allowed a greater movement of people to and from the area. The ox-drawn plough changed farming practices and as the amount of land under cultivation gradually increased, small fields started to develop. A wider variety of crops was grown, including emmer, spelt (a kind of wheat), bread wheat, oats, barley, peas and flax.

Melbourn developed into a small hamlet or village from *c*.1000 BC. The settlement would have begun close to the springs at Melbourn Bury where houses were grouped in clusters, some surrounded by ditches and banks. They would have been large solid circular structures and made of wood with no windows or smoke holes for the central fire inside.

The Romans in England

The Romans invaded England around AD 43 and occupied it for nearly 400 years. However, there is little evidence to show their occupation of Melbourn. A few Roman artifacts have been found near Portway where a possible military garrison or villa may have stood, although today nothing can be seen. The heath and forest area around Melbourn would have been put under cultivation by the Romans to produce food for the garrison. They may well have introduced the first tavern or public house. These establishments were known as 'taberna' and were commonplace along Roman roads providing lodgings for officials and other travellers.

Melbourn came under the rule of the Iceni tribe (of modern East Anglia) and the early occupation by the Romans saw many conflicts between the Iceni and other tribes. In AD 61 Boudicca raised the Iceni in rebellion against the Romans with one battle said to have been fought in 'a wooded area south of Cambridge', where Boudicca slaughtered the 9th Roman Legion. The Iceni were eventually defeated in a pitched battle in the Midlands, and Boudicca died shortly afterwards. Once the rebellion had been quelled, Rome adopted a more conciliatory attitude. The Iceni accepted Roman influence and were quickly assimilated, returning peace to Melbourn.

In AD 313 Christianity was formally adopted and paganism was outlawed. The village would have seen a Christian settlement from the earliest times and the church would have been the main

Viking warrior with his wooden shield and spear

focal point in Melbourn standing on a slight rise at the crossroads, and over the years the centre of all village activities. From AD 391 people still practising paganism faced death if caught by the authorities, and pagan temples and idols were destroyed. Twenty years later the Romans left our shores.

Saxons and Scandinavians

As Roman troops left Britain in AD 410, powerful local leaders emerged and struggles with Germanic settlers saw the end of Roman ways for the majority of the population. However, the landscape around Melbourn stayed much the same ~ primarily a farming community.

By AD 600 the area was ruled by the Anglo-Saxon Ethelbert and during the reign of Offa, AD 757–796, a mint was set up issuing the first standardised coinage, including the gold 'dinar', the first coin to be commonly used throughout southern England since Roman times.

In AD 787 Scandinavians (Vikings) began to attack the English coasts and AD 865 saw a great army of Danes land in East Anglia. England was divided in AD 886 and Melbourn was declared part of the Danish territory ~ known as the 'Danelaw' (where English and Danes were supposed to be equal in law). The Danes, together with the Romans, contributed during the first century, to the beginnings of our justice system.

The Anglo-Saxons brought their own ancestral beliefs and religion to the area, and worship was probably conducted in the open air or in a primitive building. However, religious life in the area would have been pushed underground with the coming of the Scandinavians. These 'Pagan' Danes, worshipped their own gods and destroyed churches. Harold Godwinson became the last Anglo-Saxon King in 1066. His reign was cut short when he was killed at the Battle of Hastings during the Norman invasion led by Duke William.

Normans and beyond

A stone church in the village may have been built by the Normans. This would have stood until the 12th century. With the Christian religion came the foundation of moral laws and power.

In common with most other towns and villages of medieval England, Melbourn almost certainly had only one person who could read and write. Often this would be the local priest, with his limited knowledge of Latin, as the peasantry were not encouraged to learn.

It was not until 1250 that the possession of a surname became law. Until then a peasant was identified by either 'John, son of George', 'James the Carpenter' or 'William of Melbourn'. The gentry would already have an ancestral surname. One of Melbourn's earliest recorded names is Argentine ~ lord of the Manor, whose wealth and influence played a significant part in the history of the village. In 1538, the parish was ordered to keep a register of all baptisms, marriages and burials. Every Sunday the vicar of Melbourn, Edmund Humpfrey, (still probably the only literate person in the village) would enter the details from the previous week.

Melbourn has had its fair share of troubles through the ages. The unrest during the Peasants' Revolt in 1381, the Ship Money riots which took place at the Cross in 1640, the Civil War in the 17th century, to the tragedies emerging from the Boer War and the First and Second World Wars, where many Melbourn men were injured or killed. There were a number of recorded fires in the village which destroyed many thatched cottages. The first was on St. Bartholomew's Day, 24th August 1724, when in the space of an hour ...25 *dwelling houses together with all the out houses, barns and stables and Recks of Corn were burnt down*. The devastation caused by a fire in 1915 is well documented and describes the loss of housing and the anguish it caused.

A famous landmark also disappeared from Melbourn in the late 1930s. The old Elm Tree at the Cross was the subject of many paintings, engravings, photographs and books. John Bunyan had preached nearby, and an account in a newspaper article describes how people had climbed its 'gigantic' branches to watch the procession of Queen Victoria and Prince Albert as they passed through Melbourn on their way to Cambridge. Having been the centre of village life for many centuries, the tree finally died although several attempts had been made to save it.

The village also lost a number of inhabitants as they took the opportunity of assisted passages to America and Australia during the 1800s. Melbourn was an agricultural area and employment with decent wages was very hard to come by.

The archaeology

A major prehistoric trackway, just south of the settlement at Melbourn, was formed over time and brought traders from great distances. It gave access to Norfolk and the Wash in the northeast, to Wiltshire in the southwest and became known as the Icknield Way. About half a mile to the north, and running parallel to it was another track ~ Ashwell Street (known locally as Ashwell Strete). It started at Bury Lane in Melbourn and headed towards Ashwell. Neolithic and Bronze Age finds here verify its beginnings.

A number of prehistoric ditches run across the Icknield Way. These probably marked boundaries between tribes and would have also served as primitive toll points. Bran Ditch, a Saxon example, on the parish boundary of Melbourn and Fowlmere, lies across

the Way. The boundary between Hertfordshire and Cambridgeshire was marked by the trackway and at one time cut Royston in two.

Several archaeological sites from the Bronze and Iron Age have survived to be recorded as tumuli or burial mounds on early Ordnance Survey maps.

Some of these were excavated in the 19th century, but unfortunately modern deep ploughing has reduced the mounds until today there is no visible evidence of their existence.

Impression of Saxon Melbourn from The Bury, looking towards Goffer's Knoll

Ashwell Street (known locally as Ashwell Strete), an old Neolithic and Roman road

The archaeology of Melbourn

...archaeology is the study of the past through material remains ~ effectively reconstructing events

Archaeology is the study of the past through material remains ~ effectively reconstructing events by examining, for example, bones and seeds to reconstruct ancient diets and environments, broken pots and fragments of flint with no obvious use. These may have been rubbish to those who discarded them, but are vital evidence to the archaeologist of today.

There is an indication of interest in ancient objects at least as far back as the Roman period, but there is a difference between collecting objects for their curiosity or monetary value and collecting them for the information they can provide. In Britain, the roots of what would eventually become archaeology can be found in the early studies of the 17th and 18th century.

In the early days of archaeology there were major problems with chronology. Timescale was a problem as, according to the early calculations of Archbishop Ussher, the Bible stated that the world was created in 4004 BC. Early archaeologists interpreted artefacts as being more to do with status than age and assumed that weapons or tools of stone must belong to the poorest members of society, those of iron to the middle ranks, while bronze was reserved for the higher orders.

Archaeological features around Melbourn

Barrows are mounds of earth, stone or turf placed over one or more burials, a burial practice which began in the Neolithic period (*c.* 4000 BC) and continued into the early medieval period. Depending on the shape and material used, barrows are described as round, square and long. Barrows made from piles of stones are often called 'cairns', and on old maps, round barrows are often called 'tumuli'.

The term '**bowl barrow**' is used to describe a simple hemispherical mound or round barrow, often with a surrounding ditch, mostly dated between 2400 and 1500 BC. A bowl barrow can appear as an isolated feature, or in groups of cemeteries, and although superficially similar they vary in size and excavations have revealed a diversity of burial practices.

Round barrow cemeteries comprise closely grouped round barrows, sometimes over 30 in number. Most cemeteries will have developed over centuries, often around a first large barrow and with later additions of flat graves in between the mounds.

Square barrows are round barrows which have been enclosed with a square or rectangular ditch, mostly dating to the Iron Age, between 600 and 400 BC. The central burial is often accompanied by grave goods.

Prehistory

The term prehistory, meaning the time before recorded history, started to be studied in the earlier part of the 19th century. Prehistory ends with the appearance of written records, in the case of Britain this is the Roman period in AD 43.

Aerial survey

There are many sites that show little, if any trace of the past visibly on the surface. Many sites are known only through cropmarks, and some can only be seen from the air as patterns showing the location of buried features such as ditches or walls. Crop marks are produced when crops growing over buried features develop at a different rate to those growing immediately adjacent. For example, over a soil-filled ditch the deeper soil may provide better moisture-retention and more nutrients, allowing the crop to grow faster and taller. Over a buried wall, for instance, the shallower soil may produce a stunted crop and one more liable to parching under dry conditions. In addition, earthworks such as banks and ditches can also be photographed under oblique light conditions (shadow marks).

Although crop and soil marks were first noticed as far back as the 18th century, it has only been possible to record them systematically since the introduction of aviation and the availability of faster cameras.

Controlled excavation

The excavation of a site involves its controlled destruction, either partially or completely. This type of excavation allows archaeologists to reverse the sequence of events leading to the formation of the site where, as a result of human activities, deposits have built up gradually through time.

Some individual activities may leave very obvious traces. A hearth may show only as a patch of reddened soil and a few flecks of charcoal, while a change in land use from pasture to cultivation may only be recognisable in far more subtle traces, perhaps only in the colour and texture of the soil.

In the case of total excavation, everything that is

Aerial photograph of Heath Farm showing crop marks – four rings left of centre and darker trackways, top left. The A505 is the upper road seen running from left to right in the photograph.

the result of human activity is removed until undisturbed natural bedrock or subsoil is reached over the whole site. Every change in soil colour, texture or components is observed and recorded by means of drawings, photographs and written notes, while artefacts and samples are collected for later analysis. Many sites have been left unexcavated for the future as new methods of archaeology will evolve and improved knowledge will give a better understanding of the past.

Pottery studies: shape and form

Pottery would have appeared in this area by *c.*3000 BC. It has always been invaluable to archaeologists as developments were made in manufacture and raw materials throughout the periods ~ and trends for shape and decoration changed. These all provide clues about date, function and the movement of people and ideas. Pots are classified according to shape, the type of clay used and what has been deliberately added to

Although complete pots are often discovered during excavations, many more have been found as pottery sherds such as the ones seen below. Buried pots may have collapsed due to the weight of soil, others are found on the surface of fields in pieces due to many years of deep ploughing or are just discarded broken pots. These two large pieces from a pot found in New Road in 1959 are of Deverel-Rimbury style which was a culture from southern England covering the 15th to 12th centuries BC. The sherds contained a quantity of chalk/shell tempering.

Scheduled monument at Grinnel Hill

it as well as the way in which surfaces have been decorated, for example using incised or stamped patterns, smoothing or glazes.

These changing characteristics are used to distinguish between a fragment of, for example, a handmade cooking pot made from local clay and undecorated of about 1000 BC (Bronze Age), and one of a wheel-thrown, imported, lead-glazed jug of the 13th century.

Food remains

It is possible in some cases to determine what has been cooked in a particular pot by studying burnt-on

A monument that has been scheduled is protected by law against disturbance. It is a criminal offence to damage a scheduled monument by carrying out works without consent, cause reckless or deliberate damage, use a metal detector or remove an object found with one.

food remains, and more recently, advances have been made in the analysis of the animal fats and oils and the plant waxes that impregnate porous pots. This has provided the first clues to the function of particular types of highly distinctive prehistoric vessels and more detailed information about prehistoric man's diet.

Scheduled Ancient Monuments

The Schedule of Monuments has been kept since 1882 and takes priority over other land uses, such as farming and building. It was set up to protect archaeological sites for future generations.

Archaeological remains are a crucial link with our past. They vary from the more obvious sites, such as castles and stone circles, to the buried remains of ancient settlements which are hidden below the surface. All of these are fragile and once lost, they can never be replaced.

Coins

A few ancient coins have been discovered in Melbourn, although the exact location of where many of these were found and their whereabouts today are unknown.

The earliest coins found in the area are Roman ~ they were usually issued by moneyers who used coinage rights to tell a story, express Roman ideals, or portray their family heritage. A small pot of Roman coins containing 30 1st and 2nd century silver denarii was handed in to Melbourn police in 1988. The coins were heavily encrusted and were passed on to a museum for treatment, as the metal was unstable.

2nd century brass coin of Emperor Marcus Aurelius

At Five Hill Field, Heath Farm, a 2nd century brass coin of Emperor Marcus Aurelius from AD 161~180 was uncovered. He was the adopted son of the Emperor Hadrian.

Other Roman coins found in the early 1900s were of Nero and Phillip I. The Roman bronze coin of Nero AD 54~68 (famous as the emperor who 'fiddled while Rome burned') was discovered by the Royston Road. It clearly shows the head of Nero on one side, his profile facing towards the right and reads 'NERO CAESAR AUG P MAX'. The reverse is worn and its features unclear but it has been interpreted as showing Victory rising in the air and holding a shield on which is inscribed 'SPQR'.

AD54~68 – *Bronze coin of Nero*

The fine bronze coin struck for Phillip I AD 244~249 shows Phillip facing right and it reads 'IMP. M JUL PHILLIPUS'. On the reverse Peace stands facing right holding a cornucopia.

By the end of the Roman period money had ceased to be in use, although during the 6th century gold coins from the continent arrived and began to circulate in England. Soon after this the Anglo-Saxons began producing their own coins, partly for prestige and partly for economic purposes ~ it was profitable to run a mint. Silver was imported from the continent and this in turn stimulated a dramatic growth in coin circulation and minting in England.

A small silver penny, common in everyday use at the time, was found on the west side of the Melbourn by-pass. This particular coin was struck for Archbishop Wulfred known as a radical archbishop AD 805~832 and the Diocese of Canterbury. On one side of the coin it reads VVLFREDI ARCHIEPISCOPI and on the reverse SAEBERNT MOHETA. The ruler was Egbert, who reigned from AD 802~839.

AD 805–832 – *Archbishop Wulfred and the Diocese of Canterbury*

The Scandinavian kingdom had adopted Christianity towards the end of the 9th century and many of its symbols started to appear on various

AD 899–924 – *From the reign of Edward the Elder*

AD 871–975 – *Unknown ruler*

coins. Another Anglo-Saxon coin that was discovered was dated between AD 899~924. The ruler at this time was Edward the Elder.

Also found from the Anglo-Saxon period was a coin with few visible details but is dated between AD 871~975.

Taking of Portobello, 1739

A coin or medal, found under the floor boards of a house in the village, was struck to celebrate Admiral Vernon's victory at Portobello in 1739. The coin depicts the standing figure of Admiral Edward Vernon, receiving the sword of surrender from Don Blass, the Spanish captain, who kneels before him. On the reverse the relief shows six ships entering the harbour at Portobello. This is one of 14 different medals struck to celebrate his victory.

Admiral Vernon was known as 'old grog' to his sailors due to the cloak he wore, a grogram and made from silk, mohair and wool, bound together with gum. To avoid scurvy on his ships Vernon diluted the rum served to his sailors with water and lime juice. To his men the drink became known as 'grog'. With the inclusion of lime it also gave rise to the term 'limey' which was originally used to describe British sailors, but eventually used generally to describe British men. Admiral Vernon is buried in Westminster Abbey.

Victory at Portobello in 1739

The sites

Although Melbourn cannot boast of any major archaeological sites or valuable finds, there are at least fifty sites giving us evidence of life dating back to Neolithic times. These can still be seen today as ring ditches, mostly visible from aerial photography as crop marks. Many have been well recorded, especially the sites of Bran Ditch and the Saxon cemeteries of Back Lane and Water Lane. Others have revealed little information or have yet to be excavated.

A skeleton found in the driftway near the Shant in November 1931. At the time it was thought he was possibly Mercian and was of great interest as he had been decapitated. A male of great height (1m 80cm) he was possibly a chieftain. It is known that a fierce battle was fought in the neighbourhood around the year AD 655.

Five Hill Field

Just south west of Heath Farm lies a cemetery containing five Bronze Age round barrows, an Iron Age square barrow and a cross dyke. Situated in a prominent position on a steep hill the cemetery overlooks the course of the Icknield Way. Four of the barrows are no longer visible as mounds due to ploughing.

The cemetery and cross dyke (a prehistoric earthwork which probably served as a boundary marker) was first recorded in 1847. The dyke, which runs parallel to the A505, forms the edge of the

A collection of cinerary vases and 'incense cup' from Five Hill Field, Heath Farm.
From the left: a ceramic vessel with a very irregular overhanging-rim and a few vertical incisions. This pot was incomplete with a broken rim and loose sherds inside and has been reconstructed.

A small ceramic vessel made of coarse fabric with a flat base and rim. Although incomplete, it has been glued together. This pot was sometimes called an 'accessory cup' or 'pygmy cup'.

This ceramic 'incense cup' is pierced with 7 small holes in the walls, flat-topped and decorated with incised lines.

A ceramic vessel with an overhanging-rim, about half was missing, and the rest has been reconstructed. There are a series of vertical incised chevrons on the shoulder.

Aerial photograph showing the Bronze Age cemetery and square barrow centre left at Five Hill Field, Heath Farm

cemetery and provides an insight into how the land was being used during this period. It was about 2.5m high and 200m long and the width at its widest point was 13m. Nothing of its height is visible today yet its buried remains are still preserved, showing up as a crop mark.

The tallest barrows stood over a metre high and had a diameter of about 20m. The finds from these included part of a red deer antler, cinerary vases (for cremated remains), an 'incense cup', a double bronze buckle, portions of skeletons (some of the bones of men and animals were burnt and mixed together), the bottom of a small vase and an iron pikehead.

Other finds included a 2nd century brass coin of the Emperor Marcus Aurelius ~ an indication that the barrow was possibly raided in the Roman period. Nothing is visible from the ground today of the barrows but the ditch that encircles them can still be seen from the air.

Other round barrows lie further to the south together with a square barrow from the Iron Age measuring a metre high and 15m wide. Although pottery fragments have been found when ploughing the area there is no record as to the period to which they belong. The remaining two barrows are unexcavated.

A small ditch connects the two barrows to the tallest one in the cemetery which stood about 3m high. It is now barely visible but a crop mark shows the encircling ditch is 4m wide. This barrow was partially excavated and produced three funerary vases and a small pierced cup, thought to have been used for incense.

Opposite, Five Hill Field, Heath Farm: A Bronze Age cemetery containing five round barrows can be clearly seen centre left. An Iron Age square barrow lies just above the top round barrow. Other trackways and field systems can also be seen.

Inset: This picture, taken from a different angle (rotated 90° clockwise), shows a rectangular enclosure and an adjoining linear feature which is to the right of Heath Farm (centre right of main picture).

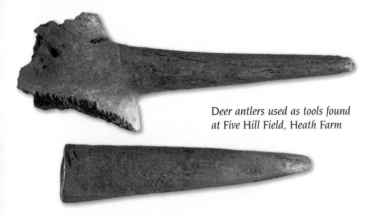

Deer antlers used as tools found at Five Hill Field, Heath Farm

Nearer the surface a bronze double buckle and two skeletons were uncovered and are thought to be later Anglo-Saxon burials.

The fifth round barrow lies to the south west of this area. The horn of a fallow deer was discovered here together with an iron pikehead and six skeletons, likely to be of Anglo-Saxon origin.

Goffer's Knoll

At Goffer's Knoll, about half a mile from Five Hill Field, is an impressive bowl barrow.

The barrow itself is circular and measures about 21m in diameter and 1.5m high. The top has been flattened although much of its original shape has been retained, shown by the angles of its sides. It was partially excavated in the 1920s on the southeastern side marked by a small pit, but this has not damaged the mound greatly.

The monument is situated within a patch of woodland on top of the knoll and would have formed a prominent landmark when it was in use, as it does today, having commanding views in all directions and as far as Cambridge. It is well preserved and will no doubt contain a great deal of historical evidence relating to its use and origins. It is, however, a rare surviving earthwork as the majority of bowl barrows have been lost through ploughing.

An example of a square barrow and a ring ditch near Goffer's Knoll. The A505 can be seen top right of the picture.

Summerhouse Farm

About 170m northeast of Summerhouse Farm lies a square barrow no longer visible from the ground. Its mound has been destroyed through deep ploughing over the years and the ditch has been filled in, but the site with its central burial pit is still preserved and can be seen as a crop mark from the air. The ditch forms a 20m square.

New Road

In January 1959 an excavation revealed a skeleton found in a Bronze Age barrow on the hill at New Road. The site was originally uncovered by deep ploughing. The excavations showed two round barrows, one of which contained a burial and a number of cremations with late Bronze Age pottery fragments known as *sherds*. The main circle is about 26m in diameter; the other is situated on the headland of the field, and so New Road cuts through it ~ but nothing was found here. The site is believed to have been used previously by Bronze Age people between 4000 and 3500 years ago.

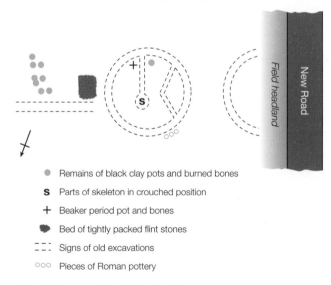

- ●   Remains of black clay pots and burned bones
- **S**   Parts of skeleton in crouched position
- **+**   Beaker period pot and bones
- ◗   Bed of tightly packed flint stones
- ---   Signs of old excavations
- ooo   Pieces of Roman pottery

Plan of the excavation at New Road

An unopened Bronze Age bowl barrow at Grinnel Hill

A skeleton was found near the centre of the main circle, in a crouched position, less than 60cm below the surface, and it is thought to be the main burial.

Outside the circle, fragments of unburned bone and pottery were found that may have been Early or Middle Bronze Age. There was also a cremation in a poor quality jar within a circular ditch. A few examples of Roman pottery were also discovered.

This was the first time in the area that the remains had been found outside the main circle. Another unusual feature was the discovery of a floor of closely packed flint stones, its purpose is unknown. Little can be seen of the site except for a dark circle that shows up after rain.

Grinnel Hill

One of the few unopened Bronze Age bowl barrows in Cambridgeshire can be found at Grinnel Hill on the Old London Road. It is about 3m high and measures 18×14m in an oval shape. Although originally it would have been bowl shaped, today it has a steep side on the northeast, the result of being eaten into by ploughing, but despite the alteration of its shape it is very well preserved. Its height has not changed much over the years, giving a good impression of how it originally looked compared to the majority of barrows in Cambridgeshire, which are now only visible from the air.

Lodge Cottage

Situated at Lodge Cottage, about 40m from Grinnel Hill is another bowl barrow. Its precise date is unknown although, as it lies in a group of Bronze Age barrows, it is possibly the same age. In its

These small pieces of pottery sherds were found at New Road. The top section shows pieces of Beaker ware which were found with buried human bones. The bottom pieces were scattered on the surface on the northwest side of the barrow circle.

original condition it would have stood out as a prominent landmark. The material used in its construction came from a ditch surrounding it, which was about 20m in diameter and 2.5m wide. Ploughing had reduced the mound to about 2m in height, but today it shows as a distinct soil mark.

New Farm

To the south of Melbourn lies New Farm, and in the south east corner is a Neolithic causewayed enclosure with two ring ditches from the Bronze Age. No evidence can be seen from the ground, but it is clearly visible from the air.

Causewayed enclosures are amongst the earliest field monuments to survive and might have been used for ceremonial and funerary purposes, defence, or settlement. They were constructed over a period of 500 years but mainly during the middle part of the Neolithic period (3000~2400 BC) and continued to be used into later periods.

Roughly circular, or ovoid, in shape the ditches were formed from a series of elongated pits, their sizes varying between 2 and 70 acres. The enclosure at New Farm is circular with a diameter of 120m. On the southwestern side is a gap of 80m which indicates a major causeway. This is flanked by 10m diameter ring ditches on either side which were possibly round barrows. A second, slightly narrower, major causeway interrupts the enclosure on the northern side with four minor ones located at irregular intervals.

No more than 70 causewayed enclosures have been recorded nationally. They are one of the few Neolithic monuments to survive and are therefore considered nationally important.

Bran Ditch

Bran Ditch (or Heydon Ditch as it is also known) was a defence system extending for just over 3 miles from Heydon to Black Peak. It marks the parish border between Melbourn and Fowlmere, running in a straight line for over a mile. Its discovery gives an insight into the violent life and times the Saxons endured during that period.

Although it was thought that such dykes had Roman connections as do similar ones at Fleam Dyke near Fulbourn and Devil's Dyke near Newmarket which have revealed Roman remains, evidence of Anglo-Saxon activity has been found here as the banks overlie Roman features.

Part of the bank was levelled and the ditch filled in when the parish was enclosed. By 1868 the ditch up to Heydon Grange and as far as Heydon Hill, had been reduced to ground level, but beyond here the rampart (or vallum) was only partially lowered; it was estimated to be about 2m high and 24m wide.

In 1925 a series of excavations revealed the true age of the ditch. Sections dug at Black Peak showed the dyke had cut through a Roman settlement. Today this settlement can only be seen during very dry periods as a crop mark which appears as a compact group of fairly rectangular enclosures with straight droves leading to a circular feature. A scattering of flint was found over an area of 200m and could have been the remains of a Roman cobbled floor, however, no evidence of any buildings has been discovered. Roman pottery sherds, two beehive quern fragments and a random scattering of tiles have been found in this area over the years.

An excavation in 1927 starting at Black Peak, revealed only Romano-British potsherds on the ground, but a new trench revealed two skeletons and further excavation uncovered more graves.

Two skeletons were underneath what would have been the rampart and it looked as if it had been constructed to avoid disturbing the burials. It appeared that under this great earthwork were the remains of a smaller earthwork as there were signs of its two smaller ditches, one running under the vallum and the second to the west of it. The burials were obviously older than the larger vallum.

Over 50 bodies were found buried between these two small ditches, mostly of men but some were of boys aged over twelve. A newly born child was found beside a post hole but it is thought to be unassociated with the others.

All but one of the bodies were naked at the time of burial; this was unusual as most Anglo-Saxons were buried fully clothed. The one body that appeared to have been clothed, was found with a small iron knife at his right side, which is typically Anglo-Saxon. He also had an iron clip, found from a belt he was wearing.

A fragment of pottery had an interesting thumbnail ornamentation on the lip, a survival of Early Iron Age decoration. Elsewhere the sherd of a late Romano-British Beaker was found under the chalk rubble.

A causewayed enclosure at New Farm. Two ring ditches can be seen flanking the larger opening on the left. No more than 70 of these have been recorded nationally. The A10 is at the top of the photo.

A gruesome end

With the exception of two of the bodies, all had been given a supposedly Christian burial as they were positioned in the traditional way with feet facing towards the east. Yet the bodies were shown to have met with a violent end. Many had been decapitated – others had experienced brutal deaths in other forms. Other graves contained two or three skulls placed at the base or at the side of the body; some were even upside down.

The head of one skeleton was bent backwards indicating that its throat had been cut, although the rest of the body had been carefully arranged. Another had a twisted body, its hands clasping its neck and its head thrown backwards. A skull had its face smashed entirely and a blow from a sharp instrument had shorn off the teeth on the right side of the jaw. Another had the back of the skull smashed and driven in.

There was a skeleton which was twisted and hunched, having no head, while in another grave the body had been carefully straightened. Some had vertebrae missing from the lower back upwards.

It is obvious that a great massacre had taken place here. The evidence suggests that a few weeks or months after the battle the plundered bodies had been collected and buried.

Later, it seems, while the position of the graves was still remembered, the line of the greater earthwork had been curved during its construction as if to avoid them.

The battle may have taken place during the period between the Anglo-Saxon conquest and AD 905. This was a turbulent time in which dyke building and renovation would have been necessary, a time of war between the East-Angles and the Mercians in the 7th century.

Portway

At the Cambridge end of Melbourn, near Portway, traces of a rectangular earthwork were found, but by 1923 all that could be seen was a small portion of a ditch (fosse) and rampart (vallum). First recorded in 1868 the evidence suggested that it formed a 200 yard rectangle and was surrounded by a vallum to the east.

Various artefacts have been found near here, the most spectacular when a farmer ploughing deep for sugar beet in 1933 found an obstruction. It turned out to be a Roman quern, top and bottom stones complete. The stones lay compactly together as though they had been carried there carefully.

It was suggested that the earthwork was constructed at the time of the first Roman advance into the district, but there is no evidence to support that the work is Roman and its purpose is unknown. However, to the east of it there was a Roman cemetery probably in use in the 1st century and definitely in the 2nd. First century pottery of coarse ware from this site is in the British Museum.

Roman querns found when a farmer was ploughing close to Portway in 1933. They were a primitive form of hand-mill for grinding corn and consisted of two flattened circular stones; the lower stone was often shaped with a rim and would have had a wooden or metal pin in the centre which passed through a hole in the upper stone; the worker poured grain through the hole with one hand, turning the upper stone with the other by means of a peg fixed into the side. These were used before the invention of windmills and watermills. The Old English word is cweorn.

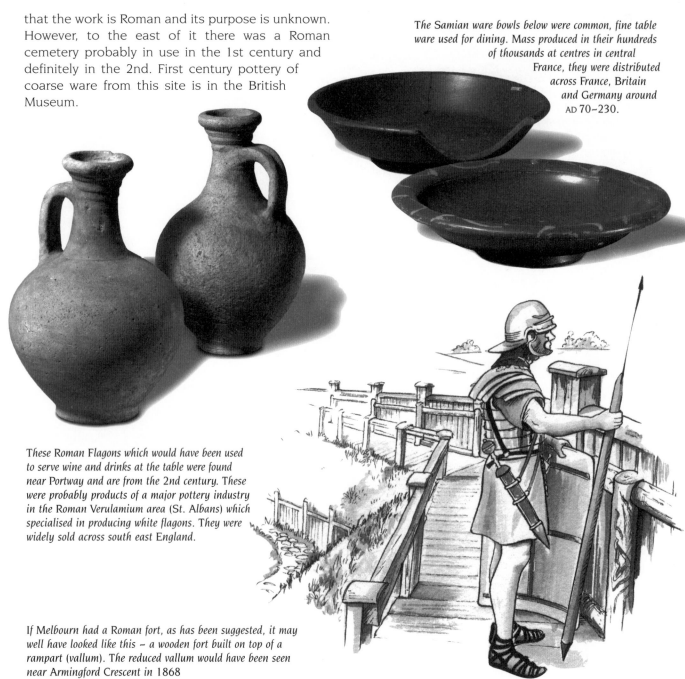

The Samian ware bowls below were common, fine table ware used for dining. Mass produced in their hundreds of thousands at centres in central France, they were distributed across France, Britain and Germany around AD 70–230.

These Roman Flagons which would have been used to serve wine and drinks at the table were found near Portway and are from the 2nd century. These were probably products of a major pottery industry in the Roman Verulamium area (St. Albans) which specialised in producing white flagons. They were widely sold across south east England.

If Melbourn had a Roman fort, as has been suggested, it may well have looked like this – a wooden fort built on top of a rampart (vallum). The reduced vallum would have been seen near Armingford Crescent in 1868

Flint Cross

Roman pottery sherds were found near Flint Cross where a rectangular soil mark was excavated and proved to be a ditch. At the same location is the course of a linear ditch which was possibly used as a boundary marker and is visible as a soil mark running from the north of Goffer's Knoll to Royston.

A10 by-pass

Before work began on the by-pass only a few worked flints had been discovered. During the construction more flints were unearthed ~ three well-made blades, an oval scraper, a stone spindle whorl (a small disc used to steady the motion in spinning wool), and sherds which were possibly examples of Iron Age and Belgic pottery wares (these were some of the first tools to become widespread imports into Britain).

Pottery sherds, dating to the 1st and 2nd centuries, were found along the line of the by-pass and a heavy concentration of Anglo-Saxon sherds were found near the Station Road junction. At the south end of the by-pass were a few tiles, nails and other iron objects, together with a small bell and a small disc with a 'strap', both in copper alloy.

Evidence of Roman occupation was discovered further north where pottery was found from the 1st ~4th centuries.

Heath Farm

In 1935 at Heath Farm, a Middle Bronze Age spearhead was found in a field during ploughing. It was leaf shaped and in good condition and a type of weapon used by the local tribes. It is not typical of a locally made spearhead but was probably imported from Iceland. The locals were well known for trading goods.

Deep ploughing in February 1953 unearthed a cake of bronze, probably from a Late Bronze Age hoard, and three ingots which were possibly formed in a crucible and were probably Roman.

Back Lane

In the 1800s a Bronze Age hoard was discovered at the southern end of Back Lane containing a gouge, socketed axe, knife, sword blade fragment, a bugle-shaped object, a hollow ring, the tip of a scabbard and a horse bit. It has been suggested that these items may have been a collection made ready for recycling.

Many earthworks in agricultural districts are, since the enclosure of the fields, gradually disappearing. Banks which were noticeable landmarks 50 years ago are now scarcely discernible unless pointed out. In these cases I have found the character of the vegetation growing on them a useful guide. For instance a Roman camp was described as being by the Portway at Melbourn. I searched in vain for traces of this until, my attention being attracted by an old furze bush, which is now very rare in these parts, growing on a hedgebank by the roadside, I examined the grass and found it consisted largely of Festuca ovina. Then on getting on to the other side of the thick hawthorn hedge it was possible, with a little imagination, to make out two sides of a camp adjoining orchard and meadow, one of which ended at the hedgebank where the furze bush grew.

W.M. Palmer

The East Anglian: or Notes and Queries Vol. 6 1895

In 1951, whilst work was being carried out for the Whiting Company in Back Lane, an Anglo-Saxon cemetery was discovered. Excavations took place in the early months of 1952 but unfortunately, before archaeologists started work, villagers became aware of the site and opened up three graves in the hope of obtaining souvenirs. The contents were never recovered.

The only structural features found at the site were two ditches. These may have defined the limits of the cemetery at different stages, the larger ditch definitely being the earlier of the two as it had a grave dug across it. The smaller one, however, is more likely to be a later medieval field boundary.

The cemetery contained over 28 male and female skeletons. There were also a number of children, two of which were infants, one aged about 18 months, determined by examination of the teeth. The other children were between 7 and 14 years of age.

A man out walking his dog along Newmarket Road by-pass was picking up sticks to throw for his dog. One was too heavy to be a stick and was discovered to be a sword covered with mud. He thought it might be worth something as scrap metal, so he washed it to find that it gleamed. It was taken to an antique dealer who thought the pommel could be removed but in the process he managed to snap the top off. In order to establish the type of metal several areas were scraped which caused further damage.

Subsequently, a metallurgist who examined the sword concluded that the grip was of cast brass and gilded. The pommel probably was made the same but had a thicker layer of gilt. It was also examined by the curator of Brewhouse Yard Museum, Nottingham who reported that the artefact was a damaged hilt and broken blade of a small sword or court sword of late 18-19th century origin. By 1800 such swords were no longer used by civilians, but were increasingly used by European and American military officers.

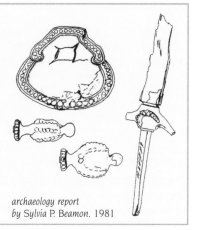

archaeology report by Sylvia P. Beamon. 1981

The graves and their contents

The only ceramic pot found in the cemetery was with one of the children and was dated to the early-7th century. Knives were also found with two other children and one child had a pin under his chin. Apart from these items nothing else was buried with the children.

A very small female was found with crossed legs and it is possible this position indicated a rich burial but in the Melbourn cemeteries it is not clear if this is the case. A box was by the side of her head together with a double-sided comb. The strengthening strips of the comb were held in place by iron rivets and attached by another rivet was a ring, both made of bronze. A pair of shears was also found together with a knife, a bronze ring and a bronze mounted wooden cup. A crack in the lip had been repaired with a small strip of folded bronze and secured by bronze pins. A small jet bead, a larger blue 'melon' bead and a bronze hook and eye were found in the same grave.

A 2cm silver disc pendant was found in another grave, the centre was bossed and may have taken the head of a pin. Around the boss was a pattern formed by a series of triangles and dots crudely stamped in a formal zigzag-reserved pattern based on the central boss. Such patterns were fairly common in Western Europe in the 7th century. This

Three single edged knives found in the grave of a rich female

pattern also appeared on a double spiral dress fastener discovered in another grave on the site. A knife lay at the side and at the ankles were two bronze lace tags. A bronze pin with an ornamental ring attached, found under the chin, would have been used as a hood or shroud fastener.

Other items included a brooch, with a serrated decoration, found on the breast, a buckle, a whorl or toggle, two beads and a pin measuring about 3cm in length.

In another grave a similar pin was found under the head of a rich female. Also in the grave was an iron handle with mounts from a wooden bucket, two bronze mounts for a gourd, and a double sided comb made of bone with strengthening strips fastened with iron rivets.

The teeth of bone combs were cut after the strengthening strips were applied, as cuts can sometimes be seen in the bevelled edge of the strip. By the 7th century combs were common with many burials and the double-sided version became more popular.

On her chest was a bronze hood fastener and complex small bronze plates by her left leg. She was buried wearing a girdle or belt with two rings – one of bronze (probably a toggle) the other was made of

Seventh century double-sided comb, common with many burials. The teeth were carved after the strengthening bar had been fitted as cut marks were found on the bevel of the bar.

iron and had two riveted bronze plates attached which may have formed the mounts for a purse or knife sheath. Between the ankles were two bronze lace tags, as found in other graves. Round her neck was a string of beads including two perfectly matched amethyst drop beads, a popular form produced in Kent.

An older female had a similar festooned dress decoration as found with the rich burial. A paper-thin silver disc, with a punched decoration of a cross, was found and is thought to have been stuck originally to a wooden or leather base. A ring, a knife and the remains of a wooden box with a spindle whorl or toggle, probably inside the box at the time of burial, were also found in the grave. A double grave, possibly dug during a very hard winter when the ground was hard, contained a male and female.

Behind the head of the male was a sheep's jawbone, the only example in the cemetery of food placed inside a grave. Also accompanying him were the remains of a small wooden bucket. Small traces of wood were still attached to the mount.

The female beneath him had, lying upon her chest, a series of five small silver rings, pendants of silver and a number of beads, which would probably have been sewn to the garment she was wearing to form a permanent decoration ~ a festoon.

Two other pendants were found ~ one of silver in the form of a hand, the fingers being illustrated by nielloed grooves. (*Niello is a black composition of sulphur with silver, lead or copper for filling engraved lines in silver or other metals.*) This hand symbol matches contemporary examples found in Germany. The other pendant was of mosaic glass in dark brown or blue, with a trellis pattern of twisted green and white glass. It was mounted onto a flat plate and turned over at the top to form a corrugated loop for hanging. A strip of silver and a length of silver wire enclosed the glass. It was oval in shape, about an inch long and very elegant. The same style pendant, though mounted on gold, was found in Kent ~ the type of mounting being very popular during the late pagan period. This pendant was obviously made at the same workshop as the gold example found in Kent as was the amethyst drop beads from the grave mentioned previously.

In one grave an iron buckle showed the imprint of a very coarse

cloth. Part of a shield was placed in another; the boss measured 13cm high by 15cm in diameter and formed a cone constructed from a flat sheet of metal. Behind it lay a plain iron bar, forming the handle of the shield, which was bound with cloth. An imprint of a linen texture was left behind by the pressure of the metal bar. It is possibly a unique type of boss, certainly unknown in Cambridgeshire, and may be the work of a smith experimenting with design. Also in the grave were a spearhead about 45cm long, a knife at its lower ribs and a small bronze buckle.

A similar spearhead, but slightly smaller at about 30cm long, was found with another old, but muscular male, shown by the build of his skeleton. With him were two fragments of cloth of fairly fine weave preserved by a buckle of bronze.

The cemetery dates from the seventh century onwards and signs were evident of the changeover from paganism to Christianity.

A selection of rings, pins and a buckle also found in Back Lane

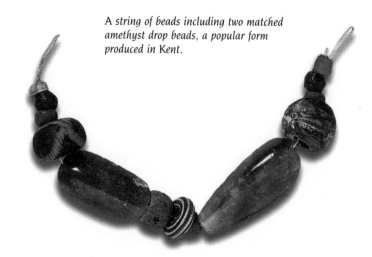

A string of beads including two matched amethyst drop beads, a popular form produced in Kent.

Churchyard excavations

Following plans for a new church hall, excavation began in the churchyard in 1989. Eighteen holes of about 1 metre square were excavated which were to be filled with concrete to act as the foundations of the building. Human remains were plentiful, especially below a level of 1m from ground level.

The deepest graves were cut into the chalk level. Others were found closer to the surface, and so, as there were numerous bodies, later burials were cut through earlier ones. In most of the holes excavated at least 5 individuals were present. Burials in the churchyard took place over a long period of time and, as the church held no records, there was no recollection of where previous burials had taken place. The layers of burials led to most of the bones being muddled and it was very difficult, if not impossible, to distinguish one individual from another.

The burials were Christian as bodies were orientated east-west. As each of the holes cut was only 1m square, whole skeletons were not recovered but it was possible to see that in a few cases two bodies had been interred together.

A spearhead about 45cm long discovered in Back Lane

Many of the bodies were of elderly people, having no teeth and the gums being worn smooth. Many of the remaining individuals were adult although the remains of a baby, possibly neonatal, was found with an adult.

There were few artefacts found during the excavation. Two gold (wedding) rings were found on one individual, both hallmarked. One was 22 carat gold, assayed in London and dated to 1862; the other possibly dates from 1858 or 1874.

The excavations showed that the graveyard was in use from medieval times, to the Victorian period. There is also a gravestone, now a listed monument remaining in the churchyard, of Benjamin Metcalfe, a central figure of the Puritan Movement 1595–1651.

The gravestone of Benjamin Metcalfe 1595–1651 now a listed monument. Metcalfe was a central figure of the Puritan Movement.

Water Lane

An area of land covered by an old orchard at the top of Water Lane was excavated in 2000 before developers moved in. Archaeologists found three main phases of activity had taken place here – early prehistoric, late prehistoric and Anglo-Saxon.

Some of the burials at Water Lane contained an assortment of interesting artifacts. The most impressive was the Melbourn great square headed brooch found in very good condition. In the same grave was a radiate brooch seen to the right, and a variety of beads at the base of the photo.

Prehistoric activity

The earliest datable activity at the site, part of a round barrow, possibly faced with flint, which had a total of eight pits, was from the late Neolithic/early Bronze Age period (c.2000 BC).

The contents of the pits may have been intentionally left by nomadic people whilst visiting the site and were not thought to represent evidence of any permanent occupation. Two of the pits contained fragments of collared urns and two bowls. They were all decorated; the collared urns with incisions or twisted cord, and the bowls had incised motifs.

The radiate brooch (below) which served as a shoulder fastening, had a small piece of leather attached to the back of the head. The design originates from Europe, but its crudeness suggests it was a copy.

The Melbourn great square headed brooch was possibly used to fasten an outer garment, such as a cloak.

After restoration, the square headed brooch revealed a magnificent example of workmanship. Made of cast copper alloy – gilded with silver sheets applied to the footplate and side lobes it is to date – the finest example in Cambridgeshire. A bird motive can be clearly seen just above each of the side lobes. A trace of woollen woven fabric is still attached to the back of the brooch (see below).

Note: The brooch featured on the front cover is to scale

A selection of jewellery from Water Lane – a pin, slip knot rings, spindle whorl and a buckle

Some graves were used more than once as this picture from Water Lane shows. The new burial has been carefully placed above the existing one.

Activity from the late Bronze Age/early Iron Age period (*c*.1000 to 800 BC) was evident from the discovery of 68 sherds of pottery and a series of four post structures which may have been used for grain storage.

The Anglo-Saxon cemetery

The excavation of the cemetery uncovered a total of 52 graves. These contained the remains of 59 individuals, including a single isolated grave which was situated about 20m from the main burial area. Grave goods were found with many of the burials, more than average for the period. A number of the graves had also been reused, one grave being reopened at least four times leaving previous burials undisturbed.

Not all finds from excavations are distinguishable at first glance. The spear heads on the right are an obvious shape – but the two single edged ones above are heavily encrusted and less discernable.

The earliest burial was that of a woman of over 45 years of age. She was buried wearing a necklace made of 57 glass and 12 amber beads, and also had three brooches and a belt or 'girdle' fastened by a copper alloy buckle. A knife and a spindle whorl were suspended from the girdle. Textile remains suggest that she may have worn a woollen cloak over a garment of linen (flax). She was from the last quarter of the 6th century.

A major change in female dress fashion took place sometime during the late 6th or early-7th century. The practice of wearing two to three brooches and long strings of polychrome and amber beads was outmoded by the occasional use of a single brooch and short necklaces from which were strung shell and monochrome glass beads, rings of silver wire and small pendants.

A female aged between 25 and

30 appeared to reflect the transition between these two fashions and may date to the final years of the 6th century. The necklace she wore contained 6 amber and 36 polychrome and monochrome glass beads along with wire rings, and spangles and a pendant of silver.

By AD 600 fashion was reflected in the objects worn by a young woman of between 19 and 25 years of age. She had a short necklace of two amber beads and a shell and a copper alloy pendant, an annular brooch and a metal dress pin. Suspended from her girdle was a knife, an antler comb and a chain of iron links from which hung an iron key and a toiletry set with an ear pick.

As the 7th century progressed the wealth or status of women at Melbourn seemed to be expressed in terms of personal possessions suspended from their girdles, such as combs, keys and shears, rather than items of jewellery. One woman in her early twenties typified this fashion. She wore no jewellery, but hanging from her girdle and extending to her knee, was a long 'chatelaine' (a chain and clasp worn at the waist by a woman to hold keys and other small items) made up of inter-

The skeleton of a male about 183cm tall. Note the crossed legs – a possible indication of a rich grave. Above the head is a ceramic jar in perfect condition.

linking iron rods, chain links, and keys, with an iron 'strike-a-light' suspended.

Not all the females were so 'richly' accompanied; some had only one or two items, such as a knife suspended from the girdle. Males are less easy to date, as fewer fashion-sensitive items were included. The normal repertoire of objects with a man comprised of a knife and buckle. The inclusion

An enlarged picture of the pot as it laid in the grave

change in burial custom has been linked to the conversion to Christianity, but may also reflect changes in the acceptable manner of expressing status of the deceased.

Less than a quarter of those buried were under the age of 18 and there are almost equal numbers of males and females. Some of the adults had reached an advanced age, with a third over 45 years and a small number probably over 60 and possibly considerably older. The large majority of males in the oldest age group is unusual for archaeological cemeteries. The people were tall, some of the tallest Anglo-Saxons yet reported.

In terms of health, there were a few fractures but there were no identifiable weapon injuries, so it appears that local conflict had become less common. One man died with a massive bladder stone, probably the cause of his death, and one woman was pregnant but her cause of death is not known.

The excavations revealed that the cemetery was in

A skeleton from the Water Lane cemetery positioned on the side

of weapons was rare and may be linked to their status. Six of the males had spears but no shields were found.

Towards the end of the 7th century there was a change in burial practices. Burials were increasingly unaccompanied by objects and the new trend was to orientate the burials in an easterly direction. The

A single-sided comb with a curved 'hog-back'. Four iron rivets along the connecting plates are still in place and the staining of a fifth can be seen. The comb had been repaired as can be seen on the left hand side. A pattern of four X's had been incised along the back.

use between AD 575 and AD 675, earlier than the Anglo-Saxon cemetery discovered in Back Lane in 1952. It is unknown if the two sites were two cemeteries or one larger one, although the 1952 site lies just 100m to the west.

Catalogue of finds from Water Lane

Festoon: an ornamental chain of flowers, leaves, or ribbons hanging in a loop or curve between two points, in this case, beads.

Beads were found to be made from five different materials from the total of 144 beads recovered from the Water Lane site. A third of the glass beads were *monochrome glass beads*. A *pale translucent blue-green glass bead* possibly fashioned from recycled Roman bottle glass. Other beads found were in the same category and also reminiscent of beads of the Roman period. Two were a *smoky yellow colour*, the other may have been colourless but was too decayed to tell.

There was a melon-shaped *black bead*. This type of bead has only been found in southern England and the Midlands. The others were barrel shaped and it is possible that these beads, having the appearance of porous pottery, may have had a black coating applied over an opaque white ground to give them the appearance of jet. *Monochrome opaque white beads* are dated between the 5th and 7th centuries.

Opaque yellow beads that were found may have originated from Frankish sources and been imported into England during the 6th century. The most numerous of the *monochrome beads* are of *green* and *turquoise glass*. Green beads were very common in the Roman period, but the majority of the Anglo-Saxon examples date from the 6th and early-7th centuries.

Translucent melon-shaped blue beads were of a common post-Roman type. The examples in Melbourn came from the second half of the 6th century. *Opaque terracotta beads* became popular in the 6th century and continued in use into the 7th century.

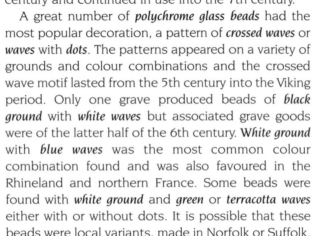

A great number of *polychrome glass beads* had the most popular decoration, a pattern of *crossed waves* or *waves* with *dots*. The patterns appeared on a variety of grounds and colour combinations and the crossed wave motif lasted from the 5th century into the Viking period. Only one grave produced beads of *black ground* with *white waves* but associated grave goods were of the latter half of the 6th century. *White ground* with *blue waves* was the most common colour combination found and was also favoured in the Rhineland and northern France. Some beads were found with *white ground* and *green* or *terracotta waves* either with or without dots. It is possible that these beads were local variants, made in Norfolk or Suffolk.

Spotted beads such as a *single opaque white* with *terracotta spots* are relatively rare and date around the early-7th century. A single example of a round bead of *black ground* with *white* and *terracotta swirls* was found, the style of which began in the 5th century and lasted into the 7th century and possibly later.

Of the **non-glass beads** there was a good collection of *amber beads* which had seven identified shapes. Some showed signs of shaping, including possible lathe-turning on the largest, *bun-shaped bead*. After the first few years of the 7th century amber beads are only generally found in ones or twos. Single *amber beads* with no accompanying beads or necklace ornaments, may have been worn to ward off evil or disease, rather than having a decorative purpose.

Seven *cowrie shell beads* were found. A cowrie is a marine snail with a highly polished shell, often coloured, fairly common on British shores. They have also been used as fertility charms. Most graves containing the shells have been dated to the 7th century.

Brooches included the *Melbourn great square headed brooch* which dates to AD 550–570. The *radiate brooch* is possibly a copy of a European style, because of its crudeness. It dates from the 1st to the 3rd quarter of the 6th century and would have been used as a shoulder fastening on a peplos-type gown. A *saucer brooch* was used to fasten the gown to an under garment and the *Melbourn great square headed brooch* would have fastened an outer garment such as a cloak. Other brooches served as shoulder fastenings.

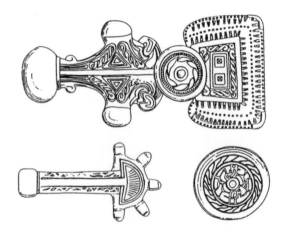

A *cast gilt saucer brooch* had an animal decoration of two stylised bodies that can be seen in the central circle with their profile heads facing in a clockwise direction on either side. This and the *Melbourn great square headed brooch* were contemporary pieces datable to the mid-6th century at the earliest.

A *circular brooch* made of cast copper alloy was the trend for burials from the late-6th century onwards. They are predominately circular in form.

Buckles were mostly placed at the waist. The one exception was situated by a hand and close to a chatelaine. It was small, elegant, and oval in shape and made of copper alloy and the most common type. Buckles were slightly D-shaped. All the iron buckles had iron tongues but the ferrous metal buckles had either iron or copper alloy tongues. The buckles could accommodate four different widths of strap ranging from 8mm to 18mm and were used by both men and women.

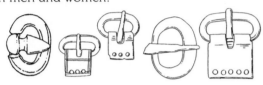

A **chatelaine** is a chain and clasp, worn by a woman at the waist, consisting of inter-linking iron rods and chain links. These held keys and other small items such as an iron 'strike-a-light', ear picks and spindle whorls.

Combs, generally double-sided, were rarely found with burials of the 5th and 6th centuries. By the 7th century they had become more common, but increasingly one sided in design.

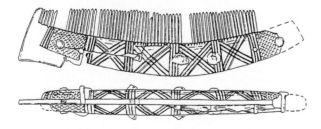

Keys were found suspended from chatelaines. These were slide keys, either L-shaped or T-shaped. Both shapes were common in the 5th and 9th century deposits in Britain. A cylindrical or barrel *padlock* was found with a hooked or bent rod which may have formed part of its bolt.

Knives were normally placed at the waist, although a few had the knife above the head. A male child and an adult female had one by the shoulder and the upper arm.

Tanged, parallel-sided, round-ended tools, with a rectangular cross section, have been identified as *sharpening steels*. Typically they date to the 7th century and were found in close association with a knife at waist level.

Pins were worn on the body and used to secure clothing. A number were used to fasten a hood or head covering. Sometimes pierced, the pin could have a ring thread through the hole, or a glass or gemstone inset. These pins were made of copper alloy. One pin was positioned on the shoulder and was the largest of the copper alloy pins ~ it would have been used to fasten a cloak.

Of the pins found, two were made of **bone** and positioned not at the shoulders or the neck but by the left ribs and right leg. Bone pins found with skeletons are rare and their use is not clear. The design of one of the pins (a small disc-headed pin characterised by a flattened head and short length) is found mainly in Scotland and only a few examples have been found further south.

Shears included in burials only became popular in the 7th century, these being full sized. In the 7th ~ 8th century in England graves containing shears were exclusively female, and here they were buried with combs and a spindle whorl suggesting a link to textile production, but they were more likely to have been multi-purpose cutting tools.

A number of **spindle whorls** were found in Melbourn. One had been fashioned from the base of a Roman ceramic vessel, the other whorl was made from a deer antler. Whorls with larger spindle holes were produced by the Anglo-Saxons whilst those from the Roman period had a smaller hole.

Triangular hooked tags used for fastenings were probably sewn onto a garment, possibly in the hoods, bags, purses, or perhaps even shrouds. They were in use for a long period, first appearing in the 7th century and extending into the 11th century.

Toiletry items found included an *ear pick* threaded onto a slip-knot ring, discernable by the shape and decorative grooves, although the end of the stem had been broken. The bowl and lower stem of an *iron spoon* ~ iron spoons may have had a domestic use, perhaps for mixing or measuring medicines and ointments.

Wire slip-knot rings were present on two spangles, and threaded through a bead would have been used as the ends of a necklace. Other *slip-knot rings*, made of copper alloy and of similar size to those worn on a necklace, were used to suspend items from a belt. Knotted *silver slip-knot rings* became popular in the 7th century and continued in use probably into the early-8th century.

Fruit pickers at The Bury 1917

Agriculture & trade
Farming

...William of Melbourn, son of the reeve, held a messuage and 20 acres of land in the 1300s

The term farming is used here to cover all aspects of crop production and animal husbandry, including management of woodlands for building materials and fuel and food for livestock. It was the employment of all but the rich and the few educated people, such as priests, until gradually, other trades evolved from servicing the needs of farmers, manors and ordinary households.

Open field cultivation

Evidence suggests that open field cultivation was practised by the Anglo-Saxons during the 8th century; using areas with little woodland, as Cambridgeshire was during this period. Melbourn had 4 open fields: West Field at the western edge of the parish and Mill (or Middle) Field situated nearer the village both of which consisted of around 1,000 acres. Cawdon (or Cawdell) Field contained around 800 acres and Fox Field about 500 acres. East of these were around 100 acres of Moor. The Common was in the north-west of the parish and was shared with Meldreth. At the south-east of the village there were about 500 acres of heathland.

The system of farming

The open fields were divided into strips known as selions, which were about half an acre and measured one furlong by two perches (220 yards by

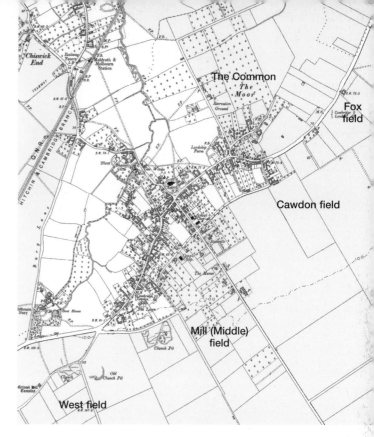

The open fields of Melbourn. Peterhouse has owned land in Melbourn since the 12th century. The following field names refer to parts of the 4 open fields (Cawdon, Fox, Mill, and West fields). Other names recur throughout the years, including: Ansden Hill, Bonny Hill Shot, Deadman's Way, Duns Hawk, Farthing Knap Spat, Foxoles, Gravel Pit Way, Grindly Hillway, Hava Hayfield, Little Bootton, Long Ditch, Long Nick, Mayfield, Middleshot, Newells Pickering Acre, Potter's Way, Pumps, Rumbold's Headway, Sotts Bottom, Sparrows, Ditch Thistle Hill, Wares, West Shortmead, and Wilsy Way. There was also Oasthouse by Millfield, next to London Way; this would indicate that hops were grown here.

11 yards). The word furlong derives from a 'furrow's length'. Each selion was separated by a track, path or sometimes a baulk (a narrow uncultivated strip or a fragment of hedge), which helped to identify individual strips.

Each farmer would have his strips distributed around the area. Strips were aggregated into

Part of a collection of documents outlining the fields surrounding Melbourn, owned by Peterhouse at the time. The one above mentions a grant of land awarded to John de Foxton, vicar of Melbourn, in 1229 during the reign of Edward I.

furlongs and then into fields. The same crop was grown by all farmers on each furlong. Crop rotation was practised ~ a system whereby each field was left fallow (ploughed but not sown), every second, third or fourth year.

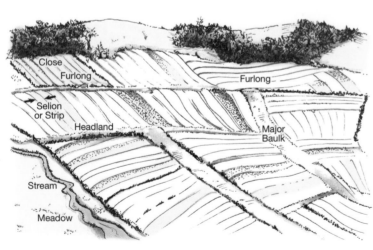

The Open-Field System

The livestock were left free to graze the stubble after each harvest and in the fallow year. This saved on pasture and provided fertilisation. The system was collective and farmers shared the cultivation of each others strips. Hedgerows were sparse and did not form enclosed fields.

Positions of the major baulks can seen today in the village by the rectangular grid of roads and small lanes which developed in their place.

Medieval ridge-and-furrow

The distinctive pattern of ridge-and-furrow developed naturally when driving a mold board plough drawn by 8 oxen, within the narrow confines of a half-acre strip. The soil would accumulate in the middle of each strip, and was therefore nudged to the ends of the strips, building up a ridge at right angles on the headland. With such cumbersome equipment it was difficult to plough in straight lines and it was better to begin the turn well before reaching the headland, giving the double curve, (a reversed-S) typical of medieval ploughland. The mold board plough caused a revolution in farming, as in earlier times the far less efficient scratch plough was used.

In some parts of the country, working the land in this way has left its mark and can be seen on aerial photos of pastureland. There is little evidence of this to be seen in Melbourn although the system persisted here until the enclosures of 1839.

Plough horses replaced oxen in the 13th century. The change was slow, and was resisted by some farmers, as the ox was superior to the horse in some respects. Having no horns to serve as tow bars the horse required an elaborate collar and harness, and oxen could be used as food after their working lives. In many areas oxen were re-introduced during the 19th and even the 20th centuries.

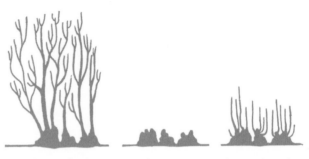

Coppicing ~ when trees are cut down or coppiced they send up shoots

Management of the woodlands

The area surrounding Melbourn was never densely forested, but wood was an essential raw material for everyday living. 'Wildwood', in England, disappeared after the prehistoric era, and all woodlands in this country have been managed since Anglo-Saxon times.

Woodlands were managed by *coppicing* and *pollarding* which promotes re-growth. When trees are cut down or *coppiced* they send up shoots. These become poles which can be cut indefinitely. In wood-pasture accessible to grazing livestock, where shoots could be eaten by the animals, trees were *pollarded*; cut 6 to 15 feet above the ground, leaving a permanent trunk which produces poles. This can be seen in pollarded willows along river banks.

Areas classed as non-woodland, such as trees in hedgerows and fields, also included orchards and plantations. Timber, as distinct from wood, was also grown as a crop, but on a much longer rotation.

The poles resulting from coppicing and pollarding were used for many essential purposes such as hurdles for pens, and wattle and daub in the construction of buildings. Archaeological evidence has shown that hurdles were also used to make roads in ancient times.

Every community would have made charcoal as this was necessary for the blacksmith. Charcoal burning, depending on the size of the clamp, could take up to 100 hours and had to be constantly attended in order that it did not burn too quickly. Charcoal burners would use 1-legged stools to deter them from falling asleep!

The Domesday Book

After the Norman Conquest in 1066, officials of William I compiled detailed records of land and property in order to assess land tax and other dues, and the findings were recorded in the Domesday Book in 1086. The survey also laid the foundations of the feudal system in England ~ the main form of social organisation in medieval times. Melbourn

(entered as Meldeburna) had at that time 2460 acres of arable land which was divided amongst various holders. There were 55 heads of family, amounting to a population of about 275 people. Bury Manor at that time was held by the Abbot of Ely and consisted of 1200 acres of land and 18 heads of family.

Argentines Manor (which belonged to Edric the Plain in pre-Norman times) was given to Guy de Rembercourt. He had also seized lands belonging to the Abbot of Ely, the total amounting to 1920 acres of which his bailiff farmed 600 and the rest was let to tenants; 6 farmers and 36 smallholders. There were two watermills on the estate and another was shared with the Abbot of Ely. Enough meadowland was enclosed to pasture 88 draft oxen (or 11 teams), there was a flock of 350 sheep and a herd of 62 swine. This estate had been worth £18 a year during King Edward the Confessor's time (1042~1066), although when Guy de Rembercourt took over it was worth only half this amount. By 1086 the value had risen to just £14. From these figures it appears that the villager suffered during the conquest of England. Even in 1086 as much as 240 acres of the lord's own land was uncultivated.

The order of society

The feudal system was based primarily on land and involved a hierarchy of authority extending from the monarchy downwards through nobility, lesser gentry, free tenants, villeins, bordars (tenants holding a cottage and usually a few acres of land at the will of the Lord and bound to menial service), cottars (peasants ranking just above a serf) and serfs or slaves.

Originally, all inhabitants of Melbourn were 'tied' to the Manor and owed services to the lord in return for their cottages, gardens and any rights they might be allowed on Common land. They were not allowed to leave the village or work elsewhere without his permission, or take any independent decision without his approval. Although treated as such, serfs could not be sold as slaves. In return for military services, the monarch allowed vassals (those who were obliged to show loyalty to a feudal lord) to hold land, to administer justice and levy taxes and they in turn sub-let these rights.

The system remained in place until King John was forced to sign the Magna Carta in 1215. This guaranteed human rights against the excessive use of royal power. The king could no longer demand enormous amounts of money from barons without their consent and no freeman was to be arrested, imprisoned or punished except by judgement of his peers or the law of the land.

It was not until after 1215 that a monetary economy began to evolve and slavery gradually diminished. A man (and his family) could be released from bondage, a process known as manumission. By 1418 at least 14 villeins in Melbourn had all their services commuted, but they were still liable for the various payments to the lord of the manor.

The bailiff's roll

Melbourn's accounts during the reign of Henry VI (1422~61, 1470~71), were compiled by William Aldyng, the 'bailiff and money collector of fixed rents and free tenements'. They contained diverse outgoings and profits of the court for 1456~7 from *the feast of St. Michael Archangel, 35th regnal year of Henry VI up to the said feast in the 36th year.*

Feudalism

As feudalism declined and gave way to the class system, the Magna Carta lost its significance, until in Tudor times it was all but forgotten. It was 're-discovered' in the 17th century when it was re-interpreted as a democratic document.

The Manors

Melbourn Bury

At the time of Domesday, The Bury (then owned by the Diocese of Ely), had 1¼ hides in demesne (the land attached to a manor).

A survey, taken at The Bury by two of the Prior's clerks in 1318, showed that the Manor house enclosure contained six acres, and with the herbage and fruit from three gardens was worth 10s a year. There was a windmill, a watermill, a dovecote, fifty acres of enclosed meadow to the north and east, and a hop ground. The arable land measured over 500 acres in pieces scattered over the parishes of Melbourn and Meldreth. This was the demesne land only; the lands of the freemen and copyholders which made up the 1,440 acres of the Domesday survey, were not included.

During the early-14th century Bury land employed 28 half-yardlanders, (people who had use of enough land to grow food to feed their family) and 12 cottars in Melbourn and Meldreth. At least 33 tenants held molland (land for which they drew lots).

A translated part of the bailiff's roll

An ornamental dovecote at the rear of The Bury, Royston Road

Old measures

The measurement of land varied depending on the quality of the soil

A hide was about 120 acres in the mid-11th century around the time of the Norman Conquest and the Domesday survey. Melbourn was assessed at about 10 hides.

A yard-land varied between 30–40 acres. A ½ yard-land was anything from 14–18 acres. and was the minimum on which a family could support itself without any other employment.

A perch, also known as a rod or a pole, originally varied, but became standardised at 16.5 feet. This inconvenient length was used to calculate the area of agricultural land that could be worked by one person in a day. The area was reckoned to be 2 perches by 2 perches (33 feet by 33 feet). Thus a *daywork* (a day's work) amounted to 4 square perches.

An acre was originally the area that a yoke of oxen (two) could plough in a day and therefore differed in size from one locality to another. It is now fixed as 160 square rods.

A furlong, originally a furrow length, measured 220 yards.

A virgate was a variable old English measure of land equal to one quarter of a hide.

And of 4s from William Chambleyns for one messuage, 2 acres and 3 rods of land formerly of Walter Lanrents, and afterwards William Aldyng, who had accounted for the same in the annual court in the 27th year of the king's reign. And of 4s 6d from William Scolar for one messuage with a adjoining croft formerly of John Groin, afterwards Thomas Cerine and lately Thomas Payne, who accounted for it in the annual court of the king's 28th regnal year.

And of 10s 9d from John Newlyn for one tenement with appurtenances, formerly (26) of John Gewney, accounted for first in the annual court held in the king's 36th regnal year.

And of 12d from William Chambleyne who rents 1 acre located in Gatonn, formerly in the tenure of John Fere and afterwards John Gervers and recently in the tenure of John Gayle. And of 12d of rent... William of which one acre of land with one... and (1?) rods is located in Foxhill next to the land of John Chambleyn, lately in the tenure of John Harnewold

Argentine Manor

In 1307 Argentine Manor employed 13 villein half-yardlanders and 4 cottars. The cottars did not work between Lammas (a Christian religious feast held on August 1st) and Michaelmas (a Christian holy day on September 29th), but a total of 240 of them brought in the harvest.

In the early 1300s the manor consisted of a splendid house with outbuildings; gardens and dovecote, worth 3s 4d a year after expenses; 100 acres of lucrative land, worth 4d an acre; a windmill and 10 free tenants who paid £4 in equal portions during the year.

When approached from the Cambridge direction, the Manor was just beyond the crossroads with the Moor. The pound was in front, with the house and herb garden behind it.

The house enclosure itself was large for the time, having about 13 acres, and within the compound were a granary, a brewhouse and barns. The kitchen and other offices were separate from the house to guard against fire. The buildings were surrounded by a moat on which swans were kept, used for the lord's table. These were prized birds as, in 1318, a

Argentine Manor (Lordship Farm), High Street

The rear of Argentine Manor, High Street

pair of swans and seven cygnets were allowed six bushels of dredge (or drage, a mixture of barley and oats) corn. There would have been a dovecote, a special privilege of the lord of the manor, and a mill. There were then two bridges over the moat; one of them may have been a drawbridge. The cottages of the bondsmen were between the Manor and the church.

The lord also employed 4 ploughmen, a carter, 2 shepherds, 2 boys and a maidservant. By 1356 feudalism was dying and some Argentine tenants were paying money in place of services for their rents. In 1381 only 20 days work during harvest and winter were recorded. This was the year of the Peasants' Revolt.

The person who kept the accounts in 1318 was the reeve, Hugh Nocky. He held an inherited tenancy

In 1318 1d (one old penny) could buy either:

25 hen's eggs, 1lb of cheese, 3 pigeons, 3–4 lbs of mutton, 1 pint of butter, 2 gallons of cider, 1 gallon of beer, 1 pint of wine, 1 horseshoe.

and his wages were 3s a year, with 1d and a gosling worth 2d at Christmas.

The receipts for the year in question were £38 1s 7½d made up of rents (£11 7s 6d), the sale of corn, fleeces, 2 horses (10s), 4 dozen pigeons (2s), etc.

The expenses for the year were £44 16s 5d, making an overall loss of £6 14s 9½d.

The expenses included: ...*to the carpenter producing new woodwork for ploughs, 7 days work 20d; to the smith for forging 12 pieces of iron into shoes and plough irons at 3d each, 3s.* The labour bill was not excessive: ...*threshing – 2d a quarter for wheat, meslin (a mixed winter crop of wheat and barley or rye), and peas, slightly less for barley and oats.* Repairs to the manor house came to 1s 8d and stock and corn were bought for 13s.

Payments were probably not in money, but by tally, a thin strip of wood with notches cut to represent pounds, shillings and pence, by which accounts could be kept. Illiterate peasants would be able to understand this system.

The main work on the 300 acre arable farm was done by the bondsmen, and the reeve calculated how many 'works' were required for the year.

One entry in the accounts reads: ...*Hoeing. Nothing was paid for hoeing this year, since it was all done by bondmen.* It took 220 days' work.

...*Harvest expenses. No further account of harvest expenses, since it was all done by bondmen, and all were fed at the table of the lord.* This took 407 days' work.

Tally sticks – thin strips of wood with notches cut to represent pounds, shillings and pence

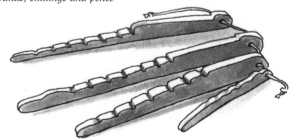

Arthur Wedd at work

The rations allotted to the labourers depended on the success of the harvest. The harvest of 1317 was a bad one and, instead of half a pint of rye and peas to half a peck each of wheat and barley, the reeve mixed together: 6 quarters of tail wheat, 14¾ quarters of meslin, 3¾ quarters of peas and 9 quarters of mill corn (the lord's perquisite from tenants' corn which was ground at his mill).

The four ploughmen, the carter and the shepherd were allowed 2½ pecks a week each, equal to 8 quartern loaves per head throughout the year. A female servant in the house was allowed 2 pecks, and a boy also allowed 2 pecks. The regular hands, in addition, received 2 quarters of oats for porridge during the winter. A quartern loaf weighed about 4 lbs.

All in a year's work

Life was a struggle for the average peasant. In the 1590s there was crop failure due to a mini ice-age. The last great famine was in 1623. Prior to that the possibility of famine was always present. The hay harvest was of vital importance since, if this failed, animals could not be kept through the winter. The most difficult months of the year were those just before the grain harvest and July was known as 'the hungry gap'.

In 'Piers Plowman' it states that July was the month when the divide between rich and poor became most apparent. The rich had barns and money to buy supplies when prices went up due to dwindling stocks. The poor were grinding up the coarsest of grains, even mouldy peas and beans, poppy seeds and other hedgerow gleanings to make bread. Wheat was not easily grown in the British Isles ~ the main crops were barley and rye. Rye, grown widely, was potentially a very dangerous grain as it was subject to ergot fungus, which poisoned flour and sent whole communities mad. The bread was known as 'crazy bread', as the fungus contained lysergic acid.

One man's duty

William of Melbourn, son of the reeve, in the 1300s held a messuage (a plot for his house) and 20 acres of land. In addition to working this for himself, he was obliged to do a number of tasks for the Abbot.

A fruit cart travelling down Station Road

Every Monday and Friday, from Michaelmas (harvest time) to Christmas (winter), he worked on the Abbot's demesne. If he was carting, spreading dung, ditching, ploughing or harrowing, he would start work from sunrise and work until the noon prayer. If he

Harvesting at the Stockbridge Farm

Transport of fruit in half sieves (baskets) along Station Road

worked through to sunset, it would count as two day's work for the Abbot. If threshing was to be done, he had to thresh 24 sheaves of wheat, peas, beans or meslin, or 30 sheaves of barley or dredge: this was considered to be 'a day's work'!

Carrying the straw from threshing to anywhere within the manor took up another full day.

He had to plough one acre of corn for winter ploughing, without it counting in the 2 days per week. If he did not plough the full acre, he had to pay a fine of 4d. For ploughing work he had to bring his own plough and oxen.

He was also required to make one perch of wall (5½ yards), 5 feet high with foundations 2 feet deep. The Abbot supplied the materials, but William had to fetch the water. For every other job, except winnowing the corn, William had to supply his own tools.

From Christmas to Lady-Day (25th March) and from Lady-Day to 1st August again he worked 2 days per week for the Abbot, but Easter Monday counted as a holiday.

From 1st August to Michaelmas he worked on Wednesdays as well, although the four feast days which fell during harvest were holidays (Holy days).

A day's work during harvest consisted of reaping ½ an acre of any kind of corn, binding it and putting it into shocks (a group of corn sheaves stood up close together).

Once every harvest he had to cart the Prior's corn from sunrise to noon-time prayer, supplying his own cart; but the Prior supplied breakfast and dinner.

Sometimes William would have to contribute to extra work when, for instance, the reeve would organise two men from the village to mow for 4 days each year for the Abbot, on top of other regular week-work. The Prior supplied rations of 3 wheaten loaves, weighing 11 ounces each, 6 herrings and one half-pennyworth of cheese. These rations were known as Water Bede-Reaps. Ale Bede-Reaps were similar; rations enough for 2 men for 4 days, receiving the same bread and cheese ration, but a plate of meat instead of fish, and as much ale as they could drink.

Transport

In addition to all this, William had to carry a 4-bushel load of the Abbot's corn to Cambridge every Tuesday, Thursday and Saturday until the harvest was in. If he was ordered to carry it on

The meeting point of Royston Road and the High Street – Townsend

Mondays, Wednesdays or Fridays as well, he was let off a day's work later on. Rules for this were quite strict. He and four other men, had to take the corn to Ely by boat. On arrival they received rations of 5 black rye loaves, 5 measures of common beer, 9 herrings or 9 eggs or, if it was a meat-day at the Abbey, 2 dishes of meat.

They were allowed to hire a boat, and pay for it out of the Abbot's corn, giving the boatman 4 sheaves of meslin and 4 of dredge. The boat owner was to supply one man for the crew and a cloth to cover the corn.

Each trip to Ely counted as 4 day's work, whether it took a week or not. If the Prior of the Abbey decided to send his men to collect the corn in Cambridge, William and the others would return to Melbourn, and that would not count as the four days' work. The allowance of food at Ely was to be the same whether they carried one quarter of corn or 30 quarters.

Malt-making

Every year William had to make 3 quarters of malt of barley or dredge, the Prior supplying the corn when William asked for it. The Prior would receive from each quarter of corn, 7 bushels of screened malt, or 8 bushels of unscreened malt. If William failed to do the job he was fined 2d per quarter.

Other rules to be obeyed included:

1   The Prior had first refusal of any bull or stallion for sale at 'a fair market price'.
2   William was not allowed to grind his corn at any other mill without licence.
3   His daughter was not allowed to marry a free-man without the Prior's licence, as any child born from this marriage would be classed as free, and not obliged to work for the Abbot.
4   If his daughter had a baby out of wedlock, she was fined. According to the Church's laws, illegitimate children were given the benefit of

the doubt and assumed to have a free father; therefore the Abbot would lose the work due! This fine was called Layerwite.

5 His eldest son was to inherit and take on his father's duties. Other sons could only live outside the village if they paid for a licence; this was called 'chevage'.

6 If he only had daughters the eldest was to inherit.

7 When William died, the Prior took his best beast as a 'heriot', a death-duty tax; but his widow was let off all duties for 40 days. She was allowed his holding for the rest of her life, on paying a fine called a 'relief'. If she remarried, she had to pay another 'relief' fine to the lord. If she died before her second husband, he had a dowry from her holding for the rest of his life.

8 If William's wife died he could marry again without licence.

9 He 'owes suit to', (i.e. has to attend) all the lord's courts.

10 William had to pay a (compulsory) Christmas gift of a cockerel; 10 eggs at Easter and 1d each quarter day.

11 If he was elected reeve ~ as was his father ~ he had to serve, but he would be excused all duties for the Abbot while acting as reeve. The reeve's job was to see that all the villagers did their duties to the Abbot.

Sheep farming: the basis of the local economy

Sheep farming increased from 1086, when there were 696 sheep in Melbourn, to around 2,200 by 1347. Sheep were obviously the most lucrative of animals to farm, as at the time of the Domesday survey the only other beasts in Melbourn were 2 horses, 11 cattle and 82 pigs. The flock, at Argentine Manor alone, numbered 200 in 1318. Fleeces from 124 of these sheep were sold and 25 were butchered. Over 225 stones of wool were produced in 1347, of which 22 stones were demanded of Lady Agnes de

Muncey's cows being taken down to Moat Meadows

Argentine from the Manor of Melbourn in order to carry on the war against France. Later, in the late-15th and early-16th century, several tenants owned sheep, and one left a flock of over 100 at his death in 1503. Wool had become extremely important to the economy although some tenants did own a few cows at this time.

The coming of the plague

The Black Death (or Plague) reached England in 1348, with terrible effects on the population and agriculture. As many as 2 million people died and the peasants fled the land. The crops were left to rot in the fields although it had been a poor harvest that year, as there was heavy rainfall throughout the summer. Cambridgeshire had been heavily populated during the late-13th century, but as people fled the plague, there were not enough workers to work the land. As a result, wages and prices rose. The *Statute of Labourers*, (an Act brought in during 1351) attempted to return wages to pre-plague levels, but the shortage of labourers meant that wages continued to rise. Landowners offered other incentives such as food, drink, and extra benefits to lure labourers back and their standard of living began to rise accordingly.

The nature of the economy changed to meet the changing social conditions. Land that had once been farmed was now given over to pasturing, which was much less labour-intensive. The increase in the

The Meadows behind All Saints' Church

number of sheep helped boost the cloth and woollen industry. With the fall in population most landowners were not getting the rental income they needed, and were forced to lease their land.

Peasants benefited through increased employment options and higher wages. Society became more mobile, as peasants moved to accept work where they could command a good wage. In some areas market towns either disappeared or suffered a decline, despite the economic boom in rural areas.

The Peasants' Revolt

In June 1381 there was a threefold increase in the poll tax, causing the peasants to riot. They demanded improved conditions and an end to serfdom and feudalism.

In Cambridgeshire the Court Rolls, recording the services due by each member of the Manor, were burned in large numbers. The burning of Manor Houses and documents is also recorded at Duxford, Bassingbourn, Steeple and Guilden Morden. Melbourn did not escape the riots. When John de Argentine died in 1382 the Inquisition, held at Cambridge, recorded that in the Manor he held at Melbourn were *...certain buildings worth nothing a year, being all ruined; a dovecote worth 40d; a windmill worth nothing, being old and ruined; two acres of pasture, worth 2s per annum; the herbage of certain gardens, worth 12d a year; 200 acres of land worth 4d an acre and no more, since half lay fallow.*

The King, Richard II, only 14 years old when first faced with the revolt, did make concessions and the rioters dispersed. Later these concessions were withdrawn.

The final outcome of the Peasants' Revolt was that quit-rents, fines and services were abolished and men paid rents in money and held lands by Copy of Court Roll. Serfdom was abolished, allowing men to move freely about the country and hire out their services to whom they could. Much of the land was put down to grass. A man would take over land from a lord, pay rent and make what profit he could out of it. His lease could run for as long as 99 years; at the end of such a period, his heirs would hand back the land in good condition.

About 40 percent of England's priests died in the plague epidemic. This left a large gap, which was hastily filled with underqualified and poorly trained applicants, accelerating the decline in church power and influence that culminated in the English Reformation. Many survivors of the plague were also disillusioned by the church's inability to explain, or deal with, the outbreak.

The economic prosperity was short-term. During the 14th century population pressure affected the distribution of land; peasants were obliged for financial reasons to forego their tenancies, and larger farms were emerging. The underlying feudal structure of society had not changed in the way the King had promised during the Peasants' Revolt, and by the mid-15th century, standards of living had fallen again.

Between 1540 and 1590 the market value of agricultural foodstuffs rose by 167 percent. Proof that some families were prospering is seen in records, mostly from wills, of new luxuries in farmhouses in the 1580s, such as pewter, glass and feather beds, as well as rebuilding and expansion of farmhouses.

But while the yeomen prospered, the labourers suffered. In the 1550s population pressure led to a shortage of housing, resulting in crude huts made of poles, being erected on wasteland and verges. Prices rose and wages could not stretch to necessities.

Geoff Catley (far left) herding sheep at The Cross

Argentine Manor during this period was being leased. In 1573 the Manor, with all its demesne lands, was let to Flower Leete, a widow, for 21 years, at a rent of just over £6 for four years and £10 per year afterwards. Twenty years later, John Harvey of Coton rented the house, lands and a sheep walk for 300 sheep, for £23 a year. Many owners were now turning their land over to sheep farming.

Land use and distribution
Melbourn from the 16th century

By the 15th century, parcels of manor lands were being leased out for years, or for life, and were continuously leased and sublet from the mid-16th century. The Harveys, Chamberlains, Hitches and Stokes, prominent yeoman families, were among the lessees in Melbourn.

On April 28th 1564, The Bury Manor, the manorial rights, the great tithes, and the advowson (the right to become the patron of a church or benefice) of the vicarage were let to Thomas Sterne for 61 years for the rent of £46 6s. He was also to supply eight quarters of best dressed wheat, a boar on St. Andrew's day and a calf at Easter. He was to keep the 200 sheep belonging to the Dean and Chapter, in his sheepfold in the summer and in his sheep yard in the winter, and was to carry out all repairs, including those of the chancel of the chapel.

In 1656 Robert Hitch was growing wheat, barley, oats, rye, pease and lentils on 220 acres. There was a trend towards the late-16th century to plant orchards, which became common in Melbourn, mostly growing apples. During this time the distinction was made between the good land, a strong white loam in the north, and the cold wetland and heathland south of it.

The growing of saffron was also introduced to the Melbourn area during the 1600s and in the 18th century hops were reintroduced. They were first grown at The Bury during 1300s.

The importance of the manor and its social structure declined due to the development of a strong central monarchy and improvement in communications. This assisted in the development of towns, and the emergence of the ruling class. The result was a large economic division between the wealthy and the poor.

Skills for sale

In 1762 twenty-five 'Hiring Fairs' were held in Cambridgeshire. Hiring usually took place at a country fair or a market once a year, at Michaelmas. Though the purpose of the fairs was to hire labourers, they also provided the chance to conduct other business and sales.

The labourers would stand on a platform or in an enclosure, to be inspected by their prospective employers for strength, general appearance and character. They would then be questioned about their skills and abilities, their previous employment and their liabilities (which could include wives and children). Finally, there would be the offer of a wage, often very low. In hard times the labourer had no bargaining power at all.

Workers skilled in a particularly useful trade, or having experience, would be able to demand good wages. People such as plough-team leaders and experienced cowmen were prized, and often the most highly valued jobs (those involving the handling of livestock) came with the benefit of a 'tied' cottage.

By the 1800s the annual Hiring Fairs became less popular, and workers were hired in a more casual way. This was usually on a daily or weekly basis, with no pay on wet days. Later, during the Victorian period, with increased farm sizes, farmers could no longer manage with just family to help out and a few live-in servants. Farmers needed more labour and greater flexibility in employment, and agricultural labourers (as did factory workers) found themselves entirely at the mercy of their employers, who could reduce their pay whenever farm prices dropped. Wages for the less skilled and experienced farm workers were very low. Most struggled for existence. In a 50-year period during the late-18th century the cost of living rose by 60 percent.

Dispossession of the peasantry accelerated between 1680 and 1780. By this time 90 percent of land was leasehold and labourers had become mostly landless. On average, yeomen (freemen with larger holdings) owned 300-400 acres. Of the husbandmen (freemen) half had less than 10 acres. Craftsmen had nothing but their tools.

In the late-18th century in Melbourn, copyhold estates (a parcel of land granted to the lord of the manor in return for agricultural services), were bought in bulk by landowners, and John Hitch, Lord of Argentine, acquired a number of its copyholds. These were several farms of between 60 and 100 acres. In 1778 the Argentine demesne was leased out.

At the beginning of the 19th century wheat, barley and oats had been the largest crops, followed by peas, rye, turnips and rape. Some seeds were sown on fallow land to make up for a shortage of hay. Each ancient cottage or house site had Rights of Common, limited to the number of sheep which grazed the fallow, but this did not apply to cattle which fed off the baulks in the open fields. In 1830 thirty farmers employed about 170 men in agriculture, but four years later there were about

---

For Enclosure

Melbourn Inclosure, notice is hereby given that application will be made to Parliament in the ensuing session, for leave to bring in a Bill for dividing, allotting and enclosing the open and common fields, commons, commonable lands, and waste grounds, in the parish of Melbourn, in the County of Cambridge, and for exonerating all the lands in the said parish from Great and Small Tithes. Christopher Pemberton.

Cambridge Chronicle 13th September 1811

WHAT THE PAPERS SAID

260 agricultural labourers over 10 years old. Times were hard and children had to supplement the family income.

In 1835 there were about 20 farms in Melbourn which included 8 owned by John and Wortham Hitch (4 each). Of the 150 landholders only 120 had a cottage and Common rights. There were 3,400 acres of arable land, 215 acres of meadow and pasture, and 850 acres of Common and waste ~ both the heathland, and the marshy meadows in the east needed improvement. A three course rotation was in practice, but land owned by Peterhouse College, Cambridge, was farmed on a four course rotation. Melbourn had 1,600 sheep and only 50 cows, but very little meadow in 1838.

Enclosure comes to Melbourn

Conditions for the agricultural labourer were desperate. The end of the Napoleonic Wars meant that many ex-soldiers were unemployed. Grain prices fell and farmers lowered wages. A landlord-dominated Parliament passed the *Corn Laws* which prevented the import of grain until the price of English wheat reached 80s a quarter.

A steep rise in the price of bread and flour during

the post war depression led to violence. Riots broke out in 1816 in demand for higher wages and many labourers destroyed agricultural machinery, which was depriving labourers of jobs.

At the other end of the scale, the larger landowners wanted to employ more scientific methods of farming, which could only be done if the land was enclosed. For this, an Act of Parliament was necessary. To enforce it, the consent of 75 percent of the owners of the land in each district had to be obtained, and as there were a large number of landowners in Melbourn, this took time. When, finally, consent was obtained, a notice was pinned to the church door in Melbourn, for three successive Sundays in August and September, to allow people to prepare their objections. The application was also published in local newspapers.

A petition was sent to Parliament asking for a Private Bill. Opponents sent up a counter petition, but stood little chance of being considered. Finally, the Bill was pushed through Parliament and became law in 1839.

The Commissioners, Thomas Uttond, Anthony Jackson and A Walford arrived in the village on 1st

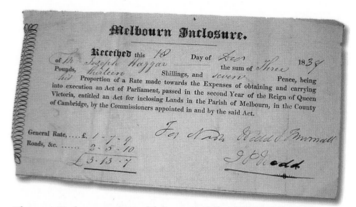

Above, an Enclosure receipt and below, part of the 1839 Enclosure map

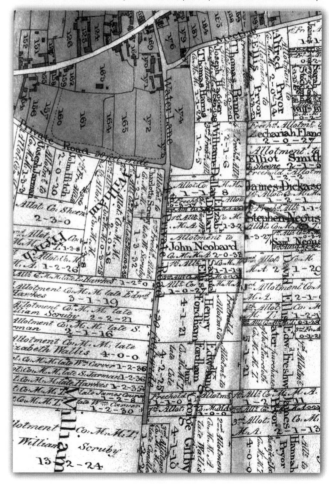

June and met at the Rose Inn. They received and determined all claims and published a Parish Award, mapping out the new arrangements. A survey of all allotments of open and Common fields, meadows and pastures, homesteads and closes, as well as roads and footways was made, and having decided how much land was required for new roads, drains, watercourses and recreation ground, the surveyors proceeded to allocate the rest.

The Lords of the Manor were allowed a certain proportion in lieu of their rights of Common, as was the Vicar, to replace his tithes. The other landowners received their portion, according to the amount of land each had held before. Each allotment had to be enclosed by a hedge, which took some time to grow, a gap being left in each hedge to allow the owner to harvest his crop. Each owner had also to pay his share of the cost of the survey.

The largest landowners in Melbourn, at the time of the Enclosure, were Messrs. Beldam, Carver, W Hitch, J Hitch, J Stanford, JE Fordham and Peterhouse College. Between them they owned 2200 acres out of a total of 4088 acres (homesteads and roadways included).

The expense of enclosing fields amounted to anything between £3 and £5 an acre, and this, plus the share of legal costs, was too much for the small farmer who often had to sell his property to a larger and wealthier owner. Before enclosure, the small owner had the use of the fallow fields and stubble for grazing his animals – this was now lost, as there was

no common fallow. Baulks and headlands were ploughed up and incorporated into the various adjoining fields.

The cottagers and squatters were worse off after the Enclosure. Previously, the cottager, with his cottage and garden, had also certain rights of Common; he could pasture his cow and geese on the Common and gather fuel in the woods. Now all such rights were taken away and he received in exchange, a tiny allotment, which he had to fence, often far from his home; this was not sufficient to provide him with a living. The squatters, who previously had had rights of Common, lost those and were left with only a house.

The position of the Pinder, who looked after the village pound used for keeping stray animals; the hayward, who arranged for periods of grazing, and the shepherd who looked after all the sheep, all disappeared from the village scene as their services were no longer required.

Herbert and Lizzie King at White House Farm, High Street

The small farmer, with the cottager and squatter, became day labourers, on wages so low that they were often thrown into the workhouse or forced to emigrate. Wages were 7s to 9s per week. The poor now had no place, or tie with the land, no interest in the village community and no ambition.

The effect on the land and society

Enclosure in Melbourn meant a number of roads and tracks, including 49 footpaths, disappeared under the plough and new roads were cut. In all, 5 public roads 30ft wide, and 13 private roads 20ft wide, were created.

Eighty families were allotted land, varying in size from less than one acre to several hundred acres; they also had their homesteads with gardens attached. The larger landowners, with their fenced-in fields, could now try out new and more scientific methods of farming. They could grow winter wheat, clover, (Armingford Crescent was once known as Clover Fields), spring wheat, root crops, etc, and since the sheep and cattle were no longer turned out together onto the common pasture, animal husbandry could be practised and breeds of cattle and sheep improved.

Noon's Folly, Newmarket Road

Summer House Farm off New Road. Originally part of W Carver's estate the farm with 185 acres of land was built by 1921.

Agricultural production increased. However, it was hard on the poor, who could no longer produce their own milk and butter and had to exist on meagre earnings. Some members of the village left to work in towns or emigrated to America, Canada or Australia. Workers were paid very low wages in winter, and none at all if the weather was bad. It was hardly surprising that articles appeared in newspapers with reports of sheep-stealing and thefts from dovecots. Hardship led to crime, and punishment often resulted in transportation to Australia.

Allotted land – who did well out of the Enclosure?

John Hitch owned the largest allotment after the Enclosure. His land, mostly freehold, was divided into three farms. Argentine (known as Lordship Farm) contained about 460 acres in the north-east of the parish; about 425 acres in the south were farmed from the Manor House and 140 acres from a homestead in Mill Lane. Lordship Farm was divided into several lots in 1916.

Wortham Hitch was allocated 440 acres, mostly freehold. White House Farm, Field Farm and a number of other smallholdings made a total of 215 acres. In 1905 his children sold White House Farm with its 180 acres to JJ Newling. It was then purchased by the County Council in 1919 and let as small holdings. Field Farm, known as Grange Farm by 1864, had 230 acres when it was sold to WJ Wedd. Peterhouse College bought the farm in 1942.

Heath Farm with windmill, Newmarket Road

Heath Farm, Newmarket Road, originally part of the Argentine estate

Holland Hall Farm, situated on the Royston Road, was held from the 1830s by the Titchmarsh family until 1922 when the Hoy family took it over.

Joseph Dickason farmed 160 acres from a house on the Moor, as did Ellis Smith with 125 acres. Peterhouse owned 190 acres, and St. John's College 56 acres also at The Moor.

Holland Hall Farm, Royston Road

William Carver, whose estate was made up of 11 different holdings, had 230 acres stretching from the High Street to the Royston-Newmarket Road. It was farmed from Townsend Farm at the west end of the village. In 1859 J E Fordham bought part of Townsend Farm where sheep, pigs and poultry were kept. Carver's estate was sold around 1862 and by 1921 Summer House Farm, with 185 acres of land, was built there.

Noon's Folly Farm had 30 acres, owned and occupied by Anne Wortham and other members of the Wortham family until the 1940s. The farm and land has been situated next to the Icknield Way since at least 1773 and was the only farm outside the village proper, pre-enclosure. It was taken over by the Wilkersons in the 1940s.

Heath Farm, built by 1851 near Noon's Folly, was sold with 422 acres in 1898 as part of the Argentine estate, to AJ Palmer, and later occupied by Collis Palmer. In 1929 it was held by the Pepper family.

Other farms included from top left clockwise: Godfrey's Farm, Cambridge Road; Wedd's Farm, Dolphin Lane; New Road Farm; Muncey's Farm, corner of Norgett's Lane; Stockbridge Farm, High Street; Wood's Farm, High Street; Fox Fields, Cambridge Road; Newling's Farm, Moat Lane

Moat House in Moat Lane

Pigs and cattle take over

The Enclosure did affect farming methods, seen by the rise in popularity of pigs and cattle. In 1864 there were four cattle dealers in the parish and a cattle dealer leased Heath Farm in 1898.

In the 1930s, The Moat House, owned by Sir Geoffrey Ellis, was a model farm with a dairy where he showed pedigree Jersey cattle. Melbourn Bury Farm and Summer House Farm produced pigs in the1920s, which had become popular. By 1929 there was also a poultry dealer in Melbourn.

Other changes in land use

Extensive orchards were planted after the arrival of the railways in the 1850s, and Melbourn became well known for its greengages and plums. JJ Newling planted 26 acres of plums and apples on the Moor, and the Palmers had 150 acres of orchards in Melbourn and Meldreth. By 1905 there were 145 acres of orchards around the parish, and in 1937, fruit was one of the main crops to be grown. In 1942 about 15,000 tons were harvested.

Springs which emerged at Black Peak provided ideal conditions for growing watercress and took up about 7 acres of land in 1919.

The Watercress beds at Black Peak

Working the land

Up to the mid-19th century, farming was a labour intensive business, everything being done by hand. Before the seed drill was invented, sowing seed was a highly-skilled job, as the seed was broadcast (scattered) by hand. When sowing with both hands, the sower had a seed bowl on his chest, secured by a leather band which went round his neck. He took the seed between his finger and thumb and sowed

in step as he walked the length of the field. Very few men knew how much of each particular seed must be sown to cover the field, as seeds vary greatly in size from turnip to various corns.

Most men were only able to sow with one hand, a much slower process, but with the advantage of being able to carry a seed hod, a much bigger container, on one side of the body.

Children, armed with slings, would then be set to defend the newly-sown seed from crows and other birds.

The seed was protected by harrowing to cover it with soil. The simplest, cheapest (and most ineffective) harrows were bundles of brushwood dragged behind a horse, sometimes even tied to its tail. Sturdier harrows consisted of wooden pegs fixed into a frame; iron-toothed harrows were virtually unknown and expensive. Sometimes the harrow was unable to break up heavy clods, so this was done with mallets.

Large seeds, such as peas and beans, were dibbled (dropped into a hole made by a pointed stick).

Farm workers during the 1940s, From the left; Reg Hunt, Frank Greatorex, Mr Chapman, Cyril Hunt and David Blackwell

Nothing was wasted – hay was also harvested from the churchyard

Cows came back into full milk as new grass took over from sparse winter fodder. Between May and Michaelmas each cow was expected to produce seven stones (98lb) of cheese and a stone (14lb) of butter.

Mr Stockbridge transporting the harvest along Station Road

Long-handled scythes were used to cut the crops close to the ground

Haymaking was the main event of June, and was a communal activity. Long-handled scythes were used to cut the grass close to the ground. Teams of men moved down the meadow in lines, each expected to mow about an acre a day. Women and children followed to turn the hay behind them to ensure it dried evenly. Finally the hay was gathered into large stacks.

The hay crop was vitally important to the village economy, for it provided the main winter fodder for animals. If the crop was bad fewer animals could be kept over winter; a good crop could mean a relatively steady supply of fresh meat over winter, a good supply of breeding stock, or a surplus for sale.

Lambs were weaned as early as possible, as sheep's milk was rich and highly prized. Shearing began late in June. The best fleeces came from wethers (castrated males), and fleeces taken earlier were often finer and more valuable than those taken later in the year.

In areas where three ploughings of the fallow field were the norm, the second generally began in late June. This ploughing was a little deeper than the first, to expose the roots of weeds, and as much manure as was available would be spread on the field before the teams began their work.

Grain stores were at their lowest in July before the forthcoming harvest in early August which weather permitting, was usually completed by the end of the month.

The last Horn Blower

The harvest day began early when the Harvest Horn was blown. William King was the last Horn Blower in Melbourn and had worked since the age of seven. He died in 1935 at the age of eighty-four.

Newlings Farm, Moat Lane

Harvesting in 1843

An account of harvesting in 1843 showed that thirty-four men mowed the wheat and in order to lay it evenly, their scythes were fitted with cradles made of iron rods. These men were each followed by two women, with a boy or girl, to gather up the corn into small sheaves. Eight teams of men followed to shock up the sheaves. Three hundred acres of wheat were cut in six days and carting took a further eight. Eighteen to 20 days were needed to complete the harvest.

The women were often the wives of the harvesters, and if they had small children to look after, had to manage as best they could. Sometimes

Horse-drawn binders were used to tie the corn into sheaves.

children were dosed with opium to keep them quiet.

In early times corn was harvested with a sickle, replaced by a scythe by the mid-19th century. The straw was either chopped and added to winter fodder, used for thatching houses, or as bedding for humans and animals. Cutting the corn was not very efficient, and some of the stalks fell to the ground.

The poorest of the community often had the rights to glean from the fields (going over a field for crops) after the harvest was brought in and before livestock was released to graze the stubble. Gleaning rights were hotly contested and were a considerable benefit to the recipients.

A church bell, known as the Gleaning Bell, was rung in Melbourn, (the last time was in 1886), signifying that all the fields were cleared and that

Bertie Pilgrim operating a steam driven tractor, at Summerhouse Farm

the remaining corn could be gathered from the fields, usually by the women and children. Families would hope to pick up enough corn to be ground for their winter supply of flour. The women took their children, who took a holiday from school at this time, to help with the gleaning. Each family put down a cloth, or mat, on which the sandwiches and drinks were placed, and then began picking up the corn stalks, which were tied together with twists of straw and stacked on the mat. Special bags were tied around the waist in which the corn heads without straw were collected. When the work was finished there was a Gleaners' tea with music and dancing. This tradition continued in Melbourn until 1882.

After harvesting, the grain was carried into large barns and was threshed on the threshing floor, usually the centre of the large barn, (the middle

A Gleaner's tea was held in a barn lent by Mr James Whitby. 73 sat down and there were children's games and adult dancing until 10 pm.

Royston Crow 28th October 1881

Corn Dollies

Near the end of reaping, only the final stand of corn was left in the middle of the field. In the past this was thought to contain the spirit of the corn, and was made up into a Corn Dolly (Dolly from Idol, the corn spirit and a fertility symbol) and was kept until the following harvest. Corn Dollies are still made, nowadays as decorative items. Cambridgeshire has 2 shapes in particular, the Bell and the Umbrella. Although these dollies no longer have any magical significance they are still tied with a witch-repellent red thread.

The Corn Dolly was carried home on the final or 'Horkey' load, with the men dressed up, some of them as women, riding on top. They all shouted, sang and rang handbells. Onlookers would throw water over them as they passed, it is thought as a rain or fertility charm for the next season.

The 'Horkey' supper, which took place after this, was a great occasion, held in barns decorated with flowers, corn and fruit. Beef and plum pudding were part of the menu and as one local farmer wrote in his day book, 'The men were sadly the worse for beer.'

stead) which had doors on either side so that a draught was created. The threshing floor was covered with clay, beaten down until it was as hard as concrete.

Handflails were used, consisting of an ash handle with a swivel on top. The part that struck the corn was called the 'swingel' and was made of tough wood, like holly or blackthorn. It was attached to the swivel on the handle by thongs of leather. The thresher swung the flail over his shoulder and brought the swingel down just below the ears so that the grains of corn

Barn at Wood's Farm and below, threshing floor at Lordship Farm

were shaken out without bruising. This was a skilful job. The draught from the open doors blew away the dust created, and the *threshhold*, (a name still in use for the modern word doorstep), across the door prevented the threshings, grain or chaff, (kept for animal fodder) from being lost. The grain was then sieved to rid it of weed seeds, which are smaller. Finally a wooden shovel was used to throw the grain high in the air, the heavy grain falling further away and the lighter dropping short, forming a kind of tail. This 'tail corn' was inferior and kept separately. The process continued well into the 19th century.

Horse-drawn technology

Thomas Wood, who lived on the High Street, and whose barns stretched as far as The Star public house, used a horse-drawn binder which tied the corn into sheaves. These were picked up by men and women and put into shocks of five, one in the middle, and four around, and stood there until dry. They were then carted back, stacked and thatched until threshing, or 'sheening' (machining), as it was called locally.

Farming from Norgett's Lane

Road sweepers near Sheepshead Row

Bill Wilson outside Wood's Farm

Harvesting, of course, was the climax of the agricultural year, and an excuse for feasting and drinking when 'all was safely gathered in'.

After threshing, the grain was ready to be stored. It would last several years if kept dry and free from vermin, but this was not always easy. Flour had a much shorter shelf-life, and milling the grain was done as and when necessary.

Families grew wheat on their allotments in Melbourn, cut by hand with a scythe and taken by horse and cart to Mill House (Sheen Mill), in operation until the mid-20th century. When flour was required, a child was sent with some corn to have it

AR Coningsby, coal merchant, in Station Road

ground and would bring it back in a pillowcase. Some villagers were still hand-flailing and winnowing their homegrown corn during the 1920s and 30s.

Although machinery was gradually replacing the use of the carthorse, horses were still used in our area in the first half of the 20th century.

After the harvest, beans and peasecods were carefully dried as a source of both human food and animal fodder over winter. Pottage was a staple of the labourer's diet, and a pot of it was generally kept cooking at all times, topped up with new ingredients as required. An old English nursery rhyme is not far off the mark …*Pease pudding hot, pease pudding cold, pease pudding in the pot, nine days old.*

Farming in the area was originally mixed, but as communications improved, by the beginning of the 19th century, crop specialisation was becoming a feature. Cambridgeshire has long been known as a corn-growing area.

Fruit farming

Fruit growing really took off after the Enclosures. Although many varieties of fruit were grown, the most important was the Melbourn gage, said to be superior to others, but in fact identical to the Cambridge gage. In 1869 according to his journal, George Palmer paid £36 7s 9d for gage trees. Later, in Water Lane, a further 650 trees were planted costing £26 14s 4d.

The manufacture of jam in Histon spurred on the planting of commercial acreages of fruit, including gages. Local names associated with fruit growing before 1914, in addition to the Palmers, were Hinkins, Howard, Prior, Fordham, Newling, and later, Hagger and Elbourn.

Fruit was sent up to London by wagon twice a week, the journey taking two days each way. However, the arrival of the railway meant that the fruit could easily be transported daily to London and the big markets. Until the 1930s a carrier still plied weekly between Melbourn and Spitalfields market.

In the summer, the wives of agricultural and other workers supplemented the family income by fruit

Fruit pickers were often the wives of agricultural workers who supplemented the family income

picking. The season usually began with gooseberry picking, followed perhaps by blackcurrants, and then by plums and apples.

The women started work at 8.30am, often having prepared a suet pudding, or a stew, that would cook all morning on the range or oil stove, and then cycled, or pushed a pram with the younger children, to the orchard. If they were on piecework they would be allocated a row of trees which had to be cleared; on

day work the atmosphere was more relaxed and pickers might work together in pairs.

The fruit picking season was looked upon by many women as a holiday, as there was companionship and ample opportunity for gossip. The fruit was picked and put into baskets called half sieves. At about 4.20pm trains from London and Cambridge passed on the local line and those working in the orchard knew that their day was almost over.

Men were also employed during the fruit harvest

Fruit picking at Palmer's orchard

Farm worker's union and wage reform

In the late-19th century agricultural workers began to make their voices heard, forming unions in order to complain about low wages and the loss of work due to the introduction of farm machinery.

In March 1892 a land Nationalisation meeting was held in the village, the speaker, Arthur Brooks, spoke of '*the evils of private ownership and owners enjoying larger profits than the labourers and workers*'. C Hinkins, a labourer, was the Chairman, and a resolution was passed in favour of returning the land to the people.

Around September that year a meeting at 'The

	Stockmen	General Workers 6 days, 7-5 pm	Harvest 7 am to dark (per month)
1912	15s	14s	men £8 boys £1 – £1 3s 0d
1913	15s	14s	£8 5s 0d
1914	16s	14s 9d	£8 5s 0d
1915	17s	15s 6d	men £10 boys £1 2s 6d – £1 3s 6d
1916	£1 – £1 1s	19s 6d	men £11 boys £1 3s – £2
1917	£1 2s 6d	£1	men £11 boys £1 3s – £2
1918	*New Wages Regulations, the beginning of the Wages Board*		
	£1 12s 0d	£1 5s 0d (+ 6d overtime)	men £13 boys £2

Farm workers' wages from 1912 onwards

promised that if any men were dismissed for joining the Federation, it would support them until other posts were found. The subscription was set at sixpence per week. The Local Secretary was Mr Adams and Alf Baker was Treasurer.

Wages in 1794 were 9s per week for rural workers, which rose to 13s per week during the period of Victorian prosperity, but dropped back to 10s per week by the 1890s.

By 1919–1922 wages had increased steadily to over £2 a week, but with the recession in farming, they fell back in 1923, exacerbated by the General Strike in 1926.

Payment was made in tokens at fruit farms. On some farms, tokens could only be used in the employer's shop.

Fruit growing
The varieties of fruit grown in the early 20th century in orchards in Melbourn

Plums; Early Rivers, Czars, Green Gages, Golden Gage, Worcester Gage, Victoria, Merry Weather Damson, Shropshire Damson, Kirk's Bleu, Orleans, Aireil, Belle de Lavien, President, Margery Seedling, Pond's Seedling.

Apples; Newton Wonder, Bramley Seedling, Blenheim Orange, Normington, Cox's Orange, Crimson Cox, James Grieve, Ellinson's Orange, Charles Ross, Laxton Early, Laxton Superb, Discovery.

Pears; Conference, William, Doyenne de Comice, Pitmaston Duchess.

Loading the half sieves ready for transport to Luton and Dunstable markets and Redbourne Jam Factory. On the left, Mark Harrup

Hoops' was held by the Eastern Counties Labour Federation. Attendance was poor to begin with, but improved as the meeting went on. The Secretary of the Federation, Mr Robinson, said that 12 shillings per week for a labourer was not enough. He also

Melbourn Bury fruit pickers were taken to London in Mr Tom Robinson's charabanc, where they went sightseeing and ended up at the London Zoo, where the Monkey House was said to be a great attraction!

Royston Crow 10th September 1926

WHAT THE PAPERS SAID

Packing fruit at Cherry Park

In 1933 farm workers' wages were set by the Agricultural Wages Committee. They were to be 37s per week for those over 21. When Christmas Day fell in the week, pay was 30s per week of 40 hours, and 48 hours on other weeks. Overtime was to be 8d an hour on weekdays and 10d on Sundays and Christmas Day. Females over 21 were to be paid 5½d per hour and 7d overtime.

From 1943 onwards, wages were set by the Wages Board, which consisted of representatives from the

Age	Pay per hr	Overtime Rates weekday	Sunday
18	5d	6d	7½d
17–18	4½d	5½d	7d
16–17	4d	5d	6d
15–16	3½d	4½d	5d
14–15	3d	4d	4½d
under 14	2½d	3d	4d

Women's wages fixed by the Agricultural Wages Board in 1918

Farmers Union, (NFU), the Agricultural Workers Union and independent members.

Women's wages were much lower, generally they did seasonal work, helping with the harvest and fruit picking. During the First World War, the government formed the Women's Land Army and women played a larger part in agriculture. After the war in 1918 a minimum wage for women was fixed.

By March 1940 agriculture had lost over 30,000 men to the Army. Another 15,000 had left the land to join other occupations, attracted by higher wages. In the summer of 1940, Ernest Bevin, the Minister of labour, under pressure from the National Union of Agricultural Workers, forced the Agricultural Wages Board to institute a minimum wage of 48s per week. This was increased to 60s in November 1941 and 65s in June 1943.

The severe shortage of labour persuaded the government to re-form the Woman's Land Army, and by 1944 there were 80,000 women working on the land. The majority already lived in the countryside, but around a third came from Britain's industrial cities.

Women in the Land Army wore green jerseys, brown breeches and brown felt slouch hats. They did a variety of jobs and a quarter were involved in milking and general farmwork. Others cut down trees or worked in sawmills and over a thousand women were employed as rat-catchers.

Ward's first workshop, High Street

Industry

...the Fire Engine House in Station Road was built, using the bricks from the old Cage on The Green

Following the breakdown of the feudal system (the main form of social organisation in medieval times), separate businesses developed alongside farming on the manors. These included leather and wood workers, thatchers, millers and blacksmiths who made ploughshares, horseshoes and other tools.

Guilds

During the middle ages the craftsmen in the village formed themselves into a Guild, known as the Guild of St. Wyburn. The Guild acquired property, land and stock, and acted much on the lines of the Friendly Societies, helping its members in need and caring for their widows and orphans. It had a Chantry, in the churchyard, where prayers were said for the souls of departed members and also a house in the

The Co-op at The Cross, once the Guildhouse and poorhouse

village, known as the Guildhouse. This stood on the Cross and was later used as a poorhouse.

Influence from outside the village

Until communications and transport improved, the majority of villagers did not travel far from home; though corn and other produce was taken from The Bury to Ely. People would have visited towns like Royston, taking produce to market. Visits were also made to the great medieval fairs, such as Stourbridge Fair (which began in 1211) bringing merchants from all over Europe to Cambridge.

From the 16th century, stagecoaches, carrying passengers, ran from London to the major cities, and passed through Melbourn en route for Cambridge. These coaches ran to a very strict timetable despite the poor conditions of the roads. Other coaches carried out the needs of merchants,

How a Melbourn lad of 1731 was apprenticed

One of Melbourn's oldest sons, (possibly a member of the Hitch family), has found in the family archives an old and faded document of particular interest; an indenture drawn up over 200 years ago when William Tompson, a poor lad of Melbourn, was apprenticed to farming with Mr William Barrance of Shepreth.

Although a system of apprenticeship existed in England from early history, it was not until 1563 that the famous Statute of Apprentices was passed. By this Act no person was allowed to carry on a trade unless he had previously served a seven year apprenticeship to it. In 1601, two years before the death of Queen Elizabeth, it was enacted that the overseers of a Parish might bind pauper children as apprentices until their 24th birthday, but in 1728, three years before the local Tompson indenture, the age was reduced to 21 years.

The legal jargon for the period is interesting, with the liberal use of capital letters, the punctuation, and the old style of spelling, notably 'Shepred' for 'Shepreth'.

This Indenture made the Sixteenth Day of September in the fifth year of the Reign of our Sovereign Lord George the Second by the Grace of God of Great Brittaine, France and Ireland King defender of the Faith Anno Dom. 1731. That the Said William Tompson the Said Apprentice shall be taught in the Art and Mistry of husbandry and shall and will during all the term aforesaid find Provide and allow unto the Said Apprentice most competent and sufficient Meat, Drink, and Apparel, Lodging, Washing and all other things necessary and fit for an Apprentice. And also Shall and Will so provide for the said Apprentice that he, be not in any way a Charge to the Parish of Melbourne or Parishioners of the same But of and from all Charge shall and will save the Said Parish and Parishioners of Melbourne harmless and indemnified during the Said Term, And at the end of the Said Term shall and will make and provide and allow and deliver unto the Said Apprentice double apparel of all sorts Good and New (a good new suit for the Holy Days and another for the Working Days).

Royston Crow Percy R Salmon

the Rose Inn, it was agreed ...*that the gravel for the upkeep of the By-ways was to be dug by the following men – William Ingrey, William Miller, Joseph Whitbey, John Smith, Job Stanford, William Winters and that the gravel be brought in, in the usual way, and that James Carter be appointed Pinder in the place of George Stockbridge, also that the Surveyor was to be instructed to remove the Moor gateposts.*

Coprolite

The short-lived coprolite industry sprang up in 1850. Commonly known as 'dinosaur dung', coprolite is the phosphatised bone of prehistoric animals. A belt of this material passed through the neighbourhood of Melbourn, and many local men were employed in

On April 20th at a Vestry meeting it was agreed to employ a number of men for stone digging. These included: Thomas James, John Winter, William Cooper, William Stanford, Joseph Day, James Whitby, William Wing, Thomas Negus, Job Stanford, William Chamberlain, David Day, John Dodkin, Joseph Smith, Jonus Hanscombe, William Huggins, Joseph Pluck, Joseph Langham, William Camp, Joseph Nacker and James Negus.

They also agreed to employ additional men and boys to level the ground: Sam Hanscombe, Eliger Freshwater, John Day, John Hale, Charles Dodkin, William Cook, William Whitemore, Philip Stanford, William Collis, Chas Chamberlain, Wm. Day, Edward Negus, Robert Chamberlain, Thomas Wood, Robert Longham, Chas Wright. Thomas Scruby and Thomas Wood were to be Overseers.

Signed Wm Baker and A.P. Jenkins Churchwardens.

Royston Crow 20th April 1835

manufacturers and businessmen, and could be chartered to carry goods and raw materials.

The local carrier was a very important person; the carriers' carts were the fore-runners of the lorries of the road hauliers.

Carriers

In 1900 there were three carriers in the village: Alice Nightingale went to Cambridge on Tuesdays and Saturdays; Arthur Wedd went to London on Thursday and returned on Saturday, he made his last journey in 1915 after twenty-four years; John Guiver went to Royston daily.

Stone and gravel

In the mid-19th century many of the Vestry meetings were concerned with digging stones and gravel on the Heath and waste land, and who was allowed to dig them. A Stones Account was kept, which showed that some loads were sold and others used for the upkeep of the roads and byways.

At the Vestry meeting, in November 1836, it was decided that no one was to dig stones or gravel on the waste lands ...*without leave being obtained from the Parish.* The Constable was ordered to tell the men who were there to leave off digging.

Two years later at another Vestry meeting held at

Coprolite train

digging it out and processing it into artificial fertiliser, (superphosphates). The land was leased to the diggers for two years, at £150 per acre, and the coprolites were found at a depth of ten to twelve feet. From one acre up to three hundred tons could be dug and sold at £3 a ton.

The railway

Real change began with the arrival of the railway in 1848. This was completed and opened in 1851, the year of the great London Exhibition at the

Meldreth and Melbourn station

Crystal Palace. Since the rail track was initially laid only as far as Shepreth, passengers went on to Cambridge by coach.

The coming of the railway coincided with the development of the fruit-growing industry and in the late-19th century and up to the Second World War many tons of fruit, especially plums and the famous Melbourn (or Cambridge) gage, were sent up to London.

Meldreth and Melbourn station staff from left to right: Mr Allen, Ernest Hale, William Vellum, Arthor Scott the Station Master, and a clerk, (possibly Charles Dodkin).
Around the time this photograph was taken there were a number of Melbourn men working at the station. These included: signalman, William Knott; porter, John Bullen; coal depot clerk, Charles Dodkin; two foreman platelayers, David Chapman and William Smith and nine platelayers, Frederick Smith, George Brown, Alfred and Thomas Abrey, Joseph Chapman, William Pearce, William Holland, William Jacklin and Stephen Chapman.

Gas & electricity

Until the 19th century the only artificial lighting available to the poor was a feeble rush light dipped in fat. Only the wealthy had easy access to light. Rush tapers, or tallow candles, were the cheapest form of lighting; beeswax candles were a luxury. Oil was not generally used until the 19th century, and even then candles were always used to light the way to bed.

Melbourn had gas as early as 1864, but only a few houses and some street lamps at the south end of the High Street were supplied. By 1869 there was a gasworks on the edge of the parish, northeast of Mill Lane, next to the bridge. This provided lighting for Melbourn and Meldreth.

On 11th October 1899 The Lighting and Machinery Act was first proposed. At a Vestry meeting it was recommended that a sum, not exceeding £30, be set aside for street lighting. (42 people were in favour and 2 against.) The discussion on street lighting went on for years. Further sums were added in 1900 and a rate of 1½d was set.

By 1904 the gasworks had expanded and came under the direction of the Meldreth and Melbourn

> The Parish Council proposes to install 14 lamps in Station Road, New Road and High Street from the Moor Corner to Townsend. The cost on the rates would be 1½d in the pound. A Parish meeting was called for 5th October to discuss the proposal.
>
> *Royston Crow 30th September 1926*
>
> The AGM was held in the Council School. The Clerk gave an account of the public lighting of 13 lamps at a cost of £42 14s 0d, or £3 1s per lamp for the 6 winter months. As 1 more lamp had been installed recently, the future cost would be £45 15s for 14 lamps.
>
> *Royston Crow 5th March 1934*

WHAT THE PAPERS SAID

District Gas and Water Order. New premises were acquired, nearer to the railway. The company was authorized to construct a well and pumping station, and a reservoir in Melbourn on land bought from Heath Farm, in order to supply gas and water to Melbourn, Meldreth and Shepreth.

The new works had been built by 1909 when the company appears to have changed hands. By 1911 it was in financial difficulties and was offered for sale. The Local Government Board was unable to help out, as Melbourn was not an Urban District Council, and was doubtful if the ownership could be transferred to the local authority. Melbourn Parish Council voted to take no action. In October 1915 it was agreed by the Parish Council that during the War, the church should not be lit by gas, and also that no lamps in shop windows or street lamps were to be lit. The company eventually ceased trading and the village reverted to oil light until the advent of mains electricity in 1925.

After the First World War there was a great deal of unemployment and hardship leading to the General Strike of 1926 in support of the Trades Union Congress. Melbourn was not greatly affected, apart from children having to be taken to school by special transport, and by the lack of trains, buses and newspapers.

Electricity comes to Melbourn

The papers found great interest in the new electric light. On 9th October 1891 the Royston Crow reported that *...the Annual Show was spoiled by heavy rain but an electric light display of 4 × 1000 candle power lights by Bailey and Grundy of Cambridge proved a huge attraction. Mr Coningsby provided the 'engine' to power the lights.*

A further report in March 1893, said that *...a talk on 'electricity' was given by Mr G A Ward at a meeting of the Mutual Improvement Society. Lamps were lit and there was also an offer for anyone who wanted an electric shock to receive one from a galvanic battery.*

The last oil lamp in Melbourn on the corner of Mortlock Street at The Cross

The Rev. J Hamilton proposed an amendment to the Act discussed in October 1899. He suggested that the lighting be by voluntary subscription, but this was overruled. A resolution was put to the vote, with 57 in favour and 24 against. It was then proposed that a sum not exceeding £30 be made available to pay for street lighting – 49 were in favour and 2 against.

Water

In 1935 piped water came to the village, though when Geoff Owen built his house on The Drift he came across old water pipes, reputed to have been laid by a wealthy benefactor wanting to pipe water to the village from Goffer's Knoll.

At Heath Farm there is a deep well by the farmhouse where a windmill pumped the water into a reservoir behind the farmyard for the use of the house and farm animals. From there, water was pumped to the top of the hill overlooking Melbourn, and was then piped to the village. Unfortunately, no-one was willing to pay for water which they could get for free in their back gardens. Mrs Cartwright at

Brown's foundry in Station Road, site of the gas company and at one time Groves' Shoe shop. Turners sweet shop was on the right. (Inset) Riverside House site of the steam laundry.

Piped water at Wood's Farm, High Street 1937

In 1925 a petition was signed by 500 people to have streets lit, but only 20 turned up to a meeting to adopt the Lighting and Watching Act, a necessary first step to obtaining lights. There was a great deal of discussion over which areas should be lit, e.g. dangerous corners, and on 11 December a filament lamp was placed on the Moor crossroads, over the clock on Howard's bakery. A second light was promised and was fitted on the corner of the building to illuminate the signpost.

By 2nd March 1928 The Parish Council had signed an agreement with the Electrical Supply Co. for lighting of the village on a seven-year contract. At an AGM held on the 5th March 1934, the Clerk gave an account of the public lighting of 13 lamps at a cost of £42 14s 0d (or £3 1s per lamp), for the six winter months. As one more lamp had been installed the future cost would be £45 15s for fourteen lamps.

By 1925-26 most houses in the village were finally provided with electricity. The older council houses had to wait another 10 years.

In 1851 Melbourn had 36 shopkeepers and craftsmen

Howard's bakery, Moor Corner

Old barn at The Cross. It later became Howard's bakery shop. Jubal Howard also had a museum in this building.

Bakers

One of the bakeries in Melbourn was Jubal Howard's at Moor End Corner. (The old pub *The Royal Oak* was incorporated into this building.) His sister Nora helped and later also Ollie Blackwell. Earlier they had baked at the house behind The Old Elm Tree and before that at Hubert Ward's house. Later Jubal rebuilt the barn on the Cross which became a bakers and confectioners. His museum was also situated here for a time. Later the bakery was taken over by OS North.

Woods' Hygenic Bakery, Mortlock Street

Woods Hygenic Bakery was also set up in School Lane (Mortlock Street), by Tom Woods and his father. Mrs Woods also had a sweet shop there.

When the Woods gave up the bakery, the Winters moved in from their premises on the High Street. Apart from selling sweets they also sold rabbit food!

Butchers

There were several butchers in Melbourn, and of course, all animals were killed on the premises.

In Victorian times one of them, a Mr Mumford, is said to have fought Sir Peter Soames of Heydon

Townsend Farm was the only exception. Water was piped as far as the Cross and at George V's Coronation celebrations it was switched on ~ it was said to have reached as high as the Church Tower!

Before the Second World War Harry Bunten was the local expert on the village pumps, a vital service before piped water was introduced.

In 1901 the Riverside Steam Laundry opened opposite to Sheen Mill. It flourished until 1914.

Bacon's butchers shop near The Cross

Grange (a famous pugilist), because he had not paid his account. Other butchers in the village were Butler, Disbrey, Emery, Oliver, Pitchford, Stockbridge and Webb.

A butcher (appropriately called Bacon) had a shop opposite the Church. Alf Bacon arrived in the village as a young man and specialised in making sausages. Before Alf Bacon came the shop was owned by Mr Butler.

Next door to the old pub, *The Hoops*, was another

Disbrey's the butchers, The Cross

butcher ~ Alf 'Moss' Huggins ~ famous throughout the area for his sausages.

Ernie Carter, whose wife kept a drapery shop, sold bacon and pork and hawked it around in his dog cart.

Alf Pryor, (known as the 'pig killer') lived in

Huggins' butchers shop, High Street

'Fessor' Hinkins and his cart outside his shop, Little Lane

A jack of all trades

Alf Hinkins, (known as 'Fessor'), had a tiny fish shop on the corner of the Cross squeezed between the thatched cottage which was the original Co-op, and the White Lion urinal! Fessor was also a chimney sweep, and made ice cream. He used the same barrow for the brushes and soot bags as he did for the fish he fetched from the station.

Meeting Lane. He would come to your house to kill and butcher your 'house pig'. He was a fine figure of a man with mutton chop whiskers and a jovial face. He wore a distinctive blue-and-white apron and carried a knife and steel.

The fish shop cottage was once occupied by a very tall couple. When asked how they managed in such a small house their reply was, 'In summer we sleep with our feet out of the window, and in the winter in the fireplace'!

Millers

Before the bridge over the stream was installed, pedestrians used the bridge by the mill, continuing through Sheen Manor garden and out by the yard

Back of Mill House and inside the Mill, Station Road

Front of the Mill, Station Road

Rawlings' Foundry, The Moor

gate. It was alleged that a white horse haunted this path. Wheeled traffic forded the mill pool.

The Sheen Mill was undershot, as were most in the area. The efficiency of this type of mill depends on clearing the water from the tail of the mill as quickly as possible, and for this reason there was a large shallow pool below the mill. This pool reached as far as the footpath to the Church Meadows (now the College playing field).

During his apprenticeship, Bert Palmer learned how to dress the millstones when they became too worn with use. This was a skilled job and involved lying on the stomach and pecking at the stone with a tool rather like a tomahawk. Tiny pieces of steel often flew off and became embedded in his hands, where they remained for the rest of his life. The Wards owned the mill at this time and later, when Jack and Billie Ward were in the army in the First World War, Joe Pepper was the miller and Laurie Handscombe the boy. Supplies of bran for pet rabbits could also be obtained from the mill.

Engineers

In the 1800s Rawlings was in business as a millwright, engineer, and iron and brass founder at the Moor End works. The company made the iron bridge over the mill stream, the kissing gates in the churchyard and those in the fields on the way to the station. These are still in place and bear the foundry mark.

The works, later known as the Vulcan Iron Works, was sold after Rawlings' death and was subsequently the site for the Walford Brothers' Engineering Works after the Second World War.

Quarrying clunch and lime

Clunch (Melbourn Rock) was quarried from a pit to the south east of the village and used for building material. In 1840 lime was being extracted from a quarry in Water Lane, and by the 1920s, the Melbourn Whiting Co. Ltd was producing calcium oxide for tanneries at Potton and Sawston.

At the chalk face

The Melbourn Whiting Co. Ltd was owned by William Wallace, from Weston near Hitchin, and the managing director was Dan Thomas, from Meldreth. The Clerk of Works was Sidney Waldock from Melbourn, who was also Clerk to the Parish Council for many years. The foreman was George Harrup.

After processing and drying in a coal furnace the chalk was sent to many parts of the country; in Manchester and Bolton it was used in carpet backing, and in London it was used in paint manufacture.

Local millers used it in their animal feed products, and a small firm just outside Shefford, in Bedfordshire, used it for making clay pigeons.

When it resumed working after the Second World War, the plant turned out 18–20 tons per day in summer and slightly less in winter, when the drying time was longer. The locals who worked there at that time were Bill Stanford, Len Smith, Arthur Cooper, Brian Cooper, Alf Harland, Archie Jacklin, Stan King, Peter Noades and Jim Winter. Alex Yates and Jock Martin were lorry drivers.

A first hand account by Wally Winter employed at Whitings

Bullen's blacksmith left of picture in High Street

Gouldthorp's blacksmith, High Street

Blacksmiths

Before the First World War a well known blacksmith was David Ellis. He lived in the thatched house behind the church and his forge faced the road.

By the 1940s there were three blacksmiths, in the village. One of these, owned by Mr Bullen, was situated where the 1915 fire started. Joe Jackson was the farrier and W Burton, an apprentice, who later owned a shop on the High Street.

Gouldthorp's was nearer the Cambridge end of the High Street and shod cart-horses. Later, Arch Sutton, a farmer during the First World War, came over from Orwell once a week to help.

Wheelwrights

There were several wheelwrights in the village, as farming was the main occupation and depended on horses and carts for transport.

The Howes lived in the cottage just beyond the Foundry at the corner of Moat Lane.

Bidwell Howes was in partnership with one of the young Gouldthorps for a while. Their workshop was in the orchard next to the smithy, and made fine carts for the Palmers.

William Ellis, kettle maker, cleaning and mending a 'tea-cattel'

Nobel Howes worked for Percy Elbourn, in a workshop at Greenlow Farm. They were experts at making Scotch carts ~ specially shaped carts built for the transport of fruit ~ mainly bushels of apples.

Harness makers

Harness-makers were important members of the community. In 1795 John Law had a shop next to the Dolphin. Besides making and repairing harness, he would clean and mend coffee mills and 'tea-cattels', mend whips, dog collars or lanterns. He also sold 'brown hesn' (hessian), 'callacho' (calico), 'blew aprons' and 'broshes' (brushes). Some of his more expensive work included making 'A good sett of plated chaise harness with raynes' for £6, while new ironwork on the Moor Gate cost 4s 7d., plus 6d for

'naels'. From his account books it is apparent that accounts were sent out annually.

Thomas Ellis (1741~1824) was described as *...Collar & Harness Maker, a Dealer in Oil, Cutlery, Ironmongery, Rope, Hemp etc.*

In 1790 Joseph Hagger, a saddler from Chishall, married Elizabeth, Thomas's daughter. Their first child, Joseph Ellis Hagger, inherited the business in 1824 on the death of his grandfather.

Early account books still exist and are of interest for their record of the prices of ironmongery and cutlery in 1795; for example, a saucepan and egg slice costing 4d. There seems to have been some diversification of the stock in 1796 when salt was

Jonah Howard, cobbler and harness maker

South Cambs Electrical and Motor Company at The Cross

Wedds garage, Flint Cross

also sold. By 1801 there were accounts for sales of thread, buttons and down from feathers. In 1812 when Joseph was about 22 years old, his records show the sale of fruit. It is not clear whether he was a middleman or if the fruit was sold in the shop.

In the mid-18th century the business was sufficiently prosperous for Joseph to pay for land to be allocated for enclosure in Meeting House Lane, opposite the orchard at the rear of his original property. A house was built on this plot to accommodate members of his family. Surviving account books go up to 1830. From that date the sources of information are letters, a few receipts and family legend. There were three JE Haggers successively in charge of the business, which grew to include, in addition to the ironmonger's shop, a harness shop, and a blacksmith's. Carpets, paint and paraffin were also sold. A horse-drawn cart would visit farms to collect work for repair and to deliver orders and finished goods.

Garages

Gradually garages took over from blacksmiths and wheelwrights. At the Cross, the garage known as the South Cambs Electrical and Motor Company was run by Jack Wedd. He also started the garage at Flint Cross; both were later bought and run by Bill Dash. There was also a garage on the High Street near Rose Lane.

Ernie Thompson's bike shop, which was situated opposite the Post Office, later became a garage and

Garage near Rose Lane

was run for years by his son-in-law John Kay. When Ernie Thompson ran the cycle shop he played a gramophone all evening to attract custom. Townsend Garage was started and run by Archie Hale.

Builders

Building had become an important trade, and in the second half of the 19th century, William French was the chief local builder. This was during the period when white bricks and Welsh slates became available, and after the railway was built.

Hale's, building contractor and decorator, Station Road

Lance Hale, Archie's son, started a business, after the Second World War, in Station Road and later managed Jacklin and Hale in Royston.

Milk rounds

There were at one time several milk rounds in the village. AR Fordham kept cows at The Bury and Ralph Day delivered milk with his horse Kitty and a float.

Jim Muncey lived in Norgett's Lane and Walter Muncey in Orchard Road. They both kept cows and people were able to collect their milk from the farm. The cows were often grazed on the roadside verges in the summer and looked after by a small boy.

Ralph Day, milkman, with his horse Kitty, High Street

Mr French built the Fire Engine House in Station Road, using the bricks from the old Cage on The Green, which he had been contracted to demolish.

Jim Pryor followed him and they probably overlapped, though he seems to have been more of a carpenter and undertaker. He bought trees from Elmdon and they were then sawn up by hand in the saw-pit at Orchard House. His workshop was later moved to the foundry, where his saw-pit was in a barn. One of his jobs was repairing The Bury roof.

His business was taken over by GA Ward & Sons, who were also painters and glaziers. This was a very successful family business for more than a hundred years.

John Hale, the grandfather of Archie of the garage, was Ward's headman. Gradually their scope extended and they took on plumbing work, made coffins, and signs for shops and inns. According to Maurice Stockbridge, who was apprenticed to them during the First World War, they made brushes for the whole area, as the company was the only one with the necessary equipment.

Top, The Post Office in the High Street owned by Ralph Ixer and above, Harry Cranfield

Mr Clear lived in a hut on the Moor in an orchard near the road to the sewage farm. He took milk round in a can hanging from the handlebars of his bike. One well known story tells of how one day, when he saw the Inspector approaching, he kicked the can over into the gutter to avoid the milk being tested.

H. CRANFIELD,

GROCER & PROVISION MERCHANT,

NEWSAGENT,   -   -   -   -

DEALER IN PATENT MEDICINES,

Cash Stores, Post Office,

MELBOURN.

Celebrated MELTON MOWBRAY Pies to order.

General stores

By 1875 Campkin's were established as a grocer's and general store near the Cross, which included a china shop, drapery and general outfitters. They manufactured mineral water on the same site and hired out open and closed carriages. S Campkin also made umbrellas. When the family business broke up, Mrs Edie Chapman ran a drapery shop at the front, and Jack Wedd took over the main premises next door as a garage and electrician's.

Campkin's shop, later Mrs Chapman's, Station Road

Buchan's shop with Mr Pickering, High Street

Bottles from Campkin & Co. dating from 1890–1900.

Ginger beer was usually sold in stoneware or dark glass bottles to protect the beer from light and prevent the purchaser from seeing the sediment. These bottles were manufactured by Price of Bristol. The internal marble stopped bottle was patented by Hiram Codd in 1873 and were generally known as 'Codds', but locally they were called 'jinklers' owing to the sound they made when shaken. A marble was inserted during manufacture of the bottle, it was then filled upside down and by turning the bottle right side up again, the gas from the carbonated drink would hold the marble tight against the neck of the bottle. A small wooden peg – known as a 'walloper' was often used to push down the marble to release the gas. The contempt of beer drinkers for the new carbonated drink may well be the origin of the saying 'What a load of Codds Wallop'.

Robinson, the tailor, The Moor

Smith's sweet shop, High Street

Thixton's shop, High Street

Apart from the Post Office there were grocery shops, bakers, a fruit and vegetable shop, shoe and boot makers, an ironmonger, a tinsmith, a clocksmith, paper and stationery shop, tailors and dressmakers. There were also many sweet shops in the village.

Sweet shops

The Tuck Shop or sweet shop, near the Dolphin, was run by Mrs Thixton and on the opposite side of the road, next to the Red Cow, another a sweet shop was kept by Dubby Smith's wife. An earlier sweet shop was kept by Mrs Winter.

Mrs Hinkins took over the Winter's shop and then moved to the laundry on Station Road; this was later taken over by Turner's. There were also sweets sold at the shop situated next to the old Legion Hall, run by Mrs Frank Thompson.

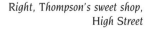

Left, Abrey's shop, Drury Lane with Maggie Stanford and son Edwin on the left and Daisy Abrey

Right, Thompson's sweet shop, High Street

Charabanc trip to Clacton

Transport & communication

...In July 1879 Alexander Hopwood, carter, was charged with 'furious driving' in Melbourn

Movement, in the prehistoric era would have been limited. The only way of travelling from one place to another was on foot. The situation did not change greatly until about 8000 BC when animal husbandry began. When possessions such as animals, crops and shelter, or the occupation of land and access to water became prized, so did the need to protect them, or to move away if they were threatened. The use of animals to transport people and belongings became a natural progression and greater distances could be covered. Routes suitable for moving animals between locations and for trading goods, were established over time.

Early vehicles

The sledge would have been used by the early settlers in Melbourn to enable larger loads to be dragged along. Over the course of the next 5000 years changes were made to this type of transport. This ultimately led to the development of the wheel.

The first known wheeled chariot, or cart, was found in Sumeria. The wheels were made of two slabs of wood fastened together with braces. Built around 3500 BC it increased the speed of travel over land. Eventually this led to the four-wheeled cart, which relieved the burden of carrying supplies.

Spoked wheels were in use in Egypt around 1500–2000 BC, and the idea was used later by the Romans for carts and chariots. A two-wheeled cart, made by Celtic woodworkers, was much admired by the Romans who called it a 'carpentum', from which the word *carpenter* derives. Later improvements included the addition of tyres ~ initially made of metal, progressing to solid rubber and then pneumatic tyres.

Tracks and roads

Around Melbourn there are two Anglo-Saxon tracks ~ simple pathways rather than roads ~ that follow the contours of the land. One of these, Icknield Way, broadly follows the line of the A505 locally, and links Salisbury Plain with the East Coast and the capital of the Iceni at Ickleham. The second track, Ashwell Street, runs partly in association with Icknield Way and under the railway arch at Melbourn. It passes along Back Lane then from Black Peak to Fowlmere and Thriplow Heath. The course of Ashwell Street in Melbourn was altered at the time of the Enclosure, so that it did not interfere with the allocation of land.

The Romans, with their more advanced civilisation, modified some of the ancient tracks. Ashwell Street is an example: it had a strategic advantage in that it was straighter than most tracks, it linked with existing routes and was also close to springs at Melbourn Bury. For the most part, the Romans constructed their own straight roads to help with the passage of chariots, horses and foot soldiers between the major Roman bases. Such improved roads also enabled easier communication between locations, not only face to face but also by signals which could be seen from a great distance.

Four-wheeled chariots from Sumeria

Beacons were one means of signalling and were used from early times to give warning of the approach of an enemy. Signals could be relayed from station to station and, for maximum effectiveness, beacons were often located on hilltops, such as Therfield Heath and Barrington Hill.

Following the departure of the Romans the roads became neglected and fell into disuse as people remained in their towns and villages working for noblemen to whom they held allegiance. There was little significant development in transport or communications until the 1500s.

Movement of goods and people

Heavy, cumbersome wagons, drawn by teams of horses or oxen were still being used up to the end of the 16th century and important communications were conveyed by messenger.

The roads were ill-defined and poorly maintained and, during bad weather, impassable. The upkeep of the public highways was generally the responsibility of the manor, a duty usually passed to the tenants. An Act of 1555, which formed the basis of road maintenance for nearly 300 years, placed the obligation of the upkeep of public highways on the parish as a whole. By 1691 the parish was required to appoint a Surveyor of Highways (or Waywarden) under the jurisdiction of the Justices and the County Quarter Sessions. The person nominated was served with a warrant by the Parish Constable, confirming his appointment as Surveyor of the Highways for the following year; acceptance of this duty was compulsory. He was fined 40s if he refused to accept office, for any default, or neglect of his duty.

His first task was to take over any balance of money from his predecessor and become acquainted with on-going works. Three times a year, at least, ... *he had to view all the roads, byways, water courses and pavements within his precinct and make presentation upon oath in what condition he finds same, to the next Justices.* He required owners of land adjacent to the highway to clear obstructions and to cleanse and scour the adjoining gutters and drains. Overhanging growth and hedges had to be cleared in order that ... *from one end of the parish to the other there might be a clear passage for travellers and carriages* and ... *that the sun may shine onto the ways to dry same.*

At all times he had to look out for ...*and waylay any waggons, wains or carts etc. that are not drawn by the statutory number of oxen or horses.* The following Sunday, after discovering any default or annoyance, he was required to stand up in the parish church, after the sermon, and name any offender in order that he might be prosecuted.

On six days of the year villagers were recruited by the Surveyor to provide labour, horses, carts and any necessary tools, to undertake highway repair. They were also bound to report any defaulter to the justices. Other duties included the collection of any cash payment due from ...*poor cottagers and niggardly farmers.*

Some parishes failed to appoint Surveyors of the Highways and, in some cases, Surveyors were unable to enforce the law on farmers ...*who beat them if they approached their houses with obnoxious demand.* The Act of 1691 also decreed that ...*the Surveyor make every cartway leading to any market town eight foot wide at least, and as near as may be even and level'* and that ...*no horse causey* [causeway] *shall be less in breadth than three feet.*

New Road, *before it was surfaced*

By 1760 travelling times had been halved compared with the previous century and were constantly improving due to changing horses at staging points and better coach design. The establishment of turnpikes also provided funds to enable better maintenance of the roads.

Turnpike roads

By the 17th century a form of privatisation had taken place. A system of toll roads and turnpikes run by Trusts, was set up by an Act of Parliament and required payment to be made by the road user before access to the road was allowed. Advertisements appeared in the press until well into the 19th century, for lessees to be selected by auction for the collection of Turnpike Tolls (amounting to £200~£400 per annum).

Toll roads were not popular; although the standard of the roads improved generally, road users were reluctant to pay. Turnpikes were in the High Street near Water Lane, and Dunsbridge Turnpike on the boundary of Melbourn and Shepreth.

By the mid-18th century toll roads were well established. The ability to move about more freely encouraged trade outside the local area and three

Position of the toll gate in the High Street, near Water Lane

distinct tiers of carrier businesses emerged: the *major carriers* operating country-wide (particularly in and out of London), the *regional carriers* who worked between towns and cities and *local carriers* who traded in and around the village.

The number of passengers able to be carried by stagecoach increased over the years. Coaches were limited to six people in the mid-18th century; by the end of the century this had increased to ten people and 16 by the early 1800s. It was cheaper to ride on top in the open.

A strong sense of competition grew between the coaching inns and the drivers and they would race against each other in order to gain the reputation of being the fastest. This sometimes meant that speed became more important than safety and, from time to time, coaches were overturned and people injured. Each of the coaches had its own name and its own following. Two well known coaches were the 'Safety' and the 'Tally-ho' that ran through Melbourn from Cambridge to London and back daily. Locals were either 'Safety' men or 'Tally-ho' men and were implacable enemies.

The turnpikes were important to the growth of trade, communication and travel. The system however, was not without its problems and the poor state of some toll roads was often due to negligence or the high cost of maintenance.

By the late-19th century the roads in Melbourn were clearly good enough to enable road users to break the law. In July 1879 Alexander Hopwood, carter, was charged with 'furious driving' in Melbourn.

With the arrival of the railway turnpikes gradually declined and eventually disappeared; road maintenance became the responsibility of local

A number of coaches passed through the village including the 'Safety' and the 'Tally-ho'

Rose Inn, High Street one of the earliest coaching inns in Melbourn

government. County Councils employed lengthsmen, or linesmen, to keep a defined length of a local lane in good condition and to ensure that landowners played their part by keeping hedges trimmed back.

Coach Accident

On Thursday night last, the Lynn Mail, which passes through this town to London, was overturned between Melbourn and Royston and the coachman (Simpson) was killed upon the spot. The cause of the accident appears to have been a quantity of mud, which had scraped to the side of the road, and being covered with snow was not discerned by the coachman who was considered a careful driver, and was justly respected by those who knew him. There were four passengers and one outside, all of whom, as well as the guard, escaped without injury.

Cambridge Chronicle 15th January 1842

WHAT THE PAPERS SAID

They were eventually replaced in the 20th century by road gangs whose area of responsibility was wider.

Arrival of the railway

The early-17th century saw the invention of the first commercial steam engine, which was improved by James Watt in 1769. However, it was not until 1804, that Richard Trevithick produced the first steam engine to run on rails. It was able to carry 70 passengers and 10 tons of iron 9 miles at 5mph. Twenty-one years later George Stephenson built the 'Locomotion' followed by the 'Rocket'.

Melbourn on track

The growth in the railway network was rapid, and in 1851 ninety railway navvies (navigators, most from outside the village) constructed the Melbourn-Meldreth line as an extension from Royston to Shepreth. The Shant public house was constructed for the navvies, after the shanty, where they met and drank previously, had burned down.

The connection to Cambridge caused some opposition from the University with regard to the route. The University believed that easy access to

Meldreth and Melbourn station

MELBOURN

CAMBRIDGESHIRE

BRITISH RAILWAYS

SEE BRITAIN BY TRAIN

London would provide too much of a temptation for students and the solution was that the train was met at Shepreth by 4-horse omnibuses to complete the journey to Cambridge. The forty mile journey from London to Shepreth by the Great Northern Railway (GNR) took 105 minutes and the 9 miles to Cambridge by omnibus took 40 minutes. Initially there were four trains daily during the week. A 1st class return fare was 10s, 2nd class ~ 7s 6d and 5s for 3rd class.

Fatal Accident

A serious accident happened at this place on Monday last, to a man named George Copperwaite, a railway labourer, who met his death under the following circumstances. The deceased was working on the Shepreth extension line, and about nine o'clock in the morning was engaged with others in filling wagons with clunch. He had filled his wagon, and was going to get some water of one of his companions, when some clunch from the bank he had been excavating gave way, and a quantity of it fell upon him. The deceased fell across the rail, and the engine to which the wagons were attached being in motion passed over him, with two or three carriages before they could be stopped. Assistance was rendered, and the deceased was found lying partly on the line and partly off, his head and the upper part of his body lying off the line, and the lower part of his body and the right leg and arm lying on the line. The carriages passed over his right leg in a line to the right shoulder, up the groin of the deceased, who survived about 10 minutes, and then died in great agony. He was about 32 years of age. No blame was attributable to any body, and an inquest having since been held before Mr Marshall, the jury returned a verdict of 'Accidental death.'

Cambridge Chronicle 24th May 1851

The extension of the line to Cambridge was approved in 1867 and thirty years later, the travelling time from Cambridge to King's Cross had been reduced to 90 minutes and by 1932 to 75 minutes.

In March 1900 the old pile bridge over the River Mel was demolished one Sunday afternoon by

Elbourn's haulage company steam lorry

50~60 navvies, after the 1 o'clock train had passed through. A new steel bridge was installed in its place and the work was complete ready for the next train, four and a half hours later!

Railway stations were originally located where they would be able to serve several nearby villages and so collection and delivery from the station was difficult. For many years villages had made their own arrangements with errand boys and carters for transport to and from the station, but with serious competion from motorised transport carrying goods, the railways found it necessary to reintroduce the parcel van delivery service in 1932.

The challenge of road vehicles

The first traction engine was produced in 1840. These engines were widely used on farms and for the carriage of goods. Some of the larger road locomotives were capable of carrying up to 120 tons. These large smoke and steam-producing monsters were not popular, particularly with the owners of horse drawn vehicles.

In August 1863, a traction engine, conveying coprolite to Royston Station frightened a horse that was drawing a phaeton (4-wheeled carriage) carrying

Sheepshead Row, High Street

George Smith and his wife and daughter. The phaeton overturned resulting in the family being injured. This was not the first accident involving steam engines and there were calls for the traction engine to be banned on the highway. Eight years

Milestone House in the High Street

later, Edward Prime, a coprolite merchant, was fined £2 with 13s costs, at Melbourn Petty Sessions, for allowing a steam traction engine to be used on a turnpike road without a person to precede it carrying a red flag.

Not only were traction engines a problem with other road users, they were clearly not the favourite form of transport for level-crossing operators either. In December 1898, Mr Elbourn complained that his traction engine was delayed at Shepreth crossing for 40–45 minutes, although the gate was opened and closed several times for other vehicles. It was explained that special precautions were required for traction engines and a man had to be sent up and down the track to place fog signals. The clerk wrote to the company asking what Act of Parliament had the power to keep a threshing machine for three quarters of an hour at the Shepreth crossing. In reply the G.N.R. said that, in one day, 90 vehicles had passed over the crossing with a total delay of only 12 minutes. If Mr Elbourn gave reasonable notice to the gate-man of the time he intended to cross, every effort would be made to prevent any inconvenience to him.

Steam lorries were in use for many years for the carriage of goods. This raised concern not only for the reasons mentioned above but because they belched out smoke and steam. There was great concern about the risk of fire posed by the vehicles to those living in thatched cottages. Drivers of open-topped cars and cyclists also disapproved.

Members of the Stockbridge family 'taking the air' in their new car

Steam lorries eventually disappeared following the development of the diesel engine in the early 1930s.

Although traction engines and steam lorries were much in evidence during the late-19th century, moving house was still entrusted to horse-drawn vehicles, though these were not without problems. Mr Law's furniture, loaded into a van which was moving his belongings to Cambridge, shifted as the van came down the hill towards Melbourn. The horses were frightened by this and bolted into the High Street. The van hit a telegraph pole and threw the driver out, breaking his hip. Then, near The Dolphin, it hit a pony and cart belonging to Mr Guiver, a general dealer, and another cart belonging to Mr Smoothy, damaging Mr Law's furniture extensively.

The motor car

The 19th century also saw the appearance of the motor car on the roads of Melbourn. In August 1898 it was reported that no fewer than three motor cars had passed through the village! One of them, owned by Messrs. Colman and Co., called at the grocer's to deliver advertising matter, and many curious villagers came out to examine the vehicle at close quarters. A year later villagers were surprised to see several well known inhabitants 'taking an airing in a petroleum motor'. Locals had been seen in horse-and-traps, and careering on cycles, but seldom in motor vehicles.

By 1920 there were 200,000 cars on Britain's roads. Drivers were being regularly apprehended in Melbourn for speeding by the police, lying in wait near The Rose. A report in January 1920 said that Henry Arnold of Stamford Hill was summoned for driving a motor car at a speed dangerous to the public in Melbourn. PC Martin reported that ... *when he was on duty near the end of Rose Lane, a car drove over the crossroads and past a notice warning of danger. The car came towards him at a speed estimated at 20mph. The driver was signalled to stop and pulled up 20 yards down the road. He*

Charabanc excursion outside the Anchor

said he was driving at no more than 12mph and couldn't go faster than 15mph as the car was running badly. He was fined 20s.

The driver of another car was told he was driving to the danger of the public. When he asked '*What speed is dangerous?*' He was told, '*Certainly anything over 15 miles an hour.*'

In October 1920 complaints about the drivers of heavy goods vehicles exceeding the speed limit were such that the police were told to pay particular attention to enforcing the law. This required that drivers of these large vehicles were not to exceed the 12mph speed limit.

The newly-tarred roads in the village, which had previously been left comparatively untreated, caused an accident in December 1921, when George Pearce was thrown from his horse and sustained serious injuries after the animal slipped on the surface.

The Automobile Association was formed in 1905 to aid the motorist. One task it undertook was to put up village name signs in order to assist touring drivers but in 1930 following the introduction of a new Road Traffic Act, the Highway Authority became responsible for erecting road signs. Other services for motorists were subsequently provided by local garages, including fuelling and servicing vehicles.

The rapid increase in car production continued and by 1939, there were more than two million private cars on the roads. Virtually all of them, of course were the same colour, thanks to Henry Ford's philosophy of offering 'any colour as long as it's black'.

Bus and coach services

In April 1914, a regular bus service was set up between Cambridge and Royston and coaches to London frequently passed through the village. Around this time day trips became possible. In September 1921 the Melbourn and Meldreth Temperance Club set out at 6.30am for an outing to Clacton in WJ Carter's 'Reliance' charabanc. They

Women and children on a charabanc outing

arrived after a 4-hour journey and spent the day enjoying themselves on the beach. They left Clacton at 6pm and stopped at Colchester and Dunmow Fair on the way home, arriving back in Melbourn at 2am ...*after a perfect day.*

By 1932 there was such demand for the bus service into Royston, particularly on Wednesday afternoon

The bus service through the village, High Street

The Rose Inn outing 1945

(market day), that large queues formed. It was not unusual for 20 or 30 people to be left behind and, on one occasion, 47 were unable to get on the bus. By 1947 it was still a problem. Children arrived early at the bus stop to ensure they would be able to get to the cinema, whereas adults arriving later were usually left behind and unable to do their weekly shopping in Royston.

Road safety

The combination of different modes of transport on the roads led to a spate of new types of accident. The extent of damage incurred with these faster vehicles became a concern. Damage to the White Lion caused by Elbourn's steam lorry crashing into it, was a good example, though the recovery operation ironically was carried out with the aid of Mr Elbourn's traction engine.

Measures were taken to reduce the risk at various parts of the village. The warning sign of a dangerous crossing ahead by the church did little to curb the zest for speed of motorists, who continued to 'hurtle' through the village at speeds in excess of 15mph. Further measures were taken and warning triangle signs were put on the wall south of the Cross, and

A crowd gathers outside the White Lion after a steam lorry crash

also on the wall at the bottom of Mortlock Street, where they were considered ...*safe from being struck by vehicles.* Here, also, a warning 'Dead Slow' was painted on the roadway. Regrettably, this could not be seen by motorists who could see little of the road from their low seats behind the long bonnets of their cars. The sign however, could be seen by horses, who would jib and shy at something that was new to them and that they were afraid to step on ~ vertical boards were then proposed as an alternative.

The steam lorry belonging to Elbourn's and driven by John Pateman, after it crashed into the White Lion

An accident outside Disbrey's (butchers), The Cross

Other measures involved lowering the kerbstones at the south-western corner of the Cross, opposite the Co-op, and lowering the fence and removing shrubs and trees at the corner of Mortlock Street. New kerbstones were laid around the grassy area by the War Memorial, to prevent motorists cutting the corner and wearing the grass away. It was also intended that they would discourage motorists from parking on the grass and up the church path. The consequence of laying the kerbstones was that safety at the corner was reduced, as motorists could not see them. The proposal to overcome this was to paint them white! The path outside the butcher's was widened and a wider curve was made at the corner to improve the angle of view.

Talk of a by-pass for the village was renewed in 1932, when two visitors from London started taking measurements, and photographs of the junctions between Water Lane and Drury Lane, and refused to discuss their reasons. Rumour was that a by-pass from near The Bury to The Bull's Head, Cambridge Road was under consideration. Further measurements were taken in April 1936 and this time the visitors admitted to being Transport

The fingerpost accident

Late one Saturday night in November 1836, an old stage wagon drawn by eight horses and driven by a sleepy wagoner, was travelling from Cambridge to London, and when passing through the village, the teamster drove his horses too near the fingerpost, when, in the words of a poem made up after the incident,

The ornamental sign by tricks
  Among the good ropes got firmly fixed.
Tearing the post from out its place
  The sign suspended in good grace.

The sleepy wagoner unconscious of the addition to his load reached Royston three and a half miles away where –

In the very narrow streets of the town,
  House after house was ripped and torn
Upon that fatal Sunday morn
  Plant pots and plants alike were strown
And gilded names were overthrown.

One man wakened from his sleep
  Upon the bedroom floor had leaped
With tasselled nightcap on his head
  In shirt and hose he quickly fled
In his first fright he faintly said,
  'T'is the resurrection of the dead!'

Not until the wagon had completed its noisy and devastating journey through the whole town, breaking many windows and doing a great deal of damage, did the post part company with the wagon.

It fell with a crash across the road, but
  Still sleepy John made his way
Towards London at dawn of day,
  Unconscious of the trouble wrought
Upon the poor Roystonians' hearts
  Nor did he learn the strange affray
Till he returned another day!

Officials. The possibility of opening Bury Lane to traffic was also considered. Residents believed that, whereas both plans would relieve traffic on the High Street, The Bury Lane plan would be the cheaper option. A survey carried out one day in October

South Cambs Electrical Motor Company in Station Road

1937 suggested that if Bury Lane were open to traffic, it would relieve the High Street of 27 heavily laden lorries, 33 cars and 47 cyclists.

A 30mph speed limit along the High Street was in place by March 1935. At this time HALT signs were also put up at the Cross. However, in 1936, they were removed and replaced with SLOW signs. Apparently, having stopped, the traffic was not sure when to go again! A traffic census, taken at the Cross in September 1937, raised hopes that perhaps consideration would be given to installing traffic lights. A count of 88 vehicles per hour was found on average.

Other road safety measures were introduced around this time, including central white lines and the imaginative invention of 'cats'-eyes'. It was said that, during the Second World War tanks travelling down the High Street caused the cats'-eyes' to be catapulted into the windows of nearby houses. These tanks were parked on a specially reinforced area at the bottom of New Road.

Ownership of a motor car was only affordable by a few people in Melbourn in the early-20th century – the main form of personal transport being the trap or cart, drawn by a horse or pony. Many who were unable to afford these, found whole new horizons opened up by the advent of the bicycle.

David Wedd with his early bicycle

The bicycle

The early bicycles were, for the most part, just novelties, unsuitable for use on the majority of roads. They lacked tyres, and were known, as 'bone-shakers'; these were first seen in Melbourn in 1870. The first rubber-covered wheels were fitted to the High-Wheel Bicycle or 'Penny-Farthing'. These were seen in Melbourn, but were probably not widespread since they would have cost about 6 months' average

pay! They too had their problems, since the rider was seated so high above the centre of gravity that, if the front wheel hit an obstruction, the back wheel would leave the ground and the rider would be rotated over the handle bars, to land on his head ~ hence the expression 'to take a header'.

The hard-tyred safety bicycle was followed by the pneumatic-tyred bicycle, and in 1893 Melbourn saw the arrival of the detachable pneumatic-tyred bicycle.

These became very popular around the village and once more brought with them a host of accidents and incidents. In 1898 J Howard's son, returning from business in Chrishall, was thrown off his bike by a pile of stones placed in the road at the bottom of Chrishall Hill. He was then approached by the man who, having laid the trap, demanded money. After a

Mr Stockbridge on a tricycle

A Stockbridge family photo ~ one of the early motor cycles

struggle, the villain was frightened away by the arrival of a man with a horse and cart.

The corner of Mortlock Street, at the Cross, became a notorious accident spot. In August 1899, a man cycling towards the Cross ran into a lady cyclist. A few months later two other cyclists collided at the same spot, resulting in bruises and a damaged bicycle. Several other accidents involving bicycles were also reported at this corner ~ George Stockbridge was driving his horse and trap to the Cross in May 1899 when a cycle ran into him as he was turning the corner. The trap wheel ran over the cyclist's arm and leg and although the cycle was damaged, no bones were broken.

Cyclists did not escape punishment for breaking the law ~ those who ventured out at night without a light on their bicycles could be fined an average of 2s 6d. Such fines did not seem to deter the enthusiasm of the Melbourn cyclist, as a Cycle Club was formed which met in The Anchor, attracting over 30 members.

Motor cycles were also in use in the village by 1903 when one offender was fined for 'furiously driving' his

A motor cycle and sidecar parked in Mortlock Street and left, the Post Office in the early 1900s, run by AT Lee

motor cycle through the village. Relatively little was heard in the press of this form of transport, though a motor cyclist with a young lady riding pillion, came off his machine at the Royston end of the village, after a thunderstorm had caused flooding. He required treatment for his injuries but the young lady escaped unscathed. Two more motor cyclists later came off their bikes at the same place, but without injury. The addition of a side-car to a motor cycle permitted family travel and was popular for a while.

Mail and the Post Office

It was not until the arrival of the stagecoach that significant improvements in communication occurred. King Charles I made the Royal Postal Service available to the public as a source of revenue, in 1635. Prior to this, mail was a royal prerogative and postmasters, usually innkeepers, received mail from royal couriers, who were provided with horses to relay the mail to the next post.

The earliest known letter and envelope can be dated to the early Babylonian times (2000 BC). The

letter was written on clay, inserted into a clay envelope and the two were baked together. This was a good security measure, as the letter could not be read without first breaking open the envelope. Seals had been used since the medieval period to authenticate letters and documents but, during the 17th century, they were used to secure letters which were placed in a folded outer covering.

The first mail coach was introduced in 1784. The guard was responsible for protecting the mail and the passengers from highwaymen, and for blowing the post horn to announce the arrival of the mail. In Melbourn these mail coaches were a common sight and welcome as a source of news. With the railway came a faster delivery service and the first mail train ran in 1830. It would be over twenty years before Melbourn had a direct rail delivery. By the time the railway did arrive at Melbourn, the penny post with

the first adhesive stamp, had already been introduced, the sender paying a rate dependent on weight. Prior to 1837, postage was paid for by those receiving the mail and charged according to the mileage. The Post Office encouraged householders to have letter boxes fitted in their doors and post-boxes were set up for the collection of mail. There were multiple collections from post-boxes daily. Stamps were cancelled with date stamps and evidence of the variety of these can be seen from old letters and post cards.

There had been a Post Office in the village since 1811. It formed part of the link for mail transport between London and Cambridge, then onward to York. Authorisation for it to become a Money Order Office was given in 1857 and provided a valuable service to the surrounding area, enabling money to be sent safely. The first building was thatched but

Post Office in the High Street

burnt down in 1866, when many documents and date stamps were destroyed. One of the early sub-postmasters and a money-lender, was a Stockbridge. the Post Office was run by the Lee family in the early 1900s, by Harry Cranfield in the 1920s and the Ixers in the 1930s.

Royal Mail continued to improve over the years

as, apart from newspapers and general gossip, it was still the principal means of contacting others. In November 1928 cycle deliveries of post from Royston stopped and were replaced by motorcycle combination from Cambridge. Outgoing mail was taken to Cambridge in the same way, in order to catch the London delivery by train.

The railways began to use the electric telegraph in the 1840s, passing messages along the line. The Station Master soon found himself acting as agent for the Post Office, which enabled urgent messages to be conveyed to the door of the addressee. The electric telegraph was eventually taken over by the Post Office in 1870.

An alternative means of communication was the development of an electric pneumatic system in 1879, which conveyed actual papers, samples or money through tubes. Attractive in principle but not in practice, it was useful for conveying official messages between nearby locations, and was also used in many shops, including Melbourn Co-op, for billing and returning change.

The first telephone exchange in Melbourn was situated in one of these houses in the High Street

The Telephone

The first telephone exchange in the village was set up in the early 1930s, in a house in the High Street belonging to Roger Willmott. He also became the 'caretaker' and ran the night-time switchboard. During the day it was run by his wife Ellen and daughter Marjory. A telephone kiosk was erected at the Cross in October 1934 and was christened 'the rabbit hutch'. Shortly afterwards, it was the source of complaint, as GPO workmen were seen painting the box on the Sabbath! Complaints were also made against the 45 telegraph poles situated at the Cross, as some were dangerously close to the road. The poles were removed from the High Street in 1936 and lines were laid underground. In 1938 the exchange was moved into a building opposite Sheen Mill in Station Road.

Home Entertainment and News

The earliest form of home entertainment was provided by the phonograph, which could be hired in

An early telephone kiosk, High Street

Adjusting the new telegraph poles near Rose Lane, High Street

primarily to hear the news. However, in order to listen to the wireless, the 'accumulator' had to be charged weekly at the garage or cycle shop, and high-tension batteries and grid bias batteries had to be replaced periodically!

The height of communication, came with the arrival of television and in 1949, both sound and pictures could be appreciated at home ~ a far cry from awaiting the arrival of the stagecoach!

An ornate telegraph pole near the Post Office

1899 from EW Stone, the Draper, in Royston. Their advertisement for ... *Edison's Largest and Best Phonographs Driven by Electric Motor* claimed ... *The most intricate parts of Band Selections, Songs, Speeches, Recitations, Banjo, Piccolo, Xylophone and Whistling Solos &c. repeated with utmost accuracy. The above must not be confused with the far less effective instruments sold under various names such as Gramophones, Graphophones, &c..*

Meanwhile an invention that transformed communications at home was the radio receiver. Devices such as the 'cat's whisker' could be found in Melbourn and ownership was the envy of many. These devices were difficult to adjust but within a few years, the radio 'valve' brought about great improvements. Development accelerated during the First World War

when radio's role in wartime communications was recognised.

It was, however, some years before the wireless became a realistic possession for the village residents, though in 1932 it was available to rent for the sum of 5s per week from shops in Cambridge.

What better Christmas present to receive than a source of home entertainment ~ a fact that did not escape Messrs. Pepper and Haywood in 1935 when they advertised a wide range of models, ranging from £7 12s 6d to 16 guineas.

In 1936 it was estimated that with Melbourn's population there would have been around 74 households with wireless sets.

The onset of the Second World War brought about a further impetus in wireless development and soon everyone in Melbourn who could afford it had one,

Buildings under repair, in the High Street, near
the Cross. The exposed clunch wall can be seen
on the left with wattle and daub on the right

A way of life –
Housing & Lifestyle

... Melbourn had about 60 tenants in 1086 and by 1377 there were 323 poll tax payers

The early inhabitants of Melbourn would have lived in wooden huts, thatched with grass or reeds. It was not until the Roman invasion that bricks were used for building in areas such as Cambridgeshire, where no stone was readily available. After the departure of the Romans, bricks were not produced in England until the 12th century and were not widely available until the late-18th century ~ around the time of the Industrial Revolution.

Stone had been imported into the area for important buildings such as churches, but due to the expense, its use was limited to quoins (cornerstones) and facings. The pillars in the parish church of All Saints', for example, are constructed of clunch. As Melbourn is on the edge of the flint belt, flints were used decoratively on the church and other buildings to face the outer walls, which are largely made of rubble, including re-used Roman bricks.

Clunch, or Melbourn Rock, is a chalk made very hard by extremes of climate and found between the layers of soft chalk blanketing much of south and east England. It was quarried from seams in a pit to the south-east of the village. Although hard, it is subject to frost damage, but, as it is easily carved, it has been used to produce very delicate church carvings, as can be seen inside Ely cathedral.

Locally made, unbaked clay-lump bricks, known as clay bats, were dug from pits in the neighbourhood. They were of no standard size but much bigger than baked bricks. The clay occurs in pockets in our locality as boulder clay underlying the chalk. When dry this material is porous and requires sealing, and so it was plastered over with a mixture of cow dung, horsehair and earth in a similar way to wattle and daub. Later on, some were tarred. It was not unusual for walls to collapse suddenly if water and frost had penetrated the plaster.

A barn with exposed clunch wall, Water Lane and below, a plastered clunch wall in Meeting House Lane

Clunch wall on the corner of Water Lane and the High Street

earlier buildings. The spaces between the timbers were then filled in, usually with wattle and daub. This method was used by the earliest settlers in the area and well into the 17th century. Sticks and branches, cut from the nearby hedgerows, were interwoven and daubed (plastered) with mud or clay mixtures. Many of these remain as interior walls in village cottages today. Later these were replaced with new infills such as brick, known as nogging.

Even wealthy people were limited in their choice

Thatched clunch building with drip boards, Little Lane

The poorest people dug out clay and chalk marl and mixed it with any spare materials lying around. This produced very unstable building material.

Timber-framed houses are still common in the village, and are regarded as the earliest type of 'pre-fab'. The timbers were all cut and numbered on the ground (usually on site in the case of houses) before being erected, and were quite often reused from

The collapsing timber-framed house in Norgett's Lane

of building materials by high transport costs, as a horse and cart on a very poor, potholed, unsurfaced road would be unlikely to cover twenty miles a day.

Bricks were originally made locally, and every community would have its own kiln. The site at Melbourn was situated near Portway and it was here in 1857 that the distinctive bricks were made for the construction of the Baptist Church.

After mechanisation, and particularly after the coming of the railway in the mid-19th century, bricks

A wall at the Baptist Church showing bricks made at the local brickworks in Portway

were more commonly available and widely used. Frequent fires, made the use of bricks more practical. This in turn attracted Brick Taxes, which were in force from 1784 to 1850.

The older, brick-built, houses in the village have 'soft red' bricks in varying shades, while 'newer'

A house using the more uniform Cambridge Whites, High Street

Flemish bond

capping bricks

tumbling in

kneeler

covered damp-damaged bricks at base of wall

Bricks are best

Bricks are an excellent building material, being heat resistant, providing good insulation as they are full of tiny air bubbles, and resist the growth of lichens and mosses. They do not decay from atmospheric pollutants, such as sulphur. The main hazard is splitting by frost, and this occurs only when rain gets in. Bricks can be made to any shape, are easily bonded and have become standardised at a size and shape which fits easily into the hand of the builder. Flemish bond (alternating headers and stretchers in staggered rows) is the most common method used in this area. A header is a brick that has only its short end showing. It is also called a bonder. Stretchers are bricks laid so that only the long face shows. Tie plates are inserted where there is damage by subsidence or weathering.

Originally the stables of the Manor belonging to Dame Mary Hatton – this converted house later became the Locomotive Inn. The upper window was inserted in the 19th century and the door was bricked up in the 1930s. The initials MH can be clearly seen in burnt header bricks

(post 1850s) houses used more uniform Cambridge Whites, made near Ely, and Burwell Whites produced near Newmarket.

Newer and cheaper materials

With the shortage of building materials after the Second World War, houses were built of concrete, using either blocks or shuttering. In the early-20th century asbestos, available from the Atlas works in Meldreth, and cement sheeting, became relatively cheap and were used extensively for repairs, especially to farm buildings.

Up on the roof

Thatched cottages can still be found in the village and thatching seems to be a reviving craft, with each thatcher having his own 'signature' for finishing a roof, in the form of the pattern on the roof ridge. Originally, roofing materials would have been reeds,

Most thatched and tiled roofs 'tip up' at the ends – an old custom to deter witches from landing

Listening in

The well known phrase 'eavesdropping' refers to a time when houses were low and had thatched roofs which extended out beyond the wall of the building. People sheltered from rain under the eaves and were thus in a good position to hear what was being said in the house. At one time it would have been possible to walk the length of a street under the eaves.

wall, protecting the most vulnerable, uppermost, wall materials. The ends of the timbers that carry the tiles are also protected, sometimes by ornately carved bargeboards, but these are subject to rotting in this exposed position.

Often the gable wall extends above the roof level, protecting the roof from wind but leaving the top bricks open to damage. Special tiles or bricks often cap these, and decorative patterns, such as 'tumbling in' are also found on gable ends. A few roofs are of mansard or hipped, gable end pattern. (In a mansard roof each face has two slopes, the lower one at a steeper angle.)

The most primitive houses would have had one low

A mansard roof seen on 'Greenbanks', commonly known as 'Dr Gregor's house', High Street

Above, the Stanford family at work, High Street and left, The Stanford 'signature' on the roof ridge, Station Road

grass or straw. Later, tiles were used, providing a more durable and safer alternative. Flat, or peg tiles are most extensively found in this area, though some pantiles (curved tiles) can be seen. Slate was imported from the 19th century and, from the mid-20th century, synthetic materials have been employed.

The join of the roof with the gable wall is important in weatherproofing, and has given builders opportunities for variation and decoration. Most commonly the roof extends beyond the gable

room with a gap for an entrance, perhaps covered with a hide, and a central hearth with a hole in the roof above it for the smoke to escape. Animals would share this room for protection from wild beasts and thieves. The floor would be rammed earth, possibly spread with chalk.

Later houses would consist of two or more rooms, giving separate accommodation away from the animals; or a loft would be built, forming a sleeping platform for the family. Evidence of some of these horizontal divisions can be seen in older cottages in Melbourn, where dormer windows have been inserted to provide light into what was originally an upper, undivided, storage space and sleeping loft.

By the end of the 19th century the new Public

Thatched cottages built at different times at different heights, corner of Water Lane and the High Street

Utilities Board had set down standards for workers' cottages, including size and height of rooms. If these standards were met the landowner could receive loans from the Public Works Loan Board. After 1918, due to a shortage of building materials, traditional thatched cottages were permitted to be built, but only to the higher standards. This can be seen in the difference in height of the newer thatched cottages in the village.

Ordinary houses were usually without glass until the late-16th century. Before then, waxed parchment, linen or even the placentas of cattle might be stretched over a window to admit some light, but exclude draughts.

The word *window* derives from 'wind eye', the opening in a wall for light, ventilation and letting the

Dormer windows were inserted into one storey attic cottages, Dolphin Lane

smoke out. The Romans introduced glass into the country centuries before; it had subsequently been used for beads and ornamentation but was very expensive. Even in the great manor houses, tall windows with few lights were needed for the hall or solar (upper room), while in the late medieval storied house, where rooms were low, horizontal runs of mullioned windows were installed in small lattices set in lead. Early glass was cut from blown discs and was usually very thin but heavily marked. Later, glass made from a disc or cylinder was set in thick wooden glazing bars. These were gradually reduced in thickness until the early-19th century, when they were sometimes replaced by bars of iron.

Centre stack on a thatched cottage in Dolphin Lane

houses, keeping them away from the flammable thatch. Later they were moved to the centre of the house, where they were more efficient, as no heat was lost to the outside. Chimney stacks were often built with ornamental brick.

In 1662 a hearth tax (or chimney money as it was

Ornamental brick chimney stack and carved barge boards on The Bury estate, Royston Road

Above, large panes of glass were used by the 19th century, Mortlock Street and left, a relic of the old window tax, High Street

In the 15th and 16th century glazed windows were designed as removable casements that could be taken away if the occupants moved. After 1840 good cheap sheet glass, became available and many earlier window frames were adapted for large panes.

The building of chimneys and fireplaces began in the 1500s, and by 1570 there were many types of chimneys sprouting up above the houses. The earliest chimneys were added to the gable ends of popularly called) was introduced by Parliament, a means of raising additional revenue for Charles II which continued until 1688.

The detailed lists of hearth tax payers, made at the time, are the most important source of population information for England between the Domesday Book and the 1801 census.

A single hearth in a house would have been situated in the hall, where it would be used for cooking and heating. At that time a kitchen was defined as a store for utensils.

The house with two hearths would have the second situated in the kitchen. Usually, this defined a person of moderate wealth, around £60 in all.

Where there were three hearths, the additional one was in the parlour. This would be in a house of six to eight rooms and the owner would be worth about £141.

A house with six hearths would have around fourteen rooms and the owner was worth around £360.

Changes in population

The Domesday Book mentions that Melbourn had about 60 tenants in 1086, and by 1377 there were 323 poll tax payers. The population varied over the next few centuries. In 1563 there were 80 households, increasing to 125 by 1672.

Ninety families were in the village in 1728 and this number had risen to 130 by 1801, with a population of 819. At the turn of the 19th century population growth was more rapid, with numbers reaching 1,931 by 1851.

The numbers increased in 1871, due to the development of the coprolite industry and agricultural prosperity, both of which meant more jobs.

Following the transfer of an area with about 200 inhabitants to Royston in 1901, when the parish boundaries were changed, the population fell

A tax on comfort

Householders were required to pay 2 shillings per year for each fire-hearth or stove within the dwelling. This was to be paid half yearly on Lady Day, 25th March, and Michaelmas, 29th September. Although the poorest people were excused from paying the tax, they were often included on lists with their exempt status noted. To be exempt, they had to obtain a certificate of exemption. This had to be signed by the parish clergyman, churchwarden or overseer of the poor, and counter-signed by two Justices of the Peace. Only those whose house was worth more than 20 shillings a year, and who paid church and poor rates, were liable for hearth tax.

In 1664 around 40 percent of the houses in Melbourn had one or two hearths. About 20 percent had three or four, and the remainder had either one hearth, or none. Thirty-one houses were excused payment of tax. Undoubtedly, the poorest families were still using the central hearth with no chimney.

The Hearth Tax Roll of 1674 for Melbourn

Name	Hearths	Name	Hearths	Name	Hearths	Discharged by Legal Certificate
Joseph Scruby	1	Widow Cooper	3	William Walman	1	Edward Watts
John Anger	1	John Andrews	1	Widow Taylor	2	Jeremy Game
Timothy Cann	2	Philip Wilcox	1	John Munsey	2	Widow Loe
Anthony French	1	Mr John Payne	12	John Hall	1	Mary Bell
John Marshall sen.	3	John Porter	2	Peter Wedd	2	William Johnson
Edward Wood	empty	Edward Kelly	1	Edward Prior	3	Sarah Crowne
William Hitch	2	Widow Carver	1	Nathaniel Blackley	1	Widow Hitch
Thomas Wright	5	Benjamin Hornold	3	William Cann	2	Edward Hutchinson
Widow Denham	3	Robert Stockbridge	2	Thomas Gum	2	Widow Oliver
Thomas Hussey	2	Nicholas Biggrave	2	Thomas Newburne	1	William Bennett
Giles Bencot	1	William Willmott	4	Edward Reynolds	1	Nathan Walker
Benjamin Medcalfe	3	Edward Chichely	1	Robert Noone	1	Mary Abby
Richard Hitch	6	Thomas Frost	2	John Chapman	1	Widow Wilcox
William Titmas	1	William Lewellen	3	Richard Badcock	3	Thomas Hutchinson
William Ellis	1	John Layton	1	Samuel Scruby	3	Widow Beomont
John Newlin	2	Henry Luck	5	William Thurlow	2	Hester Harker
John Coe	1	Thomas Huggins	3	Jonathon Stockbridge	1	Widow Orwell
Gilbert Meane	1	Widow Huggins	3	Widow Neale	1	Benjamin Ward
John Stokes	1	Mr Thomas Day (Vicar)	3	William Cherry	2	Elizabeth Constable
John Hitch	4	Widow Titmas	2	Timothy Atkinson	2	Thomas Brock
William Casboult	1	Edward Titmas	4	Widow Casbourne	3	Edward Wood
Mary Long	1	John Manfield	2	John Jarman	2	Robert Evens
Thomas Harper	2	Andrew Foscue	3	William Ashburne	1	Widow Osburne
William Wood	2	Thomas Litchfield	1	Thomas Rowell	4	Widow Parker
William Hitch	1	William Loaux	2	Robert Neale	2	Widow Cresswell
John French	1	Thom. Mumford	1	Thomas Manfield	4	William Draper
Benjamin Harris	1	John Bond	1	Nathan Andrews	1	Nathaniel Andrews
Thomas Stockbridge	1	Richard Single	1	William Wakefield	1	John Evens
John Marshall	1	John North (innkeeper)	8	Thomas Hall	2	Widow Wilcox
Philipp Wilcox	1	Timothy Hornold	2	Triamor Huggins	1	Edward French
John Hutchinson	1	George Oliver	2			Widow Sellars
Richard Anger	1	Edward Litchfield	5	Total	202	1 each Total 30

Interesting Discovery at Melbourn – 16th Century Tinder Hole

The old thatched house at the corner of Water Lane has been demolished, also the thatched wall adjoining. When the chimney corner in the living room was being pulled down, a small apse, or alcove was discovered beside the flue and behind the chimney corner seat. The recess was artistically shaped and measured about 10 inches high, 8 inches wide, and 8 inches deep, clay and brickwork being used in its construction. Such 'holes' are known to some as salt-box holes, to others as tinder-box holes, and to a few as 'squints'. The latter, however, is hardly correct, as squint holes proper are not recesses, but holes through which one may see objects beyond.

The hole discovered must have been made in the sixteenth century, and was therefore nearly 400 years old. It is thought that such holes were made for the storage of tinder boxes, hence the name tinder-box holes. Lucifer matches of a very crude make were invented in 1805, but they did not displace the tinder-box until about 1820. In many country villages cottagers used tinder boxes until the coming of friction matches in the middle of the

19th century. When the tinder box disappeared, the holes were commonly used for the storage of the household salt, especially in Melbourn, which is one of the dampest villages in the county, most of the cottages having no damp course. In many of the houses the 'hole' in the chimney corner was the only dry place in a house, and the only place in which salt could be kept in a good condition, hence 'salt-box' hole. The example which has just disappeared is believed to have been the only one in the village.

Press and News 7th August 1931

to 1,462. After the Second World War numbers rose again.

The first council houses were built after 1918. The address was 'The Council Houses', but was known locally as 'Chinatown' or 'Tipperary', as it was a long way to the shops. Some houses were built immediately after 1945, at the end of the Second World War, but the next phase of intensive building came after 1950.

Fires of Melbourn

In the past, the village mainly consisted of thatched-roofed houses and it is not surprising that a number of devastating fires destroyed many buildings.

The first reported fire was in 1730. This destroyed 25 houses, plus a number of other buildings. Smaller fires were reported in 1859, 1861 and 1894, but another devastating fire was in 1915, destroying 13 houses. However, the village still contains many houses of the 17th century with underlying timber frames.

Was on St Batholomus Day August 24th 1724 that there happened a dreadful fire in the Parish of Melbourn when in the space of one hour burnt down and consumed 25 Dwelling Houses together with all the Out houses, Barns and Stables and Recks of Corn, the which said loss upon a moderate computation amounted to the sum of six thousand eight hundred and forty two pounds and upwards.'

A statement signed by Henry Roper, Vicar and John Newman, Church Warden

Fires in Melbourn

'On Saturday afternoon last a cottage at Melbourn Heath, occupied by John Fisher, labourer, was discovered to be on fire, and was soon burned to the ground; also a barn which adjoined and a quantity of straw which formed a sheep-yard. It appears that Mrs. Fisher heated the oven, and set in the bread, when she noticed that the thatch on the top of the oven on fire.

She attempted to extinguish it, but her efforts were in vain. Several men who were at work in the fields were soon on the spot, but there being no water near, all they could do was to remove the poor mans goods, and that they succeeded in doing except the bedsteads, which were burned. The fire there was no doubt was caused through heating the oven. The barn and cottage were the property of R. Hitch, Esq., and insured in the Sun Fire Office. The barn was in the occupation of Mr. Robert Barker, farmer, and the straw belonging to Mr. Barker, who is also insured in the Sun office. Fisher's goods were not insured, and we are glad to learn most of them were saved.'

Cambridge Chronicle June 1859

'On Friday, the 4th inst., between one and two o'clock in the afternoon, the inhabitants of this village were alarmed by the (in this place) unusual cry of fire. It was soon discovered that smoke was pouring through the tiles of the farm house on the Lordship farm, in the occupation of Mr. Peter Spark. It being about dinner time there were soon several hundreds of willing hands on the spot, who went to work in good earnest; some to remove the goods of Mr. Spark (who was not at home at the time); and others got on top of the house, and removed some of the tiles to get at the fire, and in a short time, some hundreds of pails-full of water were handed up and thrown into the burning mass, and in the course of half an hour the fire was got under.

The Royston engine was sent for, and was soon on the spot, but its services were not required. It appears that during the forenoon a new stove had been fixed in one of the up-stairs rooms, and a short time before going to dinner the workmen had made a fire in it with pieces of wood, and incautiously left it burning, when a piece of wood would appear to have fallen out of the fire and ignited the flooring of the room.

The damage done to the interior and roof of the house is considerable. The house being old and principally built of wood, the only wonder of everyone who has since examined it is that the fire was got under without the aid of an engine. Considering the hold the fire had got on the top part of the house it appears almost impossible that it could have been extinguished in the way it was. The house stands close to the farm yard, which was in immediate danger, and too much praise cannot be given to both men and women, for the manner in which they exerted themselves in stopping the progress of the fire, and in removing Mr. Sparks goods from the house. The house is the property of R. W. and J. Hitch, Esqrs., of Melbourn, and is insured in the Sun Fire Office. Mr. Spark has since removed to a farm at Babraham, and we are safe in saying that he carries the good wishes of many in Melbourn with him.'

Cambridge Chronicle October 1861

'A fire broke out at a thatched cottage occupied by a man named Wing near the 'Hoops' in the High Street. Pails of water on the roof failed to control it and the fire engine with Mr Campkin and other members of the Brigade promptly put in an appearance, and with the aid of a large number of working men and women too, the engine was kept supplied by means of a water cart and a large number of pails handed on from one to another. The scene was a most exciting one for the danger of a much more serious fire was at one time very real, the 'Hoops' being a thatched building almost adjoining the cottage. The efforts of the Fire Brigade and numerous workers happily confined the fire to the one cottage which was demolished partly by the fire and partly in checking the spread of the fire. The furniture upstairs was nearly all destroyed but downstairs there was just time to get the things out. The building was insured through Mr Campkin'

Royston Crow August 1894

'In a fire at Moor End old farm houses and buildings were burned down. 'Travelling' men camping on the Moor helped as did the Fire Brigade.'

Royston Crow July 1894

Melbourn fire engine house in Station Road. The building is built of bricks from the demolished Cage on The Green

Serious Village Fire Thirteen Cottages destroyed

'A disastrous fire occurred on Thursday afternoon at the village of Melbourn, Cambridgeshire, three miles from Royston, whereby thirteen cottages and other property were destroyed. The origin of the outbreak is uncertain, but the fire was first noticed in the neighbourhood of a blacksmiths shop, and it spread with great rapidity among the thatched dwellings in Rose-lane, Police Street-lane and Dolphin-lane in the middle of the village, the inhabitants barely having time to escape with their lives, and no chance of saving their belongings. There seemed at one time to be danger of flames reaching the church. Within about an hour the thirteen cottages were destroyed, together with various outhouses and several barns belonging to Mr Clear and Miss Stockbridge. Some of the cottages were not occupied. The families rendered homeless bear the names of Guiver, Lee, Pateman, Chapman, Frost, Baker, Carrington, Thurley and Blows. One woman with some young children had just lost her husband in the war. A newly married couple who had taken one of the cottages only this week lost almost everything, while Mr Charles Frost, a well known local cyclist, has lost many valuable prizes, amounting to £60, as well as money. At the outset of the fire the Melbourn Fire Brigade got to work, but could do little with their manual engine. The Royston steam fire engine was soon on the scene, and the Baldock Fire Brigade also rendered assistance. Some adjoining property was saved by them, but the damage done amounts to several thousand pounds. The police from some distance around rendered great service, and the sufferers were looked after by a committee, which included the High Sheriff and the Vicar.'

Morning Post, June 1915

Eight families Homeless

'The village of Melbourn was visited yesterday afternoon with the most disastrous fire ever known in the locality, by which 13 cottages, several barns and between 20 and 30 outbuildings were totally destroyed and eight families rendered homeless. Fortunately the fire occurred in the daytime, and aid was quickly forthcoming, or the results might have been even more disastrous, as one eye witness described it, 'it travelled as fast as a man could walk.'

The Melbourn Fire Brigade turned out promptly under Captain J Newling, and did all they could to check the progress of the flames. The Royston Fire Brigade, with their steam Fire Engine, arrived on the scene as quickly as the horses could gallop, but their efforts and those of the Baldock Fire Brigade, whose steam fire engine was towed the 12 miles from Baldock to Melbourn by a military motor transport lorry, were directed to saving the adjacent property, the fire by the time they arrived having reduced practically all the premises involved to a heap of ruins.

The fire made a clean sweep of everything, and in an amazingly short space of time the whole of the buildings were levelled to the ground, scarcely a brick being left standing. The work of the fire brigades, the police, the Emergency Committee and the Special Constables merits high praise. But for the copious streams of water pumped up from the river by the powerful steam engines and the skilful manner in which they were directed, the damage must have been much more extensive, while the police and special Constables rendered invaluable assistance in helping the inhabitants to escape and to rescue some of their goods and chattels, and the Emergency Committee did admirable work in arranging for the temporary feeding and housing of the homeless families.

The scene of the fire was Rose-lane, Police-station lane and Dolphin-lane, in the centre of the village. Along these lanes clustered a number of old fashioned thatched cottages, barns and outbuildings, most of them built of 'clay bats', large oblong blocks of sun dried clay mixed with straw, with here and there a brick and tiled building.

The Police Station and Court House abut on Police Station-lane, and had an extremely narrow escape, being almost surrounded by burning buildings. Thanks however to the efforts of the fire brigades and to its substantial

construction, this valuable block of buildings escaped almost unscathed; but for a considerable time it was in great danger.

The origin of the fire appears to be uncertain, but the flames were first noticed in the vicinity of a blacksmith's shop, in the occupation of Mr J. Bullen, wheelwright and blacksmith. Here a man named Jackson had been at work, but had gone to dinner. The alarm was quickly given, and the Melbourn Fire Brigade turned out promptly, and did good service with their manual engine, but at first the supply of water was limited, the river being some four hundred yards away from where the fire first broke out. The flames spread with appalling rapidity and threw out an intense heat, which rendered it impossible to approach near to them except on the windward side. Flakes of burning thatch and showers of sparks were borne on the breeze, and showering down on the thatched roofs of the adjoining cottages speedily set ablaze. The flames poured across the narrow lane set trees alight, and ran from house to house with such speed that

some of the inhabitants barely had time to escape, and lost practically all their belongings.

In less than three quarters of an hour the whole of the 13 cottages were blazing furiously and an hour sufficed to level them to the ground. The buildings destroyed included part of the blacksmiths shop, some thatched cottages hard by, an unoccupied brick villa opposite the Police Station, a block of buildings at the back of the Rose public house, several barns belonging to Mr WW Clear, a number of cottages along Police Station-lane, two big barns and some stables belonging to Miss Stockbridge, two cottages belonging to Mrs Palmer, and a number of outbuildings.

Mr G.A. Ward's builder's yard in High-street, containing a large quantity of valuable materials, and some of the houses adjoining had a very narrow escape, and a thatched house on the opposite side of the High-street was only saved by covering the thatch with a large rick cloth and copious drenchings of water. The majority of the cottages it is believed, belonged to Mr WW Clear. The total damage is estimated at several thousand pounds.

At the Dolphin-lane end of Police Station-lane the Royston Fire Brigade succeeded in saving 4 slated cottages and a number of thatched cottages.

Several of the inhabitants were away at the time, the men being at their work and the women engaged in gooseberry picking. All that remains of the whole of the premises are heaps of smouldering ruins and a few twisted fragments of bedsteads and other domestic articles.

The Royston Fire Brigade received the alarm a few minutes before 2 o'clock from Mr Bentley of Royston, who happened to be motoring through Melbourn at the time, and drove off post haste to Royston. The Brigade turned out smartly under Capt. Bedwell and Second Officer Sheldrick, and were at

work on the fire by about 2.30. They placed their fire engine in a field adjoining Dolphin-lane and pumped direct from the river.

The Baldock Fire Brigade received the call about 20 minutes to three. Fortunately a military motor transport lorry was at hand, and the soldiers kindly consented to tow the fire engine to Melbourn and covered the 12 miles in such good style that the brigade were able to have their steamer at work close to the river, shortly after 4 o'clock.

Deputy-Chief Constable Webb, Supt Salmon, Sgt Connell (Melbourn) Sgt Chapman (Royston) and PC's Newell (Barrington) Martin (Harston), Frost (Fowlmere), Worboys (Arrington), and several others were seen in attendance and rendered invaluable service, and the occasion afforded an excellent example of the value of the Emergency Committee and the Special Constables who did admirable work.

The High Sheriff, Mr A R Fordham, who is Chairman of the Committee and Messrs Oscar Campkin, Rivers Smith, G.A. Ward and others were quickly on the spot and gave valuable aid to the homeless people.

A relief committee was organised on the spot, among those prominent being Mr AR Fordham, the Vicar (Rev M de Courcy-Ireland and Mrs de Courcy-Ireland), the Rev WH Wrigley and a number of local ladies, who at once took steps to feed and house those who had been rendered homeless, providing tea and temporary accommodation for them in the Congregational school-room.

It is something like 32 years since the last big fire occurred in Melbourn. On that occasion two large farmhouses and many outbuildings were destroyed.

Rev J H Grant, the Baptist Minister was also on the committee.

Royston Crow May 1915

Big Blaze At Melbourn – 13 Cottages Destroyed

A hard fight

'A piece of burning thatch alighted on some straw covering a heap of mangold wurzles in the farmyard occupied by Mr W. Stockbridge at the back of the residence of the Misses Stockbridge, in the High Street. A man in the yard hastened to trample it out but before he could do anything the straw was in a blaze, and a large barn, one of the largest barns in Melbourn was on fire, which quickly spread to other buildings, and all were soon destroyed. Several valuable horses in one of the buildings were got out uninjured. All this had taken place almost as quickly as it takes to tell the story. The spot where the fire started on Mr Bullen's premises backs onto Mr Disbrey's premises and seeing the flames he called to Mr. O. Campkin, and together with Mr Jubal Howard, they quickly had the Melbourn Fire Engine out, and then with the engine in the Dolphin

Yard, and with pails of water a hard fight ensued for the saving of Miss Stockbridges house, and this was accomplished after all the furniture had been removed. Sparks from the burning buildings flew across the street on to the thatch of the houses opposite, occupied by Mrs Thixton and Mr W. King, but men with ladders and pails of water and tarpaulins managed to keep the fire from getting a hold. At one time it looked as if that side of the High Street would suffer but fortunately the spread in this direction was prevented.

Scenes in Dolphin Lane

In Dolphin Lane the fire was spreading with alarming rapidity, and cottage after cottage soon became a raging furnace. The distracted cottagers were rushing hither and thither with their household goods, removing them from one place to another as the remorseless flames followed them up. Eventually they carried them into a meadow on the opposite side of the lane, and here heaps, some small and some fairly large, of furniture, crockery

to check the progress of the fire. Beyond this were many other thatched cottages on either side of the narrow lane, and had the fire been allowed to get any further there must have been a far more terrible loss of property. By 3.30 the progress of the fire had been stopped, and people began to bring back their property to those houses which the fire had spared.

Baldock fire brigade on the scene

A call was sent to the Baldock Fire Brigade at a time when the whole village looked like being involved. The Brigade, with their steamer, drawn by an Army Motor transport Wagon, arrived at a few minutes before 4 o'clock, and rendered valuable aid in damping down and removing dangerous parts of the ruins. The Brigade in their start from Baldock had some difficulty in finding horses. There was a R.E. Motor transport in town, and the officer in charge readily gave his consent for the men to take the Fire Engine in tow. Several of the 'Boys' in khaki from Royston and other places near by were to be seen helping the poor folk to remove their furniture.'

Herts & Cambs Reporter May 1915

and household utensils were to be seen with an occasional elderly dame sitting by with a terrified helpless expression on their withered faces, or perhaps some of the younger members of the family were left in charge of the heap whilst their elders lent a helping hand to other neighbours.

Timely arrival of the Royston fire brigade

Mr and Mrs Bentley, of Heathfield, Royston, were motoring through the village a few minutes after the fire broke out, and seeing it was likely to be a serious conflagration they drove on to Royston and gave the call to the Royston Fire Brigade. The alarm rockets went off a few minutes before two o'clock, and the Brigade with their steamer were at Melbourn by 2.20. A way through Mrs Dandy's grounds was opened for them, and they at once drove in and were able to reach the river in the quickest possible time. It however seemed hours to the anxious watchers before a stream of water was brought to play upon the burning buildings, although was only about ten minutes. The river is a goodish distance away, and many lengths of hose had to be coupled up before the fire was reached. It was useless to play upon any of the 13 cottages which were then well ablaze, in fact, many of them were cottages no more. The Brigade turned their attention to the later buildings that had caught fire. A tarred shed at the back of Rose Cottage was burning fiercely and emitting dense volumes of smoke, and two other cottages near by were ablaze, and it was here the Brigade managed

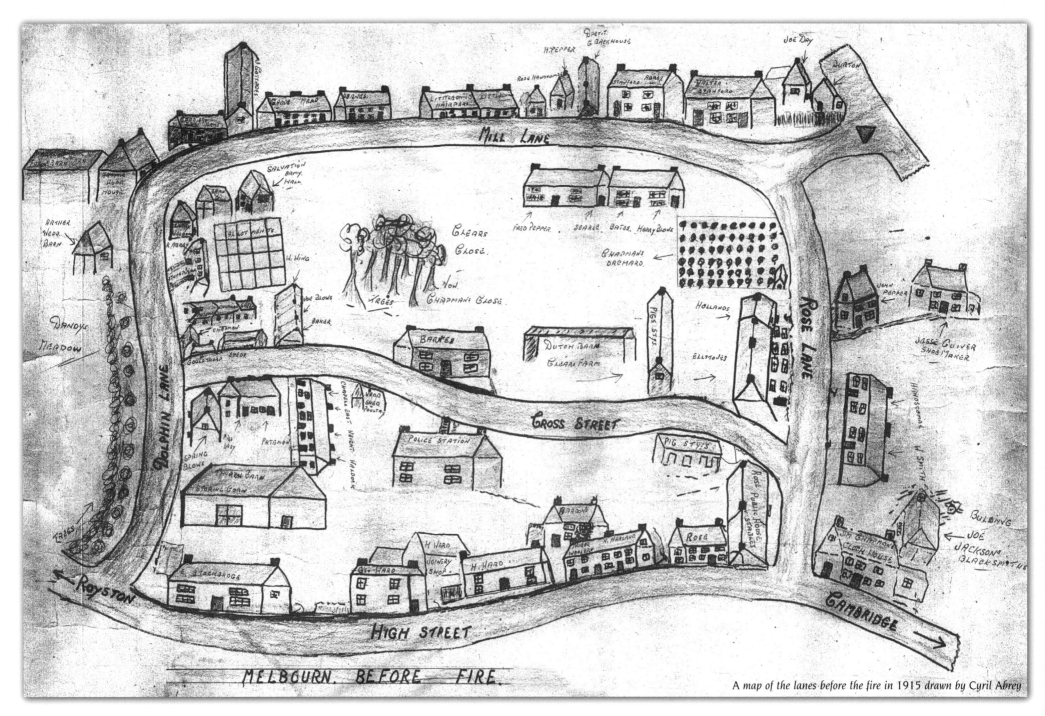

MELBOURN. BEFORE FIRE.

A map of the lanes before the fire in 1915 drawn by Cyril Abrey

Thousands visit fire scene at Melbourn

Visitors flocked into the village with motor cars, cycles, and vehicles of all descriptions lining the streets. Advantage was taken to make an appeal for the relief of the sufferers and it is understood the result was fairly good. Only one of the eight families was insured.

Ernest Carrington, son of a Royston man, had only been in the cottage a fortnight, Mrs Winifred Lee was away engaged in gooseberry picking for one of the big growers. This cottage was said to be one of the best furnished in the village and all was lost with a value of over £60. Mr D. Chapman lost the greater part of his furniture and a bicycle and all the clothing value £14 to £16, of his lodger, George Gentle, was lost. Mr. E. H. Pateman, Mrs. Rebecca Blows and Mr. William Frost have lost nearly all, and Mr. E. Thurley also lost the greater part of his possessions.

The total value of the property destroyed is now put at £3,600. Most of the people whose homes have been destroyed have been received into the homes of neighbours and friends in the village. A Relief Committee has been set up chaired by Mr A.R. Fordham. A jumble sale raised £10.1s. at the Congregational Schoolroom for the Fire Relief Fund.'

Royston Crow June 1915

'There are four houses left in the village still carrying the old 'Fire Marks' or Insurance plaques where there used to be hundreds. These are the confectioners at the Cross, the cottage opposite Howard's boot shop, Harry Anderson's at the corner of Water Lane and Mr Huggins in the High Street.'

Royston Crow 1934

Extract from the School Diary for 27th May 1915

At 1.40 p.m. just as the Headmaster was proceeding to the Woodwork Class a report of fire in Mr. Bullen's blacksmiths shop was spread in the road and playground.

The children in the proximity of the school immediately ran to the scene where a large shed was burning fiercely. In a few minutes the flames had completely enveloped the building and travelled across the lane to the outhouses at the back of The Rose.

As some seven or eight barns and houses were now in full blaze in the short time of fifteen minutes the whole village was seriously threatened owing to the great number of thatched houses and the strong east wind prevailing at the time.

The Headmaster, as soon as he reached the scene of the fire, immediately collected the children and sent them back to school where they were assembled.

As a report was spread that many houses were burning a number of scholars who reside in Dolphin and Cross Lane became very distressed.

The fire was again visited to ascertain if other children were straggling - one or two were found and immediately ordered to school.

By this time all the village was assembled and every precaution taken but in many cases it was of no avail. The flames travelled with great rapidity from thatch to thatch and soon Cross Lane was enveloped in one general conflagration.

By a varying of the wind when the whole High Street was threatened the line of fire was kept from that direction else the results would have been more calamitous, for the whole village from Cross Lane to Townsend would have fired.

Fire hazards

Thatched cottage dangers. In the opinion of some villagers, especially of those living in thatched cottages in the High Street something ought to be done to steam lorry drivers who allow their engines to emit sparks when going through the village. Often, especially at night, one may see showers of sparks coming from the steam engines, which go puffing, snorting and clanking down the street. The stentorian noises are bad enough, but the showers of sparks are even more alarming and on one of the hot and dry summer nights, which we expect to arrive very soon, some of the sparks are likely to be the cause of a big fire.

Royston Crow 8th July 1932

On Bonfire Night the children always stood by with buckets in case of fire.

Domestic Architecture

Melbourn's domestic architecture, with some overlaps, was divided into the *large house, the small house and the cottage.*

The people who lived in *large houses* were those of some local importance including: the local squire; the parson; the successful yeoman; and until the 19th century these houses formed a distinct group.

The *small house* was inhabited by those such as the tenant farmer; the miller; the smith; the poor parson; the shopkeeper; the schoolteacher; the baker; all of whom were people of significance in the community. These houses formed the main body of domestic architecture.

At the bottom of the social scale, and only just above subsistence level, were the labourers and artisans who had no wealth apart from their bodily strength or the skill of their hands. These, together with the widows and elderly lived in *cottages*. Where these have survived to the present day, later additions and improvements frequently render them indistinguishable from the *small house*.

Most of these buildings were designed by an amateur, often the owner, and were influenced by local conventions. Aesthetic considerations were minimal, practical use being the aim, resulting generally in visually pleasing buildings.

Evidence of increasing prosperity in the area can be seen in the Great Rebuilding, which occurred

The basic hall plan with central hearth, the screens passage and service rooms beyond

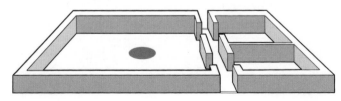

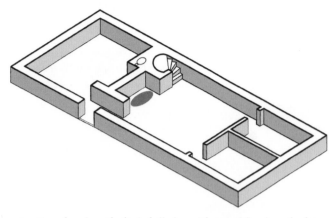

A cottage based on the basic hall plan with central fireplaces back to back, one serving the living-room which has unheated pantry and parlour opening off it, the other serving a service room

mainly between the 16th and 17th centuries, when many substandard buildings were replaced, or refaced.

Floor plans of domestic houses originally followed the medieval house plan; a hall with a hearth open to the rafters, and a screen and cross passage, behind which the service rooms were situated.

When chimneys were introduced, the plan changed, and the chimney stack frequently replaced the screen and cross passage, servicing fireplaces in back-to-back rooms. The entrance lobby was formed by the space beside the stack on one side and, often, the stairs to the upper storey would be on the opposite side. There are many variations and developments of this basic plan.

Houses of Melbourn

There were four manors in Melbourn owned by lords (hlaford) on whom their bondsmen depended. (The word 'manor' comes from the Latin 'maneo', meaning: I *remain, or* I *dwell* and 'hlaford', from the Anglo-Saxon, meaning ...*one who provides hlaford, or bread*).

Melbourn Bury

The word 'Bury' is derived from an Anglo-Saxon word 'beorgan', meaning 'fortified' or 'sheltered', and was applied to the chief house in a manor, or the chief manor house in a village. From Norman times onward this distinction passed to Lordship (or Argentines) Manor, when the diocese of Ely, and therefore The Bury, fell out of favour by supporting Hereward the Wake against the Normans.

An example of a 17th century gable at the rear of The Bury

The Bury

The source of the River Mel

Removing the arch in the medieval Hall during alterations in 1897.
Top, Alfred Prior, Archie Hale, John Chipperfield
Centre, Sid Searle, Mark Chipperfield, George Harrup
Bottom, George Ward (Wards' builders), uknown, unknown,
John Hale with axe, Dan Wing, Hubert Ward

The Bury manor was first mentioned in historical records during the reign of King Athelstan in 924–939, at which time it was part of the royal domain. It was given to the monastery of Ely in 970, when it was refounded after its earlier destruction by the Danes. When the bishopric (diocese of the bishop) of Ely was founded, and the estates of the monastery divided, Melbourn and Meldreth were governed by the Prior and convent. In 1229 the Prior had a private chapel at The Bury. The Prior was succeeded by the Dean and Chapter of Ely, who owned The Bury until the middle of the 19th century, when it was sold to the ancestors of the present owners. During its long history it was rented by several notable people, including William Ayloffe who left money for the first village school in 1691, and later John Trigg, who also left money for a non-denominational school.

During the 14th century the house consisted of a

Refectory table said to date from 1539, The Bury

hall, buttery, kitchen and chamber, the usual rooms of the era. The hall was used as a kitchen and existed until the late-19th century. A joined refectory table was placed in the hall in 1539 and is still in use at The Bury. In 1664 there were twelve hearths. By 1822, in addition to the hall, there were also two parlours and a large kitchen.

The house was remodelled and enlarged during the 19th century, and in the 1880s further modifications were made. Nothing earlier than this date is now visible externally. The River Mel, one of the tributaries of the Cam, rises in the grounds.

Argentines or Lordship Farm

Only four families owned Argentine Manor from Anglo-Saxon times until the mid-20th century. Before the Norman conquest it belonged to an Anglo-Saxon thane named Edric the Plain and was then given to Guy de Rembercourt. The Argentine family were in possession of the property in 1166, and probably eighty years earlier, presumably receiving the manor from the Normans. The last male Argentine died in the 15th century, and the heiress married an Alington of Horseheath, whose descendant in turn sold it to the Hitch family in about 1700. This was the first time it had been sold.

Argentines or Lordship Farm, High Street

Argentines or Lordship Farm

Subsequently it passed from the Hitch to the Palmer family.

The Argentines were a celebrated family, and possessed large estates soon after the conquest. Richard de Argentine, born around 1200, held several public offices. He was killed near Antioch in 1246 whilst on a pilgrimage to the Holy Land.

The Argentine family held a curious hereditary post, that of serving the king at his coronation with a covered silver-gilt cup of wine. The king paid for this cup but the server claimed it as a perquisite, and some members of the family subsequently mention these cups in their wills. The Argentines were so proud of this service that it featured in their

The Crusades ~ bounty from the East

The Crusades to the Holy Land lasted for more than 250 years, beginning in 1095, and many commodities were brought back to Europe by the crusaders. Apart from the usual plunder during these wars, the Crusaders introduced many commodities which today are taken for granted, such as rice, coffee, dates, apricots, lemons, melons, sugar and ginger.

They also brought back mirrors, carpets, cotton cloth, writing paper, ships' compasses, wheelbarrows, water wheels and water clocks.

New ideas, such as Arabic numerals, including zero, algebra, chemistry and pain killing drugs transformed society.

coat of arms, a red shield with three silver chalices. This service, known as 'sergeantry', had no connection with the manor at Melbourn, but was attached to the manor at Great Wymondley, the main Argentine seat in Hertfordshire. The owner of Great Wymondley continued to exercise this right until it was abolished, together with the accompanying banquet, after the coronation of King George IV in 1821.

There were three main building periods, which spanned the 14th to 19th centuries. The manor is timber-framed, plaster-rendered and part stuccoed (a finish for exterior walls, usually made from cement, sand, and lime) in imitation stone ashlar (square hewn stones used to face a brick or rubble

The hall of John de Argentine

wall). The steeply pitched tiled roofs are now covered with asbestos slate. There is one large chimney stack between the medieval and the 18th century section, with another side stack to the rear dating from 1699.

The plan of the building is irregular, with the gable ends facing the road and the principal front now facing the garden. It has two storeys plus a cellar and attic. Three early-19th century windows are on the first floor, and below two similar windows flank the doorway, with an early-19th century doorcase and hood.

The roof has horizontal timbers supporting the rafters. The parlour cross wing was of two storeys and the first-floor room would have been open to the rafters. Three bays, also timber-framed, were added to this end of the range in 1699. A large inglenook in the kitchen appears to have been extended when the 18th century part was added. The internal detail of this house is mostly early to mid-19th century, although there is a small room, possibly an 18th century powder room, off the main bedroom.

In 1318 there was a hall, a chamber with an outside staircase, both thatched, a chapel and offices. The buildings were surrounded by a moat fed by springs within it. Over the moat were two bridges, one of them probably a drawbridge. It is possible that the present farm buildings, within the moat, are on the line of the original buildings, and the hall and chapel were where the house now stands. There is a still a well in the cellar. In the mid-17th century the property had eight hearths. The date 1699, marked on an eastern gable, may be evidence of a reconstruction before the Alingtons sold it. It is a two-storeyed, two-winged house with several 18th and 19th century additions.

In the bailiff's account of 1318 there are several items charged for feeding men, who brought timber from their other manor at Great Wymondley, for building the 'New Chamber'. The attic has the remains of an ancient timbered roof, massive

Roof timbers at Lordship Farm

cambered, main-truss beams, principle rafters and collar, all of oak, which indicate the new chamber was possibly included in the present house. Carved brackets join the main truss to the wall post which can be traced down to the ground level. All these show signs of fire damage.

Trayles

A moated site north east of The Bury was probably the original location of Trayles Manor house, later replaced by a manor on the main street.

The house is mainly late-17th century with early-18th century extensions at the back. Its timbered frame is rendered with simple geometric pargetting (ornamental work in plaster), except for the front wall which was remodelled in the early-20th century.

There is a red brick chimney stack between the front and rear ranges, and another similar side stack. The house has two storeys, an attic and cellars. The south-east front has four cross-frame windows on the first floor with 19th and 20th century glazing, and three on the ground floor on either side of the original doorway, which has two s-shaped moulded panels. On the north-facing wall are original casement windows with later glazing. Two late-17th or early-18th century original sash windows of eighteen panes are on the ground floor and, opposite the chimney stack, is an original doorway which leads to a walled garden. In the early-18th century the rear wing was extended and this has two, original, iron casement windows.

Inside, two rooms flank the hall and the floor is set with limestone flagstones, with the original kitchen wing at the rear. The open well staircase off the hall has four flights. The two rooms flanking the hall are panelled, the room to the south has a moulded double cornice and boxed main beam. The mantel over the fireplace is original and, around 1740, a niche was inserted at the side of the fireplace.

after the death of her husband, Sir John Hatton, in 1740. Her memorial plaque can be seen in the church.

The cottage adjoining the Manor house was formerly the stable range, including a forge, of the manor, and was restored and extended in about 1740, probably by Mary Hatton. Built of red and burnt brick of Flemish bond, it features a steeply pitched tiled roof, probably originally thatched, and with plain eaves cornice and 'tumbled in' end parapet facing the road. It has one storey and an attic with inserted dormer windows, and a cellar under the central section. Originally the principal openings were in the north wall, with diaper pattern brickwork and three original window and stable door openings in segmental arches. These were bricked up when the use of the building changed, and the front of the building is now principally on the south side, which has scattered 20th century casements with small panes. The end of the building next to the road has the initials MH (Mary Hatton) in burnt brick headers and two 19th century twelve-paned sash windows. A doorway in this wall was bricked up around the 1930s. During the mid-19th century, when the railways were being constructed, it functioned as The Locomotive Inn.

Above, Trayles, and left, the side view, High Street

The room to the north has raised panelling dating from about 1740, in two heights with an s-shaped, moulded dado, double cornice and boxed main beam. There is also a corner niche with a shell-shaped hood.

In what was formerly the kitchen, in the rear wing, there is an inglenook fireplace and a main beam. On the first floor there are a number of original two-panelled doors.

The house was probably built by the Hitch family, who were tenants of Lord Alington, the Lord of the combined Argentines and Trayles manors.

Dame Mary Hatton is believed to have retired here

The rear of Trayles, High Street

The Old Manor

Built in 1710–20, this house has a slightly later parlour wing at the rear. It is built of red brick except for the rear wall, which is timber-framed. It has a cellar, two principal storeys and an attic with three hipped dormers. There is a symmetrical, five-window range framed by pilasters with red brick quoins, moulded brick capitals and bases. There are four steps up to a central doorway, with a door of eight raised and fielded panels, and flat hood on scroll brackets of a later date.

Inside there is a paved hall with a fine open-string staircase of four flights and two landings. The mid-18th century parlour is lined with raised and fielded panelling of two heights, and the adjoining room at the front has similar panelling.

It has been suggested that the house was built for Richard Hitch on his marriage to Mary Hawkes in 1704, or that it was the bailiff's house, built by the Hitch family following their purchase of the Argentines and Trayles Manors.

The adjoining house, The Maltings, was formerly a

Above, the front and left, the rear of the Old Manor, High Street

store or warehouse associated with the Manor House. It has three bays and two storeys and was originally weatherboarded. Another moated manor known as Caxtons, owned in 1086 by Hardwin de Scalers, was probably seized from Almar the priest. It was sited on the Moor but was possibly destroyed when the Moat House was built in 1939.

Old Hall House, Little Lane

A house on the basic hall plan, though now much modified, remains in the village, and is still known as the Old Hall House. This house probably originated in the late-15th century, and began as a three bay plan, with two bays to the north added in the 17th century. It has a small 20th century extension at the rear. It is of two storeys, jettied at the south end of the first floor, where the framing is exposed. The original doorway to the centre bay is now blocked. Inside, the three bays of the medieval house are intact and the timber framing is exposed. There is blackening of the roof beams, indicating the former presence of an open hearth. The timberwork of the roof is original. In 1842 the house was owned by Peterhouse College and let as two tenements.

Old Hall House in Little Lane

The Clock House

The Old Bakery, or Clock House, on Moor Corner was formerly an inn and shop, and was built around 1840. Constructed of brick or clay bat and plastered, it has a four-sided roof with sloping ends and sides known as a mansard, or 'hipped roof',

The Clock House on Moor Corner

Sheepshead Road at the northern end of the High Street

made of slate with grey brick side chimney stacks. It has wings at either side of a carriageway entry, and a shop. The façade is symmetrical and framed by decorative angled corner stones. The central doorway is flanked by two similar windows with raised key blocks, or keystones. The gabled and plastered carriageway wing is to the left. The round-headed archway has a raised surround above it, for a clock. The shop wing is a single storey with a slate roof and original later 19th century shop front.

Sheepshead Row

This row of seven cottages at the northern end of the village, was built during several periods, but mainly in the 17th and 18th centuries, and restored during the 20th century. The cottages are timber-framed with some timbers partly exposed. The timbers are varied, suggesting they have been reused, possibly from the late-17th century. The row the 1930s, but saved by the Cambridge Preservation Society in 1938, which 'brought them up to a reasonable standard of comfort and convenience'.

Originally there were fifteen separate ground floor rooms, and sixteen first-floor rooms. Four of the nine fireplaces in the downstairs rooms shared chimney stacks which stood back-to-back. Three, much larger, inglenook fireplaces are possibly of an earlier date.

There are seven staircases of various types,

Housing news

A recommendation was made that houses in the village should be numbered because of confusion over so many house names.

Royston Crow 8th December 1933

The rear of Sheepshead Row

has a long straw thatch roof and six, brick, chimney stacks. It has only one storey and an attic with nine dormer windows and twelve small window openings containing 20th century glazing.

These cottages were probably slums from the time they were built and were almost demolished in

Housing prices

A timber and thatched farmhouse on the High Street, with outbuildings, gardens, orchard etc, the property of the late Samuel Negus, sold to Mr J.G. Mortlock for £335.

Royston Crow 19th September 1890

Below, Orchard Road and right, Medcalfe Way

Medcalfe Way during construction

position and construction and it is said that ladders were in use in at least one cottage until about 1950.

The central portion of the row is raised, suggesting that it may have been a 17th century farmhouse with extra cottages added at either side at a later date.

In 1935 the row was owned by Mrs French, and the 9 cottages were inhabited by, from the right, Hinkins, Lamb, Harper, Woodcock, Webb Kilsby, Day and Negus.

There are a number of explanations as to the origin of the name Sheepshead Row. One version tells that the inhabitants stuck their heads out of the bedroom windows to look at the London to

Cambridge stagecoaches passing by. The coachman is supposed to have referred to them as looking like a row of sheep. Another is thought to have derived from the flocks of sheep which were driven along the road there. As the road narrowed it frequently caused a bottleneck.

The first council houses, built after The First World War in 1922, were in Orchard Road and then Portway.

The Hunt family, with 14 children, eventually moved into a specially adapted, large council house in Portway, where two houses were knocked into one. Previously, the children had slept in a circle with their feet in the middle of the bed. The Littlechilds also moved into a similar large house.

Houses were in very short supply between the wars and after the Second World War. One family who put their name down for a new council house had to wait eighteen years. Their daughter was sixteen when they finally moved. All the houses looked the same before gardens were established, and there were no street-lights. Airey Houses

The corner of Medcalfe Way

(prefabricated houses built of concrete shuttering) were erected in three localities: John Impey Way (formerly Ayloffe's Way), Trigg Way and Medcalfe Way.

These houses were put up so fast that people leaving for work in the morning would see nothing, but returning home in the afternoon would find new houses had sprung up!

Portway at the northern end of Melbourn

Teas Room in the High Street

Lifestyle

…residents of Sheepshead Row could put their ear to the ground and hear the Mail Coach leaving Royston

Melbourn has always benefited from good springs, which no doubt attracted the first settlers. Over most of the village, the water is only a few feet from the surface. We are so accustomed to seeing running water at the turn of a tap and to flushing the lavatory that we tend to forget that only a comparatively few years ago, the people of Melbourn were getting water from the well and using an outside privy.

Hygiene standards in the early years were poor and during the Middle Ages hygiene was virtually non existent. Night slops were just thrown out of the house, onto dung heaps or into nearby streams; in towns they might just be tossed out of the upper windows. The modern use of the word 'loo' may well date back to the custom of shouting 'gardez l'eau' (watch out for the water) before slops were thrown onto the street. The 'garderobe' (an upstairs closet with a chute into a moat) was a common device in castles. Later the 'close stool' or commode was in use and by Victorian times the chamber pot could be found under most beds. These had many colloquial names including 'potty', 'po' or 'goesunder' and became an art form in themselves. By the end of the 19th century they were highly decorated and ornamented.

More prosperous houses had a privy (a shed containing a bucket or hole in the ground) which was situated away from the house or at the bottom of the garden. Some privies would be 'two holers' (or more) with seats side by side! Rats were a hazard here, and it was not an uncommon practice to rap loudly on the door before entering, to frighten them away! Dogs and cats were usually kept, not as domestic pets, but as working animals to keep vermin down.

In October 1865 the Medical Officer in Melbourn reported that *…sanitary conditions for the village were unsatisfactory, as there were several cases of nuisance due to want of proper privy accommodation and manure heaps.*

The po, potty or goesunder

Thomas Stockbridge, the inspector of nuisances, investigated the problem and it was decided that a suitable cart would go round the village at frequent intervals and remove any muck heaps. By November the Medical Officer had given a satisfactory report.

The annual emptying of the privy into a trench in the garden, or taking the 'night soil' up to the allotments to be used as fertiliser on the vegetable patch continued well into the 20th century. However, by the end of the 19th century houses were being built with septic tanks which were emptied once a year. It was not until after the 1950s that mains sewerage came to Melbourn.

Inns or public houses had their own privies at the rear of the building, and some had a place designated as a urinal at the side of the property. A small triangular patch at the side of the former Red Cow in the High Street was one such urinal. The White Lion at The Cross had it's urinal situated between the pub and 'Fessor' Hinkins shop.

To spend a penny

In the 17th century potassium nitrate, used in gunpowder, came from rotting meat and urine. The 'petermen' would collect soil from privies and dungheaps, and by tasting the soil to check if it was ready for use, they would then cart it off to be boiled, strained and evaporated to produce saltpetre.

Wool required a 'mordant' before dyeing to hold the dye to the wool. Households dyeing their wool used urine, as a mordant, as it was as it was free and available. The wool industry, in the 17th and 18th century used 200 tonnes of urine per year, collected from towns and villages. Barrels at street corners were collected weekly for which they paid 1d a firkin (9 gallons). 'To spend a penny' originated from selling urine to the wool trade.

The drawing room of The Bury, 1891

Living conditions

The earliest houses in the village were simple shelters, often one-room dwellings where families huddled together for warmth. Floors were earthen and cooking would be done outside or on a central hearth.

In the 1300s a bondsman's cottage would be a one-roomed, beehive shaped dwelling, cruck-built, with a hole in the roof for the smoke to escape, and without windows. (Cruck-built houses used split tree trunks providing matching supports, the remains of these can sometimes be seen exposed in gable ends of cottages)

The Hall was the most important part of the manor, where the family and servants ate and some servants slept. The floor was strewn with straw or rushes, occasionally replenished, and completely renewed once a year. Sparsely furnished, the table was the most prominent piece ~ a long board on trestles (hence the expression board and lodging, or boarding house) with long wooden benches to sit on. The lord and lady may have sat on armchairs placed on a raised platform (the word 'Chairman' comes from this period). A cupboard or hutch was used to store the silver or pewter cups and another used for legal documents. Linen was stored in wooden chests. Wealthy families may have had tapestries or hangings on the walls ~ more to keep out draughts than for decorative purposes.

Lordship Farm is one such example of a 'Hall house', the gabled section on the right hand side of the building was the original hall. A hatch discovered in the gable is thought to have been used by the servants who climbed up by means of an outside ladder to sleep in the roof.

Household cleaning was carried out with brushes and a 'besom' (a bunch of flexible twigs bound round a stick). Beeswax was used for polishing the oak or elm furniture.

Soapmaking was an established craft by the seventh century. Soapmaker guilds guarded their trade secrets closely. Vegetable and animal oils were used with ashes of plants, along with fragrances. Gradually more varieties of soap became available for shaving and shampooing, as well as bathing and laundering. But it wasn't until the 17th century that washing and bathing became fashionable.

From around the 1500s, wills made by prosperous farmers and tradesmen, (as opposed to the aristocracy) leaving such items as four poster beds and hangings, linen, chests and pewter cups and plates, indicated that the lower classes were beginning to accumulate possessions. However, the ordinary village people still owned very little and what they did have, was usually homemade.

During the early 1800s, many small tenements were built in Melbourn, instigated by an increase in the village population. Crowded together, there was no room for gardens or outbuildings. In 1841, out of 54 of the better dwellings in Melbourn, 9 had been divided to house up to 22 families. Of the 306 households in the village, 204 were living in tenement (rented) accommodation and all but 29 of these had more than one family under the same roof. Tenement rows consisting of 3 to 13 units gave shelter to at least 143 families, or about 40 percent of the village population.

In 1933 a Boy Scout from Bethnal Green, East London, who was camping in Melbourn said, 'some of the houses crowded together with dark and twisting alleys between them ~ remind me of home'. By 1936 a number of houses in Dolphin Lane were condemned and the tenants were re-housed in the new council houses in Water Lane (Woodway).

Sleeping arrangements

Most cottages were built with only a few rooms, mostly 2-up and 2-down, and so it was necessary for children to sleep in the same room, and usually in the same bed. If there was only one bedroom they would sleep with their parents. There are stories of two bedroomed cottages in which families of 8 or 10 children were raised. Comparing

A washhouse showing a copper on the right, at Woods Farm, High Street

Warming pans

the population figures of 1920 to the number of dwellings in the village suggests that the average occupancy was 8 people to a cottage. They were still living in 18th century conditions with no washhouse (a washhouse contained a copper, a metal container with a fire under used for laundry) and only one fireplace in the house. Mattresses placed on the floor or on stump beds, would be filled with straw or feathers. With little heating in the house nights were cold, although in the wealthier homes a warming pan, (a copper-lidded pan with a long wooden handle), was used to warm the bed. At the end of the evening, the hot coals from the hearth would be shovelled into the pan which was then slid into the bed to warm it.

The copper warming pan was an expensive item. Poorer families would use a simple brick heated in a fire and wrapped in an old blanket. A later development was the stone hot water bottle filled with boiling water, followed by the rubber hot water bottle and much later by an electric heater.

Diet

The medieval diet consisted of coarse bread, gruel, cheese, peas, a little mutton, bacon and chicken, fish, milk, butter and ale.

Bread was a staple food; the grain used varied according to area and income. Wheat grown on good soil made the finest, most expensive white

Assorted bed warmers

bread, but the commonest bread, called maslin, was made from wheat and rye flour mixed. Darker loaves were made from rye flour alone. Weed seeds were often included with the grain, and in times of poor harvest beans, peas and even acorns were added to the cheapest bread. Types of white bread included pandemain, wastel and cocket. Cheaper breads were cheat, tourte (or trete or treet), maslin and horsebread.

In medieval times the wealthy used slices of brown bread, several days old, as trenchers, or plates. The food was served onto these and after the meal the trenchers were collected up and given to the poor to eat.

Pease pottage was another staple food. Usually a broth in which vegetables, pulses and herbs were boiled, it could be of varying consistency, from runny to thick enough to slice! The more fortunate would have meat added.

A large variety of meats were eaten, including small birds, hedgehogs or squirrels which might be wrapped in clay and thrust into the hot coals. Poaching was risky and, if caught, was punishable with severe penalties. As late as the 1800s the penalty was 10 years' penal servitude.

Fish was an important part of the diet. Before the Reformation the Catholic Church decreed that meat was not to be eaten on Wednesdays, Fridays or Saturdays. This meant that for 40 percent of the year everyone had to eat fish. The ruling was practicsed until the late medieval period, after which it applied only to Fridays. Most manors had fish ponds (called 'stews') in which they bred carp and pike, and the rivers were full of fish. Fish was usually dried, pickled, or salted in order to preserve it for use throughout the year. Salt was also used to preserve meat and its importance at the table during medieval times was reflected in the elaborate vessels used to contain it in wealthy households. This also gave rise to the saying ...*to be seated below*

From bread and cheese to a feast

For the **poor** in medieval times, meals would have been simple, consisting of bread made from rye, barley, or maslin (sometimes with pea or bean flour mixed in) broth, cheese and perhaps a bowl of curds. Servants working in households were better fed, their meal would include beef, fowl, salt or dried fish, better breads, cheese, puddings and ale.

The **middle class merchant** and **minor nobility** would have had a variety of courses, each would have offered several different dishes, brought to the table at the same time. The first course would have miniature filled pastries; a meat 'brewet' (*pieces of meat in a thin cinnamon sauce*); beef marrow fritters; eels in a spicy puree; loach in a spiced sauce; roast or boiled meat; saltwater fish. An example of the second course would be: roast meat; freshwater fish; broth with bacon; a meat tile (*pieces of chicken or veal, served in a spiced crayfish sauce*), capon pasties, bream and eel pasties. The final course might include: frumenty (*wheat boiled in milk, flavoured with sugar and spices*), venison, lampreys (fish) with hot sauce, fritters, roast bream and darioles, sturgeon, jellies. An assortment of game birds would also be included. After the meal came sweets and confections, followed by spiced wine or whole spices, to aid in digestion.

The rich aristocracy may not have had different foods from the middle class, just more of it, overall.

For the **Lords** and the **King**, the meals would have been elaborate. The feasts would have been a crowded and noisy affair; servants running around bringing wine, food, and fresh trenchers. Dogs were a common sight – gnawing on the discarded bones and scraps on the floor.

For a feast given for King Richard II in 1397 the courses included; boiled wheat in venison, cured tongue, boiled meat, boar's head, fat capons, roasted swans, herons and pheasants, large, open tarts, and two subtleties (*usually foods, like marzipan, disguised to look like something else i.e. birds covered with their feathers to appear alive or sculpted to represent religious themes, such as Samson's head on a platter*). White meat in a sweet and sour sauce, white pudding, roasted piglets, rabbits, curlews, marsh birds, venison, peacocks and teals, large custard tart, fritters, and one subtlety. Dates in relish, violets, roasted cranes, partridges, peacocks (glazed with gold), quails, plovers, large game birds, rabbits, larks, small meat pieces, apple or cheese fritters, fruit dumplings, quince dumplings, and two subtleties.

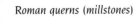
Roman querns (millstones)

the salt, as less important people were seated at the bottom of the table ~ below the salt.

The years between 1825 and 1850 were particularly difficult for the production of food in Melbourn, covering both the post-Napoleonic war period and the introduction of the enclosure system.

Until cane sugar was widely available from the Caribbean (from the mid 1600s), honey was used as a sweetener. Sugar beet was later grown locally and from 1880 became the main source of sugar. An important ingredient in many foods and preserves, sugar also initiated the sweet industry.

By the 19th century the village had several sweet shops. Sweets were sold in 'pokes' of paper ~ a

The dovecote at The Anchor

Feast Cake

In 1935 a recipe was discovered in a very old manuscript for the Feast Cake.

12 oz flour	3oz sugar
8 oz butter	2 eggs
6 oz currants	½ pint old beer
4 oz sultanas	Large teaspoon baking powder
A little mixed spice	

The only instructions given were to:
Beat butter to a cream, add other ingredients, mix well together with eggs well beaten and add the beer last of all.

---

sheet of paper rolled round into a cone and folded down over the sweets. Within living memory favourite purchases were winter mixture, bulls eyes, red-and-white striped clove sweets, sweet cigarettes, snowballs, aniseed balls, liquorice bark sticks, coconut ice, lemonade powder and sweet tobacco (toasted desiccated coconut). During the First World War Horlicks and Ovaltine tablets were popular as they could be bought without sweet coupons.

Domestic crafts

During the medieval period, cooking was done over an open fire, either on a spit, or in a suspended cauldron. The first closed range cookers did not appear until the late 18th century and it was not unusual for people to take pies and meat to be cooked at the local bakehouse. The bakery at the Moor Corner owned by the Howard's, still continued to cook this way, into the early 1900s. Girls were taught cookery skills in the home from an early age; the subject was eventually included in the school curriculum.

In 1893, a cookery lecture given in the village by a Miss Harris included subjects such as 'Why Food is Necessary' and 'Flesh Forming and Health Giving Foods'. It was reported that ...*many ladies were present but also some of the sterner sex.*

A communal pump for general use, outside the school in Mortlock Street

Keeping clean

It was not until the 1870s that the first attempts were made to bring mains water supply to the village; before then water was drawn from wells and the river. However, wells were often badly sited and contamination was commonplace. 'Melbourn Fever' as it was called, was a frequent occurrence. In 1930 an analysis was carried out of all the wells in the village and most were found to be contaminated. Jack Palmer recalled that wells were often sited without any thought of hygiene ~ some of them on the edge of dung yards! After his family moved to Cawdon House, a sample of the water was sent for analysis and he was told it was not even fit to give to animals! This was not surprising, as the well and the cess pit were close together.

Highways surveyors

On 22nd April 1847 a notice from the Surveyors of the Highways gave notice ...*to all persons to prevent their drains from their yards and premises from running into the Highway, according to the Highways Act. Also to give notice to all persons that it is not allowed to throw any slops and pails out into the Highway.*

There were numerous wells and pumps in the village. The high water table gave easy access to water without having to dig too deep. Many houses had wells in the garden, or in the cellar as did Lordship Farm, which possibly dates from the 11th century.

There were also communal pumps for general use and people also collected water from the river Mel. The 'clean' water was kept in a bucket covered with a cloth, while the 'slops' (the used water) were poured into another bucket and used to water the garden. Mains water came to the village in 1924 with the formation of the Melbourn Water Company, but many houses were not connected until long after the Second World War.

A pump in the garden of a local cottage

A cottage pump in Meeting Lane

With so many wells, accidents were bound to happen. In 1927 Violet Chapman, aged 4 years, fell down a well at 24 Council Houses (later to be named Orchard Way). She was lucky to be pulled out by Frank Chappell and was taken to Addenbrooke's hospital by horse ambulance.

In the l920s a pump was installed at the school in Mortlock Street for villagers to use. However, in October 1939 complaints were made that ...*evacuee mothers were washing their children at the pump and the churchyard was being used as a playground and as a public convenience.*

Bathing

Washing and bathing were rare events, often in the river ~ a practice that continued until the mid-20th century. Later, tin baths were used, with family

members going in one after the other, usually on Friday night, at the end of a working week.

The 19th century saw the introduction of cheap pottery washing sets, consisting of a large basin and a jug which was kept on a table upstairs. It was not unknown for the water to freeze in the jug overnight during the winter months.

Bathroom and toilet facilities were not installed into the older Council houses in the village until the 1950s.

Laundering

The Steam Laundry in Melbourn was established in the late 1800s opposite Sheen Mill, where it flourished until 1914. Before this laundering was carried out at the river, until purpose built washhouses were introduced. A wash house contained a 'copper', made of metal, containing water, under which a fire could be lit to heat the water. Washing was often laid out to dry in the meadows.

Primitive forms of washing machine, worked by hand, began to appear at the end of the 19th century, although by then most homes had a mangle through which the

The flat iron

The steam laundry, Station Road

washed laundry was fed and excess water squeezed out. A washboard with a corrugated galvanised surface was also a common item ~ wet clothes were scrubbed against the board to clean them. A 'blue bag' was put into the final rinsing water of 'whites' to enhance the whiteness. Before the advent of the electric iron, clothes were pressed with a flat iron, heated on the fire. Flat irons were heavy to use and a thick cloth had to be wrapped round the handle, as it became very hot. There were many different

Lanterns found at Woods Farm, High Street

shapes and sizes of flat iron to deal with different jobs, including goffering (crimping) irons that were used to iron intricate frills on clothing. One way to test the temperature of the iron was to spit on it.

In the early part of the 20th century home laundering in the village was done by two women well known characters ~ in Dolphin Lane, who returned the clean, ironed garments on their wooden truck.

Lighting

Until the 19th century the only artificial lighting available to the poor was a rush light dipped in fat. Rush tapers or tallow candles were the cheapest form of lighting; beeswax candles were a luxury. Oil

The public lamps

For many years past this place has been in almost total darkness during these winter months entirely from the apathy of the general public. This year the case is altered considerably for the better. The committee carrying out the object – consisting of Messrs. E.W. Parkinson, H. Coningsby, F. Smith, J. Disbrey, E. Francis, R.H. Flitton and Joseph Campkin – energetically set to work and collected sufficient voluntary contributions for paying all the expenses of lighting with gas the whole of the 22 public lamps, the effect being a brilliant appearance of the village. The committee inform us that the canvass was a very gratifying one; indeed with one or two exceptions the contributions were general. We congratulate them on their success and hope it may be an annual affair.

Royston Crow January 1876

WHAT THE PAPERS SAID

was not generally used until the 19th century, but even then candles were still used to light the way to bed. Gas was introduced into Melbourn as early as 1864, but only a few houses and some street lamps at the south end of the High Street were supplied.

In October 1915, the Parish Council agreed that during the War the church and street lamps would not be lit, and lamps were not to be used in shop windows. In 1920 it was recorded that *...every effort should be made to light the village before the next winter.* By 1925~26 many houses had electricity.

Health

Herbal remedies

Before the foundation of the College of Physicians in 1518, treatment for illness was often pure quackery. Many 'quacks' exploited this, offering noxious compounds, some based on astrology, the 'humours' of the body and guesswork.

Most villages had their 'wise woman' who prepared concoctions of herbs (especially for women in childbirth), they would also apply cobwebs and leaves to open wounds. Chilblains were a common ailment in cold weather ~ a very painful burning and itching complaint, caused by exposure to cold and poor circulation. The herbal cure was a soothing ointment of chickweed or marsh mallow. Centuries later, many of these natural remedies proved to be sound medication, *i.e.* digitalis ~ found in foxglove leaves ~ is now widely used for heart conditions. (In the raw state foxglove is extremely poisonous.)

Herbs were often mixed with the rushes on the floor which helped to keep the rooms sweet-smelling and were also an antiseptic. Sweet-smelling herbs in a pouch were also used by the wealthy, suspended just below the nose, or in a 'nosegay' (a small bunch of flowers) to protect them from street smells. This was also thought to be a protection against the plague.

The 'old medicine woman's' house in the High Street, 1929

The Plague and disease

In 1348 the Black Death, spread throughout the country and within the Diocese of Ely, 88 vicarages became vacant due to the death of the incumbant. As with many other towns and villages, Melbourn would have been affected, with land left untilled and houses standing empty and derelict. Following the great epidemic of 1666, outbreaks became less common and by 1728, had virtually disappeared, although malnutrition, smallpox, consumption and countless other ailments were still rife.

Remedies for all these diseases were mostly based on plants and herbs, with additions such as arsenic, iron, mercury and phosphorus.

Vomiting and laxatives, together with blood letting and the use of leeches were also widely used in treatment. By the 1800s a common recommendation by doctors was 'a change of air.'

Small pox was one of the most dreaded scourges, but ceased to be a threat when inoculation of cowpox, and later vaccination, proved to be effective. This success resulted in the passing of legislation around 1871, which supported compulsory vaccination requiring all children to be vaccinated with a penalty of a fine and imprisonment if it was not carried out.

Vaccination was painful, and left a large scar on the upper arm; children wore a red ribbon on the arm to warn people to avoid it. As a result of this some parents ...*took against it* and refused to have

> Arthur Woods, baker, applied for exemption on Conscientious Grounds from the Vaccination Act – he said he believed it would be a permanent injury to his child as he had come across cases where serious illness ensued after vaccination.
>
> *Royston Crow September 1898*

WHAT THE PAPERS SAID

their children vaccinated – many were fined for doing so. Outbreaks of smallpox were still common towards the end of the 19th century.

After smallpox had ceased to be a threat, consumption (tuberculosis), and childbirth became the most common causes of death. Regular reports of outbreaks of diphtheria and measles were also reported in the local press.

In 1830 the Congregational Sunday School, with 156 scholars, listed the most frequent reasons for absence as being 'illness'. Other excuses included cow-keeping, turkey-keeping, bad clothes, no shoes or pattens, (clogs or overshoes to raise the feet above the muddy ground). In May 1918 the school was closed due to an outbreak of measles.

Infant mortality

Infant mortality remained high until modern hygiene methods were adopted in the 20th century. Birth control was primitive and large families were the norm, though not many children would grow to adulthood. A typical newspaper report on 7th December 1870 stated that ...*Mary Ann Dellor, aged 6 months, daughter of Charles Dellar, an engineer, died suddenly from an effusion of serum on the brain, from congestion.* In another example, an inquest was held

> #### National Baby Week
> Infant mortality rate is 80 per 1000 which is the lowest on record. According to the Medical Officer of the Board of Education, seventy percent of the children lost to this country in the first year of life die from preventable causes. Some of the most potent dangers include: bad feeding, infection, alcoholism, feeble mindedness, industrial employment of mothers, unskilled midwifery, maternal ignorance, overcrowding and ineffectual scavenging.
>
> *Parish magazine, Melbourn July 1922*

in March 1852, on the unbaptised child of Sarah Green, aged 10 weeks ...*the mother deposed that it had suffered much from its birth and was not able to take scarcely any nourishment, and frequently appeared as if it were in a fit.* A post mortem examination found that the the baby had died from consumption.

It was also quite common for children to be born and to die in the workhouse, as did Wilfred Pryor, aged 10 months, in July 1854.

However, not all the news was grim. In October 1847 ...*the wife of Samuel Negus of Melbourn was safely delivered of three children who, with the mother, are going on as well as can be expected.*

The opium poppy

The opium poppy was cultivated, by the monks, around Ely in the Middle Ages for the treatment of Marsh Fever (Mala Aria). The importance of this plant can be seen in the 'poppyhead' carvings on the end of church pews, particularly at Snailwell and Littleport.

Opium was given to suckling children to keep them quiet whilst mothers worked; often the elder children dosed the younger ones. It was the aspirin of the day.

Opium was used in Dover's Powders from the

> ### Inquest
>
> F. Barlow, Esq., county coroner, held an inquest at the Police-station, Melbourn, on the 18th inst., touching the death of Mary, the child of William Chapman, platelayer. It appears that deceased, who was four years old, swallowed a spoonful of solution of opium which had been placed in a glass on the window-sill of its mother's bedroom for her use, and which deceased casually got hold of and drank. – Verdict, Accidental Death.
>
> *Cambridge Chronicle 23rd October 1869*

WHAT THE PAPERS SAID

> On Tuesday last, as two children were being drawn on a wash trough on wheels, by another child, on the Cambridge road, they were met by a horse and cart, the boy that was with it, we understand, being behind, but as there was no-one except the children near, it is conjectured that the horse, which was blind, put his foot upon one of the children, and when found its brains were protruding from the skull, and the bottom of the tub was knocked out. An inquest was held on the following day, at the Red Lion, by Mr. Marshall, and a verdict of 'Accidental death' was returned.
>
> *Cambridge Independent Press 1st May 1852*

WHAT THE PAPERS SAID

1700s and was later generously administered to babies by unsuspecting mothers in the form of the respectable Woodward's Gripe Water, Godfrey's Cordial and Collis Brown Powders. In 1830 the Morning Chronicle reported that opium eating in the city of Ely, ...*was the cause of infant mortality in about 11 percent of deaths generally, but in the Fens the figure rose to about 20 percent.*

In 1736 Poppy Tea was sent to Cambridge from China by Daniel Twining and became so widely used that in 1930 Dr Charles Lucas wrote ...*I do think this was the cause of the feeble minded idiotic people in the Fens!* Ely market had more stalls selling opium than any other goods.

It was said that ...*Poppy tea and Opium Pill, Are the cure for many an ill.* Laudanum (a tincture of opium), was used as an anaesthetic to deaden the pain during tooth extraction.

Accidents

Accidents were common place and often resulted in serious injury, or even death. As with any newspaper report these were often the highlight of the news.

Melbourn had a number of pits surrounding the village for the extraction of clunch and gravel – involving hazardous work. In July 1817 William Winter, working in the clunch pit ...*had been warned by his master not to work near a particular part of it on account of its danger, he had the temerity to go and work there, and a large part of the pit fell in and crushed his head to atoms.*

In 1831 Benjamin Barron, aged 6 years, took shelter from the rain beneath a wagon belonging to Messrs. Deacon & Co. Unfortunately, the horse moved and one of the wheels passed over the boy's

> An inquest was held in the parish of Melbourn, on Wednesday, the 19th inst., on view of the body of Wm. Willimott. It appears that the deceased had been living at Harston, and had lately hired a house and premises in Melbourn, and was removing his furniture. After the carts had arrived at the house, the deceased took the headstall off the head of the horse he was in charge of, with the intention, no doubt, of feeding him. As soon as the headstall was taken off, the horse attempted to bolt, and the deceased hung on to his nose, when the horse instantly turned round, and ran the deceased up against a wall on the opposite side. The deceased fell down and the near wheel of the cart (which was then laden with furniture), went over his body. He managed to raise himself up, but dropped down again. He was taken into the house, and Mr. Gray, the surgeon, was immediately sent for, but he died about twenty minutes after the accident. There appears to be no blame attaching to anyone; the horse being frightened by the headstall having been taken off. A verdict was returned in accordance with the evidence.
>
> *Cambridge Independent Press 22nd October 1859*

WHAT THE PAPERS SAID

head and chest, killing him. A verdict of accidental death was recorded and ...*a deodand of 1s was laid on the wheel.*

Gruesome details were often reported in great detail, but sometimes just a stark statement with little or no explanation would appear in the newspapers. For instance, in February 1853 ...*David Woodcock, aged four and a half, was burnt to death.*

The gravel pit was in the news in 1869 when ...*Charles Negus, a labourer aged 21, was at work in a gravel pit of Mr Bullen's, when he suffered 'instantaneous' death as the gravel fell on him.*

Tetanus, or lockjaw, was an ever-present threat in the village and in January 1918 Arthur Bell, a foreman at New Road Farm, died of lockjaw following a small wound to his hand.

Death and suicide

It was the Victorians who made much of death, with their elaborate hearses pulled by teams of black horses with plumes; the cortege would be led by a 'mute' ~ a small boy dressed in black. A period of mourning would be observed by the widow or widower (often called the relict), with black 'weeds' (veils) being worn for 6 months, followed by sombre greys, purples and finally violets. The churchyard was enclosed in 1903 and the new cemetery in Orchard Road came into use in 1904.

Paupers were unceremoniously buried on the north side of the churchyard, whereas important folk had family vaults or engraved tombstones. Interment inside the church was for the venerable ~ such as William Ayloffe whose17th century tomb slab can be seen in the floor of the church aisle. Ayloffe was a prominent figure and benefactor to Melbourn.

Suicide was not only regarded as a sin ~ it was also illegal and greatly frowned upon, no matter what the circumstances. Offenders were denied normal burial rights and were buried outside the village limits, on the southern end of Royston Road, beyond The Bury.

The coffin trolley, or bier, was made at Bullen's in the High Street

Melbourn had its fair share of suicides. A sad case was that of Alfred Huggins, aged 21, who was found hanging from a tree near French's kiln in 1869. It seemed he was a member of the Forester's Benefit Society but, having been out of work for some time, was in arrears with his payment. He was found ...*suspended by his waist-strap to the branch of a tree, quite dead and stiff.*

The medical profession

Doctors

Early doctors were known as 'barber surgeons' and were often those who had served in the army or navy. The red-and-white stripe on the pole displayed outside barber shops, symbolised the blood and white bandages.

Augustus Paul Jenkins was registered in the village as the surgeon in 1839, although little was known of him. In 1875 Edmund Wollaston Parkinson was the surgeon and medical officer for the 'Melbourn District of the Royston Union' (the workhouse), situated at The Cross, and two surgeons, Leslie Meredith Earle and Edmund Parkinson, were listed in the Kelly's Directory for Melbourn in 1883.

Surgeon Edmund Bindloss, the medical officer and public vaccinator for the No. 4 district of Royston, lived in the village in 1896 and remained here until 1900. By 1916, Dr. Edmund Gregor established a surgery at 'Greenbanks', in the High Street, in the name of Gregor and Williams. He was still practising in 1937.

The surgery was at the end of his house where he prepared medicines as required. In 1934 his waiting room only held 4 people; patients requiring his services would step up and talk through a hatch. He would write down the symptoms and then bark at the patient 'wait back, wait back', while he prepared the medicine. He would then call the patient to the hatch and hand over a bottle of medicine or paste ~ with his favourite piece of advice 'to stay in the warm'. He was also known to extract teeth. Cyril Abrey, remembered having a tooth pulled out with the instruction 'hang onto the chair'!

Dr. Hall, a former army doctor, followed Dr. Gregor at the 'Greenbanks' surgery. The practice was later moved to the building that was once the Red Cow in

The surgery was moved from 'Greenbanks' to The Red Cow

'Greenbanks', the Doctor's surgery in the High Street

the High Street. Patients sat in the old public bar. The receptionist and dispenser was Ruby Harrison, a stern lady who would hand out a tube of ointment with the strict instruction 'Do not use this all at once, only a little smear'.

There are many recorded instances of operations being carried out at home, well into the 20th century. The removal of tonsils was not uncommon, and in the 1920s Freda Camps had her appendix taken out in her bedroom.

Little was known of oral hygiene, and the absence of a good diet meant that bad teeth were commonplace. The easiest solution for an aching tooth was to have it pulled out. The barber surgeon dealt with tooth extraction, often with the use of laudanum (a tincture of opium), as an anaesthetic to deaden the pain. In the 1930s the village dentist was Mr Woods who came up from London once a week. He held a surgery in a house opposite the Old Vicarage.

Nursing

Throughout the centuries, there has always been the 'wise woman' in the village ~ she was the herbalist, nurse and midwife whose cures and potions were often hit-and-miss affairs. However, these women were well known and valued members of the community.

Nurses were often from the lower classes. On the battlefield they were the camp followers ~ the wives and girlfriends of soldiers who had followed their men, but became cooks and washer-women. After

Nurses on parade during 'Salute the Soldier' week

the Crimean War (1854-56) and with the influence of Florence Nightingale, nursing was seen as a profession and this brought great changes to public health and medical practice.

At the beginning of the 1900s Caroline Fordham, of The Bury, formed the Melbourn and District Nursing Association, with the aim of securing a membership by subscription that could support a village nurse. In 1908 with approximately 500 members in the Association, the first village nurse, Miss Lily, was appointed, with a proposed income of up to £140 per year. She was to cover both

Elsie Cox

Nurse Cox was not a native of Melbourn but came as village midwife in the early 1920s and lived in the village until she died aged 99 years.

There would have been few families who did not have a family member delivered by her. She called them all her babies.

Her stories of attending gypsies for births and of them leaving before the statuary fee was paid were well known. As was the image of her cycling around Melbourn and area in black out conditions in the Second World War. She was well respected, and even feared by some.

She married Reuben Pennicott in the 1940s towards the end of the Second World War.

Melbourn and Meldreth, either on a bicycle or on foot. She was replaced in 1912 by Miss Fryatt, until in 1921 Nurse Cox took over.

J Mortlock started the fund off with £10, and the subscription was based on the amount people earned. Labourers earning 13-15s a week were to pay 2s a year, those earning £1-£2 a week paid 4s and others paid 5s. Various events in the village in aid of the fund included a concert which raised £3 3s and a fete at The Bury in July 1910, raised £90.

In 1939 an Infant Welfare Centre was set up by Nurse Cox and held in the Village Club. 57 babies and mothers were enrolled, including 15 evacuees. Nurse Cox (later to become nurse Pennicott) remained as village nurse until 1946.

A small nursing home situated opposite the church, was run by nurse Lilian Stanford. For a fee of £5 she offered to deliver your baby and provided two weeks convalescence ...*without touching your feet to the ground.*

Hospitals

Addenbrooke's Hospital, Cambridge

The earliest hospitals were not municipal undertakings, but were often founded by individuals. Dr. John Addenbrooke, a Fellow and former Bursar of Catherine Hall in Cambridge (later to become St. Catherine's College), left over £4,500 in his will to ...*hire and fit up, purchase or erect a small, physical hospital in the town of Cambridge for poor people.* The hospital opened its doors in 1766 in Trumpington Street with 20 beds and received 11

Addenbrooke's hospital in Trumpington Street, Cambridge

patients. The beds were available to those ...*of any parish or county as long as there was room and revenue to cope.* In 1837 the hospital became a recognised School of Medicine.

Addenbrooke's was helped during the First World War by a Linen League, inaugurated by Lady Blenkinsop (who lived at Trayles), and a Local Maintenance Fund which was set up to help with finances during this period.

Royston & District Cottage Hospital

The hospital in Barkway Street, Royston, was opened in 1869 by Dr. Daniel Balding with 8 beds. It was run entirely by a matron and one sister, with infrequent visits by a doctor. Visitors were not allowed and so had to shout through a closed window.

Almost as soon as the building was complete Dr. Balding realised that it was not going to be large enough to serve the neighbourhood and he began fundraising to extend it. Sadly, in 1924 he died, a few months before the new hospital, on its present site, was opened by the Prince of Wales. It was later extended with the addition of a maternity wing. Dr. Balding lived in Melbourn for a time, in Stones Cottage in the High Street. He also served on the Bench in Melbourn for 22 years.

Mental Health

Mental health and senility were not understood in the early years; those who were unfortunate enough to lose their faculties, may well have been incarcerated in a lunatic asylum.

The upkeep of an internee, was usually the responsibility of the family, unless both were penniless, as the following event from September 1858 shows. At that time the Parish was faced with the maintenaince of Edward Jarman ('a lunatic' in the care of Fulbourn Asylum), to which they objected, as Edward was a man of property.

Edward's father, Thomas, was responsible for payment and was ordered to pay the £23 11s which was overdue. However, by March 1859 the money had still not been paid, and the Parish agreed to cover all expenses. It seems it was not a long term agreement, as in 1862, Thomas had been ordered to pay 5s per week towards his son's maintenance.

The Poor Laws

In the Middle Ages the poor were tended by the monasteries, hospitals, local charities or the Guilds. The craftsmen of Melbourn formed the Guild of St. Wyburn, acquiring property, land and stock, helping members when in need and looking after their widows and orphans. The Guild had a chantry at the church where prayers were said for departed members. They also owned a house, which was situated on the corner of Mortlock Street, later to become the site of the Parish House.

After the dissolution of the monasteries, a series of Poor Laws were passed placing the responsibility for poor relief on the parish.

Those in need who were willing and able to work, received the necessary tools and working materials from the parish. The aged, and infirm, who were unable to work, were to be supported by outdoor relief in their own homes.

The burden of poor relief became so great that those who refused to work, though able, were branded as idle rogues and vagabonds, whipped and sent back to the parish of their origin or, in larger areas, to a House of Correction. Help eventually came in the form of a compulsory Poor Rate, which was enforced by the Privy Council, levied by the Justices of the Peace and payable, in proportion to their means, by all rate payers. The rate system was the ultimate Elizabethan administrative legacy to England.

In 1801 the collection of the Poor Rates in

The poorhouse at the Cross

Melbourn totalled £1,115. A small contribution came from local charities such as the Lettice Martin Charity, which although it produced very little income, was left to accumulate until there was enough to make a small distribution of bread.

There was another step forward on 9th February 1824, when at the Vestry meeting it was agreed to provide dwellings ...*for the benefit of the poor*. An old building, (the old Guild house) on the corner of Mortlock Street at The Cross, was demolished and a double tenement, known as the 'Parish House', was built.

Widows were often destined to become paupers, having not only lost their husbands, but the family income too. In 1831 ...*Widows Chapman, Day, Stone and Pryor were all registered as paupers*. Whole families were also affected for example ...*Widow Lee with her*

Lettice Martin ~ A generous woman

Lettice Martin who lived in Chishill, left money in 1562 to charity for the poor of those parishes where the Church Towers could be seen from the Church Tower at Chishill. The area included churches in Essex, Cambridgeshire and Hertfordshire.

5 children, Widow Pluck and her 4 children, the Larkins, the Hewitts and other branches of the Chapman and Pryor families.

The Poor Law Amendment Act was passed in 1834, which established a network of Unions (workhouses) throughout the country. The Union in Royston accommodated paupers from about 30 parishes, including Melbourn. No relief was given to the poor outside the Union, and Union officials were instructed to collect the rate. During the 33 weeks, from 7th August 1835 to 25th March 1836, the total cost of maintenance of the poor for Melbourn was £344 4s 4¾d. Under the old system, the cost would have been £514 13 5d ~ a considerable saving to the parish.

After the Amendment Act, overseers naturally tried to keep their expenditure low, notably by preventing outsiders from entering the parish and becoming a liability. The poor from the village were set to work if they were able-bodied, the aged, or the very young, were paid a small weekly sum and the homeless were accommodated in the poorhouse or workhouse.

Rules in the workhouse were harsh ~ the sexes were strictly segregated, forcing elderly couples to spend their last years separated from each other. All wages were handed to the poorhouse authorities and those admitted were made to give up all their private possessions.

The overseer of the poor was appointed annually. His duties would include the provision of work, and apprenticing pauper children to a trade. Paupers either worked in the poorhouse using materials provided, or they were found work outside. Wages were low and relief was often given to supplement them. Some were employed carrying out roadwork or field drainage; collecting stones from the fields at 2d a bushel was a common task to give to children. The overseer was also responsible for attending to pauper burials, the distribution of alms to wounded soldiers or students passing through the parish holding an authorisation to beg.

Being admitted into the workhouse was not a permanent situation ~ some were often dismissed, and occasionally at short notice, as in the case of Mrs Catley and her three children in 1846 who were removed from the workhouse within 24 hours. There was always insufficient room in the poorhouse to accommodate all the needy.

Conditions improved slightly after 8th June 1847 when an Act was passed which limited the working day of women and children aged 13~18 to ten hours. However, the workhouse remained a grim place.

Welfare

Entered in the minutes of the Vestry meetings are numerous instances of almsgiving.

On 13th August 1835, with the Poor Rate set at 2s 6d in the pound ...William Carter and his wife were given 8s during their illness. The overseers at the time were William Scruby and William Woods. There were seven paupers in the parish ~ Thomas Ball, Widow Chapman, Joseph Catley, Mrs Collis, Widow Harper, Widow Pryor and Sarah Dodkin.

The Parish Officers agreed to borrow the sum of £300 from Royston Bank, for the purpose of paying the paupers. However, repayment of the loan was not allowed to come out of the Poor Rate and on 4th February 1841 at The Rose, it was agreed by the Officers, to sell parish cottages in order to repay the debt. A total of just over £330, was raised from the sale in 1844. The following year it was agreed that the ...Parish Officers should communicate with the Poor Law

Commissioners respecting the proceeds of the sale of the Parish houses in order to apply the same to its legitimate purpose. (A page from the record book covering further meetings between April and June 1846 is missing.)

Some of the more affluent members of the village were generous to the poorer families in Melbourn. On 12th January 1850; John Fordham gave ...a beautiful bullock, weighing eighty-six stone, to the poor of Melbourn parish, and Edmund Metcalf, invited ...fifty-one elderly people to dinner, tea, snuff and a glass of punch.

Although the loan previously mentioned was not allowed to be repaid from the Poor Rate, in March 1892 £2 was taken however, (and a further £2 in 1894) ...to keep the fire engine in good order.

The total expenditure from the Poor Rate during 1851 was £944 13s. Twelve parishioners donated £20 19s in 1854 to help poor families of the village, which was divided according to the number in each family.

The Union system was finally abolished in 1948. In its place the Public Assistance Act gave needy people the right to apply for relief in their own homes.

Emigration

Passage to the 'New Worlds'

Emigration to the colonies began in 1585 when a group of 108 pioneers set sail for America. However, threatened with famine and hostile Indians, the majority returned to England. From then on only small groups emigrated until 1607 when the first permanent settlement was established with settlers mostly from East Anglia.

For these early travellers life on board ship was harsh, as much of the journey would be spent below deck. Food was of poor quality and was often inedible before they arrived at their destination. Drinking water was stored in barrels previously used for wine, oil, vinegar or turpentine and epidemics of typhus and cholera were rampant.

Death was not uncommon on these long voyages especially among the young and old. Rules were often disregarded concerning personal hygiene and as a result health suffered. Sanitary conditions were crude ~ the washing and toilet procedures were to be taken on the top deck, but during bad weather the lower decks were used. The later ships did provide better accommodation and food and proper toilet facilities below deck.

Passengers were expected to cater for themselves ~ a problem during bad weather as cooking was not allowed below deck. With storms lasting days or even weeks some died from starvation.

Assisted passage

The earliest known assisted passengers set sail for the new worlds in 1620. Discontented with the corruption of the Church and persecution, Puritans ~ later known as Pilgrims or the Pilgrim Fathers ~ raised funds to emigrate to a land offering more religious freedom. Others followed throughout the centuries, together with those who had the funds to look for a better life. The prospect of a better life was widely publicised throughout the country and many families travelled to America and Canada and later to the new colonies of Australia, New Zealand and Africa.

The new colonies

With increasing prosperity in the new colonies came a growing demand for skilled labour, and so to encourage more settlers the government devised a scheme whereby a payment would be made to cover the cost of transportation. However, few took up the offer, even though incentives were applied, but by the 1820s, immigrants were departing in greater numbers. The first *free* assisted passage scheme to Australia began in 1832 when families were advanced up to £20 against future wages, but stringent conditions concerning marital status, health and moral character were attached.

Many emigrants were not from the poorest levels of society and not all received assisted passage. Much of the early emigration took place during a period when industrial development was providing increased opportunities and employment. However, Melbourn was an agricultural region and in the 19th century this meant low wages and seasonal unemployment. The decision to emigrate would have been greatly influenced by this. Of the men who left Melbourn for Melbourne in Australia between 1840 and 1866 forty-three were farm labourers, 13 were craftsmen (builders, blacksmiths, carpenters) and 4 were farmers. Two of the craftsmen and the farmers had no financial help with their passage.

Although in receipt of assisted passage many still had to contribute to the cost to secure their ticket. The amount due depended on the number in the family, their age, sex, occupation and other circumstances. For children up to the age of twelve the cost was between £1 and £3. Over 12 years of age but under 40 it was £3–£6, over 40 years up to £12 and over 50 years up to £18.

By the mid-19th century the Poor Law Unions were financing the emigration of poor families overseas. Other organisations, including the church, also offered money through collections and the use of the Poor Rate. A number of families in the village received help from the Parish, including Joseph Coningsby, William Pateman, J Bullen and J Wing who were given clothing to assist them to emigrate to Australia in March 1845. William Wedd and his wife, James Dellar, his wife and seven children also received help. In 1848 the Churchwardens and Overseers raised the £20 to help the poor to emigrate and later that year, William Dodkin was assisted to emigrate to the Cape of Good Hope in Africa.

Those who received help were obliged to stay in the Colony for four years and agree to compensate the authorities for the cost of the passage if they failed to do so. This involved the payment of up to £3 for every year or part of a year in which they failed to stay.

In addition to the contribution to the cost of the voyage, they needed to provide spending money for use on arrival. The government also insisted that an appropriate quantity of clothing was required. For males, this comprised, ...*six shirts, six pairs of stockings, two pairs shoes, two complete suits of exterior clothing, sheets, towels and soap*. It was also pointed out that as

Free passage given

Single farm labourers and female domestic servants 17–35. Men must be country resident and wholly agricultural. LAND ORDERS value £20 granted to each fee-paying passenger. For particulars, forms of application, & etc, write to ...

Local Newspapers 1890

WHAT THE PAPERS SAID

the emigrants had to pass through very hot and cold weather during their voyage lasting about four months, they should be prepared; three serge shirts were strongly recommended. The quantity of baggage was limited to twenty cubic feet; mattresses and feather beds could not be taken.

An office was set up in Royston for the 'Colonial Land and Emigration Commissioners'. It was the job of Josiah Johnson the officer in charge to recommend suitable people for emigration to Australia, and the Officer of Health and Emigration to inspect each person before they were given permission to proceed to sea. Assisted migrants had a choice of two ports, London or Plymouth. It was up to the family to make their way at their own expense, unless they could persuade the Parish to help ~ which they did in the case of sufficiently impoverished applicants.

Over a hundred and fifty people (not all assisted) left Melbourn to find a better life in the new lands. The family names included: **Baker** ~ John Baker, his wife and nine children embarked on the 'Neptune' in February 1844. Sadly his wife died before they reached Australia. Charles and Ann Baker (*née* Hagger) emigrated in 1850; **Bysouth** ~ James Bysouth emigrated with his two youngest children, Mary Ann and Henrietta in 1851. They were later joined by his four older children, Mary Marie, William, James and Ellis; **Cambridge**; **Campkin** ~ one branch of the Campkin family moved to New Zealand; **Catley**; **Chamberlain**; **Chapman** ~ John Chapman emigrated to Australia in 1852; **Collis**, **Day** ~ Joseph and Ann Day (*née* Baker) arrived in Australia in 1844 with their daughter Mary; **Coningsby**; **Dellar** ~ James Dellar, his wife and seven children emigrated to Australia in 1845; **Dodkin** ~ William Dodkin went to the Cape of Good Hope, Africa in 1848; **Elson**; **Everitt**; **Freshwater**; **Geeves** ~ William and Mary Geeves (*née* West) emigrated to Australia; **Gouldthorpe** ~ George and

Matilda Gouldthorpe and their son left in 1853; **Green**; **Greenhill**; **Hagger**; **Harper** ~ Benjamin and Lydia Harper (*née* Negus) and their six children embarked on the 'Shand' arriving in Portland in January 1851; **Howe** ~ Thomas and Keziah Howe (*née* Smith) arrived in 1849 with their children; **Johnson**; **King**; **Langham**; **Lee** ~ Amos and Harriet Lee (*née* Waldock) sailed on the 'Shand' in 1854 with their son William. Harriet's two brothers Simon and Charles were also on the voyage. Five months later July 1855 on the 'Blenheim', Amos's brother John and Elizabeth Lee (*née* Rayner) their son William aged 17 and his wife Mary (*née* Farrant) aged 22, Amos's other children were John, Charles James, Mary Anne and his youngest son Amos who died during the voyage; **Livermore** ~ James Livermore went to Australia in 1854; **Loats**; **Mortlock**; **Negus** ~ Ellis and Elizabeth Negus and their three children emigrated with the Harper family; **Oliver**; **Payne**; **Ranson**; **Smith**; **Stamford**; **Stanford** ~ Ann Stanford emigrated in 1854 to Australia; **Stockbridge**; **Theobald** Gamaliel and Elizabeth Theobold (*née* Hagger); **Waldock**; **Wayman**; **Webb**; **Wedd**; **West** (*see* Geeves); **Wootton** ~ George and Mary Wootton (*née* Baker) arrived in Australia around 1850 with their five children; **Worland** ~ Joseph and Mary Worland (*née* Stone) and their four children arrived in 1853 on the 'Othonia'. His brother Frederick and wife Elizabeth followed in 1854.

Whole families and neighbourhood groups emigrated together from the village, and many of these were young people, between the ages of 15 and 29 and most were married with young children.

The largest kin-related group left Melbourn between 1848 and 1850 and included members of the Smith, Green, Chamberlain, Gouldthorpe, Wedd and Collis families. In all 28 related emigrants travelled out in 5 groups. These groups included 2 wheelwrights, a carpenter and a blacksmith. Neighbours also emigrated together; James Dellar,

John Everitt, Simeon Smith, Benjamin Harper, and James Collis, all of Sheepshead Row lived close to Charles Catley in Drury Lane.

The qualifying rules of assisted passage changed over the years, but schemes still existed into the 1950s when the ...£10 *poms' as they were known, could travel to Australia for £10*. (The origin of 'Pom' is unknown. One explanation is that it is an acronym of 'Prisoner of Mother England' or 'Prisoner of His/Her Majesty'. The term is still used to describe anyone from England.)

The Hagger family, who emigrated to Australia. From the back, Frank, Arthur, Clara, Charles, Elizabeth (mother), Ralph and Isabel

The Francis John Clear Almshouses, Orchard Road

Almshouses

Almshouses were not built in Melbourn until 1921 when Walter Wedgborough Clear left money for the construction of four houses, to be named 'The Francis John Clear Almshouses' after his brother. The almshouses were ...*for occupation by poor and indigent ladies who had resided in the parish for more than 10 years.*

The houses were built in Orchard Road and opened by Ernest Fordham on 18th June 1924, before a gathering of the Clear family. Also present were a number of official leaders of the village and the four elderly ladies chosen to be the first occupants of the houses. The Rev. McNeice apparently ...*kept the company in somewhat hilarious mood by relating some of his previous experiences in almshouses*!

The Clear brothers had devoted themselves to the management of Fulbourn Mental Hospital, as well as being involved in educational charities and members of the County Council.

Old age pensions

In 1908 the Old Age Pensions Act granted persons of 70 years and over 10s a week in order to 'relieve poverty'. This amount was increased occasionally to keep pace with inflation; by the 1950s it had risen to the princely sum of £2 per week. It was not long before the potential for fraud was seen, and in 1909 ...*Samuel Jarman aged 74 and Fanny Jarman aged 44 were summonsed for attempting to obtain the Old Age Pension by false pretences. Fined £5 and £1 respectively, Samuel told the court he had no money and would go to prison for 14 days.*

Sick & Dividing Clubs

Workers were encouraged to save by paying in to a Friendly Society, such as the Odd Fellows' or Foresters, (associations which provided insurance against sickness and old age). Funds rose in 1910 to £3226.

The Congregational Chapel formed a Sick and Dividing Club with the intention of providing relief for families whose income had been reduced due to illness or lack of work. Subscriptions were received in the Vestry every Saturday. The Club continued until well after the Second World War, having 650 members in 1942, rising to 993 by 1948. Payments of £780 and £1228 were made in those years respectively.

The Sick & Dividing Club. Back row: Albert King, Bent Bunting, Ernest Dash, Sid Waldock, Rev. J Davis, Jubal Howard, Will Oliver. Front row: May Bunting, Hilda Catley, Eddie Stockbridge, Mrs Winter, Mrs J Howard

Bridesmaids Joyce Catley, Jessie Woods and Nora Catley

Marriage

Child betrothal and child marriage were very common in the early days ~ marriage was seen as a way of enriching the family fortunes ~ children were often used as pawns in a bartering game. Amongst the peasantry it was more of a mutual arrangement, though marriages to legalise illegitimacy were quite common. Sometimes young men were forced to pay for their illegitimate children, just as Frank Coningsby was ordered to pay 2s a week in 1883 to support the children of Clara Stamford. He was only 15 at the time and still a schoolboy!

After marriage, the woman's possessions passed into the hands of her husband. It was not until the Married Women's Property Acts of the late Victorian period that women had a right to their own inheritance. In 1918, following the First World War, when women had proved they could shoulder responsibilities and take on the work of men, married women over the age of thirty were given the right to vote.

Above, the wedding of Jubal Howard and below, bridesmaids (centre, Joyce Catley) in Station Road

Hairdressing

The earliest known barbers in the village were William Wall and John Warren, both had premises in the High Street in 1830. It was also a common practice to have your hair cut in the local pub. The 1864 Kelly's Post Office Directory listed John Hills of 'The Hoops' as a hairdresser and Jim West, landlord of the White Horse cut hair for his customers. A barber shop was opened at The Cross by Jack Jones, and Arthur Chapman cut hair on Sunday mornings for 3d, in his cottage in Dolphin Lane.

Until the 20th century women looked after their own hair, as it was seldom cut, but with the advent of new hairstyles such as the 'shingle' or 'Eton bob' in the 1920s and the invention of the 'permanent wave' ladies hairdressers became common.

Miss Martin, a hairdresser in the l920s, had premises over the baker's shop, where she washed hair, although she did not have running water.

Clothes and footwear

In early times the peasant classes in Melbourn would have worn homespun, sacking or fustian died with natural dyes taken from berries, flowers, herbs and vegetables. Synthetic dyes were not available until the 1800s.

The thriving woollen trade in Suffolk made woollen garments available, mostly to the wealthier folk. Many women with spinning and weaving skills produced simple garments at home.

Tailors and dressmakers

In 1830 there were three tailors listed in Melbourn: Ellis Baker, Henry Chapple and George Wootton followed by William Wootton in 1839, Wood & Adcock in 1864 and in 1875 John and Peter Pryor. Also in 1875 Misses Achsah & Jael Ellis ran a dressmakers and milliners. Both The Ellis' and the Pryors' were still in business in 1883 when John Gutteridge, draper and clothier, and

Dress Economy, pattern 74. 'Any girl with ordinary intelligence can make this dress up, thus saving not merely shillings, but pounds'.
Parish Magazine, Melbourn June 1920

Styles from the early 1900s, Norah Howard and William French

Richard Robinson, tailor (and grocer) set up their businesses. Robinson's premises was on Moor corner. Easter was traditionally a busy time, those who could afford it would have something new to wear. The tailor delivered clothes by horse and van on Friday nights to ensure payment, as Friday was payday!

In July 1819 there was a sale at the Dolphin Inn of 'Linen and Woollen Drapery, Hosiery, Jewellery' and 'valuable effects' which were sold by auction. The inventory of items gives a good idea of what could be purchased in Melbourn in the 1800s. These included: *silks, persians, sarsnets, ribbons, cambrics, muslins, jaconet, bombazines, a large velvet pall, 200 handsome shawls of silk, muslin and cotton, 120 yards of jean, callico, velveteen, worsted cords and corduroys, 130 yards of fustian, 120 yards of fine pelisse cloths, 480 yards of sheeting and shirting, 240 pairs of men's, women's and children's cotton and worsted stockings, 220 pairs of ladies' and girls' shoes and half boots, fur and lambswool tippets, men's and boys' hats, handsome gold brooches, earrings, eardrops and neck chains, ivory, tortoiseshell and bone combs, silver thimbles, scissors, knives and needles.*

Dress Economy, pattern 93
Parish Magazine, Melbourn January 1922

Children's clothes

Children wore smaller versions of grown-up clothing. Small boys were clothed in dresses until they were 'breeched' at about 4 or 5 years old, when they literally went into breeches. Girls wore pinafores over their dresses to protect them from daily soiling at home and at school. Most poor children wore 'hand-me-downs' and clothes would be mended and patched to extend their wear.

A well-remembered item of girl's clothing was the 'liberty bodice', a thick bodice worn over the vest. It sometimes had rubber suspenders to which black cotton stockings were secured. The liberty bodice would come into use at the beginning of the winter and be worn until spring.

A Wedd baby, dressed in a magnificent bonnet

Small boys were clothed in dresses until they were 'breeched'

A smock was a sturdy and practical garment for farm workers. In the late-19th century a farm labourer from Melbourn named John Ball was said to be the last man in the village to wear a smock. He was so attached to the garment that, he even wore it on Sundays and to hide the evidence of workday stains and grime, he wore it inside out. On Ball's death, to show his appreciation of ministerial guidance, he left the smock to the Rev. W Higgins, the Baptist Minister.

Dress Economy, pattern 64 'This little school outfit is just what little girls are looking for'. The pattern illustrated below can be purchased through the magazine.

Parish Magazine, Melbourn August 1919

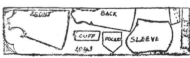

Girls wore pinafores over their dresses to protect them from daily soiling at home, and at school.

Knitted clothes

During both World Wars women knitted for the troops. Mrs Cranfield, who had owned the Post Office would distribute khaki and Air Force blue wool, to the 'village knitters' to produce *...comforts for the troops.*

From the 1920s most baby clothes were knitted ~ including pram covers. (Picture of William Wedd)

Dress Economy, pattern 80. 'Warm clothing is important especially porous woollen undergarments. These knitted bloomer-knickers are perfectly simple for a child of four to six years'.
Parish Magazine, Melbourn December 1920

From the 1920s most baby clothes were knitted ~ including pram covers. For children and adults alike socks, waistcoats, jumpers, dresses and cardigans were all knitted ~ even swimming costumes, which were uncomfortable and sagged when wet!

Dress Economy, pattern 67. 'Nothing looks prettier on a little boy of two or four years than this quaint little tunic suit.'
Parish Magazine, Melbourn November 1919

Hats

In the early 16th century, an influx of Flemish craftsmen making the fashionable beaver fur hats, threatened the traditional woollen cap. By 1570 the situation was so bad that a law was passed declaring *...that every male below a certain income should wear a cap of wool on Sundays and Holy Days knit, picked and dressed in England, under penalty of a fine of 3s 4d.*

Apart from the extravagant hats worn by the aristocracy (wimples etc.) the normal headdress for a woman in the Middle Ages was a coif or mob cap. Only young girls had their hair flowing freely. Married women generally hid their hair beneath a modest cap or kerchief.

It was in the late-17th century that women's hats began to emerge. The word 'milliner', a maker of women's hats, derives from 'Milan' in Italy, where they were well known for producing straw hats. The haberdashers who imported these highly popular straws were called 'Millaners'.

Women's hats were often decorated with ribbons and flowers. (Picture of Elizabth Wedd)

During the first half of the 19th century the bonnet dominated women's fashion, becoming very large with ribbons, flowers, feathers and gauze trims. By the end of the century, although bonnets were still prevalent, many other styles were to be found, including wide brims with flat crowns, the flower pot and the toque ~ many decorated with feathers and veils.

The style of mens' hats often reflected their status; the most notable was the formal, tall, stiff top-hat which showed the authority of the aristocracy, and those involved in the professions and trades. The informal soft trilby felt hats were generally worn by intellectuals, artists and important country folk. The bowler was worn by the important farm or works manager and the ordinary working man wore the flat cap.

Boots & Shoes

By 1873 there were five boot and shoemakers in the village: Jesse Guiver, Ishmael Howard, Joseph Liver, Edward Stanford, and Thos Wedd. Jonah Howard (who had a withered arm and could not join the family bakery) was a shoemaker in 1929. He had a shop opposite the Post Office but later moved next door to his brother's bakery on Moor corner.

Not everyone could afford new boots and it was very common to wear them second or third hand. As late as the 1940s, some children in Melbourn went to school barefoot.

Because boots and shoes were an expensive and necessary item, repairs were frequently done at home

Above, a family gathering of the Stockbridge's. The photo shows ladies' hats in an array of styles. Even children were dressed in large brimmed hats.

Left, the style of mens' hats often reflected their status. The Bury staff.

Back row, W B*aker*, King, F *Stockbridge*, W Winters, C *Stockbridge*, Guiver, R *Ayloft*, H *Webb*, G *Hillant*

Mid row standing, *Winters*, *Frost*, F *Chapman*, W *Day*, C *Holland*, J *Hinkins Jnr*, A *Greenhill*, J *Adams*

Sitting, A R *Fordham*, P *Sell*, J *Hinkins*, F *Rule*, J *Thompson*, W *Jacklin*, W *Stockbridge*, J *Catley*

Names are not available for those sitting on the ground or the gentleman far right.

Groves' shoe shop was housed in the end building in Station Road, once the site of the gas company. Turner's, and at one time Mrs Hinkins sweet shop, was on the right.

A 'hobbing' last

and a 'hobbing' last could be found in most cottages. This was a three-legged iron stand with a small, medium and large foot at each end of the legs. The boot was placed onto the appropriate leg and resoled, often using old rubber tyres. Metal 'Segs', or 'Blakeys', would be hammered into the heels and toes to prolong the life of the shoe.

Ladies' boots were fastened with laces or tiny round buttons ~ buttonhooks were used to get the small buttons into their buttonholes. Silver-handled buttonhooks would form part of a lady's dressing case, but cheaper ones were made out of base metal.

The war years

During the First World War there was a call for voluntary rationing, when it was suggested that 4lbs bread, 2½ lbs meat and ¾ lb sugar was sufficient for one person's weekly needs.

The rationing introduced during the Second World War actually brought a more balanced diet to most of the population. Gardens in Melbourn were used for growing vegetables and chickens and pigs were kept, fed on pig swill (household waste, vegetable peelings, etc.). A great deal of bartering went on.

During this time, there were regular radio broadcasts by nutritionists giving economical recipes and ideas for the best use of rations. Carrots were popular, being plentiful and easy to grow and were promoted by the Ministry of Food as *...helping you to see in the dark* ('blackout' being in force at night).

Ration coupons

In January 1918 Mrs Foley had a soup kitchen in the village and opened every day from 12.15–1pm, except Sunday. Forty gallons of soup were produced, all of which was sold, at 1d per pint.

Rationing did not end with the cessation of the war ~ for a while things became even tighter than ever and to help with cheap menu ideas the Ministry of Food issued a recipe for squirrel pie! Things did improve, and a Gallup Poll in 1947 suggested that the perfect British meal was: tomato soup, sole, roast chicken with roast potatoes, peas and sprouts, followed by trifle and cream. The government eventually introduced free milk and free school dinners.

The Second World War also brought great shortages of clothing ~ all available manufacture went into producing uniforms, overalls or parachutes. Recycling of clothing turned into an art form ~ a small boy's jacket made out of his father's trousers, dresses made from curtains etc. The Board of Trade issued strict guidelines on the amount of fabric to be used in skirts; jackets had to be single breasted with no buttons on the sleeves, turn-ups were not allowed on trousers and shirtsleeves could not have a double cuff.

Lord Woolton Pie
Ministry of Food 1940

For 5 or 6 persons.
Take 1lb each of diced potatoes, cauliflower, swedes and carrots, 3 or 4 spring onions, if possible, one teaspoonful of vegetable extract and one tablespoonful of oatmeal. Cook all together for 10 mins, with just enough water to cover. Stir occasionally to prevent the mixture from sticking. Allow to cool; put into a pie dish, sprinkle with chopped parsley and cover with a crust of potatoes or wholemeal pastry. Bake in a moderate oven until the pastry is nicely brown and serve hot with a brown gravy. Lord Woolton was the Minister for Food in 1940.

Civilian Clothing 1941

Clothing coupons were issued, and the use of only blue and grey dyes was advised for school uniforms. If a child was taller, heavier or had feet larger than expected at a given age, extra coupons would be claimed. The Utility Mark CC41 (Civilian Clothing 1941) was introduced, which was a label confirming that the item had been made to strict standards. It appeared on all items and also applied to furniture. Clothes rationing was particularly hard on brides, and there was many a wedding dress that went up the aisle more than once (sometimes made of parachute silk).

Clothing continued to be in short supply even after the war; there was still a brisk trade in old parachutes, as the silk was used to make underwear.

Rationing finally ended in March 1949 for clothes and food in 1954.

The New Look

With the end of rationing, fashion turned full circle again and the New Look was introduced by Christian Dior, with long, full skirts.

All Saints' Church c.1865

The establishment - Church and religion

...in medieval times churches were far more colourful than they appear today.

There has been a Christian settlement in Melbourn from the earliest times; the archaeological digs have revealed graves which were almost certainly Christian, the bodies having been buried in an east/west orientation. During the Saxon period worship was probably conducted in the open air or in a primitive building. However, religious life in the area would have been pushed underground with the coming of the pagan Danes in the 10th century – they worshipped their own gods and destroyed churches. With the passage of time, Danes and Saxons intermingled and the Christian religion crept back. A wooden church was constructed in Meldreth in the 11th century and was served by nine priests, who carried the Gospel to the neighbouring villages.

A Charter, which mentions a church in Melbourn at this time, was granted to the Priory of Ely by King Edgar in 959. It is possible that, by 1066, a small wooden building stood north of the site of the present Melbourn church, to serve the 50 or 60 tenants in Melbourn. The Normans may have built a stone church, which would have stood until the 12th century; all that remains of this today is the font. The church, originally in the Diocese of Lincoln, passed to the Diocese of Ely in 1193. The Rector, at the time, was Master John de Foxton, who established the first vicarage in Melbourn. Until the 14th century priests were unmarried, simple, folk and their way of life was very poor. In Melbourn, the priest's accommodation would probably have been in the room above the church porch, or in the chancel loft.

The early church of Melbourn

The early church, being the only building of substance apart from the manors, was the centre of life for the community. Inside, there were no pews and it would have been very noisy. It was here that villagers could find someone who could read and write for them. Mass was said in a part of the church reserved for this purpose; in the chancel behind the rood screen (a screen on which the Cross of Christ or crucifix is raised). The rich and more powerful people would gather by the screen to hear the consecration, while the poor, elderly and infirm had to stand at the sides; they literally 'went to the wall'.

The building would have been open to the elements as glass was extremely expensive, the windows were unglazed, allowing birds to fly in and nest. For this reason the priest would cover the chalice with a small square cover, a practice still continued to this day within the church.

Similarly, altar rails were originally introduced to keep stray animals away from the altar. It was

The only surviving Norman panel on the font

probably during the 13th century that the Norman font was cut into its present octagonal shape, possibly to fit against the western-most pillar of the south aisle where it stood until 1882. Only one Norman panel survives, the other sides were recarved in the 14th century. The east side preserves the Norman arcading; the trefoils (a three-lobed decorative pattern) on four sides are medieval. The pillars of the church are made of local clunch and the outside is flint-clad.

The power of the church

During the late medieval period the church dominated and controlled the lives of all. Everyone implicitly believed in heaven and hell; they were terrified of hell, having repeatedly heard at the weekly sermon of the horrors that would await them, should they not get to heaven.

Peasants were unpaid for their labour on churchland, in order to support the priest. They were also required to pay a tithe, or 10 percent of their earnings, to the church in addition to working. As the majority of people had little money they usually had to pay in harvested grain, seeds or animals. The peasants were told, by the church, that a failure to pay the tithe would result in their souls going to hell after they died.

Eventually the church accumulated great wealth from the tithes, and the fact it was exempt from paying taxes, but baptisms, marriages and burials remained expensive services for the ordinary people.

Medieval coffee stop!

The church of Melbourn was as appropriated to the Prior and Convent of Ely in 1225 to allow the provision of hospitality and of poor relief in connection with the pilgrimage which the Cathedral and its relics attracted.

Pro sustentacione hospitum et pauperdum domus.

Alcock's shield & bosses This shield or rebus is a representation by pictures of objects or symbols whose names resemble the intended word. This was necessary as the majority of parishioners were illiterate.

Alterations and improvements

In 1220 Sir Richard de Argentyne applied to the Bishop of Ely for permission to build a chapel within his house at Melbourn (Lordship Farm). The rector of Melbourn, John de Foxton, opposed this application and managed to have the building of the chapel deferred for some years, for fear that the appointment of a chaplain for the chapel might encroach on his dues and rights. Permission was eventually granted in 1229, with a long list of regulations. There is no evidence of the chapel at Lordship Farm today.

The first of many restorations and alterations in the church began in the 13th and 14th century. Windows were installed in the building in 1278 by Vicar George and of those, three lancet windows (narrow arched windows with a pointed head) still exist. The chancel roof was raised in 1350 and windows were placed in the chancel and north

The Parvis chamber over the porch

aisles. During the rule of Bishop Alcock in 1487, (his coat of arms may be seen in the chancel roof) the roof of the nave was raised by about 10 feet and the perpendicular windows at the east end, the clerestory (part of a wall with a series of windows above the aisle roofs) and south aisles were built and the west tower reconstructed.

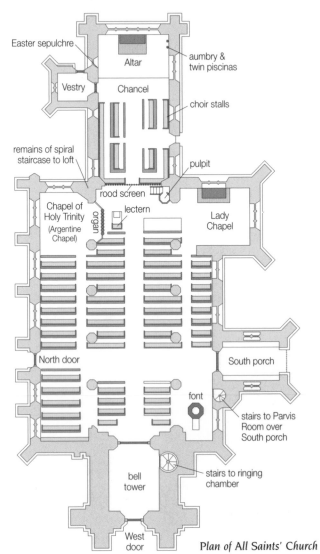

Plan of All Saints' Church

Looking towards the Chancel before the organ was repositioned

More restoration

Further restorations of the church were made in 1884. The porch with the Parvis room was rebuilt and the clerestories replaced in flint. The Sanctus bell was removed, having once hung in a cote over the junction between the roof of the nave and that of the chancel.

All the windows were re-glazed by Ward's of Melbourn, and the organ was moved, from the tower arch to the south transept, and improved. At the same time, the font was moved from the north

Aumbry (closed recess) and twin piscinas

doorway and placed on a platform of stone near the south doorway, where it still stands.

On 27th June 1884, a tea party organised by Mr Fordham, was held in the infants' room at the British School for the 62 men who worked on the restoration. Each worker was supplied with a Bible and ½lb tea for their wives.

In the chancel is an Easter sepulchre set in the north wall, an aumbry (which is in two parts) and twin piscinas of the 12th century in the south and east walls. The aumbry (closed recess in the wall) is used to store the consecrated host, (bread or a wafer representing the body of Christ and used in the Eucharist). The piscina is a sink, or drain, used for the disposal of water blessed by the priest, rather than putting it down a common sewer. At Melbourn, the double piscina allowed for one to be used for blessed water, the other for disposal of water used for ablutions.

The organ in its new position

Changes in the church fabric

In medieval times churches were far more colourful than they appear today. The walls and pillars were often painted and there would have been many statues of saints, situated in niches in the walls ~ two of these niches remain today.

The Chapel of the Holy Trinity, which was also the family Chapel of the de Argentines until 1619, was situated in the area now occupied by the organ. A singing gallery ran from the tower arch to the passageway, and would be where the church band played. The band consisted of double bass, cello, flute, hautboy (oboe) and clarinet and a fiddler who led the singing. The leader of the band was a gamekeeper, famous for his voice, as well as for his music.

The vicar of 1850 had the gallery dismantled and

The Chapel of St. Mary or Lady Chapel, originally contained a statue of the Virgin Mary

placed in the north-west corner for schoolchildren. His successor in the 1860s, then moved it to the north east corner, and, afraid that it would not stand another move, *his* successor sold it!

The rood screen was erected in 1507 with a bequest from Thomas Hitch, whose will records that it cost £1 3s 6d. Four of the church bells also date from this period and have been re-cast several times. The Chapel of St. Mary (or Lady Chapel, originally containing a statue of the Virgin Mary), also went through many changes during the 1530s. For over 100 years it was occupied by two large family pews, but, on the destruction of the singing gallery, the organ was placed in the chapel with the choir standing in front during services. The organ was

moved again ~ this time to the north side, allowing the Lady Chapel to be returned to its original use.

At the time when Henry VIII came to the throne in 1509, there were still no pews in the nave and the floor was strewn with rushes or straw. People stood for the mass at daily celebration. Few understood the words of the services but the atmosphere would have been impressive. Priests were dressed in rich, bright robes and the walls were covered with pictures and scenes from Holy Writ. The congregation took no active part in the service, but they listened to the music of the chants and were influenced by the general spirit of worship.

The Protestant church

After the break with Rome, Henry dissolved the monasteries, and the Lady Chapel in All Saints' was plundered on the orders of Bishop Goodrich. There were to be no more prayers said for the dead, no perpetual candle burning, statues were removed and services were to be in English. The country was ordered to adopt the protestant faith and 'traces of popery and superstition' were banned.

The entrance to the West tower

The development of Protestantism

The Protestant movement, beginning in the 16th century, led to the Reformation and the rift with the Catholic church. Its aim was to reform the Roman church, which had become increasingly corrupt. Hundreds of men and women had been burned at the stake as heretics or sorcerers, and the church was filling its coffers from the sale of Indulgences (people were led to believe that to buy an Indulgence would reduce their suffering in the next world).

During the 16th century, a revolt spread against the Catholic church, led by Martin Luther and John Calvin.

Luther attacked these sales of Indulgences and the blatant corruption of the Roman church. He taught that faith alone is the key to salvation, not just good deeds, and that all baptised Christians were members of the priesthood. His aim was to have a democratic constitution within the church. All rites were rejected except the baptism and sacrament of communion; the others he felt were based on superstition.

After the Reformation

Congregationalists

The first Congregationalists were the Brownists, named after Robert Brown, who defined the congregational principle in 1580. In the 17th century they were known as Independents. In 1662 hundreds of their ministers were driven from their churches and established separate congregations.

Congregationalists (and Methodists) believe that the church must be self-governing and do not adhere to the creed. Church members are the church government, and collectively determine how the church is organised. Participation in councils is voluntary.

Puritans

Rather than leave the Church of England, Puritans sought to purify it, hence their name. The movement dates from 1564 and its members wanted to eliminate Roman Catholic rituals and most of the sacraments. Later the name came to signify the purity of life they aspired to. After the Restoration they were driven from the church. They are more usually known as Dissenters and Nonconformists.

Dissenter

The term Dissenter refers to a number of Protestant denominations – Presbyterians, Baptists, Quakers, Congregationalists and others – which were subject to persecution because they refused to take the Anglican communion, or to conform to the principles of the restored Church of England in 1662. Various acts passed by Parliament between 1661 and 1665 included the *Act of Uniformity*; this required all churches in England to use the Book of Common Prayer.

In 1689 the *Toleration Act* was passed. Dissenters were allowed to hold services in licensed meeting houses and to maintain their own preachers in England and Wales, but only if they subscribed to certain oaths.

Baptists and Anabaptists

The Baptists originate from the English Dissenters in the 1600s. They stress the importance of the scripture, and members are only voluntarily baptised when they are old enough to understand the meaning of their faith. Baptism takes place in front of the whole congregation, where the person is immersed in water to symbolise their cleansing by God, in order to give them a new life.

Anabaptists retreated from society on the grounds that it was sinful and corrupt. Men were discouraged from becoming politicians and magistrates, and were pacifists, believing in the shunning of non-believers, and the simple life. They sought to create a utopian community.

Quakers

The Quakers were founded by George Fox during the 17th century. Their worship stressed meditation and the freedom of all to take part in the service called a 'meeting', held in a meeting house. They have no priests or ministers.

The name 'Quakers' may originate from Fox's demand for members to 'quake at the word of the Lord'. At meetings members would literally quake. They were easily identified by the sobriety of their dress and their use of "thee" and "thou' as a sign of equality.

Salvation Army

The Salvation Army is an evangelical social service and social reform organization, founded by William Booth in London. It was originally called the Christian Revival Association but was renamed the East London Christian Mission in 1870 and from 1878 has been known as the Salvation Army.

Protestant and Catholic monarchs

Edward VI came to the throne at the age of ten in 1547. He was a fanatical Protestant and an enthusiastic supporter of the Reformation development. It was during his short reign that Thomas Cranmer, Archbishop of Canterbury, issued the first prayer book in English.

After Edward's death in 1553, his half-sister Mary, daughter of Catherine of Aragon, came to the throne. As queen, she ordered the re-instatement of the Church of Rome. Unable to conceive, Mary blamed her inability to ensure the Catholic succession, and her bad fortune, on heretics. As a result of this, nearly three hundred Protestants were burned at the stake, earning her the name 'Bloody Mary'.

Elizabeth I ascended the throne in 1558 and the Church of England was re-established. Elizabeth tried to accommodate both Catholics and Protestants, and eventually the country became more settled, and there was a far more tolerant attitude to freedom of worship.

In 1563 records show that 80 families worshipped in the church at Melbourn. The church plate (silver or pewter dishes used in the Mass) dates from around this time. The chalice and its cover are dated 1562 and inscribed 'FOR THE TOWNE OF MELBOVRN'.

Rules remained strict however, and had to be kept. In 1599 Vicar James Scruby of Melbourn was warned, by the Archdeaconry of Cambridge and Ely, for solemnising a wedding on a Sunday.

On the death of Elizabeth in 1603, James VI of Scotland became James I of England and, thus, the first 'King of Great Britain'. He survived the

The 16th century chalice with the inscription FOR THE TOWNE OF MELBOVRN

The church and the Old Elm Tree, painted by RB Harraden

Gunpowder Plot of 5th November 1605, when Roman Catholics tried to blow up the Houses of Parliament.

In 1611 he introduced the new version of the Bible, known as the King James Bible, which was to remain in use for the next four centuries. The vicar at Melbourn during this time was Andrew Marvell (grandfather of the poet). In 1615 two bells were recast and the following year another bell was installed. In 1619 the Chapel of the de Argentines was removed. The Chapel of St. Mary (Lady Chapel), in the south aisle, was the Chapel of the Ayloffes.

A time of discontent

The accession of Charles I heralded a period of unrest. Charles dissolved Parliament because they refused him supplies and obstructed his right to tax 'his people'. For eleven years (the 'Eleven Years' Tyranny') he managed to rule alone, reviving old medieval taxes, that most people had forgotten, in order to raise his revenues.

Around 1638 a new wave of a simpler form of worship, was moving through the country. Some of the congregation in Melbourn refused to stand for the benediction/doxology (a blessing or short hymn) or refused to kneel. Puritanism had become very strong in this part of the country. The population was unhappy with the Catholic leanings of Charles I and infuriated by his constant demands for money.

The Civil War

Following the introduction of the 'Ship Tax' in 1640 unrest swept through the country and eventually led to the outbreak of the Civil War in 1642, led by Puritan Oliver Cromwell. Parliament sent a Commission to enquire into the work and activities of the parsons, who were required to make a declaration of loyalty to the Puritan cause. The vicar of Melbourn, Francis Durham, was deprived of his living ('the living' is a term used for his accommodation and assets) but allowed one third of his stipend (salary). Any vicar with 4 children was allowed to keep the vicarage and part of the benefice. In 1644 William Dowsing arrived in Melbourn with orders from the government, and assisted by Benjamin Metcalfe the churchwarden, removed and destroyed the picture of Christ over the altar, tore up the altar rails and smashed the glass windows and carved statues within the niches. William Dowsing later recorded that ...*March 14, ordered 60 superstitious pictures, one of Christ, a cross on the steeple, and the steps to be taken away by William Browne, the Parson.*

William Browne was not the Vicar of Melbourn, but he was either in agreement with Dowsing's actions, or afraid of the consequences of failing to agree.

During the Civil War, the church in Melbourn was in the hands of the Independents, although some families withdrew and formed a sect of their own, called the Anabaptists. In 1654 the families of Metcalfe, Gray, Huggins, and Briarley were entered in the church register as Anabaptists. This group, numbering about 20, met in Benjamin Metcalfe's farmhouse and, from 1660 onwards, was subject to persecution. They were looked upon as stiff-necked, troublesome disturbers of the Commonwealth, and enemies to sound doctrine.

Further persecution

John Bunyan, the Bedfordshire travelling tinker and Baptist preacher, visited Melbourn and preached on the village Green. He was later reported by a Melbourn man for unlicensed preaching, which brought about his imprisonment. It was in prison that he wrote Pilgrim's Progress.

Churchwardens in Melbourn were brought to task for not reporting people who did not attend church or did not take the sacrament, and in the same way the government set up an elaborate network of spies in almost every town. It was through them that the Rev. Joseph Oddy, fellow of Trinity College, was imprisoned in Cambridge Castle for his non-conformity.

The Rectors and Vicars of Melbourn

1229 Master John of Foxton	1582 James Scrubie
After 1250 a Vicarage	1607 Andrew Marvell MA
1305 George (Vicar)	1616 Nathl Padgett MA
1322 J de Haverelle (Vicar)	1617 Ralph Reniger MA
1356 Giles Attewell Exchange	1620 Ambrose Congham
Richard Suse	1634 Francis Durham
John Stocton & Jn Paynell	1656 Mr Cocket
1364 Will Brown	1661 Stephen Norton
1368 Geoffrey Lisse	1668 Thos Day MA
1376 Jn Wesenham	1696 Edward Griffiths BA
1384 Nicholas Blundell	1700 Will Leach BA
1385 John Ffynch	1716 Will Smeeton BA
1385 John de Langport	1722 Hy Roger MA
1395 Tho's Bolton	1755 T. W. Oldfield
1406 Oliver Shelton	1772 Robins Ellis MA
1427 Robt Bradeway	1786 Thos Heckford MA
1463 Stephen Aleyn alias Reynew	1817 J Brocklebank MA
1487 Will Towne	1824 P C W Seymour
1489 John Dobson	1833 Jonathon Trebeck MA
1505 Henry Wright (Vicar)	1846 Wm Selwyn MA
1520 Hugh Vaughan	1853 C F G Jenyns MA
1535 John Cheswright (Vicar)	1874 Jas Hamilton MA
1535 Oliver Fflynte	1911 M de Coucy Ireland MA
1544 Edmund Humphrey	1922 H H H McNiece MA
1581 Thos Pearne	1952 H A Lloyd Jukes MA

Francis Holcroft 1633-1692

Francis Holcroft was the first founder of churches run on congregational principles. The words 'Apostle of Cambridgeshire' are engraved on his tombstone.

In 1655 he accepted the 'living' at Bassingbourn, where he led the church on congregational lines, but lost it after the Restoration in 1660. He was officially silenced in 1662 under 'The Act of Uniformity' and in 1663, was imprisoned in Cambridge Castle for preaching at Great Eversden. He was then sentenced to leave the country by exile or to suffer death as a felon. A friendly gaoler let him out to preach in the woods surrounding the villages. He established thirty churches in south Cambridgeshire alone, even though most of the time he and Joseph Oddy were in prison.

In 1660 the Puritan parson, John Cockett, was forced to leave and Francis Durham, the former vicar, returned to Melbourn. The church was in a sad state of disrepair at this time and remained so for many years. In 1685 the windows were still without glass and the seats broken. Puritans lost their power and influence and so carried out their services in secrecy. In 1663 Francis Holcroft was indicted and imprisoned in Cambridge for preaching as a Congregationalist.

For several years the Independents were persecuted. Some inhabitants of Melbourn were convicted at Cambridge Assizes for not taking the sacrament; amongst them Benjamin Metcalfe's widow. Charles Turner, William Cann, William Robinson, Benjamin Hornold, Thomas Cann and the widow Hitch were also convicted. In 1665 ten people all owed £10 for not attending church. By 1671, Metcalfe's widow and the churchwarden, Timothy Cann, each owed £60 in fines, but Cann still remained the churchwarden for several more years!

In 1672 the 'Act of Indulgence' was passed, giving freedom of Worship, and Rev. Oddy was released from prison. From then on, Oddy and fellow Nonconformists went round the county at night to cottages, barns and woods teaching what they considered to be a purer religion. Despite the Declaration of Indulgence, dissenters were still considered troublemakers. The Bishop of Ely confessed that, out of a population of 240, there were 22 obstinate Dissenters in Melbourn. The Act of Indulgence was withdrawn and once again, the Puritans went underground. The following year there were 26 Nonconformists over the age of 16, and by 1679, twelve families were Congregationalists.

Francis Holcroft was arrested again and sentenced in 1681, for a year, and Rev. Oddy was ejected from his post at Trinity College, and settled in Meldreth.

The coming of stabilisation

James II became King in 1685. He was a Catholic and attempted to fill Parliament, and the army, with his supporters, but the country was not prepared to accept more religious persecution and the unrest led to the 'Glorious Revolution'. In 1688 the Protestant William of Orange and his wife Mary

Church School

William Ayloffe of The Bury left money in 1691, to provide a free school for ...*40 Boys of Melbourne & Meldreth*. The master was paid £15 annually. The Parish Clerk gave instruction on 2 evenings a week. The boys, who had to be members of the Church of England were to be taught to read, write and to answer questions on the Catechism. The schoolmaster was to be chosen by the Minister and the Churchwardens of both parishes. The school was held in the Parvis Room over the church porch and functioned for over 100 years.

In the early 1700s, constant demands were made on the parish for money to pay Briefs (collections started by authority for the relief of individuals or villages who had suffered severe losses). These were either collected countrywide or in certain dioceses. In 1730 there was a Brief totalling £6,869 for loss by fire, which occurred in Melbourn on 24th August 1728.

And as far as concerning the rests and residues of the said rents and profits of the said two parts of the said Rectory and premises over and above what shall pay the said £40 per annum before mentioned, the Parish trustees shall hold the said funds and after the decease of the said Wm Ayloffe upon the trusts following (that is to say) upon trusts they shall and will allow and pay yearly to the persons who shall be in charge – masters of Melbourn in the said County of Cambridge and his successors yearly for ever by half yearly payments after the receipts of the rents of the said Rectory £15 per annum and upon the consideration and intent that the said school master and his successors who are to enjoy the said £15 per annum will take upon him and them the mastership of a free school to be held at Melbourn aforsaid, and will there reside and instruct 40 children of the poorer sort of the Parishes of Melbourn and Meldreth being Protestants and the children of Protestants of the Church of England as it is by law established (and no other) until they can presently read English and write a plain and legible hand, and also make answers to questions of the Catechisms of the Church of England contained in the liturgy as established by law so that they may be able to make a ready distinct answer to the questions in the same in the presence of the Congregation when it shall be required of the Ministers of the Parishes aforsaid and the Trustees before mentioned shall from time to time make choice of a fit and discreet and sober : of good conversation to be Governor and Master of the said school upon the recommendation of the Ministers and Church Wardens of the said Parishes or otherwise according to their judgements of it should happen that said school master should be careless or negligent, or in any way scandalous or guilty of any crime which may be of bad example to make him unfit for the government of youths then the said school master shall be removed by the Trustees who shall place a fit person in his rooms.

The will of William Ayloffe, a great benefactor to the village

The Old Independent Chapel

(James's daughter) landed in England with an army and promised to defend the liberty of England and the Protestant religion. He marched, unopposed, on London and James fled to France. The 'Act of Settlement' in 1701, ensured that no future British Monarch would be a Catholic or marry a Catholic.

In 1689 the passing of the 'Toleration Act' allowed Nonconformist worshippers in Melbourn and Meldreth to establish a Meeting Place, together with members from Chishill.

The Congregational Ministry transferred from Meldreth to Melbourn in 1694, incorporating Bassingbourn and Great Chishill, and the first minister was John Nicholls, a strict Calvinist. He held the Ministry for over 40 years, until 1735.

The Congregational Chapel

In 1715 John Nicholls, the first pastor in Melbourn, led 400 Congregationalists. The following year, they purchased land at the top of Meeting Lane, which became the site of the first Congregational Chapel. A year later, the present Meeting House was built, originally constructed on an almost square plan. It was enlarged at the southern end before 1815, and at the northern end in 1830. It was built from local brick, with a slate roof surmounted by a low glazed cupola.

The Rev. Richard Cooper (1745–89). The south front has two doorways, and the interior has a continuous gallery, with a panelled front, supported on wooden columns. The graveyard surrounding the church, was acquired in 1789, with money left by one of the earliest ministers,

By 1728, half the population of Melbourn were either Presbyterians or Anabaptists. In 1730 a Scot, the Rev. James Watson, was appointed to the Congregational Chapel, but after 15 years service, it was reported that the members were dissatisfied with him and wished for his removal.

The interior of the Old Independent Chapel and the Parliament Clock of 1797 (centre). Following Pitt's Clock Tax, all clocks were taxed, so cheap clocks were made of the roughest materials to try to evade it.

The Old Independent Chapel

A magnificent new building

Rev. Carver was followed in 1825, by Rev. John Medway, minister until 1841 when Rev. Andrew Curr Wright took over. He lived in the Manse, which was then in New Road. During his ministry, a new chapel was built opposite the old Meeting House in Orchard Road, and the old building was then used as a Sunday school. The Congregational church flourished in Melbourn during the latter half of the 19th century. Whole families of dissenting households, and all the pupils of the two boarding schools in the village, would attend morning service.

Rev. Watson remained in the area, with a living at Great Chishill, and Rev. Richard Cooper took over at Melbourn. During his ministry (1745–1789), the Congregational members numbered 120, while in 1740 the Baptist Chapel had just 24 members.

One of the most renowned ministers of the Congregational Chapel, Rev. William Carver, became pastor in 1791 and remained for 34 years. He revived the fortunes of the church to such an extent that the building was enlarged, and in 1819 the Meeting House accommodated 800 people.

Rev. William Carver kept a boarding school for Nonconformist students and lessons were held in the barns connected to his house. The boys from the school attended the chapel, sitting in the gallery at the north end of the main building.

Independent Ministers
(Initially Chishill and Melbourn)

Rev. John Nicholls – retired 1735, died 1740
No pastor between 1735 and 1741
Rev. James Watson
Rev. Richard Cooper 1745–1789
Rev. G Scraggs 1789–1790
Rev. William Carver 1792–1824
Rev. John Medway 1824–1841
Rev. Andrew Wright 1841–1872
Rev. Burgess Wilkinson 1874–1888
Rev. Porter Chapple 1888–1913
Rev. William Wrigley 1914–1916
Rev. Jesse Davis 1917–1945
Rev. Stanley Hodges 1946–

The New Congregational Chapel, Orchard Road

The New Congregational Chapel, Orchard Road

The organ inside the New Congregational Chapel, Orchard Road

New Independent Meeting House

The memorial stone of this handsome structure was laid, in the presence of a large concourse of people, by Samuel Morley, Esq., of London. The proceedings in connexion with the event were very interesting: we refer our readers, for a report of the same to the Cambridge Independent Press. The cost of the building altogether will be £2000; through the untiring energy of the pastor, The Rev. AC Wright, the greater part of the money has been collected – a sum however of £600 is still required. The building, now being erected by Luke Gimson of Royston, is expected to be finished by next August.

Royston Crow 23rd March 1865

This imposing building remained in use until the mid-20th century, when it was demolished and the old Meeting House was used again.

The Baptist Chapel

The Dissenters, who had broken away from the Congregationalists under the banner of 'Anabaptists', continued to worship under great difficulties. William Medcalfe's farmhouse was finally

The Reverend and Mrs Grant outside the Baptist Manse

licensed in 1689, under the Toleration Act, as a place where the Baptists could freely worship.

The early records of the Baptist church have disappeared, although there is a list of ministers and lay preachers. There was an early building and burial ground situated next to the Red Lion public house in Cambridge Road, opposite Sheepshead Row. The building was demolished in 1937. Land was purchased in Mortlock Street and the present

Beating the Bounds

The Beating the Bounds of the parish was an annual event, and an occasion for much eating and drinking.

The origin of the custom

Before the enclosure of the common fields a ring of common land surrounded the parish and the villages were separated by waste ground. Very often a road ran along this common, and the boundary line would fall down the centre of the road. Where there was no artificial line of division between the common land of two villages, natural objects, such as pollarded tress or ditches, were used as markers. It was very important that the exact boundary line should be remembered, so every year, on Ascension Day, the parish priest, with cross, banners and bell, accompanied by men, women and children, walked in procession (or perambulated, as it was called) along the traditional bounds. At vital points a stop was made and the epistle read. The Town Children (that is, the children brought up at parish expense) had the situation of any particular landmark impressed upon their memory by a beating at that spot – hence the expression 'Beating the bounds'.

Beating the Bounds

'The Parish of Melbourne in the County of Cambridge, (to wit). The Bounds of this Parish were on the 4th day of June 1798 had and taken by the Churchwarden with the Principal and other Inhabitants of the said Parish as follows: Beginning at the Ashen Tree marked or cut with a Cross there on at the Melbourne End of the Bridge leading to Meldreth Town, walking from the Tree to the Mill Mouth up to the Mill Wheel marking the Mill Axel Tree with a cut Cross, taking the whole of the Mill Wheel towards the West End and advancing thro' the Mill on the West side of the River. Along the river Bank thro' The Bury mead unto the Hedghe parting the Mowed mead from the pasture, taking in the Motes on the Left, digging a Cross in the Sweard opposite The Bury Orchard, likewise another Cross a little further on the same Bank. Proceeding to The Bury Horse Pond, marking a cross on a small tree growing in the Hedge opposite the Pond, and going through the Pond under the Cartshed. Then between The Bury House and the Hen House leaving the Garden on the left hand and the Pound on the Right. Then cutting a Cross on a Timber Ash Tree growing in Mr Fordham's Hedge next the Lane. Crossing over the Hedge and the Road to the opposite side along the Bank towards Bury Rookery corner where a cross is cut on the Sweard. Proceeding up Ashwell Street along the Bank on Meldreth side as far as Kneesworth Bars, making a cross on the Corner of Bull Field, and another on the Sweard on White Hill opposite a long row of Bushes in Kneesworth field and another Cross a little below Kneesworth Bars. Proceeding straight up through one furlong at the end of the Furlong, straight up a Balk called Bonny Hill. At the further end of the same Balk is dug a Cross near to a Bush growing on the same Balk towards the Kneesworth side.

Then turning a little on the Right Hand up a Headland Piece. Then on the Left down a Headland. One Furlong along Kneesworth Joint; going up a Headland on the left, then another Headland on the Right to a Baulk making another Cross on the Sweard and going up to the Windmill leaving the Millon the left side. Then along the Miller's Path to Mr Beldam's Enclosures, going between the Park and the High Road as far as the Corner of Mr Lewer's close crossing the Road up and along the Bank as far as the Royston Towns End where another Cross is made at the corner of a field on the Sweard.

Then crossing the New Turn Pike Road going along the Bank up to Mr Wortham's Enclosure, called Great Burlows, making near the Gate Way at the bottom a Cross, and on the lower most corner of Little Burlows another Cross on the Swerard. Advancing towards the Folley House, digging several crosses on the Ends of the Baulks and Lands of the Common field which belong to the Parish of Barley. And making two more crosses about one Furlong distance, the lower Cross being at Waterdrain next to the Folley, Crossing to the outside of Waterdrain along Waldon Way to Picking Cross Way leaving the Folly on the left and Barley Field on the Right making Four Crosses, one of which is at the Corner of Barley Gravel Pits. Another Cross one Furlong further, another one Furlong further, another Cross one furlong still further and another at Picking Cross Way.

Then advancing towards Melbourne as far as Warerdraine making a Cross at the corner thereof by the side of the Baulk in little Chishall fields. Then proceeding as far as the New Bridge along Waterdraine upon the other Bank making a Cross near the Bridge on the Chissall side. Then proceeding to Branditch taking in Waterdraine making two crosses on the Foulmire side of Branditch near the Arch; one cross of each side of the Bournbridge Road. Then proceeding down Branditch as far as the Moore, taking in all the Ditch, digging a Cross where the Road from Melbourne crosses Branditch along Pottersway. Then another Cross at the Bottom of Branditch next the Moore opposite the Spring Head.

Then from the Spring Head towards Foulmire Mill along Melbourne side of the Bank crossing the water which leads from Read Well adjoining the Springs. Proceeding along the Bank as far as Foulmire Mill on the Melbourne side cutting a Cross on the West Corner of the Mill, turning short on the Left crossing the Ford down Dunsbridge Riddey to Dunsbridge Turnpike, cutting a Cross on a post of the Turnpike Gate.

Then over the Garden and Hedge along the Inner side of Dunsbridge Riddey to the bottom of Hollow Lands where a Cross is cut near Dunsbridge Riddey on the Moore going along the ditch which leads to some Willow Trees at the bottom of Hollow Sands. Along the Moore at the Bottom of Hollow as far as Hollow Baulk where a Cross is cut. Crossing the Moore to Common Downe then along the Bottom of Downe to Scollops Willows crossing the Riddey going along the Bank on Melbourne side as far as Mr Fisher's Osseys leading under the Hedge thereof upon the Right hand to Inclosures belonging to the Corporation of Chard, in the Tenure of Mr Stallabrass. Going up a ditch which divides Chard's Inclosures from Fisher's Inclosures up to the River. Then going along the River Bank Melbourne side as far as the Mill Bridge to the Ashen Tree where the Bounds were first taken.'

('Sweard' or 'sward' – a term for grass 'Osseys' are osiers i.e. young willows)

The beaters started from what is now known as Ward's Mill. Some of the village officials in 1798 were; John Hitch junr, Churchwarden, Thomas Newling and James Faircloth, Overseers; Jonathan Ellis, Constable; James Day, Pinder, and James Carter, Herdsman.

P.R. Salmon

Herts and Cambs Reporter 22 August 1932

This account of the event traces out the boundary of the parish as it was in 1798, The peculiar spelling, with capital letters, and without punctuation, is exactly as it was written then.

Baptist church was built in 1856. On 21st October a
...*neat and commodious chapel* was opened, with large
congregations attending mornings, afternoons and
evenings. England's best known Baptist preacher,
for most of the 19th century, was the charismatic
Rev. Spurgeon who visited Melbourn annually and
commanded vast congregations.

The Baptist Chapel

Melbourn Church-Rates

Sir. The Rev. A.C. Wright was preaching at the
Baptist Chapel on the evening of the day
mentioned by your correspondent. I was the
only constable present at the service, and I
attended as a hearer, and not in my official
capacity as constable. All present were quiet and
orderly until about the middle of the sermon,
when some of the congregation were much
annoyed by the fumes of tobacco smoke, upon
which some one who was sitting near informed
me of it. I immediately went out and found a
young man walking from the door with a
lighted cigar; I then stationed myself at the gate,
when about 20 others came up, several of them
having cigars. Some of those attempted to enter,
evidently for the purpose of disturbing the
congregaton, but I prevented them, and kept my
station at the gate until the service was
concluded. This I did of my own accord, and
acted on this, as on other occasions, quite
gratuitously, and am quite ready to do as much
for our Church friends, in proctecting them
from being annoyed or interrupted in their
worship.

James Wright,
Constable of Melbourn

Cambridge Chronicle 9th September 1848

The Rev. CH Spurgeon made his annual visit to
Melbourn and preached two most eloquent and
impressive sermons, in aid of the Baptist cause.
Preparations were made to accommodate 10,000
persons to hear the Rev. gentleman, and tea was
provided for 1,200. Owing to the unsettled state of
the weather, not more than 600 partook of tea, and
the evening congregation did not exceed 6,000
persons. The collections amounted to no more than
£181. On the following day, the bountiful supply of
provisions which had been left over, were taken off
the hands of the committee by J Mortlock, Esq.,
with which the children of the Infant School,
numbering about 140, were plentifully regaled. It is
impossible to speak in too high terms of this
gentleman's well known generosity to the poor, and
his extreme liberality to the cause of God in this
place".

Cambridge Chronicle 10th July 1858

A star performer

This popular preacher (the Rev. CH Spurgeon) will preach two sermons at Melbourn on July 2nd and collections will be made on behalf of the Baptist Chapel building fund. It is stated that arrangements have been made which will enable 10,000 persons to hear the preacher. Tea for 1,000 persons will be provided between the services.

Cambridge Chronicle 12th June 1858

Bunfights, concerts and festivals

During Queen Victoria's reign there was a lot of social activity in the village organised by the three churches. Sunday School treats and outings, concerts, lectures, picnics and magic lantern shows were all well-attended events in the village.

On 14th July 1859 three hundred children marched in procession to a large barn at Sheen Farm which had been lent by William Flitten. They

Baptist ministers

Benjamin Metcalfe 1675–89	Joseph Edes* 1727–64	George Wright 1875–77
John Lacy 1689–1711	Benjamin Barron* 1740–41	William Higgins 1877 –92
Solomon Hook*	Tomas Barron (Asst) 1757–64	Richard Wlbert *(?Wilbert?)*
Thomas Clack*	Tomas Barron 1764–1817	Belsham 1894–1905
Lewis Audley*	Christopher Payn (Asst) 1772–91	John Hugh Grant 1905–16
John Catlin* 1711–20	William Pepper 1818–34	William Rands Foster 1916–26
Michael Harding*	James Flood 1835–57	John Witter Appleby 1928–33
Simon Martin*	Ebeneezer Bailey 1858–61	Arthur George Brambleby 1934–36
John Cotlin* 1720–23	James Wimsett Boulding 1861–62	Neville Usher 1937–1948
Charles Hopgood* 1720–33	J Hibbert 1862–63	John Ivor Wensley 1949–
Scarlet Moody* 1720–36	Henry Wardley 1863–74	

*denotes served the four churches in Joint Leadership: Royston, Therfield, Hauxton and Melbourn

played *...several innocent games for two or three hours*. At 5 o'clock, a public tea was provided in the barn at a cost of ls each, when 400 sat down to tea ~ after which there were several addresses by Rev. John Medway and other ministers. In the same year, All Saints' Sunday School treat was held on the 21st July, when children were entertained to dinner and tea by Rev. F G Jenyns on the vicarage lawn.

On l7th June 1859, Melbourn church choir gave a concert of 27 pieces, varying from sacred to madrigals, glees and part songs. It was noted, at the time that the performance was *...admirable with spirit and expression, the intonation remarkably good and the time excellent. We noticed a slight degree of unsteadiness in a bar*

All Saints' Sunday School treat, on the left, Reverend Hamilton

or two of the opening movement of Croft's anthem 'Cry Aloud', a little uncertainty in the introduction in the minor of a Motet by Zingarelli and the time of Stevens Glee 'Ye Spotted Snakes' was a shade too fast!

Harvest Festivals in Melbourn were big events in the rural calendar. Many families were dependent on the land for their living and good harvests were celebrated with enthusiasm.

Opportunities for a celebration were never missed, and in July 1879 the Congregational Sunday School Anniversary was held, ...not withstanding the unpropitious state of the weather. It was one of the most successful for many years. The pupils from both the Melbourn and Meldreth schools assembled in the old Chapel, where dinner was served. After dinner the children were taken into two fields, where they enjoyed a variety of 'amusements'. At half past four, they were given a piece of cake and then allowed to resume their play. At half past five, the parents of the children, and a number of friends, had tea together in the old chapel. Shortly after ten, a meeting was held in the new Chapel, where the Rev. Wilkinson made a brief statement on the condition of the school over the year. During the course of this, he said that there was a deficiency of 16s. However, friends who were present spontaneously contributed this amount.

Activities were often rounded off with a homily (an address or mini-sermon), but this did not deter people from attending. There was little other entertainment and it was accepted that you would be seen at these events.

Baptisms

Prayer books of the 16th and 17th century specified that children should be baptised in the first week after birth. Baptism was usually carried out during the first month of life, but in Melbourn, between 1795 and 1830, half of the 800 children baptised were over five months old, and it was not unusual for baptisms to take place at five, ten, or fifteen years of age.

At the Congregational Chapel, the average age of baptism of the 176 children, between 1825 and 1837, was over six months.

There was often a 'season' for baptism and this included family-related children being baptised together. One reason for this seasonal event was that baptism was a semi-social affair and often associated with village festivals. In Melbourn, between 1740 and 1840, the favourite month was July; over a third of all baptisms occurred during this month. Socially this was a good time, falling between harvests, with the right weather for family gatherings from nearby villages and of course, Melbourn Feast was held in July, contributing to the sense of occasion.

Outreach work – Church societies in the community

The Temperance Society, set up nationally in the 1830s, was dedicated to curtailing the consumption of alcohol and soon the churches had societies dedicated to temperance.

Vicar stops the Feast

On the 2nd May 1882 a serious riot took place in Melbourn. William Bone the blacksmith, Walter Stanford, a wheelwright, and Daniel Barnard, a labourer, appeared at Melbourn Petty Sessions charged with breach of the peace. They and some 25 others armed with stones gathered in the street on the night of 2nd May for the 'purpose of disturbing the peace, to the terror of Her Majesty's subjects, and especially of the Rev. James Hamilton, vicar of Melbourn'.

Rev. Hamilton had tried to suppress the traditional Feast, which used to take place on The Green in front of the church over three days. The nature of the Feast had changed. It had spread all over The Green and blocked up adjoining streets and there was 'much drunkenness and unseemly behaviour'. The vicar had wanted the venue moved to the recreation ground at The Moor. Villagers were upset by this and various lewd songs were sung, including this one:

Who stopped the Feast?
I, said the Priest,
I'm a meddlesome beast,
I stopped the Feast.

A mob approached the vicarage. When Rev. Hamilton went out stones were thrown at him. After 10 minutes Mr Hamilton fired a gun into the air. Sergeant Redhouse, who was hiding in the vicarage shrubbery, caught Barnard and Stanford against the Old Elm Tree. The situation eventually calmed down and the ringleaders were bound over not to repeat the offence. The Feast was finally moved to The Moor and the date was set to be the first Thursday in July. An old Melbourn saying decrees that you plant your new potatoes on Good Friday and dig them up for Melbourn Feast!

The Rev. Hamilton and family

WHAT THE PAPERS SAID

Congregational Sunday School teachers, in 1912
Back row, Mr Wing, Mr Chapman, Mr Thurley, Mr Wing,
Mr P Elbourn, Rev. Porter Chapple, Mr A Howard, Mr B Hagger,
Mrs Hagger, Mr B Palmer, Mr Cooper, Mr Loates
Front row, Miss C Ward, Miss F Dandy, Miss E Hagger, Mrs Chapple,
Miss Elbourn, Miss Mulberry, Miss Palmer, Miss L Dandy

A branch of the Band of Hope (a society set up in Edinburgh by John Hope, aimed mainly at children, providing entertainment with a temperance message) was active in the Congregationalist church.

Fifty girl members of the Band of Hope and the Bible Club were entertained to a tea, given at The Bury, in May 1889, and an outing was arranged for 26th July, to Lowestoft.

The following year, the Church of England Temperance Society van visited, and members of the Band of Hope walked alongside it through the village. All those present at the subsequent tea party at The Bury were given an illuminated address and a bun.

Church Missionary Society

On Sunday last, a sermon was preached in the parish church by Rev. Professor Selwyn, in behalf of the above society. On the following (Monday) evening a public meeting in aid of the same society, was held in the Infants' school-room, when the Rev. FG Jenyns, Vicar, presided. After making a few introductory observations on the objects of the meeting, the chairman said he hoped there would be a good collection that evening; there was one spot in this parish where the interest taken in the poor heathen was, he thought, worthy of notice, viz., in that very room by the school children. He (the speaker) supplied them every year with a missionary box, and some time ago one of the children came to him and said, 'Please sir, can you let us have another missionary box for this one is full,' (applause): he supplied them with another, and believed that was half-full by this time. He then introduced 'an old friend to the cause,' the Rev. JB Whiting, the secretary to the Parent Society, who gave a very lucid and interesting account of the working of the society, and was listened to with very marked attention for upwards of an hour. The other speakers were the Rev. Professor Selwyn, Rev. ST Gibson, of Cambridge, and the Rev. Russell, of Whaddon. After singing the Doxology the meeting broke up. The proceeds collected at this meeting and after the sermon on Sunday afternoon, amounted to about £10.

Cambridge Chronicle 6th April 1861

WHAT THE PAPERS SAID

The Total Abstinence Society met in the Congregational schoolroom for 'improving lectures'. In 1915, there was a junior branch of the Woman's Christian Temperance Union in operation called 'The Little White Ribboners', a movement which originated in America. Older women members of the village recall how keen they were as children to join this group attracted by the clothes, especially the white shoes and hair ribbons.

Congregations were large in those days, and over 1,000 people attended the Congregational Chapel to hear the Rev. Berry of Islington preach.

Officers of the church were long-serving. Mr Hagger served for 50 years as superintendent of the Sunday School. Mr Wing was a Sunday School teacher for twenty years and when he retired, the congregation was treated to a sermon on 'The Evils of Gambling which is Polluting the Nation'.

Outside the Salvation Army Hall, Dolphin Lane

The churches were becoming increasingly unhappy about the degree of drunkenness in the country, and it was at this time that the Salvation Army came to Melbourn.

In 1888 the Meeting House in Dolphin Lane, used by the Primitive Methodists (one of the many Methodist sects which were united in 1932), was sold to the Salvation Army. With the growth of the Temperance Movement, they quickly established themselves and soon had a large number of followers.

When William Booth (founder of the Salvation Army) died, in September 1912, the Melbourn

Home of the Salvation Army and former Primitive Methodist Chapel, Dolphin Lane

Branch marched in tribute through the village playing 'Promoted to Glory'.

Royal wedding – a treat without a moral lesson

In July 1893, the Duke of York (later to become George V) married Princess May of Teck, and the parish church bells were rung in celebration. Seventy, aged, poor widows were given tea at the Vicarage, and the old men were provided with tobacco and given permission to smoke. The vicar called for three cheers for the bridal pair.

An evangelical celebration

The Congregationalists and Baptists celebrated the Dissenters' Bicentenary jointly, with full evangelical zeal in 1899. Alterations to the gallery of the Congregational Chapel were made (it was too small for the choir) the organ was repaired and the ceiling painted.

The 1899 Bicentenary celebrations

The turn of the century

The new century began badly with a large outbreak of influenza in the village. The Salvation Army captain could be found at all hours, in the houses of the poor administering earthly and spiritual comforts. In March, the Rev. Hamilton ordered the bells to be rung for the end of the Boer War.

The Death of Queen Victoria

In 1901 Queen Victoria died and the village was in mourning. The church flag was at half-mast and the tenor bell was tolled. A Memorial Service was held on February 8th, in the parish church, attended by both 'Church and Dissent', meaning all the churches.

The coronation of the new King, Edward VII, in June 1902, was postponed, as he was suffering from appendicitis, but as a Coronation Tea Party had already been planned, it went ahead on 4th July. Mothers and children attended at 4.30pm, and men at 6.30pm. Disbrey's and Oliver's, the butchers, supplied 250lbs of beef each. Winter's gave 120 loaves, Wood's gave 250 lbs of cake and Hamp's gave 104lbs cake. The coronation finally took place on 15th August.

Deaths and entrances

The Rev. James Hamilton died in 1911, aged 94, having arrived in Melbourn in 1874. He had carried out various restoration works in the church and installed a mechanical bell-ringing system, mainly at his own expense. Except for King Edward's Memorial Service, he conducted no services after 1907. Known as the beast who stopped the Feast, he seems to have weathered the bad feeling of the incident and is buried in the churchyard with his wife and daughter.

Rev. Kermode, who assisted the Rev. Hamilton during his last years, instigated 'Men Only' services in the parish church. He had intended them to be held monthly, but 150 men turned up and asked for more frequent services. The following month 200 men and lads turned up. Mr R Webb was the church organist,

Village vandals

In the parish churchyard of Melbourn, Cambridgeshire, the vicar and churchwardens recently planted a fine avenue of young lime and horse chestnut trees about twelve feet high. On Saturday night last December 23, some unappreciative rustics commenced their Christmas orgies by cutting down the whole avenue, as well as two well grown horse chestnuts in another part of the churchyard. The ruffianly work must have taken some time and, but that the solitary policeman has a beat of some ten miles, would show that the parish is badly protected by him. The population contains a large number of Dissenters, but there is no ill-feeling between them and the Church people, and the whole village is indignant at the wanton outrage the perpetrators of which will fare badly at their hands if they are discovered.

Royston Crow January 1876

Complaints were made to the church council that the trees were obscuring their view of the church clock. For many people in the village, the clock was their only means of accurate time-telling.

Trees obscuring the view of the church clock

Funeral cortege of Mildred Catley who died in May 1928, aged 18

with G Hall, T Huggins and F Wall on violins, W Goss on piccolo and F Greenhill playing the cornet.

There was also a Men's Service Social in the church room at All Saints' which resulted in a packed audience. As smoking was allowed after half-time, Mr T Myers provided ¼oz of tobacco to each man and Mr E Rivers-Smith provided cigars.

The last person to be buried in Melbourn

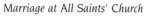

Marriage at All Saints' Church

churchyard was James King, in 1902. The new cemetery, which was to be in Orchard Road, was purchased for £200 and laid out in 1904, for another £200, of which £100 was for the Lych Gate.

King Edward VII died on the 10th May 1910, and was buried on 27th May. In Melbourn all the shops closed, the tenor bell was rung, muffled, and all denominations met at All Saints', with their ministers, for a commemorative service.

A petition was raised in the village, requesting that the Rev. Kermode be appointed as the new vicar, but in April the new incumbent was named as Rev. de Courcy Ireland, formerly vicar of Somersham. Rev. Kermode did not appear to harbour any ill will. He was in the congregation, as Priest in Charge, when the Lord Bishop of Ely

Procession to All Saints' Church

inducted Rev. de Courcy Ireland. Rev. Kermode later moved to Moggerhanger, near Bedford. Plans went ahead to celebrate the Coronation of King George V in 1911. These consisted of a cricket match, a procession of decorated cycles and prams, tea in Mr Newlyn's barn, sports in Spencer's meadows, distribution of prizes, fireworks and a bonfire on the Moor. On the day of the Coronation there was a service at 11am, with a special hymn composed by Rev. Kermode. Music in the evening was provided by the Melbourn String Band. Mr Hope, of the Riverside Laundry, installed a photograph of the King, with a waterfall effect, and GR was spelled out in electric light bulbs on The Green.

Entrance to the cemetery in Orchard Road

Donations and restorations at All Saints'

In April 1912, a collection was taken for the Titanic Fund and £6 0s 0d was raised. The cost of restoring the church tower, and re-hanging the bells, was estimated at £200. Fund-raising efforts were boosted, with £97 being collected at an August Fete and Sale of Work, but it was agreed not to start work until another £100 was raised.

At a special Vestry meeting, in March the following year, Ralph Webb, who was the church organist at the time, wanted the organ restored, but it was decided to order a new organ from Alfred Kirkland & Bryceson Bros. of Upper Holloway, London, at a cost of £430. The work was to be completed by 28th July. A generous donation of £215 was made by Andrew Carnegie, the philanthropist, and Mr Meyer gave £50.

The organ was installed and dedicated as planned, but with a deficit of £40 in the fund. Further restoration plans were outlined. The repairs to the

tower were to be carried out by Robert Wade of Doddington, near March, at a cost of £260. Bowells of Ipswich were to re-hang the bells for £140. They were in fact, hung on a steel frame, at a cost of £175! In June, the bells were removed from the tower and taken for repair by Percy Elbourn, transported on his steam lorry to the bell founders at Ipswich. Many villagers came to look at the bells as they lay in the churchyard. After all the restoration was complete, a service was held by The Bishop of Ely, and a new treble bell was dedicated. *'The Church Bells of Cambridgeshire'*, by the Rev. JJ Raven, says of Melbourn *...The Tenor is a magnificent bell.*

Ralph Webb, the organist at All Saints' Church

Dedication & Opening of the New Organ

All Saints' Melbourn

Tuesday July 22nd 1913

Two Manual Organ built by Messrs A. Kirkland & Bryceson Bros Upper Holloway, London and Wakefield

Price £430, of which Mr Andrew Carnegie has granted £215.

The organ in All Saints' Church was the last donated by Andrew Carnegie.

No excuse for lateness

Whilst the scaffolding was in place, a new clock mechanism was installed although the old dial was re-used. The new clock, from Thwaites & Reed of Clerkenwell, was started at 8pm on 25th November.

The Great War

On 9th January 1914, prayers for world peace were offered in the parish church. Britain and France declared war on Germany on 12th August, and many young Melbourn lads found themselves in uniform, travelling further afield than they would ever have thought possible.

The inscriptions on the church bells are:

1 Jesus be Our Spede 1615 R.O.
2 God Save the King 1615 R.O.
3 Praise the Lord 1616
  (generally ascribed to James Keene)
4 John Briant, Hartford, fecit 1789
5 Richard Chandler made me 1688
6 Cast by Bowell 1912

During the course of the war, all three churches played an important role in giving comfort and hope to their congregations, as the news came through of more and more dead, wounded and missing soldiers. Ladies held sewing meetings to make articles for the troops, the Salvation Army played on

Below, the Rev. de Courcy-Ireland outside the church with the re-cast bells and right, delivery in Station Road

The Green and the Rev. Kermode returned to the village to conduct services. Rev. de Courcy Ireland presided over a meeting to decide on what support should be given to Belgian refugees. It was agreed that two families should be installed in a house provided by Mr Hope of the Steam Laundry. Parishioners worked together to furnish and provision it. Later, in April 1915, Snow Fordham, from Melbourn, a west London magistrate, in a discussion on drunken behaviour of Belgian refugees, said that he had … *nothing but praise for the Belgian people as a whole … in my own village we have some refugees and their conduct is perfectly satisfactory – they give no trouble whatsoever.*

The first peal of 5040 changes was rung by the Ely Diocese Association of Bell Ringers, the bell

The establishment - Church and religion   **151**

Restoration to the West Tower and clock

The proceeds of a summer fete, in 1922, paid for the installation of radiators in All Saints', at a cost of £240. The Rev. McNeice became vicar of Melbourn and was to remain at the vicarage until the 1950s. (The poet, Louis McNeice, was his nephew.)

In 1923 the Melbourn church choir performed at the Ely Diocese choir festival, at Kings College, Cambridge. The journey was made with their friends by charabanc and, after the festival, they all had tea at the Dorothy Café.

In July 1926, E Chamberlain, T Prior, H Stanford and M Stockbridge the four choristers at All Saints' were presented with 'perseverance badges' by the vicar.

A banner for the Girls' Friendly Society was dedicated in church in April 1927 and still hangs there. There was much discussion at the Annual Parochial Church Meeting over the proposed new 1928 Prayer Book, rejected by the House of Commons in December.

Restoration continues

A new wooden screen was erected, in 1934, at the tower end of the aisle, dedicated in memory of Harry & Marianne Cranfield, who had kept the Post Office. It was the gift of their son HP Cranfield. The carving was carried out by Gus Hale.

In September 1934, a bible from Melbourn was found in Australia. The inscription read 'Ann Baker, a reward for early attendance at Melbourn Independent Sunday School, 19th May, 1833.' Ann Baker was then living in Water Lane, and it was said that she gave her bible to her sister when she emigrated. At that time it was announced that the parish church seated 400, the Congregational Chapel 800 and the Baptist Chapel 625.

The death of George V

On 20th January 1936, King George V died and the Prince of Wales was declared King Edward VIII. After

Screen to tower vestry, in memory of the Cranfields

his abdication in December, his brother, Prince Albert, was declared King George VI.

Various suggestions were made to mark the Coronation and a committee was formed to organise a carnival procession, together with sports events, children's tea, public whist drive and a dance. The day began with a united service in All Saints'. Afterwards there was a surplus of £12, enough to buy each child a mug with money left over to donate to the Local Nursing Association. The 200 Coronation mugs were presented on 1st October, 1937.

Inside All Saints' a brass plaque was unveiled in memory of Miss Gertrude Stone (a faithful church

chamber having been lined with matchwood to deaden the noise in the ringing chamber.

On Armistice Day, in 1918, the bells were rung and the flags put out, with the flag of St. George flying from the church tower.

Sadly, on this same day came the news of the death of Pioneer ER Abrey of the Royal Engineers, whose parents lived in Dolphin Lane.

A coronation mug presented to each child in the village on 1st October, 1937

member), situated above the pew where she normally sat, and an oak panel was installed bearing the names of all the vicars who had served Melbourn since 1229.

Second World War

With the threat of air attacks during 1939–45, Melbourn was subjected to blackout restrictions, gas masks, ration books and lack of street lighting.

In 1940 the Feast returned, but only to be held on two days and finishing at 10pm. The following year

A model of the Parish Church made from cardboard, matchsticks and glue by Eric Chamberlain

WHAT THE PAPERS SAID

End of the war

In 1945, with the church bells ringing for victory, it was time to assess once again the numbers of young men who would not be returning to Melbourn and whose names would be added to the 1914-18 lists on the War Memorial. It was announced that the Vicar's son, Patrick McNeice, was to be vicar of St. John's in Romford and the following year Rev. J.G. Davis retired from the Congregational church.

The Reverends McNeice, father and son

it was not held at all, but housewives still offered the traditional home-made wine and cakes.

In December, the church clock attendant, William Gouldthorpe, asked for a 'Christmas Box' as a reward for attending to the clock and winding it every Saturday. The church clock was reported to be keeping perfect time although, *...it has not had a penny spent on it since it was installed in 1913!*

A total of £115 was subscribed ~ but four years later, in January, the clock stopped because the annual subscriptions had not been paid. It was agreed that the annual 'Christmas Box' should be

scrapped and an annual salary paid, depending on a subscription list. The clock was working again by 28th January, but lack of subscriptions had again stopped the clock in February 1945. and there was talk of a small motor being purchased to wind it up.

In June 1943, a pocket bible was presented to Sidney Waldock when he returned home on leave, to mark his work as superintendent of the Baptist Church Sunday School.

The first GI Bride's wedding was at All Saints' Church on 29th April 1944, when Christina Joyce Reed, of Orchard Road, married Master Sergeant Creighton Romine of Dallas, Texas. Creighton was serving with the 91st Bomb Group at Bassingbourn.

The post-war years were difficult ~ lives had been changed dramatically. The advent of television, and more available transport, meant that the church was no longer the centre of the social life of the village. By the 1950s, church attendances had dropped, although the three churches continued to play important roles in the life of the village, and a vital role in the lives of their congregations.

The first GI Bride's wedding of Christina Reed and Master Sergeant Creighton Romine at All Saints' Church

Education

...education was only open to Church of England worshippers; Nonconformists found their children excluded from the only school in the parish

In common with most other towns and villages during the medieval period, Melbourn almost certainly had only one person who could read and write. This may not necessarily have been the lord of the manor – he may have depended upon the local priest to record details of the manor. The peasantry were not encouraged to learn and indeed, were told that learning was beyond them, a ploy to keep them in their place. Documents were also written in Latin (a language which peasants would have found incomprehensible) using quill pen with ink made from oakgall, the Ink cap mushroom, or a soot mixture.

One way of escaping peasantry and gaining a smattering of education, was to pay a fee to the diocese of Ely and enter the church.

Most who took the 'first tonsure' (head shaving) and became 'acolytes' (apprentices) probably intended to go no further in their studies. This accounts for the many uneducated 'priests' and 'chaplains' appointed during the 14th century.

There was no formal schooling in Melbourn until the late-16th century when it was reported by the Ely Visitation return of 1596, that there was one schoolmaster in Melbourn, one of only 18 in the county.

By 1690 William Ayloffe of Melbourn Bury had given the income from the rectory of Gargrave, in Yorkshire, which was divided between Trinity Hall in Cambridge, the Vicar of Meldreth and the schoolmaster of Melbourn. The latter received £15 a year for teaching poor children from Melbourn and Meldreth. Any residue was to help repair the schoolroom (the parvis room over the church porch) and to buy catechisms, religious manuals, for poor children.

The children of Meldreth were allowed to attend the school as William Ayloffe's grandfather had once owned and lived at Sheen Manor in Meldreth. He had been a Royalist during the Civil War and after the defeat of Charles I was fined for his misplaced allegiance. He had to sell Sheen Manor and took a lease on Melbourn Bury.

Although Ayloffe died in 1691, there was a delay in putting his wishes into action. In 1731 the school was held in the parvis room. In 1767 John Mayne was appointed schoolmaster by the Rev. Oldfield, Thomas Scruby the churchwarden of Melbourn, Rev. Backhouse and William Holden (or Holder) from Meldreth. He was still paid only £15 a year. By 1783, the endowment was for teaching 40 children.

During the summer months the school days began at 8am and finished at 6pm, with a break from 12.30pm to 2.30pm. In winter the day started at 9am and finished at 6.00pm. In 1790 pupils were strictly instructed to 'come with clean hands and face, hair combed and as decently dressed as budget would allow'. Those who arrived late were forced to wear a notice round their necks saying 'naughty'.

Schooling was only available to children of churchgoers; 'dissenters' were strictly barred. Children were accepted at the age of six years, continuing until fourteen. However, because of the demands of the agricultural economy, many boys left at twelve.

In 1804 the falling income from the Trust was still divided into the original proportions. In 1810 a

List showing the figures for the entire Diocese of Ely

	1338	1340	1341	1343/4	1345	1348	1349	1350	1351
Acolytes	283	105	50	188	66	8	0	26	43
Subdeacons	220	100	93	238	107	9	0	32	25
Deacons	217	77	75	20	100	12	0	18	35
Priests	159	108	63	202	108	7	0	12	55

The low figures for the years 1348 and 1349 are due to the plague – The Black Death

Porch and Parvis Room, All Saints' Church, with George Bullen

master was still being paid to teach 20 boys, but the school later fell into temporary disuse, and in 1818 the funds were used to repair the church. The former master was still paid £7 7s 0½d by the charity in 1833. The vicar and trustees re-established the school in 1849, and by 1852 the parish clerk was paid to teach boys at Sunday and evening schools, again in the parvis room.

In 1854 an infant school was built in Church Lane (Mortlock Street) from a government grant and by subscription. Money accumulated by Ayloffe's charity was also given to the new school, on condition that the new building could be used by Ayloffe's school in the evenings and on Sundays.

By 1870 there was no church schoolmaster and the vicar proposed to give a third of the income to Meldreth and two thirds to Melbourn to provide Sunday or night school teaching. In 1879 the new school had space for 122 children and an average attendance of 77. It was closed in 1887 and later used as overflow space by Trigg's Charity School (built 1855), known later as the British Schools.

Because education was only open to Church of England worshippers, Nonconformists found their children excluded from the only school in the parish. (Nonconformists were also excluded from the Universities until well into the 19th century.) In 1791 William Carver, the Pastor of the Independent Chapel, established a boarding school for Nonconformist students. This school had an excellent reputation. In fact the reputation was so good that many Church of England parents sent their children to it!

Infant School in School Lane (Mortlock Street)

Carver's school was situated on the High Street, at Greenbanks, and his land stretched as far as the Newmarket Road. The school accommodated 90 boys, who paid extra for occupation of a single bed.

A great deal of information is known about Carver's school due to one of his pupils, Samuel Morley, who became famous in later life. From his biography, written in 1881, Samuel wrote that his family made a fortune in the hosiery business. He became a politician and was active in both the temperance movement and philanthropic works. The family wealth was used to build many Congregational Chapels in England. Morley also fought for equal rights and opportunities, for Nonconformists.

Samuel, and his brother, William came to Carver's school at the age of seven in 1816. John, an older brother, was already a pupil there. Attendance at the village chapel was compulsory, and in his biography Samuel mentions that ...*it was an excellent school in every respect; the best of its kind in the country*. Carver prided himself upon being able to turn out gentlemen as well as scholars, and ...*spared no pains to train the boys in good and useful habits*, Carver's son William, a successful classics tutor, assisted him.

Trigg's Charity

While the Ayloffe School was in abeyance the need for a school was strongly felt and in 1818, John Trigg, the lessee of The Bury, left in his will the sum of £2,777 18s 10d in trust, to found a non-denominational school in Melbourn. It was to be free, and open to all children living within a 6 mile radius of the village. The school was opened in 1823, and for many years was held in two converted barns in Little Lane, supported by the charity and school pence (each child paid 1d per week to attend). In 1835 the average attendance was 165. The trustees (all dissenters) included Baker, Howard, Fordham and King.

Above, Carver's home and school, and below, barns at one time used as school rooms, High Street

Melbourn New Infant School

The infant school which has lately been erected in this parish, on a site presented by John Mortlock, Esq., was opened on Monday last, when divine service was performed in the church, and a most impressive sermon preached by the Rev. H.V. Elliott, Incumbent of St. Mary's, Brighton, from the text Galatians. VI. 2. 'Bear ye one another's burdens, and so fulfil the law of Christ.' Not withstanding the unfavourable weather, the church was well filled, and a collection made at the doors amounting to £221. 5s. 11d. After the service many of the congregation proceeded to the School, which is a spacious stone building, where a prayer was offered up by the Vicar, imploring God's blessing on the undertaking.

Cambridge Chronicle 3rd June 1854

By June 1854 the infant school had been erected on a site donated by John Mortlock. The opening was preceded by a service in the Parish Church.

Church Lane, where the two schools stood, was eventually renamed Mortlock Street, in recognition of Mr Mortlock's generous gift of land.

This second school was known as the 'British Schools' and owed allegiance to the British and Foreign Schools Society, founded to provide non-denominational education. It was administered by a Board of Managers and Trustees.

Attendance was voluntary and fluctuating and the results were less than satisfactory. The income from the trust was also insufficient to pay a suitable salary, so in 1865, Mr Fordham of The Bury offered £5 a year towards a salary for the headmaster, providing the other Trustees would do the same. Mr Few was appointed at £60 a year, plus the 1d a week from each pupil and slightly more from the children of better off families.

New School at Melbourn

On Monday last, a large number of the inhabitants of Melbourn assembled in the Church lane, at half-past ten o'clock, to witness the ceremony of laying the foundation stone of a building now erecting as Boys' and Girls' Schools, for the Trustees of the late Mr. John Trigg's charity, by Miss Fordham, of Melbourn Bury.

Mr. Nash, the architect, having explained the designs, which had been sanctioned by the Charity Commissioners, and obtained Miss Fordham's approval, requested that she would lay the foundation stone.

Mr. Mortlock, on behalf of the Ladies' Committee, presented her with a handsome silver trowel, requesting her acceptance of it as a memorial of the day, as well as a slight acknowledgement of the thanks which they felt due to Mrs Fordham and herself, for the interest and exertions they had shown in promoting education among the poor of the parish: he also deposited a bottle, containing the names of the present trustees, &c.

Miss Fordham, assisted by the builder, Mr. Wm. French, prepared the bed of mortar, and the stone inscribed;

Trigg's Charity Schools
This stone was laid by
Miss Fordham, of Melbourn Bury,
July 30, 1855

was lowered into its place; and having received three taps from her trowel, was declared duly laid.

Mr. Fordham addressed the company as follows – "Friends and Fellow-parishioners, – Allow me to congratulate you on the event of this day. More than thirty years have passed away since the establishment of a British school in this parish, during which long period many now present, many more who are absent, and some in the distant colony of Australia, have received from it blessings which are beyond all price. Although it has been in some measure superseded by more recent schools in the adjoining parishes, it appears to me to possess advantage over kindred institutions in the neighbourhood, from its unsectarian character, being open to Dissenters and Churchmen alike. Trusting the inhabitants of Melbourn and its neighbourhood will avail themselves to the utmost of all the advantages which this institution is calculated to confer, I again congratulate you on the occasion which has brought us together. In my own name and that of my brother trustees, and, I may say, in that of the parish at large, I beg to tender our grateful acknowledgements to Mr. Mortlock, for his kindness in presenting the site upon which this school is to be erected. In behalf of my daughter, I have to express her thanks for the very handsome and unexpected present she has just received, and, although the doing her duty at the school has been its own reward, she cannot but feel gratified that her labours of love have been so appreciated."

The contractor having been informed that Mr. Fordham had provided a supper for the workmen, at the Rose inn, that evening, (to which we doubt not ample justice was done,) and three cheers for Miss Fordham, and three more for Mr. Mortlock have been given, the meeting separated.

Cambridge Chronicle 4th August 1855

I give impress from this trust to invest the sum of 2,000 pounds in funds or other good and sufficient security of interest. In trust to apply the interests dividends and yearly proceeds thereof towards the education of poor children living in Melbourn and Meldreth aforsaid on six miles between the Parishes of Melbourn...

And my will is that the help of the said Annual Income of the said 2,000 pounds shall be applied to the education of boys and the other half to the education of girls and I request that the children who are to have the benefit of the education hereby provided be the children of the poor who are themselves unable to [send] their children to school...

And it is my will further that as large a number of children may receive the benefits of the premiums as can reasonable be done. And that in the plan of education to be particular attention be paid to the religious and moral improvements of the children and that the benefits of the education shall be confined to persons of the established religion of any particular religious sect, but that the same shall be open to persons of all religious denominations.

Extract from Trigg's Will 6th June 1818

School class photograph from 1898–99

20th century, the building was used in conjunction with the British Schools for older boys and girls.

The masters who followed included: Edmund Kelly (1871-86); A Matthews (1886); J Nowell (1886-1892); W Foote (1892-96); C Warren (1896-1900); W Powell (1900-03); H Harman (1903-18); F Aldridge (1918-27); C Varley (1927–1953).

School class photograph from 1898–99

Brighter pupils, called Monitors, having learned the lessons themselves, instructed the younger, or less able, pupils. Emphasis was on the learning of multiplication tables, which were chanted aloud.

William Pape was headmaster of the infant school (Trigg's) for the first five years. By 1860 his place had been taken by Henry Stringer. Henry, however, was apparently inefficient, and he and the head mistress were both dismissed. He proved to be much more successful at driving a horse and cart round the surrounding villages, selling crockery!

Following Stringer's departure, the school was run by Henry Few and R. Meldrum for a time, although exact dates are not known.

The infant school was closed in 1887, but, as the population of the villages began to rise in the early-

The Infant and British Schools in School Lane (Mortlock Street)

Education Act 1870

The Elementary Education Act of 1870 provided universal education, funded by public money. By 1872 the British Schools were providing education for 42 boys and 51 girls. This had grown to 137 by 1879, and by 1889, after the closure of the church infant school, there were 196 pupils.

However, the Act of 1870 had problems. Records of attendance were to be meticulously maintained and soon cases were being brought against parents who were not sending their children to school. In some instances absenses amounted to hundreds of days. An outstanding example was one Wortham Woods, who in May 1890, was summonsed for not sending his children to school for a total of 206 and 273 times respectively. When challenged, Woods was said to have become abusive and was subsequently fined 5s in each case.

It was difficult for some parents to lose the services of their children, especially at harvest time, when they had always helped in the fields. Young children were used as 'bird scarers' and their elder siblings worked long hours tending animals and loading wagons. The month of August, when the harvest would have been at its peak, remains a school holiday to this day.

George Mead a labourer from Melbourn was summoned by Mr. Wm. J. Webb, School Attendance Officer, for not sending his child Alfred to school. Defendant's wife appeared and stated the child had been suffering from a bad foot and could not get his boot on.

In support of her defence defendant called Martha Chapman, who corroborated. There was also a further summons respecting another child, against the same defendant. The Bench ordered defendant to pay 6d, in the first case and 2s 6d in the second.

Royston Crow 6 April 1900

WHAT THE PAPERS SAID

Inspections

The 1870 Act made provision for school inspectors, and regular visits and reports were made on the school.

The school report for July 1900 made good reading and suggested that ...*Miss Cunnningham has worked with great vigour since taking charge and the attainments have so far improved that they now deserve the highest variable grants*. The Girls' evening school was considered ...*excellent at all points*.

Adults in Melbourn were not deprived of education. A Mechanics Institute began in 1851 and other evening classes followed.

In April 1890 24 youths had attended evening classes during the winter and had been examined on their studies by Mr Bartlett with a satisfactory number of them passing.

From 1890, until 1902, the local press reported

School class photograph from 1905

School class photograph from the early 1900s

regularly on the achievements of Melbourn schools. In May 1890 Her Majesty's Inspectors reported that the British Boys' School had achieved results ...*in advance of previous years*.

As a consequence of the excellent results, in

October 1899, the Governors of the British Schools were awarded an increase in the Fee Grant of £70 13s 9d, the children were granted a half-day holiday, and the schools re-opened free after the harvest holidays.

It was suggested that, because the 1d fee was no longer payable, the money should go into a Penny Savings Bank, to aid children in future. Mr Nowell, the headmaster, was put in charge, and in October, was elected President of Royston District Teachers' Association.

Orphans were not uncommon in the village, and in March 1891, a concert in the schoolrooms raised money for Reedham Orphanage, where several children of the village were being brought up. (Reedham Orphanage was founded in Purley, Surrey, in 1844 by the Rev. Dr. Reed.)

Cambridgeshire County Council embarked on a series of lectures in February 1892 which were

School class photograph from 1911

organised by their Technical Education Department and featured a number of horticultural themes such as 'fruit growing' and 'the cultivation of plants'. A Mutual Improvement Society was also established and, at one lecture in March 1893, its speaker gave a talk on electricity and by using a galvanic battery, the audience were invited to feel what an electric shock felt like!

Other schools

As records of other schools in the village show, private education was also available, during the 19th and early-20th centuries.

In the 1850s a boarding school for girls, at Carlton House, was established by Mr Clear, with Miss Roberts as headmistress. Clear also helped in the setting up of a boys' school at the Beeches (both day and boarding). He appointed as headmaster, a Mr Orris, who had been tutor to his own sons. This school subsequently became a girls' school under the direction of the Misses Wilkerson until the end of the 1800s. At the turn of the 20th century it was led by Fanny Elbourn, who had been a pupil of Miss Roberts, at Carlton House. It remained a school until the 1920s.

A preparatory school, for both boys and girls, was run by the Campkin sisters from about 1860 to the 1880s, Miss Newling set up a Dame School

A girls' boarding school was established at Carlton House in the 1850s

which was held in the Old Church House, beside the Church and Miss Chappell, the daughter of the Congregational Minister, had a school for girls and small boys in the Manse.

In September 1895 Hugh Lupton advertised in the local press that he was opening a school for boys from the age of seven years. He promised preparation for public school, the Navy and

A school for girls and boys was held at Congregational Manse

other openings. Recent successes had gained his pupils' entry to Royal Navy cadetships and two mathematical scholarships to Rugby School.

These schools could only benefit those who could afford the tuition fees.

Sunday Schools

In June 1899 the Congregational Chapel boasted 261 scholars and 21 teachers in its Sunday School. At their annual prize giving, the guest preacher complained that ...*the English do not keep their boys at Sunday School after they have arrived at the age of 20*. In his own country of Wales both children and men at the age of 40 could be seen at school together and that influence alone, he said, had made the Welsh people the most law-abiding in the world.

The Reading Room

This building, which stood in the High Street, was opened in November 1900 donated by Mrs Hampden Fordham of The Bury. It was only available to men and boys over the age of 18 years. The rules were strict and included ...*no gambling, drinking or swearing*. It was open every evening except Sunday from 6.30pm until 10.30pm, and the subscription was 2d per week.

Northall School, only opened for short time

A new Education Act took power away from School Boards and transferred it to the County Council. In November 1903 Henry Pepper, a labourer, took out a summons against Horace Harman, the schoolmaster, for allegedly assaulting his son Joseph, with a cane, in school. The magistrates ruled that Harman was in *loco parentis* (whilst at school the teacher acted as the parent) and the case was dismissed.

By 1903 the British Schools was a council-provided school. Trigg's Charity leased the building to the Council and, under a scheme of 1908, the charity's income (about £65) was spent on prizes, books and scholarships. Attendance at the school declined slowly over the years. In 1914 there were 203 pupils, but numbers gradually fell to 130 by 1938.

Various childhood diseases, life-threatening at the time, frequently caused the school to close. An outbreak of mumps was responsible in 1893, and scarlet fever in 1907. In 1915 German measles closed the school for at least a fortnight.

Sanitary arrangements in the 1890s were primitive; the lavatories were a constant problem and the cost of clearing them appeared regularly in the school's accounts. During periods of heavy rain the 'offices', as the toilets were known, were often flooded and could not be reached. Neither was privacy considered important. In October 1912 the headmaster made an application for one of the 'offices' to be provided with a door for the exclusive use of the staff.

Good progress

Individual pupils often gained excellent results in both local and national examinations. In 1886 Emily Hagger obtained a degree of 'Licentiate of Music' at Trinity College in London. Miss G Hamilton, the niece of the Vicar and a former pupil at Carlton House School, gained a distinction in music at Cambridge University Local Examinations, in 1901. Later, in the same year, she won certificates for proficiency in music at the Royal Academy of Music and the Royal College of Music. In 1904 Mary Kirby was awarded a minor scholarship at the Cambridge and County School for Girls. This included both tuition and railway fees.

The next recorded achievement was in 1929, when Ada Adams and Newell Golding won scholarships to the County Girls' and Boys' Schools respectively, and in the following year nineteen children from the

School class photograph from 1920

Mr Aldridge and Miss Gladys Thompson (Mrs Kaye)

Kath Guiver, Brian Stockbridge, Jack Cooper, Cyril Hagger, Joffe Cooper, Harold Chapman, Alfie Day, Florrie Thompson, Nicky Barnes.

Eva Cooper, Eleanor Winter, Frances Munsey, Elsie Adams (with bow), Gertie Carter, Hilda Catley, Nellie Rumbold, Ivy Chamberlain, Elsie Goss

Audrey Knott, Elsie Dodkin, Ada Catley, May Chappell, Winnie Rumbold, Daisy Oliver, Violet Stanford, Lily Littlechild, Winnie Chamberlain

Bertie Worland, Bill Stanford, ? Rosendale, Leslie Littlechild, ? Worland, Nicky Munsey, Colin Black, Gurney Groves

county schools sat for scholarships. Nine passed high enough to be admitted as fee payers to County Secondary Schools, but Geoffrey Appleby and Kathleen Giffin obtained scholarships. In 1934 Frederick Holland and Mary Taylor won scholarships to the Technical School, and by 1936, Samuel Thurley and Kenneth Webb did the same, enabling them to go to the Boys' County School. Helen Taylor, Freda Harper, John Smith, John Gouldthorpe and Maurice Hart journeyed into Cambridge to attend the Technical School. Bernard Holland, Joyce Martin and Joyce Catley were awarded free scholarships to the Technical College.

School class photograph from 1920

Head Mr Aldridge and Miss Lesley

Fred Winter, Eddie Cooper, Daisy Cooper, Mabel Day, Noel Golding, Lily Littlechild, Joyce Winter, Muriel Cooper.

Stanley Anderson, Phyllis Rumbold, Sid Green, ?, Les Day, Geoff Catley, Ada Adams, Elsie Chapman, Dennis Cooper, ?, Wilfrid Winter, Harry Pollen

Clifford Chamberlain, Peggy Knott, Winnie Marsh, Lily Day, Winnie Ritson, Eileen Chappell, Edna Winter, Vera Prior, Kath Littlechild, Jack Chamberlain, Bill Catley, ? Munsey, Jack Waldock, Douglas Winter, ? Davis

? Clayton, Josie McCracken, Jim Catley, Dorothy or Myrtle Mead, Ivy Taylor, Edie Mead (with board), Sid Hinkins, ?, Jack Chamberlain, Bill Rumbold, Frank Davis, ?.

The Great War 1914-1918

All boys of twelve years and over were required to help on the land during the day and then attend night school in order to catch up with their studies.

In 1915 the pupils collected £1 2s 0d to provide Christmas presents for soldiers at the front. In the following year the sum of 14s 6d was contributed to the Daily News Christmas Pudding Fund for soldiers.

A New Year's Party was held in January 1918 at the Congregational Chapel schoolroom for all children of school age, and resulted in 300 attending. Mothers had to bring a baby to be admitted, and some borrowed one for the occasion! In the same year Horace Harman, having been headmaster for 15 years, announced that he was leaving and ... *was presented with a pair of binoculars and war savings certificates from the juniors and a pipe, pouch and tobacco from the infants.*

The infants received a cheque from the Prince of Wales Fund in 1920, for collecting waste paper and this was immediately sent to St. Dunstan's Home for blinded heroes.

In 1922 a different form of education began in Melbourn, with the advent of the Women's Institute. Some 78 members were enrolled and the first lecture was by a Miss Gaskell on 'Household Jobbery'.

At the sports day of 1929, the school had three houses, namely Wilberforce, Livingstone and Gordon, which competed against each other for honours. The marriage of Mr Ogden (who was to become a long standing member of staff) and Miss Norah Payne was celebrated in the same year, and Elsie Goss, the Head Girl, presented the couple with a handsome adjustable chair.

Complaints were made about bad behaviour of schoolchildren on local transport. Many Melbourn children went to school in Cambridge and the 8am bus became known as the 'bedlam bus', because of the noise and misbehaviour. It was made worse by the rivalry between villages. In 1933 there was however, a truce, following a rumour that a 'spy' from the Council was going to travel on the vehicle and single out troublemakers.

It was a huge leap forward when the school received a 'wireless set' in 1935, especially for those children who had no such luxury in their own homes. Mr Varley was said to have used the set in his history talks, and Mr Ogden for his geography

Two years full attendance medal awarded to Celia Guiver in 1922

School class photograph from 1946

School class photograph from 1925

Mr Bathe and Miss Shanklin

Back row, Gurney Groves, Jack Cooper, Wilfrid Winter, Noel Golding, Eddie Cooper, Cyril Leatson, Charlie Webb

Kath Guiver, Elsie Dodkin, Emma Negus, Eva Cooper, Eleanor Winter, Nancy Hagger, Jessie Pepper, Dorothy Richardson, Elsie Goss, Ada Catley, ?, Ivy Chamberlain, Florrie Thompson.

Violet Stanford (twin), Mabel Day, Freda Winter, Audrey Knott, Ada Adams, Phyliss Rumbold, Winnie Rumbold, Daisy Oliver, Muriel Cooper, Marjorie Wilmott, Daphne Varley.

Leslie Littlechild, Fred Taylor, Alfred Day, Gordon Drayson, Billy Stanford, Cyril Webb

Fred Winter, Eric Hinkins, Stanley Anderson, Bertie Worland, Edward Negus.

and travel talks. The travel talks on the radio, by Clifford Collinson, were great favourites ~ he was said to be ...*a breezy lecturer who knew what children liked*. His talk on the South Sea Islands interested the children of Melbourn so much that some wrote him a letter of thanks. Collinson replied saying ...*how much he had enjoyed the letters*. He did remark that ...*Lesley Catley's hope that he might live to speak about his travels for another century was rather optimistic, but he'd do his best!*

In 1938 the two villages of Melbourn and Meldreth were rocked by an incident which caused a great deal of discussion at the time. In January, the County Council ordered all Meldreth children over the age of 11 years to go to Melbourn for tuition, as it was felt that Meldreth school did not have the educational facilities required for advanced learning. There was uproar and a local dignitary, Mr H Ellis, enlisted the Meldreth parents in a campaign to have the order quashed. Meetings were held and columns written in the newspapers. The situation was not helped when Mr Fordham, Chairman of the Education Committee, branded the Meldreth parents as ...*being led by agitators*. The parents were invited to a special meeting to explain the position, but Mr Ellis, to his fury, was

Melbourn school teachers

The 'bedlam bus' became an issue again in 1940. There were many complaints of litter, throwing missiles and fights between Melbourn and Meldreth children.

Efficient blackout enabled the Council Schools to be used again in the evenings, and socials and meetings of local organisations once more became the norm. Fifty attended the first meeting of a Youth Centre at the Council Schools in 1941 and in 1942 older children were given leave to help with potato lifting for two weeks, whilst the younger ones collected horse chestnuts and rose hips.

Hot school dinners started in May 1943, which meant that many children were assured of at least one hot meal a day. In July 1944 a 'book drive' resulted in 5,892 books being collected for the Forces. Children were graded by the number of books they collected ~ 33 children were made Sergeants for collecting 25 books; 29 were Captains for collecting 50 books; 9 made it to General for collecting 150 books and 3 reached the exalted rank of Field Marshal for 250 books.

The end of the war, in 1945, saw a Victory Dance at the Council Schools which raised £52 10s 0d for the Home-Coming Fund. In 1947 it was rumoured that a Village College was being considered for Melbourn and the surrounding area, but it was confidently predicted that ...*it would be out of the village!*

Mr Barnard, of Enfield, presented a handsome trophy (The Barnard Cup for Sport) to the Council Schools in 1949, in commemoration of the welcome shown to his two daughters when they were evacuated to Melbourn during the Second World War, and to his wife in the First World War.

not admitted, because he was not a parent! He persuaded the parents to take the matter through the Courts but, when it finally arrived at the High Court of Justice, the appeal was dismissed on the grounds that the County Council's decision was quite legal. By this time, several of the children were already attending Melbourn School, others had moved to different schools and several had passed the leaving age.

Second World War 1939–45

By November 1939, children evacuated from London started to arrive in Melbourn. Some were from the Roman Catholic Brompton Oratory School and others from schools in north London, including Islington. Children were issued with gas masks, which they had to carry to school in a cardboard box with a string handle.

Melbourn school teachers and canteen staff
Back row, Mrs Ritson, Mrs Abrey, Rose Wright (Cook), Aggie Perrin, Mrs Matthews, Ada Catley, Alice Webb
Front row, Unknown, Mrs Holland, Miss E Mead, Mr W Ogden, Mr Varley, Miss Swan, Miss Jarman, Mr Saunders

Sgt. Barrett and PC Conell outside the Police Station and Court House in Cross Lane

Law & order

...in 1775 Thomas Newman was sentenced to death after he was found guilty of stealing 3 pairs of shoes

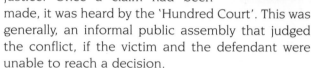

The beginnings of our justice system came from the Romans during the first century, and the introduction of 'Danelaw', established by the Viking invaders and settlers in East Anglia in the 9th century. Many of their laws were designed to protect themselves against the Britons, but, nevertheless, they would have brought peace to Melbourn.

With Christianity, and the foundation of moral laws, it was the church that held power over much of the population.

Early structure

By the 10th century much of England had been divided into shires (or counties); this was to help improve law and order and the collection of taxes. The shires were further divided into 'Hundreds' (an area of land that covered one hundred hides with each hide equal to 120 acres). The Hundreds were then sub-divided into small villages, with Melbourn in the *Armingford Hundred*. Known as a tithing (*meaning a tenth*), Melbourn was made up of ten freemen, or households. Each of these freemen was responsible for the others' conduct. A *tithingman*, or peace officer, was elected to preside over the village and he had responsibility for the other nine freemen.

In every Hundred a *hundredman*, was appointed and he, together with the peace officers (*tithingmen*) and a clerk, would meet every four weeks to discuss local issues and apportion taxes. The *hundredman* only dealt with crimes that *...broke the King's peace* which included unsolved murders. In 1158 a merchant was robbed and murdered on Ermine Street near Whaddon. As no culprit was found, the *Armingford Hundred* was fined 10 marks. In 1272 Peter and Henry de Logges and Saul the Jew, were found murdered in Melbourn fields. A fine of 600 marks was levied on the Hundred as the offender was found in the village.

The village was governed by unwritten local customs or rules; these were enforced in an arbitrary fashion. If a crime had been committed against a local, and it did not affect the King, it was up to the victim to seek justice. Once a claim had been made, it was heard by the 'Hundred Court'. This was generally, an informal public assembly that judged the conflict, if the victim and the defendant were unable to reach a decision.

The Hundred Court would meet every four weeks, in the open, and usually at a prominent local landmark known as 'Mettle' or 'Metil Hill' ~ a Saxon word meaning 'meeting hill'. The *shire-reeve* would preside over the court. Its functions were mixed; it was the 'parish council', deciding on planning enquiries and other business, and it was also the 'magistrates' court'.

Above the Hundred court was the Shire court, which met twice a year and was presided over by the *ealdorman*, the bishop and the king's senior reeve of the area, the *shire-reeve* would also attend this court. All the major landowners in the shire, or their reeves, would also have been present. Problems on which the Hundred court was unable to reach a judgement, or disputes that crossed the boundary between two hundreds, were dealt with in the Shire court.

Lord of the Manor

Following the Norman Conquest, the land was divided into 'fiefs' or manors, with each containing a village. These manors became the responsibility of the lords, or barons, chosen by the King. The Lord of the manor for Melbourn was an Argentine, and it was his job to enforce law and order and to collect the tallage (taxes).

He maintained an extensive area of land, or

The basic principle of Anglo-Saxon law – luck or justice?

The accused person had two choices, 'wager of law' or 'trial by ordeal'. In 'wager of law' the accused 'waged' or 'made' the law by producing oath-helpers. If a crime was not serious and the accused was well known in the village, he could clear his name by using oath helpers.

First, he would swear on oath saying he was innocent. He would then find the required number of oath helpers and the court would decide on how many oath helpers were required. They would be people from the village who would swear that they believed the accused to be innocent. If insufficient could be found, the defendant was found guilty. If enough *were* found, they had to repeat the words of the oath exactly, but making a mistake indicated that the accused was guilty. It was believed that God would 'twist the tongues' of oath helpers if the person was guilty.

Trial by ordeal was for people accused of more serious offences. The accused person had to undergo an 'ordeal' or test. For example, a person might be lowered into a river with their hands and feet bound by a rope. If the person sank he was innocent, if he floated he was guilty. In another ordeal, the accused person would be made to carry a red-hot iron for ten yards, or pick a stone out of boiling water. People were guilty if their hands were still burned and infected after three days.

In the Middle Ages people were reluctant to sentence a person to death without some guidance from God. A priest was present to bless the water before the ordeal, and to interpret God's decision about guilt or innocence. It was believed that God would not let an innocent person suffer.

estate, for his personal use and rented other land to 'freeholders'. The Anglo-Saxon farmer was reduced to the class of serf, or villein, and was allowed to farm the rest, although he had to give part of his produce to the lord of the manor. Villeins could not leave the manor on which they were born, but they could however, be sold. In 1377 William Batchelor, of

Melbourn paid 100 marks of silver, to Richard Cobham of Royston for a chaplain (a member of the clergy) and four villeins ~ Robert Bond, John Bond, John Wynock and his son also named John. This system of land tenure was the basis of feudalism, which became a way of life and remained so for many centuries.

By the 12th century, the name of *Shire-reeve* had evolved to *sheriff*. A sheriff was responsible for preserving the peace, as well as the collection of taxes owed to the crown and also for organising the Assizes (travelling law courts where serious criminals were tried twice a year).

During the 12th century, judges were sent out from London to the county to hear cases, and put each of the accused through a similar ordeal as was used in the Anglo-Saxon period. It was not until the 13th century that these ordeals were replaced with trial by jury; those who refused to go to trial by jury were tortured.

If found guilty, the punishment imposed was harsh.

13th century road rage

Hugh son of Ralph of Meldreth, and William le Ken of Pylarston, rode together from Walden fair in a cart. They were coming along the Icknield Way, and had got as far as the cross roads at Chrishall Grange, when it pleased them to stop in the middle of the road. A certain Henry, son of William Prude of Melbourn, who was travelling behind them, was much troubled thereat, and drawing his sword, cut off the first joint of Hugh's thumb, who retaliated with a sword slash on the shoulder. Henry appealed Hugo, but as he was the aggressor, Hugh is quit, and Henry has to pay a fine.

The Assize Roll 1285

A view of frankpledge

Lords of the Manor in the 13th century farmed land under a franchise from the Diocese, but in 1299 the King's court were ordered to investigate the running of them. Richard de Argentine of Argentine Manor (now Lordship Farm) stated that he and his ancestors had held in Melbourn, from time immemorial, 'a view of frankpledge'.

'Frankpledge was a system by which each member of a tithing was responsible for the good behaviour of the others. The 'view' held by Richard was the supervision of this system. He also had supervision of brewing and baking and all fines connected with them. His claim was allowed.

Thieves had their hands cut off. Poachers had their ears cut off. Men who robbed, or murdered, were hanged. Their dead bodies were then put in metal cages (gibbets) and hung up to rot, as a warning to everyone. Women who murdered were strangled and then burnt. Those who committed treason were punished by hanging. They were then cut down, whilst still alive, and the stomach and chest were cut open, and organs were burnt in front of their eyes. After death, the body was cut up into pieces and impaled on pikes as a warning. This was known as being 'hung, drawn and quartered'.

There would have been no prison in Melbourn or the surrounding area until the 17th century, as incarceration was not seen as a punishment. It was costly, and the villages were not prepared to pay taxes towards the upkeep. It was cheaper to execute, or mutilate miscreants, and then let them go.

The Church insisted on dealing with its priests and officers in the ecclesiastical courts. In 1260 Hugh Payn of 'Meldeburn' was called before the court on charges of theft and receiving stolen goods although he insisted he was a cleric, but before being handed over to the Bishop's officials, he was found guilty of stealing 100 sheep.

In the same year, Henry, the son of William the

Palmer, was arrested for stealing corn. He was taken to the house of the Prior of Ely (who had the 'living' of Melbourn Church), but he escaped. The village was held responsible for his escape and was fined. Although the jury decided that Henry was not guilty of the theft and could return to the village, his goods were confiscated, because he had absconded!

Sanctuary and the role of the Church

A fugitive was able to claim sanctuary in the church, knowing that the law declared him safe and free from interference for a limited period of forty days. The sanctuary boundary extended to the outskirts of the village (about a mile and a half), and was generally marked by crosses. The vicar was required to provide food for the fugitive and the responsibility for watching, to prevent his escape, was on the people of Melbourn, who were fined if they failed.

Within the church, the crime had to be confessed by the fugitive (whether or not they had actually committed it). Before the end of the forty days, the alleged criminals had either to 'foreswear the realm' (agree to leave the country) on oath before the coroner, or surrender themselves for trial. A port was then allotted to them, which had to be reached within a stated period. Clad in sackcloth and carrying a cross, fugitives were allowed to leave the King's highway for a short distance only, to seek food and shelter. If they left it permanently, or returned to the kingdom after deportation, the penalty was death on sight.

In 1298, ...*William the Cooper of Meldreth, sought sanctuary in Melbourn Church after committing a crime. He was brought before the Coroner where he confessed his crimes, dressed in sackcloth and ashes he was taken to the nearest seaport and warned that if he returned he would be executed.*

Fifty years later John Coke of Hauxton fled to the church after stealing sheep in Shepreth. He was also brought before the Coroner, then led before the altar, where he confessed. He was then taken to the port of Dover to foreswear the realm.

Those who foreswore the realm were required to leave England. However, before 1282 many went across the borders into Scotland, Ireland and Wales. By 1723 sanctuary had been completely abolished.

With the opening up of the Americas, and later Australia and New Zealand, those who foreswore the realm were sent to work in these colonies, often for trivial offences such as sheep, horse and cattle stealing or minor theft. Previously, transportation was for a capital offence but by the 1830's judges were compelled to pass sentence of transportation for life for many offences.

Sentences

Although there were only a few reports of criminals being transported from Melbourn, such as Thomas Newman and James Fordham, sentences often varied for many crimes.

In 1806 James Robertson was sentenced to three months in prison for stealing clothes; he was also publicly whipped twice. Young Maling and Thomas Munns also received three months imprisonment in 1808 for burglary. They were also fined 1s each. James Fordham was convicted of assaulting Mary Jarman in 1817. He was imprisoned for 14 days, paid a fine of 20s, and was bound over to keep the peace for one year. Stealing a quantity of barley from the tithe stocks in Melbourn in 1817, landed Sarah Wilkinson, Ann and Sussanna Wilkinson, and Ann Smith with a sentence of nine months each.

In 1859 John Miller was charged with a ...*brutal assault on his wife Eliza, by kicking her in the body and threatening to put her on the fire and burn her.* He was sentenced of two months in prison with hard labour.

Reported as a 'nuisance case' in 1867, ...*Louisa Douse was given the choice of 14 days' imprisonment or pay a fine of 12s 6d for throwing water into the face of a neighbour and using offensive language.* Also that year George Jarman received a sentence of 3 months for stealing 4 ducks to the value of 4s. He also received a further 3 months for stealing coals and wood worth 2d.

The following year, George Worland was charged with ...*being drunk at the 'Star beer house', despite the landlady Lydia Gouldthorpe asking him to leave.* He was fined 10s 6d but, as he was unable to pay the fine, he was jailed for 14 days.

At the same sessions Ward Stamford was charged with ...*having a foul dung-pit near his house.* He was ordered to remove the mess and fill in the pit; he also had to pay 6s 6d costs.

William West was charged with being ...*drunk and riotous* and fined 1s, and 9s costs. C King was jailed for 21 days for assaulting Sarah Whitmore.

Transportation

Those who foreswore the realm were often sent to work in the colonies ~ in many cases for trivial offences such as sheep, horse and cattle stealing or theft of no more than £5.

Prisoners were transferred from the county jail to prison hulks, to await their passage to America, or Canada where in 1660, a convict from Melbourn was sent for cutting out a sheep's tongue. Later, convicts were sent to Australia.

Not all prisoners were sent to the colonies; those

House-breaking

On Thursday the 6th inst. Edward Smith, William Handscombe, Jonathan Reeder, James Fordham, William Collis, John Whitby, and James Peters, all of Melbourne in this county, labourers, were committed to the county gaol to take their trials at the next assizes, charged with house-breaking, sheep-stealing and other felonies. It appears by the communications of the above named prisoners that extensive depredations are made upon the corn, sheep, poultry, and other productions of the farmyard, without the proprietors knowing that they have suffered any loss. It is recommended to farmers to look attentively to their barns, granaries, locks and keys, and frequently, at least weekly, to number their flocks and poultry, both on account of their own personal interest, and of diminishing the temptation of those who, seeing their culpable negligence, steal their property for the purpose of drunkenness and other kinds of dissipation.

Cambridge Chronicle 14th June 1822

Burglary

Edward Smith aged 26, and William Handscombe aged 21, were indicted for a burglary in the house of James King, of Melbourne, and stealing there out 2 silver table spoons, 4 tea spoons, and divers other articles; and James Fordham aged 24, was indicted for having received such articles, knowing them to be stolen. On the part of the prosecution it appeared that the prisoners, Smith and Handscombe, to effect the robbery, had broken a hole in the wall of the prosecutor's house, and stole the articles mentioned in the indictment, in the night; and the spoons were proved to have been sold by Fordham to a man in London for 14s. through the medium of a porter. Their several confessions, taken by the magistrate, fully proved their guilt, such confessions being taken without any promise or threat. Guilty. His Lordship in passing sentence on the prisoner Fordham said, that was it not for such bad characters as him, crime would not be so prevalent, for were their no receivers there would not be so many depredations committed on the property of the honest man; he should therefore make an example of him, and sentenced him to be transported 14 years.

Cambridge Chronicle 26th July 1822

with a 7-year sentence could serve their entire term on the prison hulks. These end-of-the-line battleships, or frigates with their masts removed, were moored near a dockyard, so that the labour of the convicts could be used for public service. Alongside these hulks would be a hospital ship. On their arrival the convicts were immediately made to strip and wash. They were clothed in coarse grey jackets and breeches, and irons placed on their legs.

Discipline on board was harsh and very strict, with extreme cleanliness enforced. The daily diet was: 1¼lb of bread, a quart of thick gruel in the morning and evening, on four days of the week a piece of meat weighing 14ozs before cooking, and on the other three days, in lieu of meat, a quarter of a pound of cheese. Also an allowance of small beer, and on certain occasions a portion of strong beer, was served to those engaged in hard labour.

Sent ashore in gangs, prisoners were hired out to work and each could earn one penny for every shilling the government received for his labour. He was paid one-third of the money he earned weekly and the remainder was kept until the end of his sentence. A prisoner who had served seven years on the hulks could have up to £15 on his release. These hulks were also sent out to the colonies to be used as prisons.

Prisoners who had been sentenced to seven years transportation, could find their sentences cut to only three or four years if they behaved well. Other inducements, to keep order on the hulks, included having the irons lightened and being promoted, which relieved them from severe labour. One ship was used exclusively for boys under the age of sixteen, where they were taught various trades such as bookbinding, shoemaking, tailoring etc.

A perhaps more realistic view of life on prison hulks can be seen in a letter on the right.

The journey

Although the first convicts to sail arrived in relatively good condition, those that followed were not so fortunate. Conditions on board the ships were primitive; prisoners were held below decks; often confined behind bars and, in many cases, restrained in chains.

Cruel masters, harsh discipline and scurvy, dysentery and typhoid resulted in a huge loss of life, but by 1801, the system had changed. To avoid the dangerous winters of the southern hemisphere, the ships were sent twice a year, at the end of May and the beginning of September. Independent Surgeon Superintendents, whose sole responsibility was for the wellbeing of the convicts, replaced the doctor-surgeon employed by early contractors. New procedures were developed, and the surgeons were supplied with instructions as to how life on board was to be organised. By this time, the company charged to deliver the prisoners was also paid a bonus to land them, safe and sound, at the end of the voyage. Later, a Religious Instructor was sent on these ships to educate the convicts and attend to their spiritual needs.

Strict rules and regulations varied from ship to ship. The prisoners were not allowed to talk to guards or any of the ship's company. The prison deck was to be kept clean and dry, and any water spilt was a punishable offence; prisoners were not allowed to wash themselves, or their clothes, below deck. Any prisoner caught stealing ship's stores, smoking or striking a light on the prison deck, quarrelling or fighting, was severely punished. They were not allowed to exchange, or sell, their clothing and gambling was prohibited. Swearing, the use of obscene language and the singing of immoral songs were also banned. After 8.30pm, singing, speaking or noise of any kind was not permitted.

With only two stops on the 3-month voyage the daily routine would have been mundane. On arrival at their destination, convicts kept the flock mattresses and blankets they had used on the passage out. By 1861 punishment by transportation was reduced to penal servitude (forced labour) not exceeding 14 years.

The colonies

Convicts were first sent to the North American plantations, where they became bondsmen, or slaves. Conditions for many prisoners were harsh; for the slightest offence, real or otherwise, they would be flogged, or put to labour in chains on the roads. Following the American War of Independence, transportation came to a halt, but by 1787, prisons and prison hulks had begun to overflow. A number of attempts in 1781 and 1782, to establish a convict colony in West Africa ended in disaster, when most of the convicts died from disease and neglect, or escaped.

In 1787 the government chose the newly claimed colony of New South Wales as a destination for the convicts. The first ships left Portsmouth on 13 May 1787 with about 1,350 people; 780 convicts and 570 freemen, women and children. The fleet arrived in Botany Bay on 18 January 1788 but decided the site was not good enough and so sailed on to Sydney Cove.

Many prisoners sent to Australia suffered similar treatment to those in other colonies, as this letter from a prisoner in 1828 shows:

…Hunger is our sauce; we grind in a hand mill, we bake in the ashes, and live in miserable huts, which admit both wind and rain. A sheet of bark and a bundle of straw is our bed, and a blanket our covering. The slightest offence provokes flogging. A man calls himself a settler, first imposes upon his slaves, goads them on to speak and then drags them before a magistrate to be lashed and tortured for insolence. It is useless to murmer, for complaint is crime in this dreadful country. We all feel a twofold degradation here; we feel that we are slaves to paltry tyrants, who seem as if they where born to add to the stings and tortures of a wretched criminal.

For others life was very different. On arrival prisoners were assigned to the services of Settlers. Those with a trade, or who had been in domestic service in England, could be given the same occupation in the new colony, and instead of working in a state of slavery, some found life easier with only minor punishment – and often received a fair wage. Prisoners who behaved well, after a few years were treated as free men and went on to enjoy the freedom to work for themselves; others received conditional, or even free, pardons.

Elizabethan constable

In 1775 Thomas Newman was sentenced to death after he was found guilty of stealing 3 pairs of shoes. This was later commuted to 14 years transportation. In 1822 Edward Smith and William Handscombe were found guilty of stealing cutlery and other items from a house. However, it was James Fordham who received a sentence of 14 years transportation for selling the items.

Coroner's inquests

After the Norman Conquest, to deter the local communities from the ongoing slaughter the Normans, a heavy fine, known as the 'Murdrum' (from which the word 'murder' is derived), was levied upon the village, should a corpse be found and presumed to be Norman (unless it could be 'proved' to be English).

From 1194 it was the duty of the coroner to investigate the circumstances of these unnatural, sudden, or suspicious deaths, including deaths in prison. Suicides were also investigated, on the grounds that the goods and chattels (property) of those found guilty of the crime of *'felo de se'*, or *'self murder'*, would then be forfeit to the crown. It was the custom for suicides to be buried outside the boundary of the village, with a stake driven through the body. There would be no funeral service, nor was the burial registered. In 1818 Edward Neaves hanged himself and was buried at the south end of the village. An Act of 1823 put an end to this practice.

The coroner was charged with keeping local records of legal proceedings. He was also a tax collector and would raise money for the crown by funnelling the property of executed criminals into the king's treasury

The village was bound by law to send representatives to inquests on fatalities and in 1285, Melbourn suffered a fine of 100 shillings for not doing so. At an inquest held in Melbourn on 11th July 1346, the following villagers formed a jury: Robert Hakere (Harper); Robert Prest; Peter Faby (Fabian); John Pearson; John Richold (Richards); Nicholas Pearson; Lawrence Heydon; George Ware; Robert Ferour (Farrow); Simon Iremonger; William Marchal (Marshall).

The deceased was Hugh Hulot who had been run over by his own cart. Under the law, the objects that caused the death had to be sold and the money given to charity, or for religious purposes. This was known as a deodand. The horses were valued at 16s 4d, the cart and harness at 7s 6d and the cargo (a pipe of wine) at 20s. (A pipe of wine, was a cask containing a measure of two hogsheads, equal to 105 gallons.) This law was not changed until 1846. Inquests were held before a jury until 1926.

In the 18th and 19th century many inquests were held in local public houses, often because they were the only buildings in the village that had room to accommodate a large group of people.

An inquest in 1883, was held on a child born with six fingers on each hand, six toes on each foot and a double upper lip. It was described as a ...*monstrosity*.

The following year, Edward Thurley Bridges, aged 1½ years, died from ...*being scalded by boiling water. His condition was made worse when the person looking after the baby put flour on the scalds.* The verdict of the inquest was death by 'asphysia' caused by scalding water.

In April 1885 a verdict on Simeon Bass, aged 69, recorded an accidental death after he had been crushed by a load of potatoes. It was noted that ...*the horse ran back and tipped the cart.*

William Day was equally unfortunate in May 1886 when he ...*was buried under a fall at the clunch pits and suffered a fractured spine and internal injuries.* In September 1891, a man called Paine ...*was kicked and knocked down by a horse he was holding for Mr. Titchmarsh.* Both verdicts were of accidental death.

A sad, but not uncommon event, took place in June 1902, when a newborn baby was found buried in a garden in the village. The child belonged to Annie Mary Smith Holland who told the court that ...*the child had been born dead. She had given birth unaided which did not help the child's condition.* She was remanded on bail of £5.

In October 1929 a verdict of ...*suicide whilst insane* was recorded on Beatrice Cooper, who was found hanged in a barn in the High Street.

The Parish constables

The word 'constable' has Norman origins, coming from the Latin 'Comes Stabuli' meaning Count of the Stables, or Master of the Horse. The Anglo-Saxons used the term 'Tithingman' or 'Head Borough'.

The early village constables were freemen, and ordinary farmers, shopkeepers and craftsman but ...*of good character*. They were appointed to the office by the Manorial Court set up by the Argentines, and sworn in by the Justices. The position was usually for one year and the constable was given a staff of office that had the appearance of a truncheon. Two fellow villagers, known as 'Headboroughs', were appointed to keep the peace and were aided by an Aleconner, whose main responsibility was checking the quality of the ale and beer and ensuring that they were sold to the proper weight and measure.

The constable's tasks included the supervision of the 'Watch and Ward' ~ the 'watch' being night time

and the 'ward', daytime patrols. He would organise the watchmen, and was responsible for the welfare of the poor, the apprenticing of poor children, the removal of vagrants and beggars and inspecting alehouses. He also collected taxes, conveyed those being held in court, served writs and summonses, supported bailiffs at evictions, checked weights and measures, supervised military arms supply and military training, and ensured the upkeep of the local means of punishment, such as the stocks. He would also organise the 'Hue and Cry'. This was the method by which a person wishing to make an arrest could call on the rest of the village to join him in pursuit of

Nightwatchman

the offender. Everyone was obliged to join the hue (pursuit) and to cry aloud to attract other people's attention. It was illegal to start an unnecessary hue. Public participation in the arrest of criminals was encouraged by rewards and failure to carry a 'hue and cry' was a punishable offence.

Other duties included public health and the early 'manual' given to the constable included instructions on how to deal with the plague: *...constables may command and oblige persons infected with the plague to keep within their houses; and if after such command, they wilfully go abroad, having any infectious sores upon them, it is felony; and if they have no sores, they may be bound to good behaviour, and punished as vagabonds, by whipping, etc.* The manual also explains how to administer the punishment.

Where a child, or expected child, might become a burden on the parish, it would be up to the parish constable to put pressure on the father of the child and compel him to marry the pregnant girl. The groom would then be escorted to the church by two parish officers carrying heavy cudgels with strong knobs at one end. These forced marriages were known as 'Knobstick weddings'.

The Parish Constable of Melbourn

Before 1839 there was no police force in the modern sense; policing was a local matter. The early parish constables were volunteers and unpaid, although they received payment for special duties and expenses. With no proper qualifications, every householder in the village was liable to serve. If the

Watchman

Melbourns Parish Constables

List of expenses claimed for the year

1719 Peter Dunham (£9 1s 6d)
1721 Thomas Barton (£8 13s 1½d)
1722 James Lee
1723 Thomas Munsey
1725 Richard Badcock (£8 18s 7d)
1726 Thomas Jarman (£11 19s 5½d)
1728 John Hitch (£11 1s 4½d)
1729 Thomas Letchfield (£9 1s 0d)
1731 William Ellis (£11 11s 11½d)
1732 John Huggins (£18 8s 6d)
1735 John Hitch (£9 14s 11d)
1737 E Chapman
1739 E Chapman (£6 12s 4d)
1744 James Miller (£2 17s 0d)
1747 T Huggins (£8 11s 6½d)
1751 W Munsey (£2 6s 10d)
1754 T Huggins (£3 7s 6d)
1757 W Ellis (£2 13s 2d)
1763 Jonathan Ellis and son (1763–1805, 1823–24)
1811 Robert King
1825 George Stanford
1828 Joseph Hagger and Stoughton Campkin
1877 Ishmael Howard (1877–1886)
1888 Charles Harrup
1889 Charles Gouldthorpe
1889 J Bullen
1891 Ernest Carter
1892 Joseph Hodge
1894 Ernest Eustace French

Truncheon given to Melbourn Parish Constables

parish could not find enough volunteers to fill the parish offices, they would combine a number of the jobs, and the constable could also be the surveyor of the highways. His duties as a constable meant that he was responsible to the village authorities

and the church authorities. He would not only appear at quarter sessions court or assizes but also at the church courts. He watched over the conditions of the church and reported on many aspects of the lives of parishioners, such as attendance at church and the birth of illegitimate children.

In 1894 with the advent of the new parish council, the office of the parish constable disappeared. Maintenance of law and order became the responsibility of the official police force. The last constable to serve in the village, Ernest French was charged for selling short weights on his coal deliveries; he was heavily fined.

The Militia

In 1757, an Act was passed *...for the better ordering of the Militia Forces in England* and it was the parish constable's job to draw up a list of all able-bodied men between the ages of 18 and 50 living in Melbourn, who were 'liable to serve' in the militia (an early form of National Service). The number of taxable houses determined the number of men required from the village.

Men were chosen by ballot and were required to serve for three years. However, those drawn in the ballot could either provide a substitute, or pay £10 towards

Old London Road, part of Drift Way, reputed to be the meeting place of the infamous highwaymen Dick Turpin and Tom King

the provision of one. After three years, both the drawn man, and any substitute, would again be liable for service by way of the ballot.

Footpads and highwaymen

The crimes that attracted the greatest coverage, in the late-17th and early-18th centuries, were those perpetrated by footpads and highwaymen, who frequented the roads leading out of the village. It was reputed that two of the most infamous highwaymen Dick Turpin and Tom King, visited the village. However, there is no documented evidence to prove this.

By the beginning of the 18th century, turnpikes and tollbooths were introduced. The turnpikes surrounding the village enabled money to be collected from road users, to help pay for their upkeep. The tolls continued into the 19th century when, in 1818, an additional Toll Gate was erected in Mill Lane. Early toll keepers were also sworn in as Parish Constables. They were able to detain felons within the tollhouse, or escort them to the parish lockup. This led to a decline in Highway robbery.

On Tuesday, William Beard, of Meldreth, was brought up in custody of Supt. Stretten, before J.E. Fordham, Esq., charged with violently assaulting and wounding William Baillee, of Melbourn. Complainant is suffering from paralysis, but occupies a beerhouse, his wife managing the business. Prisoner was drinking there in the morning, and on being left alone with the old man, without the slightest provocation, threatened to kill him, at the same time commencing a furious attack with a pair of tongs, inflicting several blows upon his head, one of which cut completely through the scalp. The old man defended himself as well as his infirmity would allow, until the arrival of his wife, who very courageously seized his assailant, until the arrival of a police officer, by whom he was at once secured. No reason can be assigned for this cowardly attack, other than that Beard, who is usually very quiet, is slightly deranged, and may have imagined himself injured.

Cambridge Chronicle 2th July 1855

Inspecting the accident at the Cross

Cambridgeshire Constabulary

The introduction of the 'real' policemen in the village began in 1838, although the role of the parish constable did not disappear altogether. The post continued to be filled each year at the Vestry meeting.

A top hat, stick, blue jacket and trousers made up the new police uniform. The pay was good in comparison to other jobs, starting at 17s a week for a constable; a sergeant could expect £1 2s 6d.

Court sessions were usually held in Melbourn and Arrington but, in November 1896, the local magistrate Mr Fordham suggested there was little point in sitting in two courts and that

A policeman with his top-hat and staff

Sheep-slaughtering has become very prevalent in this district; and it is thus accounted for. The farmers find their sheep dead in the fields, either by having been thrown on their backs, or by their throats being cut: this being thought to be malicious damage, the farmers order the mutton to be cut up and sold to the poor at a low price; and we are informed by the County Constabulary that there is no doubt but that this is the very object for which the sheep have been killed. Three or four instances have occurred in which it is proved that the animals have been killed for their skins, and the meat has been sold for a trifle.

Cambridge Independent Press 19th March 1853

all cases should be heard at the Cross Lane court in Melbourn. His proposal was defeated by four votes to two. A few years later, a report on Melbourn Police Station, showed that Sergeant Ding, who was in charge of the station, also lived in the building but had to vacate his bedroom in order that the magistrates could use it as a retiring room. It was eventually agreed that urgent alterations should be made.

The Old Cage lockup and stocks

The old cage, or lockup, was on the Green at the Cross and was designed as a gaol to hold criminals overnight before they were brought to the magistrates court. It was a small one-room building,

The Cage and Stocks at The Cross.
(*Based on an original drawing*)

In the Cage

We know there were the stocks on The Green, the round cage with the extinguisher like top was there too. One man, who was put in the cage, not for his good qualities you may depend, spent a good deal of an evening's imprisonment industrially kicking out the bricks, and would have succeeded in escaping only the constable was informed and defeated his design by staying with him. Another offender was not so audacious; his wife went to the cage, called him but got no response. However, early in the morning she was at the cage with a jug of hot tea and a saucer. He answered all right in the morning, and he drank the tea, a saucerful at a time, pushed between the iron bars of the cell window. In the morning he was taken before a magistrate, who sat in The Rose Inn parlour, and was fined, the magistrate out of the goodness of his heart paying the fine himself and then our hero slipped round and joined his pals in the taproom, and he was put in the cage again at night.

Jubal Howard

WHAT THE PAPERS SAID

soundly built with bars on the window and a good strong door. Next to the cage would have been the stocks. These were used for vagrants, shopkeepers who gave short weight and landlords who sold more water than ale. The offenders were then a target at which local folk would throw rotten food. The cage was finally demolished in 1847, when it was decided that criminals were to be taken to Cambridge for judgement. The materials were used to build the fire engine house in Station Road.

Melbourn and crime

Melbourn has had its fair share of offenders in the past! Crimes ranged from theft to domestic disturbances and most were recorded in a very interesting manner in the local newspapers.

School attendance

Following the Education Act in 1870, school attendance became compulsory and many parents were brought before the courts for failing to send their children. Records were meticulously maintained and, in some cases, show hundreds of days when children were recorded as being absent.

Only a few children attended school at the beginning of this period; most poor children worked, as their earnings were an important part of the family income.

In May 1890 Wortham Woods was summonsed to the court for not sending two of his children to school for a total of 206, and 273, times respectively. He was fined 5s in each case.

In some instances the fine was paid, but often the plea was, ...*there was no money to pay the fine although there might have been if the children had been allowed to work!*

Juvenile behaviour

Drunkenness in the village was a common occurrence in the 1800s; alcohol was cheap and easily available to the young. In 1877 the young Charles Thurley, convicted of being drunk and disorderly, was fined 14s 6d including costs.

In September 1881, at the age of 13, Ralph Carter was charged with stealing 10 apples from an orchard. However, he had also been caught taking money from the school and so the punishment he received was harsh. He was sentenced to have six strokes of the birch (a large cane), which was given immediately after the case had been heard.

Other juvenile problems involved 'child support'. In March 1883 Frank Coningsby, aged 15, was ordered to pay 2s, a week plus 16s in costs, to support the children of Clara Stamford. No other details were given with this report.

Ralph Carter was again in court in May 1884; this time for stealing a fowl valued at 2s. He was sentenced to 14 days in prison, but having already served twelve days awaiting the trial, he served one extra day and was released.

That month also saw Frederick Waldock, George Gray, James Potman, John King and Henry Plum accused of damaging wheat to the value of 6d. They were each fined 3s 6d for the offence, 6d for the damage and a further 6s costs; in total 10s. The newspapers at the time complained bitterly that *...young men were going about on Sunday evenings and causing mischief.*

In 1885 William Barnes, a young boy, was charged with throwing a stone at Susan Chapman – he was fined 30s, plus 10s 6d costs or given the option of going to prison for a month; it was not recorded if he paid or went to jail. In the same year James Handscombe aged 16, George Harrup aged 15 and Herbert Dodkin also aged 15, were convicted of assaulting Fanny Jarman. Each was sentenced to six months imprisonment with hard labour.

Young travelling hawkers also proved a problem when Walter Kettle, aged 15, was charged with stealing a ham to the value of 5s from the publican Thomas Wedd. He had already been in prison for ten days and was sent for another fourteen with hard labour. The Chairman of the Bench *...urged upon him the necessity of turning over a new leaf.*

The Vicar, James Hamilton, (the beast who stopped the feast) was not slow in prosecuting people who damaged his property. In 1888 Henry Gadd aged 15, Walter Harry Harper and Henry French both aged 18, were charged with damaging an iron frame said to be the property of the church. They were each fined 11s 6d with 14s 6d costs.

The Melbourn Musical Society gave the last concert of their season in April 1895. The programme included an organ recital by Mr Landergan from Northampton but the concert did not go smoothly.

The newspaper reported that *...it is especially to be regretted that numbers of Melbourn boys who crowded into one of the galleries and seemed to think that a place of worship makes an excellent playground, should have made the concert an opportunity for indulging in loud conversation, whistling and horseplay. During the last voluntary, Mr Landergan had to cease playing until the disturbance partially subsided. The lecturers of the County Council have complained of similar occurrences and it is very desirable that steps should be taken to put a stop to what is becoming an intolerable nuisance. The formation of a 'Discipline Committee' to maintain order at Melbourn meetings would be a step in the right direction.*

A 'curious case' occurred in February 1898 when William Adams, David Eversden and Charles William Mead were charged with *...sliding in Mortlock Street,* each was fined 5s. Ralph Lee, Frederick Rumbold and Ernest Robinson followed them into court the next month on the count of *...obstructing the footpath and making horrible screaming noises.* The fine was 1s, with 4s costs.

In June 1899 Charles Harper aged 10, Percy Robinson and Albert Stanford both aged 11, were

Glass panes in the church

charged with damaging the glass panes in the church to the value of 1s each. Henry Pepper aged 11, a witness to the incident, said that he saw Robinson shoot at the window with a catapult and break it. The three were each fined 5s each for costs and damages.

A 'serious offence' was reported in the papers in 1909, when Alfred Mead aged 20 and Joseph Pepper also aged 20, were charged with throwing fireworks causing ...*James West's horse to fall and his trap was smashed*. They were fined 10s each.

Melbourn Youth Club

In November 1916, the names of Mead and Pepper were in court again. This time it was Fred Mead aged 17 and John Pepper aged 15, who were convicted of stealing 4s 2d from Melbourn Conservative Club. Mead was bound over for twelve months on probation, but Pepper was sent to a reformatory school until he reached the age of 19 years, ...*he was said to have liked the sea and it was hoped to find a ship of a reformatory school character for him to attend.*

The firing of steel balls from catapults became a common problem in the village in 1924. Thomas and James Cooper both aged 12 and Harry Adams and Stanley Cooper aged 13, were convicted of breaking windows. Each was fined 11s. The practice was said to be ...*rife, especially on Sunday evenings, when there was nothing else to do.* The same excuse was possibly given by Hadley Dodkin aged 18 and Charles Agar aged 16 when they were convicted of throwing apples at cars on Newmarket Road. Each was fined 5s with 2s 6d costs.

During the Second World War regular complaints were received of ...*bad behaviour, horseplay, and pelting of elderly people with fruit and pellets* on the 'bedlam bus', which ran from Cambridge at 4.10pm carrying schoolchildren home to Melbourn.

When the iron railings surrounding many gardens and properties were removed in February 1943 for aircraft and tank production, gangs of youths were reported to be running wild through the village and across gardens. Residents resolved the problem by plugging the gaps with hurdles. There were also complaints about ...*rowdyism every Thursday, following the evening dances at the Council Schools.* It was reported that ...*there was much noise and vandalism including an effort to uproot the fingerpost at The Cross.*

Even the Victory in Europe Day celebrations, in May 1945 were marred, ...*hobbledehoys'* (foolish boys) *had thrown fireworks into bonfires and through letterboxes in the village.*

The fingerpost at The Cross

In May 1950 the Vicar, Rev. McNeice, publicly blamed ...*youths who use The Green as a supper room and were too lazy to walk a few yards and place their waste in the basket provided.*

Vagabonds, tramps and gypsies

The unemployment rate for Melbourn in 1834 was 33 percent and rising. With destitution and the workhouse looming, beggars and tramps became a common sight in the village. A report in the Royston Crow suggested that ...*local farmers and other landowners might put unemployed men to work in order to clear stumps*

Ashwell Street (Strete) and a small gypsy caravan

Begging Extraordinary

On the morning of Sunday week, a bill of large dimensions was exhibited at a conspicuous place in this village, to the following effect:– "Notice – Whereas sundry persons of the sect Amphibia have forfeited all claim to sanity and respectability by becoming amateur beggars of the most importunate class, they are hereby cautioned that they are infringing the Act passed for the suppression of vagrancy, and are warned that all persons found begging, on any pretence, in Melbourn, or parishes adjoining, will at once be removed to Fulbourn asylum. By order." We do not see much personality in the above elaborate announcement; but one of our worthies, who (we suppose) believed himself to belong to the sect there in mentioned, pulled it down, and there would have been no more notice taken of it, and many of the inhabitants would never have known that there had been such a thing in existance, had it not been for the ostentatious manner in which the offended party acted. The next we hear of it is at a prayer-meeting the following evening in the Baptist Chapel, where the minister read it for the benefit of his flock, and afterwards exhibited it for their inspection, with what motive we cannot solve, unless to make it publicly known.

Cambridge Chronicle 9th April 1859

and roots of trees which they might sell for firewood to obtain money to get them through the winter without aid.

James Smith was found begging in the High Street in February 1877 and was sentenced to hard labour for one month. John Williams, well known as a professional beggar and described as ...*a decrepit looking individual, was charged with begging* and given a 14-day prison sentence.

The Moor road

The Moor was a popular site for a gypsy encampment, despite a notice warning against making a camp. In May 1891 the Vestry meeting received a complaint about a gypsy site and ordered the police to remove it. However, it was not until owners of adjoining properties also complained that the police eventually agreed to act. In June that year, William Stockbridge, the owner of the property, had successfully ejected a travelling showman from the recreation ground, at The Moor. The next month James Worland, described as a travelling hawker, was charged by William Stockbridge for the ...*reprehensible crime of allowing his horse to rub paint off his fence.* The damage was valued at 6d. However, Worland, declared ...*he had only been summonsed because they*

Begging in the parish

George Curtis, a tramp, was brought up in custody, and charged by Sergeant Levitt with begging in the parish of Melbourn, on Sunday last. Two shillings and a penny was found on the prisoner, and he was committed for 7 days. Several persons were in attendance in answer to their summonses, but only one Magistrate being present the cases were all adjourned for one month.

Cambridge Independent Press 17th April 1869

wanted him off The Moor. There was no conviction as the court decided it was a civil case.

Worland was again charged in November 1898, this time for driving his van onto the recreation ground. The charge was levied by the newly formed Parish Council. On the first day of the Feast, all vehicles were to pay a fee to park on the recreation ground, but Worland declared ...*he had been on the ground for 30 years and had never paid.* He was fined 2s 6d with 7s 6d costs.

In 1921 William Smith, a travelling showman was ordered to move on after he parked his two caravans in a space near The Shant public house before going on to the Feast. However, he was found there the next morning. When he was charged he replied ...*all right, I suppose I shall be fined half a crown.* He received a 20s fine!

Poaching

Landowners and their gamekeepers waged a truceless war against poachers who were always on the lookout for rabbits and more exotic game, such as pheasants and partridges. In many cases, poachers were just trying to feed their families but this was not seen as an excuse and punishment was often severe. It was not unknown for the landowner

or his gamekeeper to use mantraps ~ metal devices with powerful springs and serrated jaws, which sprang shut when stepped upon by a poacher and were difficult to open. These were placed where poachers were most likely to operate.

In July 1883 William Barnard was fined 8s 6d with 11s 6d costs for trespassing on Albert Spencer's land ...*in search of conies* (rabbits). A few years later, Edward and George Harper, were caught poaching with a net, they were given a 3 months prison sentence and fined £3. Using a net was regarded as a very serious crime!

An odd case, found in the papers in January 1895, involved Frank Carter, a soldier. He was ...*charged by his brother, with stealing a number of nets, a ferret line and a bag, the 'tools' of a poacher.* His brother tried later to withdraw the

A *man trap*

charge but this was refused. However, the magistrates agreed that he had only 'borrowed' the equipment for rabbiting, and the charge was dismissed, but he was charged with trespassing in search of rabbits and fined 10s. His brother paid the fine!

Henry Carter was discovered in February 1898 with a dead rabbit in his hand. He was charged with using two dogs for poaching and received one month's imprisonment.

Dogs featured again in an article in September 1904, when Thomas Smith and Arthur Winter were ...*charged by John Stockbridge for using the animals to take game.* They were each fined £1 3s 9d, which included costs.

Joseph Hodge tried to fool the authorities when he claimed that he had a gun licence but ...*it was subsequently discovered that the licence was dated after the offence.* He was fined 40s in May 1905.

Trouble on the highway

In July 1878 William Harris of Gamlingay was fined £1 7s 6d costs for ...*erecting a steam circus less than 25 yards from the highway during the Melbourn Feast.*

The following year, Alexander Hopwood of Shepreth was charged with furious driving. It was said ...*he was going so fast that he ran into a pony and trap in which some ladies were travelling.* He suffered a fine of 30s.

Riding without reins could incur a fine of 7s 6d, and also falling asleep whilst in charge of a horse, as Arthur Wing found to his cost, in June 1886.

Charles Gouldthorpe, who was appointed the parish constable in 1889, was found in a ditch in January the following year. He alleged *... he had been robbed of £60, entrusted to him by the Oddfellows Society, and offered no assistance to the Police investigating the missing money. He was also accused of not involving himself*

during a local fight, and was said to have stood by and watched. In April of that year his name was put forward for re-election as constable, but with considerable objections to the choice, he was not elected.

In June 1899 there was consternation when several well known inhabitants were seen *...taking an airing in a petroleum motor.* July 1903 saw local magistrates dealing with speeding vehicles and one case involved *...a car being driven over the speed limit of 12mph* and *...a motor bicycle being furiously driven* although the speed is not recorded.

In May 1908 Vernon Taylor was convicted of dangerous driving. He had caused *...serious damage to a pony and trap, the pony having had both legs broken, had to be put down.* Taylor's licence was suspended for six months and he was fined £5, with costs of £5 14s 6d. The accused appealed against the sentence saying *...a licence was necessary for his work* but there is no record of the outcome.

In November 1923 Alfred Chapman, Jack Cooper and Ernest Stanford *...tied twine across the High Street as a joke to catch mates.* However, they caught PC Henry Martin instead and were each fined 2s 6d!

Neighbourly disputes and assaults

Disputes between neighbours or families were not uncommon. In 1855 *...George Miller stabbed Sylvester Barrow at Mr Pullen's farm after a quarrel,* and a few years later, in March 1859, John Miller was charged with *...assaulting his wife Eliza by kicking her and threatening to put her on the fire.* He was given two months hard labour and bound over to keep the peace for six months.

William Hales was fined 10s 6d, with 11s costs, for assaulting William Huggins in May 1884. The following year, William Hales became the victim himself when Walter Stanford was fined £3 for a similar offence. In the same month, Stanford and Samuel Carter also assaulted Joseph Worland, for

which they both received one month's hard labour.

George Winters was given 21 days hard labour, without the option of a fine, after he assaulted Joseph Barnard in May 1887. *...Winters insulted Barnard for becoming a Salvationist, and the language of Winter was described as something dreadful;* he was also described as *...the worst man in the place for making a disturbance.*

In March 1898 Harriet Wing was accused of using *...abusive language to her neighbours in Elm Tree Court after they had accused her of keeping a brothel.* By April things had become worse and Harriet Wing threatened Agnes Stanford. She was given 14 days imprisonment as she was unable to pay a fine, although it was said that *...she broke down in tears and begged and prayed not to be sent to prison.*

Love romance and tragedy

Many years ago in a cottage near the Church dwelt a young shepherd with his widowed mother, and his name was Stockbridge. He was a man of fine physique, observant, and intelligent, and respectful. In fact he was one of nature's gentleman. He had charge of a flock of sheep on the grazing ground of Melbourn Heath. There were no houses up Mortlock Street, after you passed the village poorhouse, a poor thatched building. There was no new road in the sense, as we know it, there may have been a bridle path. Of course, our shepherd had to personally report at times to his master who lived down at old farm. No doubt by the shepherd's manly and upright bearing, his visits were welcomed, until he began to find it necessary to go up and discuss matters that appeared on the surface trivial affairs.

There was an only daughter, who turned down many a farmer's son, until it began to dawn upon them that a mere shepherd a menial, was not despised by the farmer's daughter. One night, the young lady of the house went down to the shepherd's cottage in some agitation, and asked why their son had not been up to see father? "He has not been home." was the old lady's reply, "for three nights, but don't worry Miss he has been away like that before when the sheep were troublesome." and with that she had to be content. But days and days went by, and the shepherd never returned. A search party was formed and scoured the Heath with no success. It was a pathetic sight to see the shepherd's mother leaning on the arm of the young girl tramping over the heath land in her endeavours to find her son and calling out his name. His employer was deeply grieved at the turn of events and took the old lady into his house until she died. Many years afterwards the tumuli, which can be seen from Newmarket road was explored, they are called the five old monuments. Near one was discovered the skeleton of a tall man, a decayed shepherd's crook and the skeleton of a dog. Who committed the outrage was never known.

Jubal Howard

Assaulting the police, in May 1903, cost Sarah Ann Worland 5s and David Worland 15s. They had both been drunk and disorderly and attacked PC Snelling.

Fines were obviously hard to find for people on low income and sometimes they were given time to pay. In September 1903, Frank Blows and Arthur Mead were ...*found guilty of threatening behaviour towards Arthur Holland, and both given three hours to find 40s, or go to prison for 14 days*; the fine was paid!

Attacking teachers was a problem in November 1903. Henry Pepper was charged with assaulting Horace Harman, the schoolmaster. ...*Pepper accused the teacher of assaulting his son Joseph with a cane. The magistrates ruled that the teacher was in loco parentis*, meaning that, while at school, the teacher was acting as a parent and could administer punishment where necessary; the case was dismissed.

Frederick Handscombe, said to be newly returned from the Boer War, was ...*drunk and disorderly near the Church and tried to pick a with fight another soldier. He was using filthy language and had to be carried away by four men!* He was fined 10s.

The Winter and Cooper families were involved in a dispute outside The Dolphin Inn, in October 1908, resulting in ...*Joseph Littlechild, Albert Winter, Frank Stanford and James Stanford being arrested for using filthy and obscene language*. It seems that the Coopers had wisely withdrawn from the scene. Fines between 7s 6d, and 10s were levied.

In November 1921, Amy Day accused Edward Stanford of assault. She alleged ...*he came out and knocked her down like a bullock with his fist.* However, Stanford said she was already on the ground and she must have laid down herself! His wife told the court there had been no assault; the Bench dismissed the case.

A month later, Amy Day was involved in an wrangle with Elizabeth Stanford, ...*Stanford alleged that she met Day coming into Melbourn and was called a murderer*. Day was fined £5 and bound over to keep the peace for twelve months.

A domestic dispute cost Ellis Gill his licence as landlord of The Rose Inn in October 1923, following reports that ...*he and his wife often sported black eyes and other injuries as a result of both parties hitting each other!*

Wanted

Some young ladies in this village have received a card, which professed to come from a member of the 'Anti-poke-your-Nose-into-other-People's-Business-Society,' and of which the following is a copy:

'Wanted immediately,

A Person of Fair Character,
(Age or Sex immaterial,)

Salary, £500. per annum,
Merely to mind their own business;

With a Periodical Increase,
equivalent to £1000 per annum.
Only to leave other people's alone.

Applications, with testimonials, to be addressed to the Honorary Secretary of the 'Neglected Home Department.'

Cambridge Independent Press 27th March 1852

'Salute the Soldier' week parade in the High Street

Wars & riots

...to lay before the men of Melbourn their patriotic duty of helping their country through the present crisis

The early 1300s saw a period of unrest between England and Scotland. Several campaigns were launched in order to subdue or conquer the north, and money had to be found to finance them. In August 1316 the village of 'Meldeburn' was levied 30s 8d, in order to send a soldier to the Scottish Wars. Out of this sum, 5s was allocated to the purchase of one akaton (a well-padded garment covering the body from neck to knees), and 20d for a bacinet (a basin-shaped helmet or head covering of metal).

In 1381 the Peasants' Revolt shook the country and was sparked off by the imposition of a new 'poll tax', which was three times the rate of that imposed in the late 1370s. Rebels from south-east England marched on London and demanded reforms from Richard II. The main ringleader in Cambridgeshire seems to have been a man called Hanchach, of Shudy Camps near Cambridge who, between 15th and 17th June of that year, marched a band of peasants along Ashwell Street. Around this time, John Stanford, a saddler of London, described as *...that common leader and notorious congregator of malefactors* arrived in Melbourn, where he told the people *...that he had the King's Commission to destroy traitors*. He fled on the arrival of the actual King's Commissioners.

The Wars of the Roses began in full, during the reign of Henry VI. In 1453 the king became ill, and Richard, Duke of York, was made protector of the realm. Henry's wife, Queen Margaret of Anjou, a rather headstrong woman, alienated Richard upon Henry's recovery, and Richard responded by attacking and defeating the queen's forces at St. Albans in 1455. During the War troops were obviously moved to and from the north of England and St. Albans and came through Melbourn. A disorderly host of Lancastrians, under the command of Margaret, is said to have destroyed the village in search of food. Such an army carried little food and had to 'live off the land'.

Ship money riots

In 1635 Charles I faced a financial crisis and was unwilling to summon another Parliament. He resorted to demanding Ship Money, a system whereby the monarch was able to order towns and villages to provide money to build ships, whenever invasion was feared.

Letters were sent out to sheriffs reminding them of a possibility of invasion and instructing them to collect the Ship Money. Encouraged by the large contributions he received, Charles demanded more the following year. In the past Ship Money had only been raised when the kingdom was threatened by war. It was now clear that collections would be made year upon year. Sheriffs wrote to the king complaining that their counties were being asked to pay too much.

The county of Cambridgeshire was told it had to raise £3500 in the year 1639–1640 *...for the setting forth of one ship for the safeguard of the seas*. The Armingford Hundreds was rated at £233 13s 4d with Melbourn's contribution fixed at £25 10s. A resistance in Melbourn to this 'illegal tax', or Ship Money, was organised by Benjamin Metcalfe and on 12 June 1640, when the Sheriff's bailiffs arrived at the village green to collect the toll, they were met by a crowd of a hundred or more men, women and children, led by Metcalfe. The 'collectors' ~ those who had been assigned to collect the money from the village ~ were arrested by the bailiffs. The official report stated that:

...The collectors, John Pettitt, John Neale, Benjamin Metcalfe, Leonard Evens, Edmond Jefferson, Roger Andrews, Nathaniel Andrews, John Thurgood, John Hitch, brother of William Hitch and William French the older, with a number of a hundred more men, women and children, assembled together against the said bailiffs, who sought for the constables and desired their aid to keep the peace, which was denied and ill words given. Then the bailiffs and sheriff's men, fearing some hurt would be done, made a proclamation that all should depart ...notwithstanding the whole multitude rescued the collectors and fell upon the bailiffs and sheriff's men with

stones and staves, and hedge staves and forkes and beat them and wounded divers [several] of them, and did drive them into a woman's yard ... her house for their safeguard, and were forced to get out of town the back way, some thirty or forty able men and boys pursued them about a quarter of a mile, stoning them and driving the bailiffs into a ditch where some of the horses stuck fast, and the said multitude got some of the bailiffs' horses and carried them away. Parliament abolished the Ship Money in July 1641.

It was inevitable that events such as these would lead to a Civil War. During the 1640s, Melbourn had a leaning towards the Puritan cause, and the movement was certainly reinforced by the Royalist Army, which in 1643, had plundered the area in search of food.

By contrast, there is no record of any such action when Cromwell's Army was encamped on Thriplow Heath in June 1647. In that year Oliver Cromwell, with Fairfax and others, marched his army into East Anglia and set up his headquarters in Saffron Walden. He then billeted some 20,000 soldiers in and around Thriplow. A council of war took place ...*in a fair green meadow four miles from Royston, on the down called Thriplow Heath. From east and south-east all roads converge there.* These roads have been identified as 'The Bridgefoot' and 'The Flint', which were on the boundary of the parish of Melbourn.

By the 10th June 1647, the army moved on to London, by way of Royston and St. Albans; a fortnight later Charles was under escort from Newmarket to Royston and later to Hampton Court, still a King but also a prisoner.

The Boer War

The latter part of the 19th century saw a great deal of military activity in the village. In May 1891 soldiers from the Hertfordshire and Bedfordshire Regiment marched from the station, drilled in the centre of Melbourn and were then entertained at Mulberry Hall before marching to Royston station.

A local baker, Mr T Woods, was reported to be

supplying bread to a militia encampment at Royston in April 1897. By this time the Boer War was imminent and local men became involved.

In December 1898, a welcome home public tea was given to Privates Frank Day and John Catley who had taken part in General Kitchener's campaign in the Sudan. Both returned unwounded, but were suffering from the effects of the campaign. They were marched 146 miles in 5 days and rested for only 24 hours before battle. Before coming home they had been recovering at the Army Hospital at Netley, near Southampton.

By 1900 the war had been in full progress for several years and was not going well for the British Army.

Doctor Unwin, a former assistant to Doctor Bindloss in Melbourn, had become a medical officer in the Warwickshire Yeomanry and had been commended in dispatches for coolness in treating the wounded under fire. In September of that year, Sergeant J Handscombe and Private H Harper (Suffolk Regiment) were released from a prisoner of war camp at Nooitgedacht. They had been wounded and taken prisoner on 8th January.

In April 1900, Mrs Woodcock, living in Water Lane at

A ten shilling note issued during the siege of Mafeking

the time, received a box of the Queen's chocolate from her son at the front with a request to preserve the contents and the box. Queen Victoria had sent a box to all members of her forces for Christmas 1899.

Alfred Chapman, a private in the 18th Hussars, sent a letter to his mother describing the privations suffered during a siege at Ladysmith. His Christmas dinner had consisted of one and a half dog biscuits and a piece of horseflesh, but he cheerfully said, '*rough fare was nothing once you got used to it*'.

The end of another siege, probably the most famous in the Boer War, caused great celebration in the village in May 1900. When the news came through of the relief of Mafeking (a British held town under siege for 7 months), the whole community joined in paying homage to Colonel Robert Baden-Powell, the commander of the garrison. Flags of all sizes were put out, the church bells were rung. In the evening ...*the young men of the village paraded with an impromptu band and sang patriotic songs.* The evening finished at about 1am with a Union Jack being placed on The Green. The crowd gave three cheers for 'Bathing Towel' (a nickname for Baden-Powell) and sang the national anthem.

The turn of the century

In January 1901, following the death of Queen Victoria, the Volunteers, under the command of Surgeon-Captain Bindloss, paraded at the parish church for a memorial service. In the following October, a collection was made at the church for men serving in the Army in South Africa. It was reported that twelve Melbourn men were in the ranks and each was to receive a pipe, plus ½lb of tobacco, two pairs of socks, two handkerchiefs, a 1lb plum pudding, a box of soap, stationery and a Christmas card.

Reasons to celebrate

By March 1902 the war was over. There was much rejoicing in the village. The Post Office had three Union Jacks flying, there were flags and bunting in the High Street. The church bells rang all day and three banners flew from the church tower. All businesses closed at 1pm and a meeting on The Green, was followed by a torchlit procession and a photograph taken by Mr Bishop. This ended at the chalk pit on the Old Royston Road, where a bonfire was built and lit. The crowd dispersed when the fire had died.

Territorial Army. Back row, Arthur Chapman, Quiler Waldock, Jack Ward, Alf Harland, Oliver (from Whaddon).
Front row, Law (from Whaddon) Alex King and George Connel

By August Private H Woodcock (Suffolk Regiment) returned from South Africa with a fine collection of ostrich feathers. The following month, Private John Catley of the Lincolnshire Regiment came home after 2¾ years' service, having been wounded at Paardsberg. In October, Sergeant Handscombe finally reached Melbourn, having been wounded and held prisoner. By November, he had celebrated even further by marrying Rose Gouldthorp at the Congregational Chapel. Also in November, Private Alfred Chapman of the 18th Hussars, who had seen a great deal of action, returned home. He had at one time been reported killed.

The First World War

Prayers for peace were said in the Parish Church at the beginning of 1914 but, by 4th August, the First World War had been declared and many flocked to enlist. At first the Army relied on volunteers but as casualties mounted conscription was brought in.

During the month that war was declared, daily sewing meetings were held to make articles for the wounded and families of servicemen. Twenty-six pounds was collected to help the work continue. Services were held on behalf of all sailors and soldiers at the church. After one of the services the Salvation Army Band played on The Green and collected 19s on behalf of the Prince of Wales National Relief Fund. A public meeting was held in September *...to lay before the men of Melbourn their patriotic duty of helping their country through the present crisis.*

In October 1914 J Catley, E Waldock and R Waldock were amongst the first to leave Melbourn, as they had taken part in previous engagements.

A public meeting of Melbourn and Meldreth parishioners was held to consider the plight of the invaded Belgians. A fund was raised and it was agreed to house two of the families in a house supplied by Mr Hope, which had been furnished by gifts from parishioners.

William Jackson 1913

Many wounded and killed

By the end of the month advertisements in the newspapers were calling for a second half-million soldiers to reinforce the first, already recruited. The ages required were 19–35, with the pay set at 6s 8d a week.

Sergeant Thomas Guiver (Dragoon Guards) was the first man from Melbourn to die. He was killed in action on 6th November 1914.

There were no further casualties until the following year when, in April 1915, Private Albert (Alfred) Negus was killed and during May, Private Frank Chapman of Dolphin Lane was wounded in the head and hip by a bursting shell and was reported to be in a French hospital.

Lance Corporal Frederick King (Bedfordshire Regiment) was killed in action on 25th September.

The death of Sergeant Albert Holland of New Road, serving in the Bedfordshire Regiment, who had been killed on 18th December, was widely mourned. He had been a member of the Baptist Church choir and a memorial service was held there in January. The same month saw the deaths of Sapper WC Howes (Royal Engineers), Gunner Ernest Green (Royal Artillery), and Private Samuel Northrop (Suffolk Regiment).

The twenty-four Belgian refugees, who had been looked after in the village for 15 months were preparing to leave and the work of the Melbourn & Meldreth War Refugee Committee was declared to be at an end. The final refugees to depart were Madame and Mlle. Langeau.

Reverend W H Wrigley, the Minister of the Congregational Church, read 'letters from the trenches' from Melbourn and Meldreth soldiers, at a service in February.

Frank Greatorex 1914–18 War

By June 1916 there was an acute shortage of farm workers. Mr Thomas Titchmarsh of Holland Hall Farm had the help of seven men from the Hertfordshire Regiment with the hay harvest. More news came of war casualties and of death. From the Hertfordshire Regiment, Private Charles Dodkin was reported to have died of wounds, and Private Willis Ward was in hospital having been wounded. Also wounded was Frederick Smith of the Cambridgeshire Regiment.

More men were killed in action over the summer months; Private James Saunderson (Suffolk Regiment) and Lance Sergeant Charles Fordham (Royal Fusiliers, City of London Regiment) in July and Private Lionel Frost (Suffolk Regiment) in August. Private Frank Brunton, of the Suffolk Regiment, was wounded in July and Private Ernest Abrey of Dolphin Lane had been wounded, gassed and blown up. There was no further news of him.

By September, news had come through that Private Walter Littlechild (Suffolk Regiment) had been killed on 1st July, the first day of the infamous Somme offensive, and Walter Lee of the Army Service Corps had died from the wounds he received whilst unloading ammunition. He is buried in the Congregational Chapel cemetery, having died in this country. Private Jack Fuller (Suffolk Regiment) was also listed as wounded. September also saw the death of Private Fred Pepper (Suffolk Regiment).

A break from the news of casualties came in the same month when Private Henry Crabtree of Clun Grange won the Military Medal for carrying despatches under fire. By October, it was reported that Private Fred Holland was wounded, and Gunner Richard Guiver of Orchard Road was in hospital, suffering from shell shock and other complications.

Scrimping, saving and sorrow

In February 1917, a call for voluntary rationing was made, otherwise a rationing service would have to be enforced. It was suggested that 4lbs of bread, 2½lbs of meat and ¾lb of sugar was sufficient for weekly needs.

In March a War Savings Committee was formed, with Mr WH Taylor (Chairman of the Parish Council) as Treasurer and Miss H Brett as Secretary. Sixty names were enrolled who contributed a total of £25 12s 6d. Numbers had increased to 79 members by May and 188 certificates had been sold. The war had an effect on the delivery of mail and Sunday deliveries were stopped. Trains delivering mail from Royston were now later than usual. In April, Private Frank Day of East Terrace was shot and killed by a sniper.

Further bad news

The spring of 1917 saw the deaths of Rifleman Frederick Saunderson (King's Royal Rifles Corps.) in February, Private Jesse Guiver (Nottinghamshire and Derbyshire Regiment) in March and Private William Jacklin (East Kent Regiment), was killed in action on 9th April. May and June were also bad months for casualties, with the deaths of Privates John Reed and Frederick Winter, both of the Cambridgeshire Regiment and Private Harry Squires (Australian Contingent). Harry had emigrated to Australia from Melbourn two years before the war but returned to England to serve.

Four deaths occurred in August; Arthur King (Gloucester Regiment), Private Alfred Winter (Essex Regiment), Private Charles Huggins (Lincolnshire Regiment) of New Road (described as a well known local footballer and runner) and Lance Corporal Stanley Waldock (King's Royal Rifles). All were killed in action.

The year drew to a sad close with the death of Private Robert (Bob) Reed on 30th September and

the wounding of Privates Douglas Gouldthorpe and B Wedd of Dolphin Lane. The latter was moved from France to Bournemouth to recuperate and then granted twelve days leave before being sent back to France. Private Rydal (Jack) Wing (East Lancashire Regiment) died in October, as did Private Alfred Smith (Suffolk or Cambridgeshire Regiment), followed by Gunner Lewis Robinson of New Road in November.

'Our Day' was an occasion in Melbourn, where house-to-house collections and the sale of flags raised £13 2s 0d for soldiers. Mrs Foley, from Manor House, arranged two concerts with the orchestra of the 31st Middlesex Regiment. The proceeds were used to send a postal order and Christmas presents to all Melbourn men serving at the front.

Not all the news coming through was bad, when it was announced that Corporal AC Blows (Machine Gun Corps) had been awarded the Military Medal.

New year, new hope

Private Percy Wedd (Grenadier Guards) was killed in March 1918. Corporal William Pullen, who had escaped from a prisoner of war camp, and returned to service only to be killed in action. He was married with three children.

There were two deaths in April ~ Private Edgar Brown (Northumberland Fusiliers, T.A. Regiment) and Sergeant William Harper (Hertfordshire Regiment).

Sergeant Alfred Blows (Machine Gun Corps) had had his right leg badly shattered in May, and Private William Willings (Royal Berkshire

Lewis Robinson 1914–18 War

Regiment) died on 24th June. Private Bertie Wedd (Royal Warwickshire Regiment) was reported to be a prisoner of war in Germany. Reported wounded were Private Chris Handscombe, Private Frank Harper (Royal West Kent Regiment), of the High Street and Gunner Joseph Henry Stockbridge (Royal Field Artillery), who was married with four children.

The War Weapons week, in August, realised £625 purchased in War Bonds and a further £947 in War Savings Certificates.

Frederick Green (Lancashire Fusiliers) died on 28th August ~ he was born in Melbourn, and enlisted in Royston, but lived in Kilowna, British Columbia, Canada. In September, Corporal GW Catley (Army Service Corps) died. Private John Burton (Royal Warickshire Regiment) died the following month and Private Harold Rumbold (Royal Inniskilling Fusiliers) died 4th November, only eight days away from armistice.

JE Hagger was reported to be engaged on secret Admiralty work and was returning to this country from Ireland when his ship, SS Leinster, was torpedoed and he died.

Peace at last

The Armistice was signed on 11th November 1918 and flags were flown in the village, the bells rung and St. George's flag flown on the church tower. At the same time, the sad news came through that a shell splinter had killed Private Edgar Abrey (Royal Engineers) on 28th October. Despite an epidemic of Spanish influenza in the village, a service of thanksgiving for the end of the war went ahead.

Even after the Armistice, reports of casualties continued to be received. Private Ernest Pateman, of the Machine Gun Corps, had been killed on 23rd October. He had joined under age (as had so many other young men), had been discovered and was sent home, only to return when he was eighteen years old.

As late as February 1919, Private Job Stanford (Northamptonshire Regiment) was reported as having been killed in action on 29th September 1918. He had worked with his brother as a thatcher.

In April 1919, a 'Discharged and Demobilised Soldiers' and Sailors' Fund' had been organised and 21 members enrolled. In May a Smoking Concert for returned servicemen was held in the schoolrooms and organised by those who had not served.

In September, details were made known of a Military Medal awarded to Sergeant King who, despite being wounded, when his officer was killed, had taken charge of a party removing German soldiers from a farmhouse. Lance Corporal JH Dickson (Military Police) was awarded the Meritorious Service Medal.

Also during September, an appeal was placed in the newspapers for a list of the Melbourn men who had given their lives for their country. It had been reported that 44 names were listed, and any omissions should be submitted, so that the correct names could be inscribed on a Memorial at The Cross. This figure was later increased to 46.

In November, the possibility of installing a stained glass window in the south transept (or in the south window of the side chapel), and a brass tablet on the wall, was discussed at a meeting of Parish Church members, to record the names of Melbourn men who had died. The cost was estimated at £140, and some promises of donations had been made.

In May 1920, the Harry Brodie Day memorial window was placed in position in the Lady Chapel and a brass tablet commemorating all the Melbourn men who died, was also installed. Second Lieutenant Harry Brodie Day of Roseleigh, was killed by shellfire on 4th February 1918 when returning from the trenches.

The window was dedicated by the Assistant Archbishop and Archdeacon of Ely. It represented 'The resurrection of our Lord' and was made by Martin and Young of Stratford, as was the tablet. It was described as follows:

...In the upper lights the arms of the Diocese of Ely, of All Saints' Melbourn, the red cross of St. George, the Rose of England, the fleur de lys of France and the emblem of the Blessed Trinity. The central light contains the glorious Saint and Martyr St. George, the patron saint of England and especially of soldiers, depicting his victory over evil by treading the dragon under his feet. In the left light St. Michael the Archangel, the Prince of the Church Militant, is shown in armour with a fiery sword and other emblems of defence or protection; in the right St. Martin, Bishop of Tours, on whose festival 11th November the armistice was signed and the actual warfare came to an end. He is the emblem of charity.

The Harry Brodie Day memorial window, in the Lady Chapel

Memorial service on Armistice Day, at The Cross

Unveiling of the War Memorial

On Sunday afternoon last, notwithstanding the inclement weather, some 400 or 500 people gathered at The Cross at Melbourn for the unveiling and dedication of the beautiful Memorial Cross which had been erected to the men of Melbourn who had given their lives in the Great War.

The flag on the Church tower was at half-mast and a half-muffled peal was rung on the bells. For a quarter of an hour immediately prior to the commencement of the service the bell was tolled. The ex-service men of Melbourn, numbering about 50, in charge of Regt-Sergt. Major L. Hale, paraded in Mortlock Street near the schools. The Boy Scouts, in charge of Scoutmaster Maurice de Wolfe; the Girl Guides, under Mrs Swain, the Brownies in charge of Mrs Gregor, with the school children, marshalled by Mr F. Aldridge, and the teachers, were all on parade, marching down to the Memorial. The ex-service men, with Captain G.S. Wilkinson at their head, were drawn up on the north side of the Memorial, the Scouts, Guides and Brownies on the east, and on the west side were seats for the relatives of the fallen men. At their back were the school children. The hymns were led by the choirs from the three places of worship, and P.S.A. Band with Mr R. Webb at the organ.

There were present and taking part in the service Rev. M. de Courcy Ireland (Vicar), Rev. R.W. Foster (Baptist), Rev. J.G. Davis (Congregational), and Mr A.R. Fordham. The service opened with the hymn, announced by the Rev R.W. Foster, 'O God our help in ages past,' and a portion of scriptures was read by the Rev. J. G. Davis.

Mr A.R. Fordham then stepped forward, and removing the Union Jack which veiled part of the Memorial on which were inscribed the names of the fallen, said they had erected that Cross in memory of the men of Melbourn who had died in the Great War. He then read out the name of each man inscribed upon

On Sunday 5th December 1920, the Melbourn War Memorial was unveiled and dedicated. All ex-service men were asked to assemble opposite the schools and take part in the ceremony under the direction of ex-Regimental Sergeant Major L Hale.

A memorial tablet was also unveiled at the Congregational Chapel in May 1921, containing the names of seventeen men who were members there.

Four years later, the OBE (Military Division) was awarded to Sergeant Major Reuben Pennicott of the Royal Air Force, whose home was at Ferndale in Mortlock Street. He was serving on the north-west frontier in India at the time, where the Royal Air Force was 'policing' the area.

the Memorial. Those men, he said, had died for their country, they died for us, and they died to save England in the greatest peril that ever befell her. We could never repay what we owed them, but he hoped that the Memorial would keep their names green in the memory of all for many years to come. Whilst they honoured their dead they did not wish to forget the honour due to those who came through all that terrible time and were with them once more.

Captain G.S. Wilkinson, on behalf of the ex-service men, said they had just unveiled that beautiful Cross in Melbourn in memory of those men who many of them knew so well, and who had died for them. It required no Memorial of that kind to keep green the memory of them in the hearts of those dear ones they had left behind, but to others such a Memorial would serve for all time and point to the heroic deeds they did, and the sacrifice they made for their country. Theirs was an example of true patriotism which should surely be followed by every one of us by doing all we could for those who were disabled or suffering. This patriotic spirit was still needed by us all in pulling together and in helping one another to make this country better and brighter for all who lived in it.

The Rev. M. de Courcy Ireland then offered the dedicatory prayer and prayers for the relatives of the fallen and all those in distress.

This was followed by the concluding hymn (announced by Rev. R.W. Foster) 'For all the saints who from their labours rest.' The ex-service men then marched past the front of the Memorial with the order, 'eyes right', then followed the little Brownies, the Girl Guides, and the Boy Scouts, each group being halted as they came to the front of the Memorial while three of their number deposited a wreath on the steps, saluting and withdrawing. The 'Last Post' was then sounded by an unseen bugler from a distance, and the Benediction by the Vicar concluded a memorable service.

Many beautiful wreaths were placed round the base of the Cross by relatives and friends of the fallen men, the most conspicuous being a large artificial one under a glass shade bearing the words: In memory of our fallen comrades, from the ex-service men of Melbourn.'

They fought for King and Country,
They never missed the call;
Now they have gone to be with
The highest King of all.

Amongst the other wreaths were: 'In loving memory from All Saints' Parish Church'; 'In affectionate and grateful remembrance from the Melbourn Congregational Chuch and Sunday School'; 'A token of esteem and remembrance of all those connected with the Baptist Church, who laid down their lives in the Great War, from the members and congregation, 'Peace perfect peace'; 'In loving memory of those who laid down their lives for us, 1914–1919, from the teachers and scholars, Melbourn Council School'; 'From the Melbourn Girl Guides, in proud and grateful memory, 'Service'; 'In grateful memory of those who died for us, from the Melbourn Brownie Pack'; 'In Memoriam, from the 4th Cambs District Troop (Melbourn and Meldreth) B.P. Boy Scouts'.

A very large wreath was also deposited amongst others by General Cotgrave of the Middlesex Regiment, bearing the inscription: 'To the glorious memory of 2nd Lieut. E.L. Hall, Royal North Lancs., Pt. Ernest Waldock, and all their comrades of this village who gave their lives for their country in the Great War'.

The Memorial is erected on The Green near the Parish Church and the cross roads, and is composed entirely of Portland stone. The whole stands on a stone base 10ft 3in square, from which are three steps on each side of the square up to the pedestal of the shaft, which

is about 18 feet high, and surmounted by a small Latin Cross. On the base of the shaft fronting the main road is a small laurel wreath in relief on the stone. Cut on the four sides of the pedestal are the words, 'In memory 1914–1918', and the names of the fallen as follows:

Edgar R Abrey	George Pateman
Edgar E Brown	Frederick G Pepper
John Burton	William H. Pullen
Arthur H Carter	
William G Catley	John W Reed
Henry B Day	Robert H Reed
Frank W Day	Louis Robinson
Charles Dodkin	Harold E Rumbold
Charles Fordham	Frederick Saunderson
Lionel B Frost	James Saunderson
Ernest J Green	Alfred H Smith
Frederick C Green	
Jesse Guiver	Joseph Smith
Thomas Guiver	Harry Squires
William C Harper	Job Stanford
Albert Holland	
William C Howes	Frederick Throssell
Charles H Huggins	Stanley J Waldock
William. T Jacklin	Percy Wedd
Arthur King	
Frederick J King	William Willings
Walter Lee	Rydal SL Wing
Walter A Littlechild	
Alfred Negus	Alfred J Winter
Samuel Northrop	Fred Winter

The Memorial was obtained ready worked by Messrs. G.A. Ward & Sons, of Melbourn, and erected by Mr William Whitehead, of Royston.

Herts and Cambs Reporter 10th December 1920

Forty-five men are mentioned in the newspaper report, although church records list forty-six men. The missing name is Edward L Hall.

Further discord

During the 1920s, and part of the 1930s, Great Britain reduced its armed forces, trusting in the League of Nations for protection against a future war.

The League of Nations had a local branch in Melbourn but, by 1930, it was in decline although the Rev. Appleby agreed to stand as secretary.

In May 1938, Bassingbourn airfield was opened. Melbourn was on a direct line between Bassingbourn and Duxford airfields and villagers became worried as as there was a possiblity of war. A less-than-comforting report suggested that the distance between the two airfields was 7¾ miles, and a straight line would be ... 10 *furlongs north-east of Melbourn Church.*

By August the residents had experienced a Precautions Exercise, when all lights had to be extinguished or screened by dark curtains between 1pm and 3pm on Sunday 7th. On the 12th of August, a Demon two-seater plane crashed in the grounds of The Lodge owned by Mrs Duff, opposite The Dolphin. The pilot, S Robinson, parachuted to safety, landing in the Congregational Minister's garden, and the observer, S Macadam, landed in Muncey's farm.

Plane Wrecked at Melbourn

Two aeroplanes which had been engaged in the air defence manoeuvres crashed in Cambridgeshire in the early hours of Sunday morning, but in both cases the pilot and his observer escaped by parachute.

It was shortly after 4 a.m. when what one of them described as a "terrific crash" awoke the occupants of The Lodge, Melbourn. One of the planes had landed in the front garden there, missing the house by a few yards. In its fall the machine caught some tall trees, or it must have struck the house.

Mrs. Duff, who lives at the Lodge, told a reporter that the crash broke the windows of her room.

Meanwhile, the pilot, P.O., S.J.D. Robinson, had landed safely near Cawdon House, Melbourn, which is occupied by Mr. B.A. Palmer. After a 3½ hours search it was discovered that his observer, A. C., S.F. Macadam, had come down in a field near Royston.

The machine, A Demon two-seater fighter, had apparently run out of petrol. The occupants were men of the 64th Squadron, stationed at Digby, Lincs.

At about the same time a plane of the same type, which had also run out of petrol, came down in a wheat field at Little Chishill, about a mile from the Flint crossroads.

The pilot and observer jumped and parachuted to safety.

WHAT THE PAPERS SAID

Reports of the Prime Minister's visit to Hitler in Munich filled the local newspapers in September, but the relief of that visit did not stop the digging of trenches at places in the village.

In October an ARP exercise was held in the village when gas masks were supplied and fitted. After the

There were a number shelters in the village, some situated in back gardens. Known as Anderson shelters, they could accommodate up to 6 people. A large hole 6' × 4' 6" × 6' 6" was dug in the garden and covered with galvanised corrugated steel. For those on low incomes they were issued free of charge, but for those on higher incomes, there was a charge of £7. Morrison shelters took the form of a sturdy metal table with mesh sides, which were housed indoors.

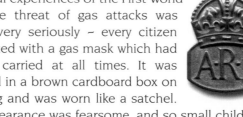

dreadful experiences of the First World War the threat of gas attacks was taken very seriously ~ every citizen was fitted with a gas mask which had to be carried at all times. It was housed in a brown cardboard box on a string and was worn like a satchel. Its appearance was fearsome, and so small children were issued with Mickey Mouse masks.

Appointments of air raid wardens were made, and were named as AW Bacon (Head Warden), G Pearce, F Ward, A Woods, W Winter, CA Frost, S Reed, A King, H Lee, A Harland, A Dodkin, F Hickman, E Stanford, G Dockerill, A Handscombe, AJ Day, C Gouldthorp, E French, N H Watson, E Cooper and F Hurst.

It was their job to get people off the streets, marshal them to safety, and make sure that the 'blackout' was observed.

Also in October, a report appeared in a national newspaper of Walter and Donald Littlechild as brothers, who had joined the Army on the condition that they would serve together at all times.

Walter and Don Littlechild

By December 1938, the wardens had checked all 1400 gas masks issued to the villagers and all were reported to be in working order. On that sombre note the last year of peace ended with heavy snowfalls necessitating the use of snowploughs.

There were complaints about low-flying aircraft over the village from Duxford, but it was said that they were taking aerial photographs to determine the route of the new by-pass.

On 1st September, the kerbstones in the High Street were painted white in readiness for the blackouts.

The Second World War
Life at home

War was declared against Germany on Sunday 3rd September. Four days later, a large crowd assembled to see off 54 members of 18th Platoon of the 2nd Cambridgeshire Regiment, as they left the village to join their regiment.

At the same time 200 evacuees arrived and were billeted in the village, and later followed by a further 50 mothers and children from Islington and 92 children from the Brompton Oratory Roman Catholic school in Chelsea. The priest in charge of the school was billetted with John Buchan of the Congregational Chapel. Mr Buchan, who ran the general stores, was a strict teetotaller and took exception to the priest's frequent visits to the local pub! The children from Chelsea stayed only until November, having found more suitable accommodation in Clacton.

The police station had been sandbagged and only regular policemen were issued with steel helmets, which caused some friction with the special constables.

Nurse Cox set up an infant welfare clinic in December, and enrolled 57 mothers and children (including 15 evacuees). Also in December, there was a panic over reported 'mines' in the River Mel ~ these

Daphne Black in the ATS

turned out to be two sacks of corn that had fallen off a lorry into the river!

The blackout had prevented many village organisations from meeting in the evening; there was no street lighting at night and everyone had to put up blackout curtains to cut out the light. Brown paper was stuck criss-cross over the windows in case of bomb blast. By February 1940, the Council schools had been successfully fitted with blackout curtains and evening events could again be held.

Following the introduction of the National Savings Scheme, Melbourn set up a committee in May; Mr C Varley was appointed as secretary and Mr A Thompson as treasurer. Friday evenings, between 6.30–7.30pm were agreed as collection times. The scheme, slow to get off the ground at first, had only reached £99 by June. A 'thriftometer' was installed in the Post Office window which obviously did the trick as, by the end of June, £500 had been collected, rising to £1000 in July, and £3000 by the end of November.

All for the war effort

When women were conscripted, they had the choice of joining the Auxiliary Territorial Service (ATS), Women's Royal Naval Service (WRENS) or Women's Auxiliary Air Force (WAAF), becoming land girls or working in factories producing munitions. Quite a few Melbourn girls worked at Atlas in Whaddon, or in the old Kayser Bondor factory in Baldock where they made parachutes. When they came back in the evening they had a nerve-racking walk home, from the station across the Meads in the dark, through a herd of cows.

There was fear of an invasion and of spies, foreigners were viewed with suspicion and all signposts were removed throughout Britain, the

LOCAL DEFENCE VOLUNTEERS
CAMBRIDGESHIRE

No. 4/ 747

This is to certify that the Bearer

Cecil Joseph Jackson

has been duly enrolled as a Member of the above Armed Force of the Crown and is hereby authorised to act as such.

W. Phillips

Major

June, 1940

Commanding Cambridgeshire Zone

theory being that an invading force would get lost. Buildings and landmarks which could easily be distinguished from the air, were painted with camouflage. All letters to and from servicemen were opened, and censored if it was thought necessary. Government posters told you that *Careless Talk Costs Lives* and warned you to *be like Dad, keep Mum*. Phrases such as *Dig for Victory* and *Put That Light Out* were propaganda slogans seen in buses and trains. *There's a war on* became the excuse for everything.

The wireless, or radio, had great importance being the main source of news and entertainment. 'Monday Night at Eight' and 'ITMA' (It's That Man Again) with Tommy Handley, kept the nation's spirits up, whilst children listened to 'Toytown' and 'Children's Hour'. Vera Lynn, the Forces sweetheart, travelled abroad to entertain the troops with ENSA (Entertainments National Service Association but unofficially it was known as 'Every Night Something Awful'), and Forces Favourites on the radio provided links between home and abroad. Workers' Playtime took music to the factories daily, aimed at keeping up morale. Local girls would go to dances at Bassingbourn or Duxford, especially if the Glen Miller band was playing!

The war takes hold

The first Melbourn casualty of the Second World War was Corporal William Wilkins (Royal Army Service Corps.), who died on 17th June 1940.

After the evacuation at Dunkirk, in May, a National Day of Prayer was organised and all three churches in the village were full.

The formation of the Local Defence Volunteers, swiftly re-named the Home Guard, enabled many men over call-up age to do their bit. The first weeks were chaotic and the only uniform was an armband marked LDV, but eventually they became organised and the following description written at the time gives some idea of those early days:

…As more arms and ammunition came through, LDV officers loaded them into their own cars and distributed them around. Usually, it was a matter of two or three rifles and a handful of cartridges to each village. An officer who did this in south-west Cambridgeshire recalled:

Three hundred and fifty rifles, with ten rounds each, and 350 denim overalls were rushed out and left at Melbourn police station, from where they were collected by the battalion commander and issued through companies to the homes of village detachment commanders, often without even a chit to say their number, or a signature to show who had them. One remembers a handful of rifles dumped on the billiard table of the village inn, with ducklings waddling through the door, and the air of subdued excitement and anticipation everywhere one went. The conversation often went as follows:

'Any news of the invasion, sir?'

'No'.

'Well I suppose it will be coming along in due course' and everybody thought it was, and appeared to be utterly unafraid, although we were raising an army as ill-equipped as that of Monmouth at Sedgemoor to face the most highly trained and mechanised troops in the world.

The first bombs fell on the village on 31st August, when one or more enemy planes started bombing over Fowlmere and then travelled north of the village over Shepreth, Meldreth and Barrington.

Many of the bombs fell within the parish, in Corrie Stanford's fields and Bert Palmer's orchards. On 16th October, three more bombs were dropped near The Moor Corner and one at Heath Farm. On 20th October, a large bomb was dropped on Percy Elbourn's field at Townsend. This broke several windows and knocked items from shelves in houses at the Royston end of the village. Five days later, four bombs were dropped on Hoy's farm.

Jubal Howard's dog, Carlo, featured in the newspapers in November, was said to bark only at enemy planes, never at friendly planes! The following month there was a debate on the installation of an air-raid siren in the village and queries about who was to pay and where it would be positioned. It was eventually installed at the Atlas factory in Whaddon. It could be clearly heard in

Melbourn ~ it sounded a loud up and down wail when enemy planes were approaching ~ and at the sound, mothers would run to the school to take their children home! The 'all clear' was a long, unbroken signal, always greeted with relief.

Featured in a newspaper the following month was a list of the names of Melbourn men serving in the forces.

The low point of the war is generally thought to be 1941, when there were few victories to be celebrated. Great Britain was 'hanging on'.

By March, 200 members of the Melbourn National Savings Scheme had contributed £5000 and, in May, villagers had the chance to make a real contribution to the war effort with 'War Weapons Week'. There was a great parade, with several Army and Royal Air Force units involved as well as local organisations.

The village had set a target of £2500, but the final total was the huge sum of £19,064, which was remarkable for a village of Melbourn's size.

Rationing throughout the war

Rationing began in 1940, although registration for some commodities was urged in the autumn of 1939. By the end of 1940, bacon, ham, butter, cheese, margarine, cooking fat, sugar and jam were rationed and, in 1942, eggs were added to the list. One egg was allowed per adult per week or one packet of dried (powdered) eggs each every four weeks. Sweets were confined to 12ozs each month.

There was much trading of 'coupons'. If someone did not take sugar, they might trade their sugar coupons for a butter ration, although being an agricultural community, Melbourn suffered little real shortage.

Babies and toddlers were issued with coupons for Virol (a sticky malt extract paste), concentrated orange juice and rosehip syrup ~ in the autumn people were encouraged to collect hips from the hedgerows to be made into syrup. Clothes and footwear and were rationed from 1st June 1941.

More casualties

News came of the death of Lance Corporal Cyril Webb (Cambridgeshire Regiment), who died on 11th October 1941. He is buried in Melbourn Cemetery.

The following year, whilst there was rejoicing at victories in the Middle East and the entry of America into the war, it also proved to be tragic for Melbourn families. Many of the local men had joined the Cambridgeshire Regiment and were sent to the Far East ~ to Hong Kong and Singapore. Many arrived in time to be involved in the badly-led sieges and were taken prisoner by the Japanese, a fate which was to prove horrific for them.

Civil Defence Group later known as the ARP's

Red Cross nurses on parade during 'Salute the Soldier' week in the High Street

In February, B Palmer, an air gunner in Bomber Command, was shot down over Germany and, after some initial worries, was reported a prisoner of war.

On 27th March a report was received that Warrant Officer Smith (Royal Army Service Corps) had been taken prisoner in Malaya.

Also that month the Warships Week set the village a target of £10,000 to raise. It was surpassed in April when a final figure of £12,467 was announced.

The Invasion Committee, under the direction of Lance Hale, met to consider reports on local food depots and calls for men to volunteer to dig emergency trenches.

In May Sergeant Ernest Butcher was reported missing in action. The following month Reginald Bunten qualified as a pilot after training in the USA.

June saw the final attack from Germany, when a flying bomb fell on Mr Stanford's field near Black Peak. This missile shook the village, cracked ceilings and windows and greatly alarmed the queue of people waiting at The Green for the Royston bus!

Gunner (Kenneth) Robert Lee (Royal Artillery) died on 7th August 1942 and was buried in Calcutta, India.

October saw yet another fund-raising effort when 'Tanks for Attack' raised £4,837, which was the highest in South Cambridgeshire, but not quite up to the target of £5,000.

There was a huge Military and Civil Defence Exercise in and around the village, but by November the victory at El Alamein meant that the church bells, silent since Dunkirk and only to be rung in the event of invasion, were ringing again.

Keeping spirits up

1943 – and the New Year began with a dance, held in aid of prisoners of war, which raised £20.

Gangs of workmen descended on the village in February and removed iron railings which, the population was told, were intended for aircraft and tank production. Later reports suggested that a great deal of the metal collected was never used – the whole event being a propaganda exercise. The only adverse effect it had in Melbourn was that the youth of the village ran wild through gardens causing some householders hastily to replace the gaps with hurdles.

Under a scheme which allowed towns and villages to 'adopt' a Royal Navy ship, Melbourn was given HMS P52 and a certificate was displayed in the Post Office window.

The Government, satisfied that an invasion was not imminent, allowed church bells to be rung again on Sundays and on days of special importance.

In May 'Wings for Victory' week targeted the sum of £10,000, but such was the enthusiasm for the scheme that £11,838, (which represented £8 16s 0d per head of population) was reached and was the third highest total in South Cambridgeshire, after Sawston and Linton.

The Home Guard on parade during 'Salute the Soldier' week in the High Street

The Home Guard on parade during 'Salute the Soldier' week

By May reports of Melbourn men in Japanese hands started to come through, usually in the form of a simple postcard, which spoke of being in good health and *...working for pay*. These were palpable lies, as later events revealed, as any correspondence with prisoners was often non-existent. Warrant Officer Ernest Waldock (Royal Engineers) was amongst the first to be reported, followed by Private Tom Wright of the ill-fated Cambridgeshire Regiment. Many servicemen died working on the Burma Railway.

Wing Commander Howard Burton (RAF) died in June. His name is commemorated on the Runnymede Memorial.

In July reports came in that Sergeant Percy Holland and Privates Eric Stanford, Charles Frost and Leslie Littlechild were prisoners of war in Japanese hands, and Pilot Officer Jim Taylor was a prisoner of war in France. Warrant Officer Reginald Bunten was awarded the Distinguished Flying Cross in November. William Smith, driver with the Royal Army Service Corps/Anti Tank Regiment, died in October. He was buried in Thailand.

By the end of 1943 there was a note of cautious optimism, although not for those villagers with relatives in Japanese hands.

The battle goes on

In January the following year, Oswald Smith (Royal Army Medical Corps) sent a postcard saying he was *...in excellent health and working for pay* although by now reports filtering through suggested that these conditions were very far from the truth. On a happier note, a letter from India told the village that Jim Catley and Joe Chamberlain had met up and spent 24 hours together.

Deaths during the year included Flying Officer Douglas Bacon (RAF Volunteer Reserve) in May, Sergeant Percival Holland (Cambridgeshire Regiment) in September and Lance Corporal Roy Stamford (York and Lancaster Regiment), who died on 5th November.

In May 'Salute the Soldier' week set a target of £10,000, and again this total was easily reached and passed with a final total of £13,021. In June, the 20th platoon of C Company of Cambridgeshire's Home Guard won the Challenge Cup for best battle platoon and the trophy was displayed in Howard Brothers' shop opposite the church. This was almost the last throw for the 'Dads' Army' because, in December 1944, with the allied invasion of Europe reaching ever nearer towards Germany, the Home Guard was stood down. Over 1,800,000 men had enlisted nationwide, and, although the early days of 1940 had earned them a certain amount of ridicule, there is no doubt that, had Germany invaded, they would have stubbornly resisted the enemy. A 'stand down' dinner, at The Bull Hotel in Royston, was held in December. when Lieutenant DA Elbourn, the officer in charge, was presented with a copper inkstand on behalf of the NCOs and men.

Sergeant Major Waldock sent three letters in his own handwriting from his Japanese prisoner of war camp in August, which must have cheered up his relatives.

The ill-fated operation at Arnhem resulted in many losses and prisoners, amongst whom was

The 20th platoon of C Company of Cambridgeshire's Home Guard with the Challenge Cup for best battle platoon

Lance Corporal Frederick Holland, who was wounded and taken prisoner. Fusilier Arthur Waldock (Royal Scots) was a prisoner of war in Germany.

Peace on the horizon

Six Mustangs crashed, within an hour of each other, shortly after take-off on 13th January 1945, due to bad weather. One came down in Rose Lane and the 2 families involved were fortunate to escape, as the engine was buried just feet away in the front garden. The aircraft were to have escorted heavy bomber planes on their way to bomb German bridges and marshalling yards. The pilot, who was killed, was Lt. Thomas Ksanznak.

In this last year of the war, a letter arrived from Private Ernest Frost saying again that ...*he was well and working for pay* in Thailand.

In March 1945, Sergeant Percy Holland was declared missing at sea, after the Japanese transport, taking men from Thailand to Japan, was sunk by allied aircraft. Also that month, Corporal Cecil Winter (Royal Army Service Corps) was killed by a shell in Italy, whilst taking supplies up to the line.

Victory in Europe Day was celebrated on 8th May, with a service in church, a bonfire in Collis Palmer's meadow and a tea in Portway. The occasion was marred by ...'*hobbledehoys' throwing fireworks through letter boxes in the village.*

In the same month, Jim Palmer, Fred Holland and Arthur Waldock ~ the first prisoners of war held in Europe ~ returned to a warm welcome from village residents.

The war in the Far East continued to rage, and in June it was announced that Oswald Smith had died, in October 1943, in Japanese hands.

A Victory Dance in July raised £52 10s 0d. for the Homecoming Fund, to add to over £3,000 collected since the fund was first started in November 1944.

Victory in Japan was celebrated in August with another service, a dance, a bonfire in Collis Palmer's meadow, and, this time, dancing in the streets to music supplied from The Rose Public house. The street lights were on again in September and news began to come through about prisoners in Japanese hands.

Private Ernest Frost was reported safe in Rangoon, and Eric Stanford in Colombo, Ceylon, but Private Tom Wright had died in September 1943 and Sergeant F Butcher had been killed as long ago as February 1942, in the siege of Singapore. The receipt of this late news had a devastating effect on those families hoping their men were still alive.

The additional names were included on the War Memorial and a book was placed in the Parish Church noting the names of the fallen. Their names, together with the fallen from the First World War, are still read out every Armistice Day at The Cross. They are:

Douglas A Bacon	William OI Smith
William Barron	Roy W Stamford
Howard Burton	William Thompson
Frederick EC Butcher	Cyril J Webb
Percival L Holland	William G Wilkins
(Kenneth) Robert Lee	Cecil Winter
Leslie A Littlechild	Thomas A Wright

In addition to those engraved on the war memorial, three others names are included in the church records. These are Clifford and Kenneth Chamberlain and Basil Stockbridge, who was a police constable in Somerset and died receiving a direct hit from a German bomb during the war.

End of War Celebrations 1945

The VJ celebrations last week, brought about by the surrender of Japan and the coming of peace to a troubled world after 6 years of war, will be looked upon as red-letter events in the history of our country, and the doings in Melbourn in the two days of rejoicing will long be remembered by villagers, as never before in living memory had such a notable and enjoyable programme of local events been so well organised and carried out, no untoward incident being recorded.

Very few people in the village heard at midnight on Tuesday of Japan's surrender, and it was not until a little before 7am on Wednesday that a prolonged ringing of the church bells awakened villagers to the fact that something special had happened. In a very short time flags were out and notices of coming events appeared in shop windows.

Limited space this week prevents the publication of a detailed report of all the doings, arranged mainly by the committee of the local Homecoming Fund, of which our live wire, Mr Jeff Puddock, is Hon. Sec.to whom and to many other enthusiastic workers, great credit is due.

On Wednesday evening there was a well attended dance in the Council School, where the necessary music was supplied by a radiogram and other electrical devices, under the direction of Mr Maurice Stockbridge. Amusements for children during the afternoon in the school grounds had been arranged, but owing to a pouring rain this part of the programme was abandoned. Thursday however, was a day of big doings, the weather having improved.

The St. George's Cross flag appeared on the tower of the parish church, and at 3pm there was a United Service at which the officiating clergy were the vicar, (Rev H.H. McNeice) and his son the Rev. Desmond McNeice, Rev. J.G. Davis of the Congregational Church and the Rev. H.T.N. Usher of the Baptist Church, and among the congregation were members of the British Legion and various other bodies. The two bowling greens were occupied most of the day, and many contests were staged. In the evening there was a whist drive at the Council School, when 17 tables were occupied, Mr A. Holland acting as MC. There were also many other attractions at the school.

At 9.30pm a large bonfire was lighted in Mr Collis Palmer's meadow, and this was supplemented by a display of fireworks, probably the finest show of its kind ever seen in the district. And of particular interest to children, the majority of whom had never before seen a proper pyrotechnic display. The final and crowning item of the 2 days' celebration was music and dancing in the street, the High Street at the Rose Inn corner being specially floodlit for the dance. Mr Charlie Bird, the host at the Rose and accomplished musician bringing his grand piano out onto the street, and playing dance music in his well known manner.

The event, which continued till midnight, was well conducted and most orderly, and at one time there was said to be nearly, if not quite, one thousand persons present, even the most sedate villagers venturing to show spectators what they knew of the terpsichorean art. Verily a most memorable ending to a perfect day.

Welcome home boys! – outside the Anchor pub in the High Street

Melbourn Thanks giving Week

The National Savings Thanksgiving Week in Melbourn ended last Saturday, November 13th, and a busy week it was for its organisers. The baby show, flower show and other attractions in the village during the first three days of the week. On Wednesday there was a concert in the Council School, arranged by Mr A.W. Whydale of Royston, a notable event in which 15 items were contributed by talented performers, they consisted of pianoforte and violin solos, songs, readings, conjuring and dances, all of which were most artistically produced. On Thursday thirty tables were occupied at a whist drive, when Mr O Palmer Howard officiated as M.C., assisted by Mr C. A. Leech. Refreshments were supplied under the management of Mesdames F. Winter, C.A. Leech, W. Wedd and G.H. Bunten.

On Friday there was a free M.O.I. Film Show, when the Council School was filled to capacity. The pictures shown were unquestionably the finest ever presented in the village, telling in a most impressive manner of the doings in Japan, West African villages, Italy, Coventry, and the making of a mosquito aeroplane. Verily a first class show and an admirable exposition of the National Savings Movement.

The final event of a memorable week was a dance under the management of Mesdames V Pettit and G. Kay of the local Homecoming Fund Committee. The school room was specially decorated for the dance, Dick Palmer's quartet (R.A.F) supplying the music. During the evening a banana, presented by Mrs Greatorex, was auctioned and finally sold for 11s 6d.

Old Folk's Victory tea

It has been decided to give the old folks a Victory tea on Saturday October 27th. For further particulars see notices in the window at the Post Office.

Brownie outing to Wicksteed Park, outside South Cambs garage

Recreation Leisure & sport

...the arrival of extra beer and the dusting of many wine glasses by housewives are evidences of feast time

There is little evidence from early times of sport and leisure activities in the village. However, there were numerous Feast Days were associated with the church and these provided both leisure and entertainment for everyone. Religious Festivals included colourful processions, miracle plays and feasting.

Some sports developed from military practice, such as archery and swordsmanship. The lord of the manor required men to hone their skills in case they were needed to defend his domain, or in the event that he was asked to supply soldiers to the King.

In pre-Norman England, hunting was still a democratic pastime (for all but slaves) and every free-born Anglo-Saxon had the right to bring home game for the pot. Medieval hunting was also a preparation for war. Horse and man were kept fit and a bond was formed between the warriors.

It is said that in 1314 Edward II banned the game known as football, as so many men of fighting age were getting injured and were therefore unable to fight in the King's army.

Leisure and work activities were determined by sex. A boy would be expected to help his father and acquire skills in the process, while a girl helped her mother with domestic chores. Boys still had some time for play, however, and would make bows and arrows, bowl hoops with the metal bands used in barrel-making, play 'dice' with knuckle bones, use a pig's bladder as a ball, throw horseshoes round a post and improvise many other 'home made' games, many of which persisted until the recent past. A girl would have a rag doll and imitate her mother in looking after the newest baby, while an old piece of rope could be used for skipping. There would also have been singing and ring games. By the age of 12 or 13 boys would be apprenticed or learning a trade, and girls would be employed as maids in the house or dairy.

Seasonal Celebrations

Originating from the agricultural or pre-Christian calendar, seasonal celebrations were universally popular. The harvest was one of the most important, and can be traced back many centuries.

Our ancestors were directly dependent on agriculture and their survival was conditional on a successful harvest.

In Victorian times, there was a clerical attempt to sanitise these rites by introducing elaborate church Harvest Festivals.

Hallowe'en was originally the Celtic Fire Festival of Samhain, the end of summer, the beginning of the new year and a time when the souls of the dead were supposed to visit their homes. The festival acquired sinister significance and jokes and pranks were played. The 'Trick or Treat' was originally 'Trick or Trete', trete being a type of tourt bread made from rye, so named in Yorkshire.

In the church this became All Hallows' Eve, followed by All Hallows' Day, a celebration of all the redeemed. November 2nd, or *All Souls' Day*, is a day of prayer for those souls in purgatory, for whom prayer is the only salvation.

'Souling', on these days involved going from house to house singing in return for alms, in order to pay for prayers to be said for the dead. After the

Irene Cooper, crowned May Queen in Vicarage gardens

Reformation, buying prayers for the dead was outlawed instead, people went round singing for soul cakes. The cakes were usually small and spiced and said to bring luck. They may have derived from the pagan practice of putting aside food for those who had recently died. Many families kept old soul cakes, sometimes for many years.

Christmas combines the Roman Feast of Saturnalia and the Norse Yule Festival covering the shortest day. Many of the characteristics of these Festivals were transferred to Christmas. Sometimes a King was elected from among the servants, and servants were waited on by their masters. Like the pre-Christian festivities, which lasted for several days, Christmas and New Year celebrations lasted for twelve days at the darkest time of the year.

Plough Monday was the first Monday after Twelfth Night, and on this day the ploughmen dressed up, often as women, and called at every house singing and dancing in a crude manner. If they were not given money and something to eat and drink, they would plough up the ground in front of the house.

On *Shrove Tuesday*, the day before Lent began, when people were 'shriven' or cleansed, they feasted, using up ingredients which were forbidden in the Lenten Fast, and played games. Shrove Tuesday is more commonly known as Pancake Day, and pancake-tossing races became usual. In some places 'pancake bells' were rung, and various other, often rough, games were played.

In Melbourn, until Victorian times, this was the big day for cockfighting, introduced into the country by the Romans. Hundreds of people went to a pit on a farm within walking distance of the village.

Easter, a moveable celebration which follows the lunar calendar, can fall anywhere between 22nd March and 25th April. Although this is the most important festival in the church, several traditions follow pre-Christian customs, notably the eating of Hot Cross Buns to break the Lent Fast on

Good Friday. The bun derives from the moon shape of the Roman equivalent, which was cross-marked to show the 4 quarters of the moon. It was thought that hanging up a dried bun would protect the house from fire for the next year.

Gifts of Easter eggs, painted hens' or ducks' eggs, were originally pagan symbols of the new life to be born in the Spring.

April 1st has been a day for playing tricks on family and friends since Roman times, and may originate in Hilaria, the end-of-winter Roman orgy.

St. George's Day is on April 23rd, and everyone knows that St. George killed the Dragon and saved a Princess; but this was in Palestine in the 4th century. The story was heard later, during the crusades, and brought back to England, where George was made Patron Saint, by Edward III, in the 14th century.

St. George survives in the Mummers' Plays which were often enacted at Easter as well as Christmas.

May Day, or Beltane, is another Celtic, or even pre-Celtic, Fire Festival. The fertility connotations are evident in the phallic appearance of the Maypole, danced round on the first day of summer, when 'spring fever' is prevalent. The original maypoles were extremely tall and without ribbons; these were added by the Victorians. The King and Queen of the May were chosen and paraded the village, bedecked with flowers gathered from the surrounding fields. A beautiful complexion is assured by washing in the dew on May Day morning.

Ascension Day, or Holy Thursday, forty days after Easter Sunday, is the day for Beating the Bounds of

May Day celebrations organised by the Guides, Vicarage gardens

a parish and has its origins in the Roman festival of the god Terminus, the boundary god.

Whit Monday, the seventh Monday after Easter, is a traditional time for fairs and sports and was the biggest day of the year for Morris dancing.

Summer Solstice, the longest day of the year, was the time to gather plants and herbs, dance and party all night.

Congregational Chapel Celebrations

Saints' Days

A glance at the calendar of the Catholic Church reveals many Saints' Days, and before the Reformation, Saints' Days were supposedly holidays for everyone. Had this really been so the work in an agricultural community would never have been finished. When the workload was heavy, many peasants were expected to work, even on Sundays. However, it is clear that everyone including the peasants, joined in with the fun and games on several occasions throughout the year.

Entertainment from outside the village

As Melbourn lies on the main route between London and Cambridge there were many opportunities to see bands of travelling players, with musicians, acrobats, and jugglers, often accompanied by performing bears, dogs or horses. These groups carried all the news of important events as well as gossip, new fashions and songs. During the 17th century, when James 1st had his

hunting lodge at Royston, he would have ridden through Melbourn on more than one occasion, on his way to Newmarket or Fowlmere Heath race courses, causing a good deal of excitement among the villagers.

There were the big fairs, such as the Stourbridge and Midsummer Fairs in Cambridge. These attracted people from all over Europe, bringing traders with exotic goods to the area. People from the village would have visited these spectacles several times in their lives, even if they had to walk there and back.

Big celebrations were held in villages in 1815 to celebrate the victory over Napoleon at Waterloo. Some of the games mentioned were: a Sack Race, 1st prize a leg of mutton, 2nd prize a gallon of porter; a pound of tobacco to the man who made the ugliest face; climbing up a greasy pole; a sirloin of beef to the winner of the donkey race. However, the donkey was not to be whipped, slapped, kicked, sworn at or urged on in any way!

In the 1800s an annual fair was held in a meadow at the back of Old Farm. One of the events was the 'greasy pole'.

The meadow was bought by Mr Stockbridge in 1935 and was put to use during the Second World War when ten acres were ploughed. Older members of the village warned Mr Stockbridge to look out for a wagon wheel sunk into the ground, into which the greasy pole was stuck. Sure enough, the iron rim and remains of the wheel were found!

Over the stiles on the Sabbath

Despite the fact that most people worked hard physically, and had to walk, or cycle, wherever they needed to go, many people 'went for a walk' on Sunday, the only day off. One of the favourites was 'The Stile Walk'. This began in the lane by the church and finished in Meldreth, taking in 19 or 20 stiles on the way.

The Village Feast

The Melbourn Village Feast has, from medieval times, started on the first Thursday after the 1st July, unless that day is also a Thursday, in which case it would be a week later. It was originally held on The Green in the centre of the village, and was an ideal opportunity for bawdy merry-making, sports and games, including archery, bowling, dice, quoits, skittles and wrestling. In 1859 there were five or six side shows depicting the wonders of the world: a pig with two heads and a sheep with six

The Feast

Our village feast took place on Thursday week, and was kept up till Saturday night. There was the usual quantity of stalls and spice cakes, toys, &c., and a large quantity of shooting galleries and swinging boats. There were also five or six shows (which made it look like a large fair), the owners of which appeared to try who could make the most noise, inviting the juveniles to walk up and see the wonders of the world, acting monkeys and dogs, a pig with two heads, a sheep with six legs, and a legion of other wonderful things, for the charge of only one penny. There was one called a juvenile circus, where a tom-fool was on the stage, making ugly faces, and requesting those who stopped to listen to listen to him, to recollect that it was the only juvenile circus in the known world. There were two photographic establishments, which we believe did a good deal of business. We are happy to add, that we did not notice any drunkenness or quarrelling amongst our own townspeople; peace and good-will appeared to be the order of the day, during the time the feast lasted.

Cambridge Chronicle 16th July 1859

Shadows of coming events

The whitewashing and colouring of houses, the putting up of clean curtains at windows, the arrival of extra beer and the dusting of many wine glasses by housewives are evidences of feast time. The last three days of this week will witness the annual village feast on a Moor field, while next Sunday will be Feast Sunday. We look like having a passably good feast as modern feasts go, but it will be a poor thing compared with the feasts held on the green and along the High Street in the good old days before motor traffic came to worry and stifle us.

Royston Crow 8th July 1932

Joe Cooper, playing the clown

Womens' Institute fancy dress competition, late 1920s

legs, for example. Shooting galleries and travelling photographers also had stalls. The Feast was a special time, as relatives from all around would try to get home for the fun. In 1882, due to excessive rowdyism, the Feast was obliged to move from The Green to the Recreation Ground on the Moor.

Many baptisms took place at this time as family members returned home for the Feast.

Sunday last was Feast Sunday, when many visitors came to the village to renew old friendships, and to sample the many varieties of home-made wines, which usually flow so freely at feast times. The feast, which since about the year 1877 has been held on the Moor, was, on preceding days, the scene of much merry-making, and all passed off orderly and well. The feast itself seems to have been larger and more successful than usual, it starting in earnest on the Thursday, a day earlier than in recent years. According to those who profess to be 'in the know' the larger feast was due to altered conditions of letting the sites. There are no signs of Melbourn feast disappearing, as so many like events have done.

Royston Crow 15th July 1932

Rough Sports

In earlier times, cockfighting and badger-baiting were common in the area.

One of the most popular sports was wrestling. Matches were held between villages, and Melbourn contended against Bassingbourn, the Mordens, Whaddon and Meldreth. Frequently the match would deteriorate into a general fight between villages.

In the early-19th century, a group of 'professional' fighters from Cambridge would go to the surrounding village Feasts and encourage the locals to place wagers. Of course, they expected to win. On one occasion two well known fighters, 'Soapy Dan' and a big black man known as Malone, were brought to Melbourn by the Hon. George Fitzwilliam of Trinity College. At that time, Melbourn had a famous pugilist in the form of J King and, to the amazement of all, King floored both of them and won ten guineas. He subsequently had a brief success in London, once going 47 rounds before being beaten.

There was also a fight at Noon's Folly, in 1838, which ended in the death of a young man of 20. Apparently about 3000 people were present, so

although the event was illegal it was well advertised.

Most village celebrations seemed to involve large quantities of food!

Eating also featured in 1902 in celebrations for Edward VII's Coronation. A tea was held in two barns and a marquee in Mr Browning's yard. Mothers and children were entertained at 4.30pm and the men at 6.30pm. Disbrey and Oliver each supplied 250lbs of beef. Winters gave 120 loaves and Harrups 104lbs of cake. Messrs Campkin, WH Lee and AT Lee gave sundries. There is no record of where, or how, these vast quantities of ingredients were cooked and prepared.

The programme for celebrating the coronation of George VI, in 1936, included a united service held in the Parish Church at 9.30am, and a carnival

Left, picnic at the clunch pit and right, taking a dip in the Mel

Loyal and royal: wedding celebrations

Melbourn held celebrations for the wedding of the Prince of Wales and Princess Alexandra. The whole day was a holiday; bells were rung at intervals, younger children were given buns and medals at The Bury, and at 1pm nearly 100 people over 60 assembled under the elm tree in the centre of the village from where they marched behind the village band to the British schoolroom for a substantial dinner.

The procession was in itself an amusement as many of the aged men, for the first time since their marriage, gave their arms to their spouses. After dinner some went to a field where the youth of the village were assembled for athletic sports.

Legs of mutton suspended on high poles in vain invited the young men to climb and win them. Many acquitted themselves creditably in other contests such as hurdle races, sack races and gathering 50 stones a yard apart.

At four and half past five o'clock about 300 persons under 60 joined those in the British schoolroom for tea. Addresses were made by the Vicar, JE Fordham Esq, and the Rev AC Wright.

In the evening there was a very successful display of fireworks. When this concluded, the band, who had been employed during the afternoon and evening, led the multitude in singing the National Anthem. The vicar then proposed three cheers for the Queen, three for the Prince and Princess of Wales and then three cheers were given for the vicar, to whose exertions the successful issue of the day's proceedings was in a great measure due.

Royston Crow March 1863

WHAT THE PAPERS SAID

procession at 1pm. At 3pm there were sports in Collis Palmer's field, and at 5pm children's teas. A public whist drive was held at 8pm, and from 9pm to 1am, there was a carnival dance in the Council Schools. Later, each child was given a coronation beaker. Two hundred in all were presented.

Sports Reports

Melbourn Ladies' Hockey Club 7, Homerton College 0. The team consisted of Misses AE Elbourn (goal), Misses Stockbridge and Warboys (backs); Misses Nash, Palmer and Chappell (half-backs); Misses Gibbs, L Campkin, Disbrey, Nash and M Wedd (forwards).

Royston Crow 23rd November 1906

was played in The Bury meadow and this arrangement lasted into the 1940s.

There were men's, women's and mixed, cricket, tennis, bowls and hockey teams, athletics, and a quoits club, started in 1907. There were two tennis clubs, both attached to churches. The Congregationalists played on courts situated where Beechwood Avenue is now, and the Parish Church courts were at the Vicarage. There were several other private courts.

Billiards and darts were played, by men, in the public houses.

Less strenuous pastimes were whist drives, bridge drives, magic lantern shows and local dances. Often

Atlas Football Club 1933–34

Victory Celebrations

At the end of the Second World War, despite rationing and the shortage of money, preparations were made for welcoming the heroes and heroines home from the war, and a Victory Dance, held at the Council Schools, raised £52 10s for the Homecoming Fund.

The Victory celebrations in the village consisted of a service, a bonfire in Collis Palmer's meadow, music and dancing in the street, with the music courtesy of the piano from The Rose public house.

Sports

By the 19th century there were an amazing number of documented sports' clubs in the village, not all of them in existence at the same time, though cricket, football, tennis and bowls seem to have been permanent fixtures, being discontinued only during the two World Wars.

Three acres of land on the Moor were allocated for the Recreation Ground in 1842, which have been well used since then. In the early-20th century, when A R Fordham was the President of the Club, football

Melbourn Cricket Club Junior cup winners 1949

Congregational Chapel Tennis Club

Gilbert Harding at Melbourn Bowls' Club

these were held to raise money for worthy causes. There were also occasional visits from a circus, which caused great excitement.

There were local flower and produce shows, horse shows and ploughing matches, as well as shooting game and vermin on the farms.

The Melbourn Gardens' and Allotments' Society was founded in 1942 and The Young Farmers' Club in 1944.

Baptist Chapel Girls' Brigade marching behind the Boys' Brigade

The Mutual Improvement Society began in 1885 and held educational lectures. Other groups and clubs included: Guides, Scouts, Ranger Guides, a Young Peoples' Guild and a Youth Centre which was set up in the 1940s.

The Women's Institute started in 1922. It was part education and part entertainment and was very popular during the Second World War when housewives banded together to can fruit etc.

Attached to the various churches were societies, including: The Boys' Brigade, the Girls' Brigade, the Band of Hope, the White Ribboners, the Girls' Friendly Society, a Bible Society, the Christian Improvement Society and Church Missionary Societies.

Mutual Help societies, which included social activities, and can be traced back to the old Guilds, included the Ancient Order of Foresters, the Atlas Lodge of Buffaloes, the Oddfellows and the Sick and Dividing Club.

The annual school concert programme, 1936

Music and Drama

Drama and music were well catered for in the village. Plays were produced at the school and in the churches, and all the churches had a choir. There was also a Village Band. The Bicentennial Anniversary of the Congregational Church, in 1894, was a splendid 2-day affair and provided entertainment for the entire community.

Melbourn Choral Society has existed under several different names since 1842, when it was started by George Ward and friends. It met in the Congregational Church and also The Hoops public house. In the 1890s, Hugh Allen, (later to become Sir Hugh Allen

Fancy Dress Pageant at the Congregational Chapel

The Mikado 1911

Fishing in the Mel

conductor of the Bach Choir and Principal of the Royal College of Music in 1918) was the conductor for a while. He conducted a St. Cecilia's Day concert in 1895 and brought some members of Cambridge University Musical Society (CUMS) with him to supplement the singing. On one occasion he persuaded the LNER to stop the northbound express at Meldreth so that he could get back to Cambridge before the College gates closed for the night!

In the 1920s, the Choir entered the newly-formed Cambridge Festival of Music and won many cups and certificates for madrigal singing, mixed voice choruses and sight-reading. The conductor was George Ward, the grandson of the founder. The choir was discontinued during The Second World War but restarted soon afterwards.

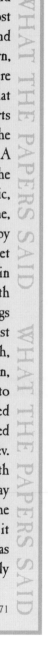

Melbourn. Cottagers' Flower Show and Harvest Thanksgiving. On Tuesday last a most satisfactory show of fruit, flowers, and vegetables, grown by the cottagers of Melbourn, was held in the Vicarage gardens, which were kindly thrown open to the public on that occasion. During the afternoon, various sports were going on in the grounds adjoining the vicarage, under the able superintendence of Mr A Coningsby, who distributed suitable prizes to the successful competitors. In the gardens, music, both vocal and instrumental, enlivened the scene, after which an excellent tea was enjoyed by upwards of 950 visitors, and we must not forget to thank Mrs Oliver for the efficient manner in which so large an assembly was provided with that refreshing meal. The festive proceedings were brought to an appropriate close by a Harvest Thanksgiving service in the Parish Church, which was suitably decorated for the occasion, and which we were pleased to find filled to overflowing by a congregation who joined heartily in the service, and listened with marked attention to an impressive sermon by the Rev. H.M. Lower, rector of Foulmire, from the 12th chap. St. John, 24th verse: 'Verily, verily, I say unto you, except that a grain of wheat fall into the ground and die, it abideth alone; but if it die, it bringeth forth much fruit.' Special music was also chosen for the occasion, Dr Garrett kindly presiding at the organ with his usual talent.

Cambridge Chronicle 30th September 1871

WHAT THE PAPERS SAID WHAT THE PAPERS SAID WHAT THE PAPERS SAID

THOMAS WEDD,
LICENSED RETAILER OF
BEER & TOBACCO. To be
consumed on the premises

The Red Lion, High Street

Taverns, inns, and ale houses

...the earliest mention of an inn in Melbourn was in 1622, and in 1686 one of the inns had stabling for thirty horses and beds for seven guests

The first tavern, or public house, in Melbourn was probably built by the Romans when they set up a camp in the village. It would have been a small establishment known as a 'taberna', from which the word tavern is derived. These were commonplace along the roads of Roman Britain, providing lodgings for officials and others passing through the village. After the Romans withdrew from England the public house continued to flourish.

Grape wines were imported in vast quantities and sold alongside ales in the taberna. Although the Romans may have established some vineyards in England, it was not until the late-11th century that grapes were grown to any extent. By the 14th century, almost every large castle and monastery in East Anglia and southern England had its own vineyard. Wines continued to be produced, together with other traditional drinks including cider, ale, mead and fruit wines such as verjuice (a sour juice made from crab apples or unripened fruit). These drinks would be made from food grown locally. Vineyards declined in numbers over the centuries and eventually only small areas were cultivating grapes.

Brewsters and alewives

Simple alehouses appeared in the village and took the place of the relatively sophisticated taverns. These alehouses, run by women known as brewsters or alewives, brewed their own ale, and indicated that it was available for sale by a broom stuck out over the door.

Demand for alehouses grew rapidly and, in the early-7th century, the number of ale-sellers was restricted. Three centuries later, a decree was issued making drinking vessels in alehouses a standard size i.e. the 'pottle' (4 pints). Each pottle was to be sub-divided into eight parts by means of pegs set inside the tankard. No one was to drink down further than one peg at a sitting. This, naturally, was seen as a challenge to try and drink more than one peg's worth – hence 'to take him down a peg or two'.

By the Middle Ages, many inns had become disreputable places, harbouring criminals and political malcontents. However, it was in these inns, the forerunners of modern restaurants, that the custom of providing a meal at a set time originated.

Inns and public houses were, of course, originally owned by individuals, and made their own beers and ales. Later, as breweries developed, they owned and maintained the fabric of the building. Two of the local breweries were Phillips, at Royston, and Fordhams, at Ashwell.

The unrest leading to the English Civil War during the 17th century saw the rise of the Puritans. They had strict rules against the ...*evils and excesses* of drink and they introduced laws to govern the inns and taverns, which included ...*no person or persons licensed for common entertainment shall suffer any to be drunk or drink excessively, that is above half a pint of wine, or continue drinking for more than half an hour, or at unreasonable times, or after 9 o'clock at night, on penalty of five shillings for every such offence. Any person found drunk, that is so that they are disabled of understanding in their speech or gesture, shall forfeit ten shillings; for excessive drinking, three shillings fourpence; continued drinking for more than half an hour, two shillings six pence and drinking at unreasonable times or after nine a clock at night, five shillings.*

During the conflict alehouses, taverns and inns were taxed to pay for the war. With Oliver Cromwell came religious and intellectual tolerance, but everyday enjoyment such as games, sport, dancing and singing (except in church) was banned. Many alehouses and taverns had their licences withdrawn or refused, and illegal drinking outlets were closed.

Ale parties

In medieval Melbourn, ale had become a central feature in the celebration of holidays, and huge festivals were held during various important events, with the entire family 'partaking of the merriment'. These festivals were called 'ales'.

There were *parish-ales*, a parish festival of 'merry-making', at which ale was the chief drink. In *Church-ales*, parishioners were asked to make a contribution

The early medieval brew

Before the 19th century, water was so polluted that people avoided drinking it whenever possible. Ale became one of the staple foods because of its availability. It was typical for most people, including children, to consume at least a quart of ale for breakfast. The ale for daily use was generally weak, although recipes existed for stronger ales. The strong version was only used on special occasions, primarily because it took twice as much grain to produce.

Ale was simple to produce. Although a cloudy drink, it was full of proteins and carbohydrates, making it a good source of nutrition. The ale created by the boiling and fermentation also killed any germs the water may have contained. Many homes produced ale for their own consumption and sometimes for the community. Local farms were still producing beer well into the 19th century.

Simple ale production

Almost any cereal was used for ale making. It was soaked over a few days and then laid out to dry. Once germination had begun, the grain was very roughly crushed or ground until the husks were just starting to break away from the grains. This process is called malting.

A cauldron (possibly made from copper) was then used to boil the malt in water for around two hours. It was then transferred to a wooden barrel or similar container and left to cool.

Flavouring known as gruit was then mixed with the liquid. This would have been obtained from plants such as bog myrtle, yarrow, cinnamon, garlic, ginger, rosemary, and berries. Oak bark and honey were also used and sometimes a mix or a blend of these ingredients. A blossom was often incorporated which gave additional yeast to the brew.

The mixture was then covered with a thin material and left to ferment in a warm area for about six hours. About 24 hours later the mix had formed a mash which was strained using a coarse sieve, leaving a yellowish opaque liquid. Nothing was wasted. The mash, which contained a lot of yeast, was then used to make bread. The liquid was left to stand for an hour or so to allow any yeast left in the liquid to drop to the bottom of the container. Yeast in the brew created alcohol.

Although it would have been drinkable at this point it was often strained again through a finer mesh which would have caught much of the yeast left at the bottom of the barrel. The yeast from this second straining was then used to start the fermentation of the next brew and for each subsequent brew. An abbey in Belgium that produces beer, has been using the same yeast for over eight hundred years.

After the third and final straining the ale was ready to drink. It had to be consumed quickly, as after a day or so it began to go off. One Saxon writer of his time wrote ...*after two days only the bravest or silliest men of the village would drink the ale, but usually it was only fit for pigs*. The stale brew was often fed to the pigs as it was said to improve the flavour of the meat (and also gave rise to the saying 'a drunken swine').

Ale used for medicinal purposes was often flavoured with hyssop, sage, wormwood or rosemary, while a restorative brew, known as 'cock-ale' would consist of parboiling a cock, steeping it in sherry, and adding it to the ale with fruit and spice. Over the centuries the cures invented were often worse than the diseases.

The early ale 'bottles' were made of leather and were used throughout the Middle Ages. If the alcohol needed to be stored for a longer period of time, it was put into a keg or barrel.

Ale and beer were measured in gallons. A gallon was itself divided into 8 pints, 4 quarts, or 2 pottles. Brewed drink was also measured in barrels, each containing usually 32 gallons of ale or 36 gallons of beer (ale made with hops). A barrel was divided into 4 firkins, or 2 kilderkins. Grain and malt were measured in quarters, each quarter containing 8 bushels.

Many of these alcoholic drinks were believed to nourish the body, restore health, aid digestion, clarify ideas, open the arteries, cure melancholy and help in procreation!

to the church. These festivals were as much for the church, as for the social life of the village, and were used as fundraisers and for entertainment. The chief purpose of *church-ales* and *clerk-ales* was to collect the parish dues and to make a profit for the church from the sale of liquor by the churchwardens. These profits either kept the parish church in good repair, or were distributed as alms to the poor. During this period alewives were banned from making their own brews. The Church would hold *tithe-ales*, festivals serving beer, to bring the people of the village in and persuade them to pay their tithes. *Leet-ales* were held on leet, or manorial, court days, a time for the lord of the manor and those from his estate to get together.

During the *bride-ale* or *bachelor-ale* (the forerunners of the modern hen night or bachelor party) ale was produced by the bride and a tankard of this was exchanged for gifts or money. The term 'bride ale' was shortened and became 'bridal'. On the wedding day, the mother of the bride would brew an ale which was served at the *weddyn-ale*, or what we now refer to as the wedding reception. As with most ales, the purpose was to exchange beer for money and gifts. Even at childbirth, a celebration was held for the new addition to the family. This was known as *groaning-ale*, and if the child was the first son born, the parents would celebrate the arrival by having a *give-ale*.

Lamb-ale was a celebration of springtime during the lambing season, when the baby lambs were born. In the autumn, when the harvest was done, they had a *harvest-ale*. Farmers could now afford to celebrate, and plenty of grain was available for brewing.

Bid-ales, once very common throughout the country, were 'benefit' feasts. A general invitation was given out, and all the neighbours attending were expected to make some contribution to help the object of the 'benefit'.

Haslingfield this Seventeenth of June 1622

Petition for an Ale House in Melbourn
To the Right Honourable Sir Albert Morten the clerk of the Privy Counsel
Sir
This bearer William Neale of Melbourne in the County of Cambridgeshire heretofore to his great charge obteyned a Licence under the great Seal of England for the keepinge of a common Inn in Melbourne, and having also to his further great charge prepared and filled his house by new buildings and furnishinge the same for that purpose, his patent of Licence being resumed by proclaimation, his whole charges were lost, and the man much impoverished. We are now desired to signify unto you that his house standeth in the greate towne, and in a visual and common frequented road leading to and from divers [other] shires and places of travell, the house as it is now prepared, and the person also, are fit and convenient for the usage and continuance of an Inn as we conceave. All which we leave to you further preceeding and wisdome, and Ristinge.
Your lovinge fends
William Wendy

Seen on a gallery in a church is this poem:

God speed the plough
And give us good ale now ...
Be merry and glade,
With good ale was this work made.

During the 12th century it was noted that *...the English were greatly addicted to drinking*. By Tudor times, English behaviour was often described by the three bs: beer, bread, and beef.

The 13th century saw the introduction of the bread-assize, which controlled the price and sale of grain. The sale of ale was included in this law some years later. The ale-assize strictly controlled the price of ale, depending on the amount of grain used in a pint. These laws were enforced by the local bailiff.

Although the word 'beer' is used to define a traditional alcoholic drink, the term was not generally used until the introduction of hops in the brewing process. Hops had been grown at The Bury in the 1300s for a short period, indicated by the presence of an Oasthouse, next to London Way. However, it was not until the 16th century, when hops were imported from the Netherlands and commercially grown in England, that beer became a common drink. Before this time the beverage was known as ale. Hops were reintroduced at The Bury in the 18th century.

From London to Cambridge

Innkeeping has always grown alongside trade, travel and industry, and Melbourn was no exception to this, lying on a major route between London and Cambridge. As more people began to travel, so the inns offered stabling where horses could be changed.

The earliest mention of an inn in Melbourn was in 1622, and in 1686 one of the inns had stabling for thirty horses and beds for seven guests. However, most inns in the village date from the 19th century.

Many of the public houses in Melbourn were used as meeting houses or as auction rooms, selling land, property, livestock and an assortment of goods including haberdashery. In the mid-19th century they were also used for inquests.

The demon drink – temperance and the poor

More than one-fourth of the daily earnings of the citizens of the slums goes over the bars of the public-houses and gin-palaces. On a Saturday night, butchers, bakers, greengrocers, clothiers, furniture dealers, all the caterers for the wants of the populace, are open till a late hour: there are hundreds of them trading around and about, but the whole lot do not take as much money as three publicans – that is a fact ghastly enough in all conscience. Enter the public-houses, and you will see them crammed. Here are artisans and labourers drinking away the wages that ought to clothe their little ones. Here are the women squandering the money that would purchase food, for the lack of which the children are dying.

The time to see the result of a Saturday night's heavy drinking in a low neighbourhood is after the houses are closed. Then you meet dozens of poor wretches reeling home to their miserable dens; some of them roll across the roadway and fall, cutting themselves till the blood flows. Every penny in some instances has gone in drink.

All honour to the brave temperance workers who have already done so much to diminish the evil. In this district such men are labouring night and day. No one now disputes the good which temperance can accomplish. It will strengthen the hands of those who are trying to wean the thriftless poor from drink, if we give the people better homes and enforce sanitary laws.

The temperance advocates have accomplished much – they will accomplish more; but if they wish to check the evil in its hotbed, they must be among the strongest advocates of the proper housing of the poor. To say, because a certain proportion of the poor are drunkards, it is useless to try and improve the social conditions of the masses, is like refusing to send the lifeboat to a sinking ship because half the crew are already known to be drowned.

George Sims, 1889

George Sims, writer and journalist

The rise of the Temperance movement

During the 19th century, public houses were often the only buildings able to house the meetings of a growing number of groups or clubs such as the 'Friendly' or 'Mutual Aid' Societies. Friendly Societies were set up, in the 17th century, as a solution to financial problems facing families during illness, or after death, leaving their, children or spouse with limited resources. Workers saw membership as a means of reducing their chances of ending their days in the workhouse.

In the 1800s these societies covered all manner of trades including agriculture, gardening, shepherds and railway workers, many of which laid the foundations for the trade union movement. As membership of these groups grew, so did the problem of drinking caused by the frequent meetings in pubs.

Temperance Garden Party ~ Melbourn Bury June 1910

Miss Gillanders,　Miss Winter,　Mr Stockbridge,　Mr Farnham,　Mr A Woods,　Rev. Grant,　Messrs A King,　F Handscombe,　J Camp,　F Winter,　L Hale,
Mr Hall,　Mrs Crabtree,　Mrs N Winter,　Miss Anderson,　W Burton,　G Pullen,　R Reynolds,　Messrs J Pepper,　W Gray,　G Holland,　E West,　F Abrahams,　A?

? Gillings,　Miss Chappel,　Miss Price,　Miss Wedd,　Miss Waldock,　_____ _____　Miss J Day,　Mr E Rumbold,　Miss Hinkins,　Miss Woodcock,　Miss Chamberlain,　Miss ?
? R, Wilkinson,　Miss Brett,　Miss Chappel,　Mr A R Fordham,　Mrs Fordham,　Miss Mulberry,　Mrs Grant,　G Hale,　Rev. Porter Chappel,　Mrs A Chappel,　Mrs Jackson?
Miss Joyce　　　Mrs W ?

The names above have been placed as they appeared, handwritten on the back of the original photograph, as the order seems to be confusing.
Question marks indicate where the names have been cut off on either side and are not available. The dashes are as they appear on the photograph.

It is thought that friendly societies may have developed directly from 'harmonious clubs' promoted at the end of the 18th century by the proprietors of public houses themselves. These harmonious clubs simply existed to encourage drinking. Drunkenness and alcoholism were becoming a major problem in cities and villages alike.

It was due to the problems of drunkenness and alcoholism that the temperance movements spread throughout the country. Some activists saw that there was an advantage in linking temperance with mutual aid.

The mid 1800s saw the first working class men

Cider

Cider became a popular drink from the middle ages. Apple growing had been introduced into Britain before the Roman conquest in the 1st century AD. Druids often planted apple trees near sacred oak groves, these served as hosts for mistletoe, a very important plant to the Druids. But it was during the Roman invasion that the practice of growing apples in orchards was first introduced. Army veterans were given settlements on which to grow fruit trees as an inducement to stay.

The Normans in 1066 brought with them different and improved varieties. One variety was the Costard, from which the word costermonger comes, meaning a seller of Costard apples.

In the 17th century cider had become the drink of the people. Melbourn had extensive orchards of apple and other fruit trees and many of the farms would have had their own cider press. A tradition found on many of these farms was to pay part of the farm labourer's wages in cider. A typical allowance would be 3–4 pints per day, increased to 6–8 pints in August, during the harvest! The outlawing of this practice in 1887, together with profound changes in farming, led to a decline in consumption.

Mead

Mead has a long history and is probably the most ancient of all fermented beverages. Honey was used in cooking as a sweetener and a drink.

Beehives were placed in many of the orchards surrounding the village to help with the pollination of blossom but they also provided honey, collected from the hives just before harvest. The 'comb' which contained the honey was squeezed out and stored for use by the lords of the manor as a sweetener. The wax was used for candles, medicinal salves, jewellery-making, and a host of other uses. It was processed by throwing it into large vats of boiling water where the wax melted, and the residues of honey dissolved into the water. When cool, slabs of wax were lifted from the surface for re-melting and other processing.

The weak sugar solution in the pots was allowed to ferment with the naturally occurring yeast in the air and was ready for drinking when the harvest of the grain began. This thin, honey drink (mead) known as Meth or Hydromel was liberally passed out to the workers.

A portion of the honey that had been pressed from the comb was made into a much stronger and sweeter drink, known as 'high mead', destined for the Lord's table, and would have been prepared by the 'manor brewer'.

The strongest mead was Methaeglen, a favourite drink of Queen Elizabeth I, and it is from here that the word medicine is derived. Such was the importance of the drink to the Royal Court that royal mead makers were immune from all prosecution while making it!

In medieval times it was customary for a newly married couple to be given enough mead to drink a glass every night for the first month (or moon cycle) of their marriage. If the wife became pregnant and bore a son, the mead maker was congratulated and held in great esteem for his potent nectar. This is the origin of the term 'honeymoon'.

sign a pledge that they would never again drink alcohol. Groups of working men throughout the country followed the example and by 1835 the British Association for the Promotion of Temperance was formed.

Membership usually involved a promise not to drink spirits, although consumption of wine and beer continued. By the early 1840s, the society was advocating teetotalism, which was a much stronger position than previously held, as it not only included the pledge to abstain from all alcohol for life, but also a promise not to provide it to others.

As the Temperance Movement grew, many societies built their own halls. The teetotal 'Independent Order of Rechabites' (an organisation established in 1835) was foremost among those who refused to meet on licensed premises. The Rechabites were a secret society, who met in tents and advocated total abstinence. However, many other societies that did permit drinking also had their own buildings.

The Women's Temperance Association was formed in 1876. They spread the message of total abstinence along with the gospel. They made it their responsibility to persuade men to promise never to drink alcohol again. The Band of Hope, a temperance organisation for working class children, founded in 1847, helped to increase the number of teetotallers.

Quakers and members of the Salvation Army also played an active role in the Temperance Movement, and these groups tried to persuade the government to pass legislation to restrict the sale of alcohol. In some parts of the country public houses were forced to close on Sundays and permission was rarely granted to allow new ones to open.

Nonconformists were also very active in this movement, and the mid 1870s saw most young ministers setting an example by abstaining from alcohol. In 1886 over 1000 Baptist ministers and 2500 Congregational ministers had signed the Pledge. By 1900 an estimated tenth of the adult population had become total abstainers from alcohol.

The War years

Before the outbreak of War, in 1914, there were no laws in force governing licensing hours. During the conflict the Government decided there was a need to keep workers from drinking too much, as munitions production was suffering because of drink. David Lloyd George, said in 1915, that ...*Britain was fighting three enemies – Germans, Austrians and Drink, and as far as I can see the greatest of these foes is Drink.* He began a campaign to persuade national dignitaries to pledge that they would not drink alcohol during the war. In April 1915, King George V supported the campaign when he promised that no

alcohol would be drunk in the Royal household until the war was over.

In 1915 the Government introduced laws limiting opening times between 12noon to 2.30pm and 6.30 to 9.30pm – these times remained in place for many years. It also became illegal to buy drinks for other people. Alcohol was taxed more heavily, and the strength of beer reduced. Consumption was cut by more than a half and convictions for drunkenness fell.

The origin of names and signs

It was the Romans who began the tradition of the inn sign. The 'Tabernae' would hang vine leaves outside to show that they sold wine; in England, small evergreen bushes were used. Early pubs hung long poles, or ale stakes (used to stir the ale during production), outside their doors. If both wine and ale were sold, then both a bush and a pole would be displayed.

The naming of inns and pubs became common by the 12th century, but as the majority of the population could not read or write, Richard II, in 1393, passed an Act making it compulsory for pubs and inns to display a sign, in order to identify them to the official Ale Taster.

Before Henry VIII and the Reformation, many names had religious themes, but, after the split with the catholic church, names were changed to royal or heraldic subjects such as 'The Royal Oak', 'The King's Head' or 'The Rose' etc.

The 'Red Lion' is the most common name for a pub, and originates from the time of James I, and VI of Scotland, who came to the throne in 1603. James ordered that the heraldic red lion of Scotland be displayed on all buildings of importance ~ including taverns! Many pub signs had other royal links ~ the 'White Lion' dates from the time of Edward IV.

In the 18th century, the word 'Arms' was added to many pub names, indicating that the establishment was under the protection of a particular noble family.

The abolition of the beer tax, in 1830, meant that any ratepayer could sell beer without a licence. During this period there was a dramatic increase in beerhouses. Beer was now being sold in the kitchens of people's homes. Gradually the drinking space in the house was separated, seating became available in the 'taproom' and a counter was placed in another room providing standing room only in the 'bar room'.

The 'free for all' in ale stopped in 1869 with tighter regulations of the brewing trade. Smaller alehouses fell by the wayside while larger brewers extended their control over drinking establishments as brewing was transformed into an 'industry'.

Melbourn's pubs

Most of the public houses in Melbourn were situated on the main road. **The Bull's Head** was at the northern part of the village, on the Cambridge Road. A fire partly destroyed the building in the early-20th century but it was rebuilt to closely match the original. The Bull is an ancient sign. It is thought that the name was originally derived from a reference to a papal bull ~ the seal attached to the pope's edicts (the Latin name being *bulla*). A bull's head was introduced into the arms of Henry VIII after he had defied the papal bull of 1538, which

The Bull's Head on Cambridge Road

may give an approximate date to the origins of the pub sign. **The Coach and Horses**, was situated at Flint Cross, on Newmarket Road. This marked the parish boundary and was said to be the meeting place for the men of Melbourn on Sunday evenings. It was a popular pub name and many of these old coaching inns went on to be named after famous stage-coaches. **The Red Lion**, the heraldic symbol of James I, stood opposite Sheepshead Row and was a coaching inn for about three hundred years. It was demolished in 1937. The first Baptist chapel

and burial ground was next door. In 1851 Mary Pearman of *The Red Lion* was fined for giving short measure!

The Royal Oak was at The Moor corner and was kept by William Dellar, who was also a shoemaker and farmed several acres. This pub later became part of Howard's Bakery.

Further down the High Street was **The Star**, built in the mid-19th century. It was possibly named after

The Coach & Horses, Newmarket Road

The Red Lion, High Street demolished in 1937

Below, The Royal Oak on Moor corner

INQUEST

On Friday (yesterday) an inquest was holden at The Rose inn, in this village, before J.E. Marshall, on view of the body of Mr. Wortham Hitch, aged 52 years. It appeared that the deceased was subject to fits, but had not had an attack for 9 months, until Thursday, and on that day he appeared in his usual health up to about 6 o'clock, when he was found by his daughter lying on his face in his dining-room, and quite dead. He had been observed to enter the dining-room about half-past 3, and close the door after him. A pair of nut-crackers lay by his side, and blood had issued from the nose of the deceased. It appeared from the medical testimony that the deceased died of apoplexy, and a verdict to that effect was returned.

Cambridge Chronicle 4th October 1851

The Spotted Dog in the High Street

Above, The Star in the High Street, and left, the Cambridge to London coach that stopped at Melbourn

'The Star Coach' that ran through Melbourn on its way to Cambridge. On the opposite side of the road was **The Spotted Dog** or **Dog**. It is said that the name may have originated from the landlord's ownership of a pet spotted dog. Opposite Vicarage Lane was **The Anchor.** This sign, normally found on the coast, is thought to have emerged when ex-sailors took over a pub, or wanted to attract sailors as customers. Originally, it was a farm house, until the Enclosure Act, when it was sold. At the rear of the pub was a large dovecote.

Inset, The Anchor
Background picture, The Elm Tree on
the right and The Anchor on the left

A few yards from the Anchor was **The Old Elm Tree**, sitting opposite the elm tree that stood outside the church. This building could be identified by the bargeboards under the roof line, which were uncommon for this area.

At the top of Station Road, opposite the church, was **The Tailor's Arms**. Campkin's grocery and Burton's hardware shop also occupied this building.

The White Lion stood at The Cross between Mortlock Street and Little Lane. The sign dates from

An egg weighing 5½ ozs, had been laid by a hen belonging to Moss Huggins of the Red Cow. People were allowed to view the egg on payment of a small fee, which was donated to the Red Cross!

Royston Crow May 1916

Right, The Old Elm, High Street and below, The Tailor's Arms (right of picture) in Station Road

SUICIDE

An inquest was held at The Rose, Melbourn, on Wednesday last, by F. Barlow, Esq., on the body of James Langham, a man who had hanged himself. From the evidence, it appeared that as a man named Webb was walking along the road between Newmarket and Royston, when he saw the deceased hanging by his neck in a tree, at the distance of about two miles from Melbourn: he had on only a shirt and a pair of trousers. Webb went and fetched his elder brother, and they cut deceased down: he had hanged himself with one of his braces and was quite dead. The man had the character of being half-witted, and when this fact had been deposed to and some other circumstances elicited, the Jury gave a verdict that deceased hanged himself when in a state of temporary insanity.

Cambridge Chronicle 20th June 1863

Above, The White Lion after an accident in 1930, and during the repair. Top right, The Rose can be seen in the background

the period of Edward IV. The landlady, Annie Walls (who ran the pub with her husband Frank), was reputed to be very slow. It was said that you could order a pint, go down the road to *The Red Cow*, drink a pint there and return to *The White Lion* just as Annie was putting the drink on the bar! She would go down to the cellar to get each drink. On 29 April 1930, a steam traction lorry belonging to Elbourns, and driven by John Pateman, crashed into the building and partly demolished it. It was rebuilt and functioned for several more years until it was finally demolished.

The Rose was one of the larger inns in the High Street which had stabling. *The Rose* was the most common flower to appear on pub signboards and possibly dates from the 15th century, following the Wars of the Roses, a battle between the House of York, whose symbol was the white rose, and the House of Lancaster whose coat of arms included a red rose. Further down the road, and on the opposite side, was **The Hoops**. This pub was next to a pork butcher's shop owned by Albert Huggins. *The Hoops* was named after the rings that hung outside the pub. These circular bands of metal or wood were known as 'hoops' and used to hold the 'staves' together around a cask or barrel. Many publicans of the time had several other skills. Peter Wedd of *The Hoops* was also a harness maker, took in lodgers and gave magic lantern shows! *The Hoops*, which apparently had a large club room, was used by several organisations including the Melbourn Choral Society.

The Rose, High Street

The Hoops in the High Street. The circular bands of metal or wood were known as 'hoops' and used to hold the 'staves' together around a cask or barrel

Odd Fellows' Anniversary

The members of the loyal Pride of Melbourn Lodge of the Manchester Unity of Odd Fellows celebrated their fourth anniversary on Friday, the 15th inst. At two o'clock the members emerged from The Hoops Inn, and proceeded by a brass band from Cambridge, went in procession through the village, every officer dressed in his peculiar costume, and carrying with them all the paraphernalia of the order; they then returned to the Hoops, where a public dinner of a first-rate character was provided by host Hill, in a booth erected for the occasion, when about 50 sat down. The Grand Master of the district (Bro. J. Fleet,) occupied the chair, and Bro. J. Camp was vice-chairman. After dinner the usual toasts were drunk, and at seven o'clock there was another procession around the village, accompanied by the band, when our usual quiet village appeared all alive. The party again returned to the booth, where a pleasing evening was enjoyed, intermingled with toasts, songs, and the enlivening strains of the Cambridge band. The company dispersed soon after eleven o'clock, everything having passed off in a very agreeable manner.

Cambridge Chronicle 23rd July 1859

The Dolphin has been a public house for many years, and its name may have derived from the French word 'Dauphin', the title given to the eldest son of the king of France, heir to the crown. It was current until 1830. *The Dolphin* was used for parish meetings and often inquests were held there in

The Dolphin, High Street

Above and left, The Red Cow in the High Street

Victorian times, as indeed they were in several other public houses in the village. On the other side of the road was **The Red Cow**, at one time run by Moss Huggins. Later, and for many years *The Red Cow* was used as a doctor's surgery.

Just before Water Lane came **The White Horse**. The sign, and name, probably date from the 14th century. Most pub signs were carvings and horses were a very common and popular subject.

The White Horse in the High Street

The Locomotive Inn, High Street

The Oak Tree. The Locomotive Inn can be seen in the background

Further down the road was **The Locomotive Inn**, named after the coming of the railway. Originally the stables and servant quarters of the Old Manor House, it was at various times a pub, and garaging, before reverting to a private house. **The Oak Tree** was a little further along, on the same side of the road. Also on the High Street was **The Rising Sun**, the heraldic symbol of Edward III. However, most signs of *The Rising Sun* tended to simply illustrate the start of the day, with the sun emerging above the horizon. The promise of a new day dawning is probably of more significance than a coat-of-arms! The site of this pub is unknown.

The Carrier's Arms in Dolphin Lane, was reputed to be haunted ~ at 10pm a door was said to have

The Carrier's Arms, Dolphin Lane

Suspicious Death

Yesterday (Friday), an inquest was held at the Police Station, before C.W. Palmer, Esq., deputy coroner, concerning the death of Samuel Carter, a labourer, aged 58. The inquiry lasted over two hours and a half, and the evidence went to establish the following facts:– The deceased left his home on the evening of Sunday, August 30th, and was not seen again by his wife until following Tuesday evening. Witnesses were called to prove that he was at work machining on Monday, August 31st, and he was last seen on that night between 9 and 10 at the Black Horse at Melbourn, by Benjamin Hawkins, who considered him perfectly sober. On leaving the Black Horse, the deceased was observed to turn away from the direction of his own home. At 6 o'clock the next morning he was seen coming out of a straw stack near to his work, and looked very ill. One of his mates asked him what was the matter, and noticing a scratch upon his left temple said, "You must have been drunk over night and tumbled down." Deceased replied that he was not drunk, nor had he fallen down; he had been in a worse scrape than either one of them. The witness asked him where he had been, to which the deceased replied, "I shan't tell you, you will hear that time enough." He went home and to bed, and was attended by a doctor. It was ultimately found that his collar-bone was broken, and there was no doubt that several of his ribs had been fractured. The doctor, when he first visited the deceased, noticed a wound on the back of his hand where an abscess had subsequently formed; this appeared to have been caused by a blow, given or received. The deceased lived until Wednesday last. Several persons who visited him (including his wife and the doctor) asked him about the matter, but all that he would reveal was that he had been knocked about by three men. Nothing could be got out of him as to where and when or by whom. One of the witnesses stated that about a week before the injuries were occasioned the deceased had told him he had had a row with three men, one of whom he had knocked about. – Thereupon, the Deputy-Coroner adjourned the inquest for a week, in order that the police might institute inquiries.

Cambridge Chronicle 10th October 1874

The Shant, Royston Road

The Black Horse in Orchard Road

opened of its own accord. Orchard Road had two pubs: **The Black Horse** (as with *The White Horse* the sign probably dates from the 14th century) and **The Beech House,** which stood about 500 metres along from *The Black Horse*.

At the south end of the village, on the Royston Road, stood **The Shant**, used by railway workers when the line was being laid from Royston to Shepreth during the 19th century. The word Shant, or Shanty, means a roughly built and often ramshackle old shack.

Three other pubs were said to be in the village: **The Catherine Wheel**, **The Grave Digger's Arms** and **The Chequers**. The sign for the latter is said to be one of the most ancient, introduced to Britain by the Romans. It possibly indicated that the game of draughts was played in the tavern. The sign was later associated with a money table, because the word 'Exchequer' originally meant a chessboard. In the early days many pubs offered simple banking services and exchange systems so the sign was used to advertise this additional activity. It is not known where these three pubs stood.

Not all of these pubs were operating at the same time, but Melbourn did have its fair share, especially since the population was no more than 1500 until after the mid-20th century.

Taverns, inns & ale houses **229**

The Muncey family at Farm Corner, Norgetts Lane

Village names & personalities

...Mary a child of a woman that harvested at Capt Hitch indigent born 9 days before Sept 25 1698

Although the recording of family names began in the 17th century, with the introduction of Church records, it was not until 1250, due to fiscal and legal requirements, that possession of a surname became law. The first surnames often referred to the father's name or occupation, or a place name. It would have been the usual custom to specify the family, or greet the individual, by simply saying 'John, son of George', 'James the Carpenter' or 'William of Melbourn'.

By the 14th century the common way of distinguishing between families was to add the words 'son of'. Thus David, son of John, became David **Johnson**. Similarly, son of Thomas became **Thomson**. In Melbourn there were also **Dickerson, Richardson, Robinson, Williamson** etc. A shorter form was also used: **Adams** (on), **Bowes, Collis, Dix**(s)**on, Edwards, Harris, Peters, Phillips** and **Reynolds**, but this was not always the case. **Collins** is said to be a diminutive of Nicholas. Many people used their occupations as a surname, such as: **Baker**, bread maker; **Butler**, a bottle bearer; **Carter**, a maker or driver of carts; **Chapman**, a pedlar, merchant or trader (from the Anglo-Saxon word meaning to

barter); **Cooper**, a barrel or bucket maker; **Jackman**, a horse soldier; **Fletcher**, an arrow maker; **Miller**, one who ground the grain into flour; **Pateman**, a headman of the village; **Shepherd**, a sheep farmer; **Smith**, a blacksmith; **Taylor**, a garment maker. The name **Cooper** (barrel maker) first appeared in the Melbourn records in 1298, when William the Cooper sought sanctuary in All Saints' church. (Names shown in bold can be found in Melbourn; those shown in italic can be found in the county.)

Other occupations included *Alderman, Archer, Bishop, Butcher, Clark, Farmer, Fisher, Potter, Outlaw* and *Wainwright*, to name but a few. However, these names were not always passed down through the family line. John Blacksmith may have had a son who decided not to follow in the family trade. During the 14th century a person could be baptised John *Blacksmith* but buried John *Carpenter*.

During the time of the feudal system of the early Anglo-Saxon and Norman period, titles or names were given to high officials. Many of these names still exist today and include: **Chamberlain**, an officer who managed the household of the manor; **Marshall**, a law officer or high sheriff; **Palmer**, a wandering religious man who wore two crossed palm leaves from the Holy Land; **Reeve**, a bailiff or steward of a manor; **Steward**, a man employed to look after the manor or estate and **Squire**, a young nobleman attendant upon a knight.

Others would use names indicating their place of origin, such as a village or town. These include **Ashwell, Cambridge, Baldock, Bolton, Durham, Letchworth, Lancaster, Lincoln, Melbourn, Nottingham, Royston, Triplow, Ware, Weymouth, Whitby** and **York**. Even county names were used, such as **Cornish** and **Cornwall**. Others include *Kent, Midlands, Norfolk, Suffolk* and *Yorkshire*. From further afield there are names such as

Flanders, **French**, **Holland** and **Norman**. The direction from which they came would also serve as a surname: **Coast**, **East**, **Eastham (from 'ham' a village)**, **Eastman**, **Bysouth**, **North**, **Norton**, (northern or north-facing), **Norris**, (northerner), **South**, **West**, **Westley** and **Weston**. It is important to note that the use of names such as those above may in itself come from an earlier old English word; *Sheffield*, for instance, may have derived from Shed-field, or sheep-field, or field bordering the River Sheaf.

Natural landmarks would also add to the diversity of names: **Banks**, a slope of land; **Bourn**, small stream or brook; **Creek**, a small inlet in a shoreline; **Dale**, a low place between hills, a valley; **Deller**, from the low lands; **Field**, an expanse of land or meadow; **Ford**, a shallow area in a river; **Fordham**, a place near a ford; **Moore**, a broad area of open land; **Underwood**, small trees growing beneath taller trees; **Ward**, a district within an English county; **Vale**, a valley with a stream. Other descriptive names include **Greenhill**, **Freshwater** and **Wood**.

Man-made landmarks have also been used, and include **Bridge**, **Bell**, **Castle** and **Hall**.

Sometimes a surname could be derived from the physical condition or characteristics of the man. These descriptive names are thought to have evolved, originally, as nicknames during the Middle Ages. Michael the Strong would become Michael **Strong**, and brown-haired Peter, Peter **Brown**; **Armstrong**, strong in the arm; **Balding** may have derived from the Germanic word Baldo-lug, meaning descendant of the young, bold one. Others are: *Stout*, a large person, *Broadhead*, a person with a large head; *Baines*, (bones) a thin man; *Moody*, a moody individual; *Whitehead*, *Longfellow* and *Goodbody*.

Personality traits and animal names are often found in this category. Their use may reflect the type of animal or its original meaning. They include **Sparrow**, which is an old English word 'spearwa' and means to quiver or flutter; **Fox**, was a fox hunter, but it also meant sly or crafty; **Peacock** meant arrogant. Others are **Beaver**, **Bird**, **Bull**, **Crow**, **Goslin(g)**, **Nightingale**, **Pigg** and **Salmon**. Even the months of the year have been used, such as **January**. **May** has been used but its interpretation varies. One version is 'to be strong or able' (an Old English word), another is 'blossoms of the hawthorn' which come out in May. **Christmas**, **Summer** and **Winter** are also to be found.

Relationships were also adapted as names in Melbourn. There was a **Neave**, the medieval word for nephew, and **Godson**. The Bible became a good source of names following the publication of the King James Bible in 1611. Such names include **Adam**, **Cain**, **Eve**, **Hagger**, **Lucas** and **Luke**.

Everyday objects and items used as names are: **Chapple**, a place of worship; **Dodkin**, a small Dutch or Scottish coin; **Farthing**, rent payment or a foreign traveller; **Hale**, a nook or retreat; **Mead**, a drink made from honey; **Negus**, a wine that included hot water, lemon juice, sugar and nutmeg; **Puddock**, a small enclosure; **Vellum**, fine parchment made from calfskin or lambskin.

The study of any list of names will reveal how they may have originated. As shown above, the links can appear obvious ~ a place name, an occupation, the father's first name ~ others may have been combined, **Cakebread**, **Dearman**, **Goodman**, **Hereman** and **Mansfield**. These examples may have obvious meanings, but it is important to note that, over the years, names have become corrupted, misspelt or totally different from their original meaning. Names may have come from Old English or medieval language which has been lost over time. Historians can only speculate as to the origin of many names and some that appear to be derived from an obvious occupation can be misleading. For instance, in medieval days, a 'farmer', was not an agricultural worker, he collected taxes.

Other old English words used for names include: **Burton**, a Manor house enclosure or a fortified farm; **Cain**, a field of combat; **Campion**, to strive or fight; **Cyllyn** (Cylin), a kiln or oven; **Dunn**, a dingy or dark brown; **Geapes**, wide or width; **Gee** (Gea), foolishness or light-mindedness; **Hagger**, (a name previously mentioned), is possibly a biblical name, but could be a corruption of an Old English word, Haga, meaning hedge or enclosure; **Ludgate**, a side gate, and **Wed**(d), a pledge or security.

Many names have remained in the area and a number have had streets named after them: **Drury**, **Fordham**, **Medcalfe**, **Mortlock** and **Trigg**.

The development of church registers

In 1538, following the reformation of the church, Thomas Cromwell (Chancellor to Henry VIII) ordered that every parish keep a register of all baptisms, marriages and burials. Every Sunday the vicar of Melbourn, Edmund Humpfrey, in the presence of the wardens, was to enter the details from the previous week. Few instructions were given on the details to be recorded, so very little information was entered in the early books. The first entry in the All Saints' register was a burial and simply read, ...*Jone wife of Thomas Campion Jany 1558*. A marriage in the same month read ...*John Johnson and Agnes Campyon Jany 16 1558*. The earliest christening had even less detail ~ it simply read ...*Rebecca dau. of RD Dec 6 1558*.

Details in the church records varied. Some gave very few clues ...*Ales dau. of S Apr 13 1559*; others were more detailed ...*Jone dau. of John Hitch the younger Dec 25 1560* and ...*Mary a child of a woman that harvested at Capt Hitch indigent* (destitute person) *born 9 days before Sept 25 1698*. When it came to burials they often included other information,

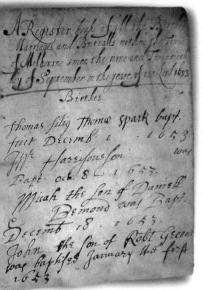

Part of the first page of baptisms from the Church Register. Unfortunately, the original book containing entries from 1558 to 1598 has been lost. However, before it disappeared the entries were copied into this book – at a later date and so appear further on. Some children baptised in Melbourn during this period had unusual names including: Abigail, Damaris, Obadiah, Phineneas, Tryamor and Zacchareus.

...Thomas Wygs slain with clunch in the pit June 13 1607; ...Henrye Dockrell slain with a loaded cart Aug 14 1607 and ...Mary Pratt a poor maid that came casually from Shepreth July 3 1639.

Records in this early period were written in Latin. ...Katalina (Katarina) filia Robertus Jarment baptizatus Aug 1 1562, translated into English reads; 'Katherine daughter of Robert Jarment (I have) baptised August 1 1562'; a marriage would read ...Richardus Medcalfe nupsit Marg. Purdewe July 28 1560 translated; 'Richard Medcalfe married Margrett Purdewe July 28 1560'; and, for a burial, ...Johannes filius Nicholaus Robertes dormit Jany 31 1558 in English reads, 'John son of Nicholas Roberts sleeping January 31 1558'. Although some clergy had been educated in the classics and preferred Latin, others had it thrust upon them and, possibly, the first time they used it was when they took up their new position in the village. It is because of this that the grammar and spelling varied. This can be seen in names such as 'Williamus'. The letters 'us' were added to 'William' instead of using the Latin equivalent Gulielmus. Other Latin words included filia, daughter; filius, son, and uxor, wife. Baptisms were recorded in a number of ways, including baptizatus, baptizat and renatus (meaning reborn). A marriage was written as nupsit, matrimonium solemnizat, copulati or coniuncti erant and for burial the words dormit, sepultat, sepultatus erat, in tumulo sep and inhumebat were used. It was not until 1733 that a law was passed forbidding the use of Latin in parish registers.

The information gathered in these records depended entirely on the clergyman or parish clerk. The clerks were often uneducated. They would have other jobs to tend to, or farms to look after, and the books were often written in a hurry. Different dialects confused the matter further and a name would often be written as it sounded. A person travelling to the village with the name **Higgins** may appear in the records as **Hinkins**, or **Garrett** may become **Jarrett**. This corruption can be seen throughout the register and examples include **Adelson**, **Aldleston** and **Addleston**; **Anscombe** and **Handscombe**; **Baisley** and **Bazeley**; **Beamond**, **Beaman**, **Bemont** and **Beaumont**; **Dranfield**, **Branfield** and **Tranfield**. Many of these names would have continued in their new spelling to run alongside the original. It was not until the 19th century that fixed spelling of the surname was adopted.

The register was to be kept in a coffer (strong box) with two locks – one key to be kept by the vicar and the other by the church warden. Failure to comply with these rules would mean that the vicar, Edmund Humpfrey, would be fined 3s 4d, which would be spent on the upkeep of the church.

The order to keep a parish register was received with great suspicion. Most people believed it to be a new tax and so most parishes ignored it. First given in 1538, it was renewed again, in 1547, during the reign of Edward VI, but this time the fine was to go towards poor relief. As with All Saints', most registers began around 1558, but due to a lack of money to

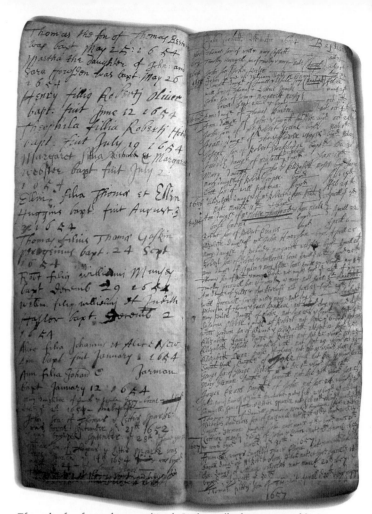

The early church records were written in Latin, until a law was passed in 1733 forbidding its use, although English was used occasionally before this date. These pages containing baptisms, show a change in hand writing in the entries.

The left hand page has entries from 1654 with one from 1652; some are written in Latin, others in English. The right hand page starts in 1651 through to 1657 and is completely in English.

Names entered on both pages are from the top left: Beeton, Housden, Oliver, Hitch, Webster, Huggins, Gaskin, Munsey, Hasler, Newlin, Jarmin, Gray, Sparke(1652), Sparke. From the top right: Casbolt, Hornwell, Porter, Nash, Gray, Sparke, Munsey, Parker, Housden, Greene, Wigges, Stockbridge, Dockerill, Moses, Cooper, Patman, Hitch, Evans, Harrison, Webster, Noone, Allen,ornwell, Bencroft, Hornwell (Hornold), Dunham, Porter, Oliver, Goodwin, Game, Casbolt, Dunn, Hall, Oliver, German (Jarment), Evans (Ewins) Beamond, Sparke, Norket, Andrewes, German (Jarment), Munsey, Wiggs, Hitch, Willcocks, Pitty

Christening charts for All Saints' Church

pay for material and the reluctance of the vicar, the first twenty years of the original register were omitted. In 1557 Edmund Humpfrey, was instructed to record the names of the Godfather and Godmother at Baptisms. Godparents were sometimes referred to as 'sureties', 'witnesses' or the old English 'gossib' or 'gossip'.

Elizabeth I, in 1597, ordered that all records were to be kept in parchment books (made from animal skins). All earlier paper records were to be transcribed onto parchment and copies (or 'Bishop's Transcripts') of all new entries were to be sent each month to the dioceses. It was not until 1603 that the Act was finally enforced throughout the country and each parish ordered to finance its registers. James Scrubie, the vicar of Melbourn at that time, was to keep the books in a chest, now with *three* locks. To ensure that records were kept properly he was to read the entries out each Sunday

after evensong. Despite this, the records of Melbourn are patchy. Although the Bishop's Transcripts date from 1599–1782, missing entries throughout this period span fifty years. Also missing from the church registers are burials from 1679–1696, marriages from 1698–1700 and a few baptisms in the 1680s and 1690s.

Melbourn continued to maintain the parish register during the Civil War, 1643–1647, but throughout the rest of the country many towns and villages abandoned them altogether. Others made scant entries and, in some cases, books were hidden by the clergy ~ some of these have been completely lost. During this period a civil register was set up and civil marriages allowed. The fee charged for a birth was 4d, a marriage 12d, and a burial 4d. The practice of holding registers returned to the church after the restoration of the monarchy in 1660.

Entries in the church register were used to raise a tax, in 1694, for money for a war against France. For a birth the charge was 2s, a marriage 2s 6d and a burial 4s. A tax of 1s per year was also levied on all unmarried men! In 1696 a fine of £2 was to be imposed on those who did not report the birth of a child to the vicar within 5 days, and the family of an un-christened child was liable to a tax of 6d. If the vicar of Melbourn, Edward Griffith *also* failed to record a birth, *he* was fined £2 for neglect.

The effects of Nonconformity and civil registration

With the increase of Nonconformist churches in the late-16th century, many began to conduct their own baptisms and marriages, often clandestinely, but few possessed their own burial grounds until much later. Following the Toleration Act of 1688, chapels could operate openly and, although Catholicism continued to be suppressed, Catholic priests continued to operate in secret. A new law, in 1754,

prevented marriages in Nonconformist Chapels, although a number of baptisms and burials were still carried out and recorded in Nonconformist registers. The Methodist church registers began earlier, in 1738, but since the church was an illegal institution at that time, what records were kept had to be hidden.

The records for baptisms for the Independent Chapel in Melbourn date from 1800, when '*Henry son of William and Sarah Drew. Aged 3 months on Nov 11 1800*' was baptised. The records for burials are from 1810. The first one simply reads '*Child of John Smith Aug 3 1810*'.

By 1837, a large number of churchgoers went to Nonconformist churches, rather than to the Church of England. This was one of the driving forces behind the introduction of a national registration system and, on 1 July 1837, civil registration was introduced. Following its introduction, Nonconformist churches were offered the opportunity to submit their registers for authentification. This gave their contents a legal status for such purposes as disputes over inheritance.

The coffer (strong box) at All Saints' Church

The census

Study of the church and census records shows how many names have changed slightly ~ for example, an 's' is often added on the end of the name or an extra 't' put in the middle. The different accents of those moving around the country, and illiteracy, added to these variations.

Melbourn has had a census every ten years since 1801. The first four were little more than a simple head count of the village. These were the responsibility of the overseers of the poor, and the clergy, therefore only a small amount of information was gathered.

The first full census took place in Melbourn during Sunday 6th and Monday 7th June 1841. Each householder was required to complete a 'census schedule', sent to them in the week preceding the census day, with simple questions that included: street name; the occupants first and last name; age; marital status; profession or trade; if of independent means, and whether they were born in the county. Answers to some of these could be indicated by ticking a box. As many in the village were illiterate, it was left to those conducting the census, the 'enumerators', to fill in the forms. Once again, the accent of the person would have caused problems or, if the enumerator had just come from a person with a similar-sounding name, for instance, the name **Alger**, spoken quietly or quickly, could easily sound like **Auger**, **Ilger** or **Iljer**. These problems can be seen throughout the census. In the 1851 census a family appears as **Handscom**; by 1861 the name is spelt **Hanscomb** and **Handscomb**; but 1881 saw an additional spelling, **Handscombe**. It is worth noting that, in the 1861 census, the *Hanscomb* and *Handscomb* were probably related.

The 1851 census had similar questions to those of its predecessor but with a few additions. These included the relationship with the head of the

The 1891 Bury Census group. Catherine Fordham, a widow, was head of the household at the time of the 1891 census taken on 21 April. As the transcription of the records below shows, her three sons and sister were also staying at the house at the time. Servants working at the house on the day include – a housekeeper, three housemaids, a footman and a gardener.

Name	Relation to Head	Condition	Age	Profession or Occupation	Where born	
Catherine Fordham	Head	Widow	52	Living on her own income	Cumberland, Broyton	*F3
Alfred Fordham	Son	S	18	Student	London, Kensington	*F2
Edward W. Fordham	Son	S	16	Scholar	London, Kensington	*B9
John G. Fordham	Son	S	14	Scholar	London, Kensington	*B3
Elizabeth Lawson	Sister	S	64	Living on her own income	Cumberland, Broyton	*F1
Ellen W. Price	Servant	S	57	Housekeeper and domestic	London, St Luke's	*B5
Emily Jackson	Servant	S	20	Housemaid and domestic	Cambs, Whaddon	*B7
Annie Jane Harrop	Servant	S	24	Housemaid and domestic	Cambs, Melbourn	*B6
Elizabeth Turtlebury	Servant	S	19	Housemaid and domestic	Cambs, Thriplow	*B2
Dan Chapman	Servant	S	24	Footman	Cambs, Melbourn	*B8
Edward J Stockbridge	Servant	S	25	Gardner	Cambs, Melbourn	*B1
Anne Orbiston	Visitor	S	46	Lady's Maid	Norfolk, King's Lynn	*B4

*F = Front row seated from the left, B = Backrow from the left

The 1901 Bury Census group. By 1901 the family line up had changed and only two members of the Fordham family were living at The Bury.

Name	Age	Occupation	Born
Alfred Fordham	28	Barrister	London
Caroline Fordham	25		Cumberland
Jane Gillanders	33	Housemaid	Scotland
Mary King	29	Ladys Maid	London
Lizzie Kippist	23	Domestic Cook	London
Lourie Pateman	20	Scullery Maid	Meldreth
Chales Morcer	20	Footman	London

Right, a facsimile of the 1901 census covering Sheen Mill, Station Road and part of The Cross. Questions on this form asked if the person was an 'imbecile, idiot or feebleminded'. Amongst the families listed are the Campkins. Walter Campkin, who was well known as a grocer and draper, and Nina Campkin, whose research was instrumental in the production of this book.

household, whether the person was a lodger or just visiting and, in the case of the boarding school in the High Street, each child was recorded as a scholar. Instead of the yes/no answer to 'Born in County', the question was 'Where born' i.e. the county or place. In the last column was a box to enter whether the person was blind, deaf or dumb. By 1881 this heading had been changed to: 'deaf and dumb, blind, imbecile/idiot or lunatic', but, in 1901, 'idiot' had been omitted and 'feebleminded' added.

The 1881 census was later the first to be fully collated and indexed by the Mormon Church based in Salt Lake City, America ('The Church of Jesus Christ of Latter-day Saints'). Mormons believe in 'posthumous baptism', where members are able to have their deceased ancestor baptised in order to see them in the after life. It was from this that the church made the most comprehensive collection of names and information for the entire world.

The 1931 census, stored in London during the early part of Second World War, was destroyed by fire, and 1941 saw a 'national registration' instead of a census. The information on the census is not available to the general public for 100 year.

No of Schedule	ROAD, STREET &c. and No or NAME of HOUSE	HOUSES — In habited	HOUSES — Uninhabited — In Occupation	HOUSES — Uninhabited — Not in Occupation	HOUSES — Building	Number of rooms occupied if less than five	Name and Surname of each Person	RELATION to HEAD of Family	Condition as to Marriage	Age last Birthday — Male	Age last Birthday — Female	PROFESSION OR OCCUPATION	Employer, Worker, or Own account	If Worker at Home	WHERE BORN	(1) Deaf and Dumb (2) Blind (3) Lunatic (4) Imbecile, feeble-minded
1	Sheen Mill	1				4	Samuel Hopley	Head	M	20		Miller & Corn Merchant	Employer		Little Budworth Cheshire	
							Mary Jane Hopley	Wife	M		28				Cheshire Whitegate	
							Ada Mary Hopley	Daughter			2				Cambs Melbourn	
							Laura C Hopley	Daughter			1				Do Do	
							Charlotte Lowe	Servant	S		17	General Servant Domestic			Ely Cambs	
2	Station Road	1				2	Sarah Webb	Head	Wid		85	Living on own means			Cambs Melbourn	
3	Ditto	1				4	Ralph Webb	Head	M	38		Coal Merchant	Employer		Cambs Melbourn	
							Louisa Webb	Wife	M		35				Herts Ashwell	
4	Do	1				3	Ruth Handscomb	Head	Wid		64	Laundress Wash	Own account home		Cambs Shepreth	
							Walter Handscomb	Son	S	36		Labourer Ord agricultural	Worker		Cambs Melbourn	
							Clara Lee	Daughter	M		39	Laundress Wash	Worker		Herts Sawbridgeworth	
5	Do	1				2	William Harper	Head		61		Labourer on Highway	Worker		Cambs Melbourn	
							Louisa Harper	D-in-law	M		26				Gloucestershire	
							Frederick A Harper	Grandson		1					Cambs Melbourn	
6	Do	1				3	Wilfred C Winter	Head	M	24		Baker Journeyman Bread	Worker		Cambs Melbourn	
							Rosetta Winter	Wife			25				Cambs Melbourn	
7		1				4	John Gouldthorpe	Head	M	67		Gardener (not domestic)	on own account		Cambs Melbourn	
							Emma Gouldthorpe	Wife			65				Cambs Melbourn	
							Lewis Gouldthorpe	Son	S	31		Labourer Agricultural	Worker		Cambs Melbourn	
							Herbert Gouldthorpe	Grandson	S	26		Labourer Do	Worker		Cambs Melbourn	
8	Do	1					Harry Gouldthorpe	Head	S	35		Manager of Public House	Worker		Cambs Melbourn	
9	Do	1					Walter C Campkin	Head	M	61		Grocer Draper & Min. Water man	Employer		Cambs Melbourn	
							Masie Campkin	S-in-law	Wid		53	School Mistress	on own account		Germany Hessen Darmstard	
							Winifred Campkin	Niece	S		17	Dressmaker	Worker		Cambs Melbourn	
							Nina Campkin	Niece	S		15	School girl stu			Cambs Melbourn	
							Reginald Campkin	Nephew	S	12					Cambs Melbourn	
							Lilian Campkin	Niece			9				Cambs Melbourn	
10	The Cross	1					Elizabeth Disbrey	Head	Wid		53	Purveyor of meat Butcher	Employer		Cambs Melbourn	
							John C Disbrey	Son	S	21		Butcher Slaughterman	Worker		Cambs Melbourn	
							Minnie E Disbrey	Daughter	S		18				Cambs Melbourn	
							William Johnson	Boarder	S	38		Butcher Journeyman	Worker		Cambs Orwell	
10	Total of Scedules of Houses and Tenements with less than Five Rooms	10			7		Total of Males and of Females ...			14	17					

Administrative County **Cambridge** — The undermentioned Houses are situate within the boundaries of the

Civil Parish of *Melbourn* — Ecclesiastical Parish of *All Saints' (part of)* Melbourn — County Borough, Municipal Borough, or Urban District of ___ — Ward of Municipal Borough, or Urban District of ___ — Rural District of *Melbourn (part of)* — Parliamentary Borough Chester Division of *West Cambridge (Part of)* — Town or Village or Hamlet of *Melbourn (part of)*

Personalities

...the novelty of having electricity! We switched the lights on and off just to see them work

Because of their wealth, and therefore influence, many of the people who have owned the Manors (Argentines, later Lordship, The Bury, Trayles and the Old Manor) have played a significant part in the history of Melbourn.

One of the earliest names is probably **Argentine**, who held the manor from the early-12th century.

The manor was sold in the early 1700s to the **Hitch** family, who also bought Trayles manor in 1703. By 1891 the Hitches had sold the manorial rights (*the land and all its privileges*) and, in 1898, they also sold nearly 1000 acres of land in Melbourn and Meldreth, mostly to the **Palmers** who were fruit growers. The Hitches retained the Manor House in the High Street and continued to live in Melbourn. The rood screen in All Saints' Church was donated by Thomas Hitch in 1507.

In 1700 the lease for Melbourn Bury was held by Sir Benjamin **Ayloffe**, who left money to found the first school in the village. By 1725 the lease had passed to Sir John **Hatton** and after his death to his widow Mary, in 1740. The Bury was sold in 1784 to John **Trigg** and held by Mary Trigg until 1806, when she sold it to John **Fordham.** The Triggs were great benefactors and Trigg's Charity still exists in the village. In his will, dated 6th June 1818, he instructed that on his death all his goods should be converted into cash and distributed to various charitable and religious institutions. It was through this that the first free village school was established.

In 1864 the freehold of The Bury estate was sold to the **Fordham** family, also great benefactors to the village. They supported all three churches, donated a Reading Room and held many sporting and charitable events in the grounds of The Bury. They also ran a dairy and milk round and employed local men on the farm and in the fruit orchards.

Benjamin **Metcalfe** (**Medcalfe**), a dissenter and founder of the Baptist Church in 1654, was famous for being involved in the Ship Tax riots which took place in Melbourn in June 1640.

William **Carver** became minister of the Congregational Church in 1792. He took over the ministry after dissension among the church members over the conduct of a minister, Samuel Bull. Following the death of the Rev. Richard Cooper it was thought that his young assistant Samuel Bull,

The rood screen in All Saints' Church

Grave of Benjamin Metcalfe in the churchyard of All Saints' Church

a former student at Homerton College, would be appointed in his place, but objections from the congregation led by Mary Newling and her family caused Bull to be rejected. He had married a widow who was ...*somewhat penurious and irritable and far older than he.* The union was not regarded as a happy one. Bull went on to become the first Minister of Bassingbourn.

Carver remained at the ministry in Melbourn for 32 years. The Congregational Church was in some difficulties when he took over and attendance was low. However, by 1819 he had revived its fortunes to such an extent that the Meeting House was enlarged.

Because public schools were barred to Nonconformists, he founded a boarding school for 200 boys, 90 of whom were boarders. The school gained such a good reputation that children from other denominations were also sent there. Carver was also a member of the Parish Council.

He held only one pastorate and died in Melbourn on 3rd August 1825. In his long years of ministry it was noted that ...*there was never anything unpleasant between minister and people.*

The Penny Bank

The total number of depositors has been 223; of these 41 have withdrawn part of their deposits or having withdrawn all have again become depositors; and 36 have ceased to be depositors but of these many had good sums in before they took any out and several have told me they intend to put in again soon. There are now therefore 187 persons who have sums in the bank varying from a few pence to several pounds; but this includes about 15 who can hardly be reckoned in the number of depositors having only put in small trifles some time ago and now seem to be tired of it. The total amount of money put into the bank has been £145 7s 3d; of this £25 2s 5d has been withdrawn so that there is now £120 4s 10d in the bank; and since there are as I have said 187 persons who have money in, the average amount belonging to each is about 13s. The total number of deposits has been 3,781 and as the bank was open 51 nights the average number each night has been 74 – the average amount of each deposit being 9d. Of the 3781 deposits, 247 were of 1d each; 744 of 2d; 523 of 3d; 233 of 4d; 1028 of 6d; 522 of 1s; 81 of 2s; 35 of 5s; 23 of 10s; 16 of £1 and the remaining 390 of various sums. The friends of the poor will rejoice on reading this interesting intelligence.

Royston Crow February 1860

His son William and other village notables, such as George Ward, were involved in the formation of the Melbourn Choral Society, in 1842. The Society was still in existence in the 1950s.

The Rev. **de Courcy-Ireland** was vicar of Melbourn between 1911 and 1921 and an enthusiastic follower of country sports. During a shooting party in 1921 at Abington Piggots, one of the shooting party accidentally shot the vicar in the eye. The Reverend gentleman bound up his eye and although in great pain drove himself home to Melbourn and then to hospital in Cambridge, where the eye was found to be so severely damaged it was immediately removed.

Rev F M **Jenyns**, known as ...*The excellent vicar of Melbourn,* encouraged the village to join a savings scheme known as the Penny Bank. By 1860, 223 depositors had joined the bank.

One of the longest-serving vicars of the village was the Rev. James **Hamilton**. He carried on well into his nineties. Although not originally from the village the Rev. Hamilton became vicar of Melbourn in 1874. He finally gave up his work in 1907 but continued to be involved in village projects. In 1910 he worked on the Memorial Service for King Edward VII. He also became involved in the restoration of parts of the church and the installation of the mechanical system of ringing the bells, was mainly at his own expense, but he will be remembered as ...*the beast who stopped the Feast.* This well-reported incident took place in 1882 when he tried to stop the Feast and caused a riot.

Rev. James Hamilton
'Beast who stopped the Feast'

I remember it well…

Reminiscences of village life in the early-20th century including *interviews with local inhabitants.*

Abrey, Peggy (*née* **Robinson**) *b.*1930

I attended Melbourn Village School until the age of fourteen when I started work at the village Post Office. Later I moved to Cambridge Trinity Street Post Office.

My grandfather, Harry Robinson, owned the tailor's shop at the corner of the Moor, next door to the bakery. He had three sons who worked with him, one of the sons was my father. They made and repaired garments for all the villages in the area.

The cloth was ordered from London and came by train to Meldreth station. The tailors sat cross-legged on a large table and stitched the fabric by hand. The irons for pressing were heated on a stove in a corner of the room.

The work was very tiring on the eyes as the tailors worked by the light of oil lamps until electricity came into the village.

Easter was the busiest time as everyone had new clothes then. It was a great event when a boy had his first pair of long trousers. The tailor delivered the garments to the customers in all the villages by pony and trap. The best day for this was Friday, as it was payday.

The business closed for good in the 50s when ready-made clothing was easily available in the shops.

I married Gerald Abrey, a skilled carpenter, whose grandfather, Ryal, kept a shop in Drury Lane which stocked almost everything. His two daughters served in the shop. Ryal Abrey was well known in the surrounding areas as he sold provisions from his horse and cart. He had a patter, naming all his wares, and when a customer asked for something he didn't stock he would say: '*That's the very thing mother forgot to put on the cart this morning!*'

The horse knew the route and would stop at all the right houses and venues. When Ryal returned to the shop he would leave the horse outside; one day it disappeared and was found eating hay in the stable with the cart still attached, having knocked down the gateposts on its way!

Black, Daphne *b.*1915

Local resident Daphne Black started her studies at the local school in Melbourn in 1920. On the first day she screamed all the way there. All the children were standing outside wondering where the noise was coming from but once the headmaster, Fred Aldridge, had taken her by the hand and said 'Come on my little dear', she stopped crying at once. Daphne had ambitions to be a White Ribboner (a Temperance group for children) and asked her mother if she might go to school dressed in a similar fashion. Her mother had not checked the qualifications and when Daphne arrived, dressed from head to toe in white, she was told she wasn't allowed to join as she went to the 'wrong church'. The White Ribboners were Baptists and the Black family were Congregationalists.

Daphne recalls that the infants' school was in the extension at the back of the school. The infants wrote on slates with what she describes as '*thin squeaky things*' but at 7 or 8 years of age they were promoted to paper. She learned to make letters on specially printed papers. Learning was by 'rote', or the mechanical use of the memory, and no reasons were ever given. In the same classroom was the village library run by Wilf Ogden. He was much liked and went on to teach for many years. One of Daphne's boyfriends was Cyril Hagger, and she still has a note he sent her.

Daphne moved schools to be educated in Cambridge travelling at first on an open top bus.

She remembers well the end of the Second World War. Having been de-mobbed from the ATS, she caught a train as far as Royston, and had to walk the rest of the way to Melbourn, but '*the local RAF were putting everything they could find into the sky in one giant firework display*', which helped with the three mile walk home.

Brooksbank, Ron *b.*1924

Ron arrived in the village after the Second World War, and his account of village life, and the duties of the village policeman at that time, make very interesting reading!

Melbourn then had a population of around 1,400 inhabitants, and the Police Station was located in the Magistrates' Court in Cross Lane, a red-brick, Victorian building.

The Magistrate sat on a raised dais with an iron rail set with brass knobs. One of Ron's first jobs was to polish these knobs. His first cycle patrol was with the Section Motor Cyclist, also on a cycle, when they visited all the lanes and main areas of the village.

All policemen had to get a case in their notebooks. After a fortnight when he had drawn a blank, he stopped and reported a cyclist for having no rear red light.

Cane, Norah (*née* **Catley**) *b.*1914

Father died of cancer when I was seven. He worked with cows, and it was believed that he got the disease from them. Mother had to bring up four girls on very little money.

At school I learned cookery and needlework while the boys did woodwork. We didn't make whole garments in needlework as the cloth was too expensive. We also did drawing and art. I stayed on at school until I was fifteen, as I had been ill for a year with inflammation of the kidneys.

There was a lovely meadow near our house on

New Road where we played at houses and other games. Children played with balls and tops on the road, but it was not so good once the surface was Tarmacked, as the loose gravel prevented the balls bouncing properly.

Mother had a sewing machine and was able to make clothes for us, often from cut-down garments. We belonged to a clothing club and were able to have some clothes from there.

At the time we didn't know that we were poor.

At Christmas we had very few presents, but had a chicken and some boiled salted beef, which was lovely.

Clear

The Clear family were great benefactors of the village. The neat row of cottages in Orchard Road opposite the URC Chapel was built as almshouses with a donation in memory of Francis Clear. The family were well known and respected members of the village community. Amongst his many roles, Francis Clear was an active member of the Cambridgeshire Education Committee, and also represented Melbourn and Meldreth on the County Council for many years. Francis Clear died in 1905.

Cooper, Ada (née **Catley**) b.1916

At one time there were 500 Coopers in the village and surrounds.

I was born at Campkins in a cottage belonging to the Campkin family. It had been part of a pub called The Tailor's Arms. My parents paid 3s 6d a week rent. I was delivered by nurse Ada Guiver; she was not a real nurse but an unqualified midwife for the village. Nurse Cox, a qualified nurse, delivered my 4 brothers. My parents were both born in the village, my mother was a Chipperfield. My father worked for the Campkin family putting the glass marbles (known as jintlers) into glass pop bottles. I was educated at the local school in Melbourn and

passed my scholarship exam, but the family did not have enough money to send me to school in Cambridge, and the yearly scholarship was awarded to Daphne Hagger, so at 14 I left school. I went to work for Mrs George Palmer at Sheen Farm earning 5s a week. I ran errands for Mrs Campkin and thought I was rich when she paid me 1½d. After 4 years of service I was earning 4s a week. When I left to get married the Palmers gave me a dozen eggs as a wedding gift.

I love singing and playing the piano and organ and attending the Baptist Chapel.

Chamberlain, Molly (née **Greatorex**) b.1927

During the Second World War, I, and some other children and young people, were strafed by a German fighter whilst walking in the High Street. We jumped into a nearby hedge and came out to shout 'Missed us!' as the fighter disappeared.

My father was a member of the Melbourn Home Guard platoon. The Home Guard practised around the village, once turning The Cross into a large bomb crater marked out with chalk with 'casualties'. No one was allowed to walk into the chalked area, until Jack Palmer wanted to get into Station Road. Then the order was given that, as it was 'Master Jack' who wanted to get through, they had to let him walk in the 'bomb crater'.

The platoon frequently mounted guard in the church, some members of the platoon on patrol, some resting in the pews, and others plane spotting from the tower.

One night, three members of the platoon were plane spotting from the tower. They decided to creep down to the back of the church, put the choir robes over their heads and run up and down the pews where the rest of the platoon were sleeping. The platoon woke up and fled the church thinking that they were seeing ghosts!

The Melbourn Home Guard were to go on night

manoeuvres, but they were back in their homes within two hours as the Sandon Home Guard forgot to turn up for the exercise.

Chapman, Arthur b.1905

During the First World War, each farmer was allowed to keep only one worker of conscription age. All the other men had to join the forces. I was taken out of school at the age of twelve, in order to work on the land. I went to night school to keep up my school work.

Later I worked on Wedd's farm, and then Muncey's farm, before going on to the Atlas works. During the Second World War, I and some of the other machine workers were not conscripted but stayed to do essential work at the factory.

Ellis, Helena (née **East**) b.1924

I was the second of 4 children; my mother was an Abrey and my father worked at the Cam factory in Meldreth. We lived in a terrace of 8 houses in Dolphin Lane. The terrace, long since demolished, had 4 toilets at each end of the row and no back doors. To the rear of the row were the allotments and, beyond them, the Court House and police station. We had fields on the lane side of the house, and we children spent many happy hours and carefree days playing in the stream at the bottom of the field. It was also a good source of duck eggs. We played at Wedd's Farm, also in Dolphin Lane, with the Wedd boys ~ Arthur, Roy, Bertie and Tommy. One lasting memory I have is of the day father got us up early one morning, to watch the R101 airship gliding over the village en route, from Cardington to India; sadly it crashed in France. When I was 11, my family moved from Dolphin Lane to Turnpike Cottage, in the High Street just opposite Water Lane. At first we rented the cottage then later my father bought it for £250! The novelty of having electricity! We switched the lights on and off just to see them work. In those days we knew everyone in the village which was a close-knit community. When the church bell was tolled at the death of a villager, word soon spread as to who had passed away. I went to the local school in Melbourn. On leaving school I eventually found a job at the Burlington Press in Foxton ~ there was very little employment locally. My friend and I cycled 6 miles a day to work and back and my weekly wage was 7s 6d. On Saturdays, for entertainment, we cycled to Cambridge to go to the Regal Cinema matinée, costing 2d. At that time, Marks and Spencer was a Five Shilling store, with many nice dresses at that price. Woolworths was a 3d and 6d store. I married Claude Ellis from Foxton, in June 1942. Being surrounded by orchards of fruit trees, we young mothers found employment in the picking gangs, as we could take the younger children with us. It was hard work, but as a group we had a lot of fun.

Gillings, Morag (*née* **Hagger**) *b.*1920

I was born in Rothsay on the Isle of Bute. My father, who was a constructional engineer, went up there to do a job and stayed in my grandmother's house. He met my mother when she was 14, and married her at 19. As he was always working abroad, at that time in Calcutta, we lived up there until 1923. When my great grandmother died and we moved down to this house (in Orchard Road), I was 3 and my sister was 18 months younger. We travelled by train, with Grandmother Patterson, and spent a night in Glasgow, where uncle brought a lot of balloons into the bathroom!

My father had sent money home to have the house built, and our Scottish grandmother came to live with us. Grandmother Hagger was living in the Maples at that time ~ but she moved out and lived where the business was, in the High Street. This was the saddlery business (Joseph Hagger and Son), which had started around 1790. By the time I remember it, it was in decline, as horses were no longer used as

much on the farms and the business didn't move with the times, although they did own an ironmongery shop and a blacksmith's.

My father, Cyril was the 5th child of Joseph Hagger. Another Cyril Hagger was my cousin, whose father Bert managed the saddlery business. My mother ran the orchards while my father was abroad. After Calcutta my father went out to Aden, so he was home only for a few months.

By the time my parents had been married for 10 years, they had only spent 18 months together! Usually my father went overseas alone, but my mother did go to Ceylon for 18 months, when I was 16. My father was intent on saving money and building up the orchards for his retirement. He was in Ceylon when the Second World War started and came home in 1941, via South Africa, to America and then across the Atlantic. He then retired and stayed at home.

I started school at Hop Mallions, a Dame school run by 2 single ladies. One of them had stomach pains and always held onto a hot-water bottle. After that I went to Dorothy Palmer's school for a bit, and then to the Village School when I was 8. At Dorothy Palmer's school we had long breaks. There were the sons of 2 butchers at the school, Dudley Hoy and Douglas Bacon, and we had to be the animals which they herded around and slaughtered! I didn't enjoy that. We had dolls and other toys and played the seasonal games, such as skipping, marbles, tops etc.

We went to the Congregational Church, as did all the farmers, all Nonconformists.

We would go to Royston, and Cambridge, on the bus which was open-topped, with an apron. You could also sit with the driver, which doesn't sound very safe now; there were 3 seats there in the front. I went to the County School on East Road at 11.

I was 18 in 1938, the year of the Munich Crisis, and went up to London and stayed near Clapham Common, where they were digging trenches. I was at the Battersea Polytechnic doing Domestic Science. As

mother was in Ceylon I had to organise myself. After a year we were evacuated to Shrewsbury, but it was so expensive and we all came back to London for the Blitz! They made us sleep in the basement, and take our mattresses down there every night. I had a friend who wouldn't do this, but hung out of her bedroom window looking at the bombs ~ she thought it was exciting.

My sister read Biology at Newnham. Then, after working in Pest Control, she eventually became a teacher when the war was over.

We had a telephone quite early on, the number was 53 ~ we had it because mother used to phone Uncle Mark in Meldreth when he was ill. Other people used to come and ask to use it in emergencies.

My father occasionally sent us cables when he was overseas. Mother would cable him if she had problems and he would reply 'Do *as you think fit, dear.*' The dear, cost him extra of course, and it became a family saying!

My Grandmother Hagger was very authoritative and tried to rule mother. She sat in the dining room with a bell and the maid had to answer immediately.

We went to church (Congregational) every Sunday, wearing our Sunday clothes. These were made by Mrs Anderson who lived at the bottom of Water Lane; she had worked in London previously. She made my clothes from when I was 3, till I was 29, and she also made my wedding dress.

When my father retired, he was on the District and County Councils for many years. He took a great interest in getting a sewerage system for Melbourn, and visited the continent to find the best possible system. He worked as the chairman at Cambridgeshire Growers, until he was 87, as fruit was doing very badly and he needed the money.

After training, I had to come back and work in the County for 3 years for very little money and after that, when I was 24, I got a job at Leicester Domestic Science College.

It was there I met Gilly, (Ken Gillings) who was finishing his pharmaceutical training, which had been interrupted by the War. He had joined up as a boy soldier, aged 14, and started pharmacy then. He was in the army for 7 years. I gave up my job when we got married so we were both jobless for a time.

I remember the Sunday School treats we had before the War, in Collis Palmer's orchard opposite the Star pub ~ there were swings on the trees, and races. The Christmas party was in the URC, with a magic lantern show and lots to eat and drink. To 'spend a penny' you had to go across the road to a little shack, but I never went there as we were so close to home. I never 'spent a penny' at the Village School either; the toilets were nasty places so I always went home at lunch time.

We didn't really have summer holidays, as that was the fruit picking season and we all went up to the orchards to help. Later on, we grew daffodils and tulips and then asparagus; I liked that!

Every day at school we had 3 hymns in the morning, and had to say grace before and after lunch every single day.

Oh yes, and I remember the landlord of the Black Horse cutting his throat when I was very young. I shall never forget the groans.

Gregor

The first notable Doctor to live in the village was Doctor Gregor. He and his family lived in a large house, in the High Street, known as Greenbanks. The surgery could be found at the end of the house.

Hagger

The Hagger family were fruit farmers and were involved in many aspects of village life. The family owned a saddler's shop in the High Street, of which the earliest accounts date from 1790. J Hagger was a member of the Congregational Church, and, in 1890, he received an illuminated address on retiring after 50 years of service as the Superintendent of the Congregational Chapel Sunday School. Miss Hagger was a well known pianist and accompanied musical events in the village for many years.

Hale

Gus Hale is remembered for his numerous talents some of which can be seen in the Parish Church, and was well reported in the local newspapers for his achievements. He also made an altar piece for the church. This has since disappeared. Gus was a choirmaster at the church for some years.

> The Mothers' Union banner, made by Mr Gus Hale was dedicated in the Church by the Vicar.
>
> *Royston Crow 6th July 1923*
>
> The Tower screen in the Parish Church in memory of Henry Cranfield, the former postmaster, and his wife was made by Mr Gus Hale.
>
> *Royston Crow 21st November 1930*
>
> Harvest Service and Dedication of Ringing Board. At the conclusion of the sermon the Vicar thanked the ringers and complimented them on the success in completing the peal and proceeded to dedicate the ringing board in commemoration which had been designed and painted by Mr A G Hale and contains the inscription 'Peal of Plain Bob Minor – 5040 changes – rung on July 20th 1920 in 2 hours 44 minutes by S Wedd, A Austin (conductor), C Gouldthorpe, J Ward, E Hibbins, and tenor F Harper.'
>
> *Royston Crow 8th October 1920*
>
> A handpainted list of Melbourn Vicars, framed in oak, has been made and placed in the church by Mr Gus Hale.
>
> *Royston Crow 7th June 1935*

WHAT THE PAPERS SAID

Harper, Violet (*née* Hale) *b.*1905

My father had two allotments as there were seven children to feed. He grew vegetables on one allotment and wheat on the other, enough to last the year. The wheat was cut by scythe, and Mr French's horse and cart were hired to take the corn to Sheen Mill where it was stored until it was needed. One of the children would then be sent with a pillow case to bring home some of the ground corn to make into bread.

One of my brothers used to go out with Bert Howard, the baker, and would hold the horse while he collected the money. Jubal Howard delivered the bread in the village using a handcart, and often it would be my bedtime before he got to our house.

My mother used to buy 'Beehive' wool, to knit our socks, from Miss Pryor who lived at Crossways. In the room to the right of the front door she had a shop where she sold books, stationery, wool and haberdashery. She also sold thimbles ~ we were always losing ours. She would ask to see our fingers and say 'You need a size 5', which we would try on, and she was always right!

The fish shop was owned by 'Fessor' Hinkins, a very happy man. He was also the chimney sweep and sold ice cream! A small door next to the White Lion Pub was used as a lavatory by the men (hygiene was not then as it is today!). In the summertime it was very smelly; we used to turn our heads away as we passed by. There is a similar little area next to what was The Red Cow.

My grandfather told me that he was up in the elm tree, with his friends, in 1843 when Queen Victoria and Prince Albert came through, by coach, on their way to Cambridge to open an exhibition. Just after the procession had passed underneath the bough snapped off, and the boys fell into the road. My grandfather laughingly said '*If that branch had broken a minute earlier we would all have landed in the coach, and had an even better view!*'

Hinkins, Alf

Alf Hinkins, known to all as '*Fessor*' Hinkins, had a small fish shop at The Cross squeezed between a thatched cottage, once known as the Guildhall, and the old White Lion pub. As the local chimney sweep it was not unusual for Fessor Hinkins to be seen using the same barrow for his brushes and soot bags, as he did for the fish he collected from the railway station. Later, Alf sold the fish shop and opened a fruit and vegetable shop on the corner of Little Lane, where he sold home-made ice cream and fizzy pop in old-fashioned glass bottles.

Housden, John (Jack) *b*.1914

Shepherds' tales

The last shepherd in the village was John Housden, known locally as Jack. He worked as a shepherd for 18 years, from 1942, and was well known throughout the area for his knowledge and skills of shearing sheep by hand, which brought him extra money. Jack would often drive the sheep nine miles to market on foot and, if the sheep did not sell, they were walked back again.

One of Jack's memories was of early one May, a local farmer who kept a few sheep in his orchard asked Jack to shear them, despite being warned that the weather could turn cold, which was dangerous for newly-shorn animals. Finally, he agreed to do the work for 9d per sheep, on condition that he was not blamed if they died. The weather did turn cold and four sheep died. After this the farmer took his advice and went back to June shearing like everyone else.

Following his many years as a shepherd, Jack went on to work at The Bury with cattle. Before the services of a veterinary surgeon were readily available Jack, a registered castrator, was used by many farms in the district, not only for neutering farm animals but for pets too.

There were seven in Jack Housden's family and he was the second eldest. This meant that he had to help his mother with the little ones when she was busy, and he often fell asleep holding the baby. This happened once when his mother was visited by the wife of the boss, who, concerned that he would drop the baby, insisted that his mother wake him up. Of course, the minute his mother tried to take the baby, he *did* wake up.

This so impressed the lady, that she immediately wanted to employ him as a houseboy, and he helped in her house from the age of 10 to 14. His duties included cleaning the range, lighting it with paper and sticks and boiling the kettle. At this point he called up the stairs, '*Water is boiling Ma'am*', and Madam came down, in her dressing gown, to make tea for her husband and three little daughters. All this took place before 7am, when the maids arrived.

He also cleaned all the shoes, including the farmer's muddy boots, and had to do jobs like scrubbing the cellar steps. Since he was so young one of the maids would often help him when no one was looking. And all this for a wage of seven shillings a week! The family also employed a cook and nursemaid as house servants.

At the age of 14, when he left school, he went to work with farm animals under the instruction of his brother. This meant an increase in his wages from

7s, to 12s a week. The money he earned was not kept by him as pocket money, but was given to his mother to help with household expenses.

One of his clearest memories is of the time when, one after the other, the children in the family were sent to the Isolation Hospital in Royston. First his older brother became ill and was diagnosed as having Scarlet Fever; he was kept in isolation for six weeks. After this time it was considered that there was no risk of infection and he was sent home. However, all the children, one after the other, fell ill and were carried off in the horse-drawn ambulance to the hospital. Neither his parents, nor anyone else in the village caught the disease. Jack was about 15 at the time and his 6-year-old sister was there with him.

He has clear memories of his time there; how the entire place was run only by a Matron and a Sister, with infrequent visits by a doctor; how visitors had to shout through the window, and how, rather oddly, they had to soak their feet in hot water and then have them scrubbed with a pumice stone. One of his most poignant memories of this time is of the boys from the orphanage which was situated in Barley on the Barkway Road. These boys sang a very plaintive song and must have repeated it frequently as Mr Housden remembers it perfectly:

'Mammy come and fetch me home
From this convalescent home
I will stay a day or two
If you bring me home with you
I went down the lane to buy a penny whistle
The copper came along and took my penny whistle
I asked him for it back but he said he hadn't got it
I know the Curly-Wig had got it in his pocket.
Tap-Tap-Tapping on the window
I saw a copper at the door.
If you don't let me in
Then I'll bash your door right in
And you won't see your Mammy any more.

Howard

On the corner of the Moor stood the old bakery, home to the Howard family. This building also included a bootmaker's, run by Ishmael Howard.

The Howards were a religious family, and this was reflected in the biblical names they gave to their children. Jubal Howard was the baker of the family and a very keen historian, collecting many photographs, books and artifacts of the village. His collection was exhibited at a museum, in a reconstructed barn, near The Cross.

Hunt, Sid *b.1922*

Sid was born in Dolphin Lane. The family moved to a council house in Orchard Way and then to a specially built new house in Portway. There were 12 children in the family. Sid attended Melbourn Village School until he was 14 years old.

The older boys helped Miss Disbrey at the butcher's shop on the way home from school. The butcher would throw out a rope from the slaughter house window and the boys would pull on the rope to bring the animal to its knees, when it would be shot. The blood ran down the gutter in the street

Jubal Howard on his bread round

The Howard family

from the butcher's shop at the Cross as far as the shop opposite the Vicarage. Miss Disbrey owned the butcher's shop and sold three penn'orth of bits, which was quite a bit of meat. Mr Johnson chopped up the meat in the shop, and Mr Leech came as an assistant. When Miss Disbrey died Mr Leech took over the shop.

When he left school Sid started work at the South Cambs Motors garage at The Cross, where he worked for three and a half years. He left to work at a farm in Shepreth for 2 years and then moved to work on a farm with Will Muncey. Sid later bought his farm and started to grow his wonderful vegetables.

During the Second World War, one of Sid's brothers took over his work at Will Muncey's farm.

MELBOURN MUSEUM

The exhibition of local and other antiquities collected by Mr Jubal Howard, along with many others loaned by villagers, is attracting many visitors and will remain open for a short time. As stated last week the exhibits are to be found in a room belonging to Miss Forcey's confectionery establishment, and admission is free.

The following are a few of the many objects that should be examined by visitors:

Roman quern or handmill used for grinding corn. Ploughed up in Melbourn in November 1930. This is at least 1,500 years old.

Several rounded stones or 'bullets' used in slings by the Romans; discovered with the quern.

Several flint-lock pistols as were used before the days of percussion caps, usually carried by drivers of mail coaches.

Dibbling irons and flail, used in pre-machinery days for sowing and threshing corn.

Mantrap used for catching trespassers. The use of this trap in fields was prohibited by an Act passed in 1861.

Stone weight for weighing trusses of straw. By an Act of George III (1796) a truss of straw must weigh 36lbs.

Baker's watch, a stone built in the back of a baker's oven. When at white heat the oven was right for baking.

Holy Bible dated 1620.

Book describing the wonderful adventures of a Captain W.J. Barry, who was born in Melbourn in 1819 etc.

Pewter tankards used in the time of King William IV.

A very fine earthenware jug, 500 years old, found at Haslingfield.

A pair of 'Baxter' prints etc.

A very fine sampler worked in Melbourn School by Catharine Harris, 97 years ago.

Shekel, used in Jerusalem, about AD 66. This was about the same value as the English half crown.

Nine coins of Cnut, better known as Canute, who reigned from AD 1017 to 1025.

Silver penny of Alfred the Great who died AD 901.

Silver penny of Edward I AD 1272-1317.

Half-crown of Oliver Cromwell AD 1658.

Tom-tom, bows and arrows, assagai (a light spear or lance), and other articles from Central Africa.

Arrow heads and other worked flints. Relics of pre-historic times.

Tea caddies and sugar cutters, used in the days when tea and sugar were expensive luxuries. The cutters to cut up 'loaves' of sugar before 'lump' sugar was an article of commerce.

Among the many articles kindly loaned Mr Howard by villagers the following may be mentioned:

Old wooden scales for weighing butter – Mr Bert Palmer.

Bassoon used a century or more ago to start the singing in the Old Chapel – Mr Oscar Campkin.

Crystoleum picture (painting on glass) showing Napoleon going to Marengo. Dated November 1800 – Mr Reg. Slater.

Fossilised tortoise found in a well at the Cross – Mrs Nursey.

Greek peasant's coat, waistcoat and shoes

Royston Crow 25th August 1933

Additions to Museum

Several interesting objects have been added to the local museum during the past week. Mrs Addison of Moss Vale, Whaddon, has kindly loaned two sections of fossilized vertebrae, which were found in the village, these are parts of an ichthyosaurus, a prehistoric reptile something like a lizard, whose length was about twenty-four feet. Other objects loaned by Mrs Addison are an old clay pipe of monster size, a Roman urn and a miniature bible, said to be the smallest in the world.

Mr E O Cooper, of Melbourn, has loaned a fine old cavalry sabre and scabbard as used by the old Dragoons, also a wooden Calvary in a wine bottle.

Royston Crow 15th September 1933

Mr Jubal Howard has lent to the village school his valuable collection of coins and tokens all arranged in a specially made glass topped case. The history of tokens is described and the collection contains some of the best.

Royston Crow 20th May 1932

Death of Mr Jubal Howard on Feb 27th aged 66. He was born in Melbourn in 1881, educated in the village school and was employed as the village baker. He was devoted to serious literature and local history and had a wide knowledge of numismatics. He was also a connoisseur of grandfather clocks, old furniture and prints. Although deaf, he had an excellent memory, was a fine calligraphist and an avid reader. He acquired the ability to decipher ancient documents in Latin and English and could quote lengthy passages from Chaucer, Burns and Shakespeare. He lectured to the Women's Institute on a range of subjects including the Bayeux Tapestry and for many years was the Crow's reporter for Melbourn. Numerous mourners attended his funeral.

Royston Crow 7th March 1947

Littlechild, Don *b.*1921

I was born in East Terrace, Drury Lane, in a cottage owned by the Palmers. My brother Walt was also born there. Our mother died when I was 9 and we lived with our granny until our father remarried. I have 9 half-brothers and sisters, a great family and all friends. I was educated at the local school in Melbourn. When I left school I went to work at a grocery shop in Royston as an errand boy. I was paid 10s for a 53 hour week. I cycled to and from work and even came home for my midday meal. I delivered groceries to Ashwell, The Mordens, Bassingbourn, Melbourn, Royston and Therfield on a grocery delivery cycle. Therfield was the hard one; it took two boys to push the bike up the hills. There was a different delivery day of the week for each village, except Thursdays when we stayed in the shop and did chores like polishing the big brass weighing scales.

Walt and I joined the Army, The Royal Fusiliers, on September 26th 1938. We asked not to be split up and did our training together, even getting our names in the national press. In 1942 we were posted abroad with the 8th Army in North Africa. We later landed at the Salerno Beaches with the 5th American Army. When I married Gwen we lived in a cottage in the High Street and then moved to Portway, until we moved again to Mortlock Street.

Owen, Geoffrey *b.*1919

I was born at Vine Farm, High Street, Melbourn. At the age of three I moved to Royston and went to Queen's Road School. At the age of 11, I went to Hitchin Grammar school until 1935, when I went on to the Hertfordshire Institute of Agriculture.

In the holidays I came back to Melbourn to work at Old Farm for Charles Stockbridge, especially at harvest time. The harvest took a month. Men were 'in their harvest' for that month, working from early morning until 8pm at night.

They were paid their normal wage, plus extra money in a lump sum at the end of the month. In 1936, after College, I started work at Old Farm. There were then six men employed: Bob and Billy Wilson, Bill Basham, Bob Baxter, Fred Chapman and Albert Smith. The farm had horses, sheep, cattle and a cow for the house.

I was chosen to stay at the farm in the Second World War.

It was a bit of a lottery; for example, at Summer House Farm, Chris Wedd went to war, but Peter Wedd was allowed to stay to work the farm.

Page, Joan (*née* **Smith**) *b.*1923

I have happy memories of my schooldays in the village where both Mr Varley and Mr Ogden kindled my desire to learn. Due to the fact that we lived at North Hall, there was no chance to take part in after-school activities and I remember being disappointed not to be in the school play. However, the teachers were kind and allowed me to recite the Prologue.

Children today (or at least their parents) would be horrified to see the somewhat decrepit old grey van in which the dozen or so North Hall children were transported to and from Melbourn school. There were no windows and we sat on bare wooden benches along each side. Len Smith was the contractor and I think that he kept a pub not far from the Old Congregational Chapel. There was sometimes straw on the floor which might indicate animals going to market! Better than walking though!

Daphne Wedd (*née* Vellam) was my special friend and often took me to White House Farm in the lunch hour. The garden was beautiful and her mother would take me round and name every one of her many roses. Occasionally Norah Machon invited me to lunch at her aunt's cottage 'down the moor' (as was then the description), and I will always remember the delicious meat pudding which included morels (a type of wild mushroom). I have never tasted any since and wonder whether they are still to be found locally.

I loved every moment of those 7 years, and after leaving the village school had to cycle each day to catch the bus at the Cross. As we waited for it we were sometimes entertained by a Mrs Harper singing hymns as she swept up horse droppings for her garden! In winter it was dark as I rode home along the somewhat lonely road to North Hall. Another memory is of gypsies who often camped for the night and cooked their supper in a big iron pot. Rabbit or hedgehog? Whatever it was it made me feel hungry.

My recollections of the early part of the War were when my father, and some of the farm workers, were loading corn sheaves on to a wagon, prior to making a corn stack, and they were suddenly targeted by a German fighter plane and machine-gunned. Luckily no one was hurt as they all dived under the trailer for cover.

A somewhat more amusing incident was when an aged aunt and her daughter, who had experienced London bombing, rolled out of a taxi from Royston station with no warning. Next morning, when taking them an early cup of tea, my father was horrified to see them sitting up in bed wearing gas masks. Evidently they had mistaken his alarm clock for a siren. Life proved too quiet for them and it was not long before they departed.

Palmer

The Palmer family were strong supporters of the Congregational Church, and were involved in many village activities including the Parish Council, Scouts, Guides and Brownies. They managed many fruit orchards employing village people, and, throughout the 1800s and 1900s, the name of Palmer was never absent from stories of the village.

Palmer, Jack *b.*1905

Jack was born in Melbourn and lived there all his life. The family lived at The Campkins until they moved to Orchard house which was built by Jack's grandfather. The family moved again to Cawdon House in 1920, where Jack and his sister Peggy lived for many years. The family home had been a Dame school run by the Misses Elbourn and Jack and his sisters, Peggy and Molly started their education at the school. He later went to the Perse School in Cambridge. At the end of his schooling Jack and his brother Jim, joined their father in the fruit growing business. They became one of the biggest orchard owners in the area employing 12 men and a team of 20 women in the picking teams. The Palmer family has lived in the area for several hundred years and local history was one of Jack's hobbies. A lifelong teetotaller and a staunch member of the Melbourn Congregational Chapel, he was a generous man donating his time and means to the village. Early in the 1930's, until 1950, Jack was the Scoutmaster of the Melbourn Troop, after which he became Assistant District Commissioner for the Scout movement. An accomplished sportsman, Jack played hockey for the county, sailed, walked, enjoyed tennis and rugby, and skied for nearly 40 years. Jack served on the Melbourn Parish Council and was Chairman for several years. He was also a school Governor. When the Palmers Way playground was built he donated all the play equipment for the area.

Salmon, Percy *b.*1872

Known as 'Peepbo', Percy came late to the village. He had a colourful career as a photographer and journalist (often using the name Richard Penlake) travelling widely throughout the world. Living at the Cross proved a great vantage point from which to keep an eye on village life and to photograph the comings and goings of the village. His photographs can be seen on many postcards of the village.

A Journalist's Jubilee – Fifty Years of News-Gathering

For the past ten years Mr Percy R. Salmon, our Melbourn correspondent, with his pithy pars, his fun and sobriety, his pathos and humour, and his faithful recording of village happenings, has caused his weekly column to be looked upon as a leading feature with our readers, yet few realise he is anything but the inexperienced scribe he would have folks believe.

His recent account (when village news was scarce) of how he once photographed and reported the doings of Queen Victoria when on a visit to the French Riviera let the cat out of the bag a little, and learning from another source that this year he celebrates his 50th year of professional news-gathering, we have endeavoured to find something about his doings in bygone days. He was, however, too modest and retiring to say very much, but thanks to 'Who's Who' and other reference books, volumes of literary cuttings and items from other sources, we are able to pen the story of how a village lad, overcoming the handicap of primitive schooling fought his way to London by untiring self-effort to become a front-rank journalist and an authority in the photographic world.

Born of Farming Stock
A son of the late W. Salmon, subsequently of Cambridge Borough Police, and a nephew of the late Superintendent C. Salmon, Cambs County Police, 'P.R.S.' first saw the light of day 71 years ago at Waterbeach Cambs. His forebears were all farmers and market gardeners, and his first grains of knowledge were derived from his grandfather who had a night school at the farm, teaching all adults who cared to attend.

Very soon he escaped (as his father and uncle had done) from the farm to Cambridge, where he continued to make a close study of photography. He joined the Cambridge Camera Club, and won the Club's Silver Cup in 1892. He made a speciality of genre and country life pictures, winning the cup for a picture of a girl at a farmyard well, Miss Eliza Dickerson of Little Abington, whom he married 9 years later.

He used his camera so skilfully and artistically that in all he has won 16 medals for photographic studies, mainly scenes of country life.

He was elected a member of the Royal Photographic Society in 1897, and was admitted a Fellow of the Society (F.R.P.S.) the following year and is now one of the oldest members.

A magic lantern show
Mr Salmon gave a lantern slide show to the Men's Society. This included two views of Dolphin Lane which had won approval by judges in Australia and on the continent.

Eliza and Percy 'Peepbo' Salmon

Royston Crow 10th March 1933

Stanford, Harry *b.*1882

Harry Stanford, was a great authority on Melbourn and its past; few people could speak of it with greater authority than Harry who was born in the village and owned a cycle shop at The Cross for 62 years. He could recall with some ease the names of all the 17 pubs which Melbourn could once boast.

Harry was born in February 1882, in the Old Elm Tree public house which was run by his father until it closed down in around 1910. Harry's father was in charge of the Melbourn voluntary fire brigade, and as

Melbourn Auxiliary Fire Service during the Second World War.
Back row, Albert Chapman, William Ellis, Arthur Smith,
Front row, Jack Jones, Harry Stanford, Douglas Gouldthorpe

a young boy Harry would have to run to all parts of the village to call out the men in emergencies – the beginning of a voluntary association with the fire service which lasted 52 years.

He was in charge of the fire service during the Second World War putting out many chimney fires in Melbourn, although he would have to call the Royston Brigade if the fire was beyond his control. He recalled: '*One Christmas Eve I was called out to 3 chimney fires, and there wasn't one person offered me a mince pie. Not that I would have taken one, I don't care for pastry!*' In Harry's day the fire engine was a manual one and he remembered the time that water had to be fetched from a horse pond in Meldreth to fight a Melbourn farm fire in 1904. On that occasion he went to the fire on Friday and didn't get home until Sunday. All his work for the fire service was entirely voluntary.

He ran a cycle shop from the building next door to his home which opened in 1912, but two years later went to fight in France with the Royal Army Ordnance Corps. He remembered the date he left for France (13th August) with clarity. He was the last survivor of 'Melbourn and Meldreth Old Contemptibles'.

On his return from the war in 1918 Harry re-opened his shop. Around the shop, the face of The Cross had changed considerably during Harry's time; there used to be a farmyard next to his cycle shop, where Harry remembered corn threshing when he was a boy. He would be told to stand at the door and wait for the mice to run out so he could kill them. Not content with this, Harry would go in where all the activity was, and would return home with his pockets bulging with mice. '*Our old cat would shove its head in my pocket trying to get at the mice*', he said.

Another boyhood memory was of a menagerie that was set up on The Green at The Cross. Harry got into trouble when he upset the lions by serenading them with a watering can.

His wife, Mildred, was well known in the area as the District Nurse.

Joseph Stockbridge and family

Stockbridge, Joseph *b.*1837

Joseph Stockbridge was a farmer and horse dealer who was not only well known in the village, but throughout the country, for his horse dealing. The Stockbridge family had been in Melbourn for many years and had farmed some 200 acres of land in Melbourn and Meldreth. As a horse dealer his jolly face and figure used to be seen at every horse fair in the country. He supplied horses for the big London breweries, and in the old days for the coaches plying between Cambridge and London.

His memories included the coming of the railway from Hitchin to Cambridge, which he used to transport many of his horses. One delivery to Royston station included a retired hunter. The horse was ridden home with no saddle, just on a halter. After hearing the sound of a local hunt the horse took off at high speed to join in the fun, with rider clinging on over hedge and ditch. He could also remember when Melbourn Heath Farm was just pastureland. Although Joseph enjoyed remarkably good health throughout his life, in 1936 he caught a cold whilst in his farmyard and died a week later at the age of 99 years.

His coffin was laid on a black draped dray, pulled by a black horse dressed with black feathers. It was led down the High Street to Melbourn church by an employee dressed in a black frock coat and top hat.

The shop in the High Street
Owned by Frank Stockbridge

In 1940 Frank Stockbridge came to Melbourn and bought the shop in the High Street near the Post Office from Mrs Looms. At first he lodged in Melbourn and took his meals at The Rose. He had lunch at the pub most days with Jack Ward, the owner of Sheene Mill.

The shop sold everything, men's wear, ladies' wear, shoes, boots, haberdashery and white goods, and across the road from the shop, where the fish and chip shop now stands, carpets and rugs. Freda Harper, was born September 22nd 1924 in Bristol. Her father was in the army. Freda, her mother and the other children followed him around the world.

The family moved to Melbourn when Freda was 11 yrs old. She started working in the shop for Frank Stockbridge in 1947. Muriel (Topsy) Cooper, was born at New Road Farm in 1917. She was educated at Melbourn Village School until the age of 15. In her spare time she helped her mother around the house and worked on the farm. After leaving school Topsy started work at Marks & Spencer, and then Woolworths, in Cambridge. On the death of her mother she gave up work to look after her father and her brother. She started working at the shop in the 1950s.

During Second World War both Freda and Topsy had to do war work, Topsy on the farm and Freda at Royston Laundry and Atlas.

The shop assistants worked from 9am until 6pm Monday to Saturday, with a half day on Thursday. Each department was responsible for the ordering of goods and for dressing part of the shop window. The shop had very little heating.

Mr Stockbridge, who attended Chapel, was a perfect gentleman. He was good to his staff and never uttered an unkind word. He added two more shops to his empire, one at the corner of Little Lane and one in Mortlock Street, he also bought a house in the High Street, The Hollies, to live in. Over the years the High Street shop was burgled twice. The first time the thieves stole the dry cleaning and threw stock around. The second time all the goods were packed into boxes, but the thieves were disturbed and left empty-handed.

by Freda **Kefford** (*née* **Harper**) and Muriel (Topsy) **Pluck** (*née* **Cooper**)

Thurley, Gwen (*née* **Vellum**) *b.*1921

I was born in Melbourn. My mother's family was full of local names like Blows, King and Carter. My father's family were from Lincolnshire and grandfather moved to the Melbourn area with the coming of the railway. My mother, father, younger sister Daphne and I lived in New Road until 1926, when we moved to White House Farm. My family attended the Congregational Chapel and I started Sunday school at the age of 5 and went on to sing in the choir. I was educated at Melbourn School, gaining a Trigg's Scholarship to study Business Training at Cambridgeshire Technical College.

I enjoyed playing tennis on the Chapel courts near Martin's Farm on New Road. Melbourn had a Ladies, cricket team in which I played along with team mates H Cooper, G Holford, I Adams, E Dodkin, E Adams, M Stamford, M Day, D Pettit, W Dodkin, E Thompson and D Taylor. I was taught to play the piano by Emily Hagger.

After Technical College I worked for the Electricity Board in Royston until 1939.

When the Head Office of the Atlas Stone Company was evacuated from London to the Meldreth factory site I was sent to work there. In 1942 I was 'called up' to the ATS (Auxiliary Territorial Service). I stayed until 1944 when I left to get married to Derrick. My wedding dress was made of parachute silk and I passed it on to my sister for her wedding day.

Titchmarsh

The Titchmarsh family can be found in documents going back over many centuries. Older residents of the village used to refer to the hill, known as Hill Farm, which stands between Melbourn and Royston, as '*Tommy's Hill*', after Thomas Titchmarsh.

Walford, Brothers

John and Michael Walford were demobbed in 1945 and decided that they would set up an engineering business. They cycled around the country and eventually came up to Melbourn, as their second cousin Essie Stack lived in the village, and set about finding suitable premises. With the aid of Jack Wedd they found a site off Station Road, where the Parish Office is now, and where Ted Cox subsequently had his excellent engineering works.

Jack Wedd helped them by offering the use of his buildings and cowsheds at the top of The Moor. It was here, in a cowshed, that they repaired their first tractor.

Ward, George *b.*1867

George Ward was one of Melbourn's best known tradesmen and ran a business in the village ~ GA Ward & Sons, Builders, Decorators and Undertakers.

In his youth 'Master George', as he was known, was a keen cyclist and owned one of the first Penny Farthing bicycles in the district. An enthusiastic sportsman, he was also involved in many village activities, including that of organist and choirmaster

The passing of Mr George Ward of Melbourn

The death took place on Sep 7th 1942 of Mr George Andrew Ward, one of Melbourn's best-known and most highly respected tradesman; he died at the home of his brother in Newmarket at the age of 75 years.

Mr George Ward, widely known as 'Master George' was the eldest son of the late Mr and Mrs George Andrew Ward, who died in 1893-5. With his brother Hubert, who predeceased him in January 1937, he owned the well known business of G. A. Ward and Sons, builders, decorators, etc, a firm established by their great-grandfather in the year 1819.

The deceased had been in failing health for about 2 years, and he will be long remembered by all those who knew him for his very quiet and unassuming disposition. Outside his business he was perhaps most outstanding for his musical talents, and until his semi-retirement a few years ago there was nothing in the village or district in connection with music in which he did not take part with the keenest interest. He personally trained and conducted the Melbourn Choral Society, founded in 1842 by his father and friends, and records are still held of this Society's outstanding performances and achievements; at the annual music festival, the Society, also the string band, have always earned the highest praise and merit, thanks to his careful training and enthusiasm.

At the morning service at Melbourn Congregational Chapel on Sunday last, touching tribute was paid by the Rev. J.G. Davis, who told of what the chapel owed to Mr Ward, who was voluntary organist and choirmaster for well over 45 years (he retired in 1933) and always ready and willing with kindly advice and help relating to matters connected with the chapel.

In his youthful days he was one of the earliest and certainly the most ardent cyclists in the district, and had many tales to tell of thrilling rides on his 'penny farthing' bicycle. He was also a keen and clever tennis player, and a particularly fine shot, being a member of the Old Volunteers for many years. During the Great War of 1914–18 he was a special constable. Yet another of his activities deserves special mention, namely that of magic lantern operator. Over 40 years ago Mr Ward was sent to London to purchase a magic lantern for use in the village and he became a most expert worker of it. The lantern is still frequently in use and let out on hire, despite the rivalry and popularity of the cinematograph; the old oil illuminant so carefully nurtured by Mr Ward, however, has now given place to a more easily worked electric lamp, but the old lantern still remains a faithful and popular servant. Evidence of the great respect with which the deceased was held was evinced by the large number of relatives and friends present at the funeral last Thursday, one of the simplest character carried out at his own particular wish. The plain coffin with only the inscription 'GAW aged 75' cut out in lead, was borne by the present day employees of the firm: W. Chapman, J. Cooper, G. King, W. Day and J. Baker. By the deceased's request there was neither mourning nor floral tributes. The only flowers being a bunch from the garden he loved so much.

The service was conducted by Rev. G Davis and no hymns were sung. Mr E Byre, who was staying in the district and who had had musical associations with Mr Ward for many years, played appropriate organ music before and after the service.

at the Congregational Chapel. He also trained and conducted the Melbourn Choral Society. One of his main hobbies was as a magic lantern operator of which he became an expert after purchasing a lantern in London for use in the village.

Wedd

The Wedd family ran a farm in Dolphin Lane. On Wednesdays Arthur Wedd would travel around Melbourn and Meldreth collecting chickens, turkeys, other poultry and their eggs to take to the London market. At 8am every Thursday morning he made his way to London by pony and cart. The journey to London would take most of the day and the produce was sold on the Friday. He would return to Melbourn on Saturday night at 6pm. Arthur Wedd made his last run on 16th July 1915.

Wedd, Bob b.1922

I was born on 18th September 1922, one of six children, four boys and two girls. My parents were country people living in a tiny hamlet just outside Melbourn. There were about twelve cottages, two farmhouses, a garage and pub, all spread over half a mile or so. My father, on being invalided out of the army in the First World War, was a farm worker. We were, as were most others around us, a poor family, but we children had very good parents so we did not feel deprived. We had enough to eat, and warm clothes.

My earliest memory was sitting beneath the kitchen table and seeing my father's leather leggings and huge boots moving around. On the floor would be cheap, thin lino, the pattern worn off in many places.

A school, [Bridgefoot], had been built around the time of my birth and all the children from 5–14 years were in the same classroom, about 25 altogether. The only water was rainwater. However, the school only lasted a few years and then we were all taken to the nearest village, Melbourn, by an old Ford van, driven by one Len Smith. He kept pigs in an orchard and, as I was one of the first out of school, I would go along to help clean out the van from carrying the pigs and put the side benches back in. If you looked closely at the van you could faintly see 'Salvation Army' on the side.

We were picked up at 8.30am, took sandwiches, and were home again at 4.30pm. I was small, thin and very shy, as the only other children I had played with were my own family. It was not a very happy time to begin with.

I did well at school, became house captain and, in 1936, the best boy in the school. Then I made the biggest mistake, probably, of my life. I was offered a scholarship and turned it down. I couldn't face the two and a half mile walk, morning and night, and the bus trip to and from Cambridge.

My father was horse keeper on a farm, and as such, by 1939, was earning 35s a week That was it – the entire family income! He would go to get the horses fed and groomed at 5.30 in the morning, which would take about an hour. He then did 9 hours work each day (On Saturdays – five and a half hours).

He would sometimes bring home a bundle of horsehair, from his grooming. My mother would take it to the village and sell it for about 9d and then buy some bones for soup or stew.

Sometimes we were fortunate when my father brought home a rabbit or hare that he had managed to catch during his work. Ploughmen were very good at this. They would see one sitting in a 'form' or nest, and they gradually ploughed closer and closer pretending to ignore it. Then they walloped it with the 'spud' (plough scraper).

On windy or foggy days we children would search beneath the telephone wires which were stretched along the road verges, and it was surprising how often we could pick up a partridge that had broken its neck on the wires.

A rabbit skin could be sold for 9d and later 1s. My uncle used to trap moles, as moleskins were even more valuable.

Saturday evening was the high point in the week as Gouldthorpe would come. He came in an old Ford van which would be loaded with practically everything: paraffin, sweets, tin baths, chamber pots, saucepans, coconut matting, and many other things hanging all over it. You could buy a Double Six chocolate bar for 6d. It had twelve small squares and was made to look like a domino. They were my favourite but not always affordable. I don't ever remember Gouldthorpe missing a visit but suppose he must have missed one or two.

On winter evenings we would often play cards or darts. The dartboard hung on the stair door, which was riddled with holes. My father loved to join in these games but mother never would. She would be busy doing needlework or knitting.

Another winter evening task was making cloth hearth rugs. It was started by opening up a sugar sack, giving an area of 4ft × 3ft. We children then cut up strips of cloth about 3ins × 1in, and these were pegged into the sacking with wooden pegs or rug-making tools. The finished rug was extremely heavy but warm.

I remember Foden steam wagons and open-topped, single-deck buses or charabancs on excursions to Newmarket Races. We would stand by the roadside and wave to them.

We would wait for Shepherd Rule to feed the sheep with what were known to us as Locust beans. As soon as he was gone, we were over the hurdle eating as many as we could cram into our mouths. I've often wondered since what we were actually eating! They were very sweet and tasty. I remember steam engines dragging huge ploughshares across the fields by steel cables and the eerie sound of them whistling up for more water through the autumn fog.

On Sunday evening walks, my parents would meet and chat to the folk from across the fields. They had a daughter about my age. She had huge eyes and I would just stand and stare at her. She would gaze back at me. I never did speak to her. I think it was true love.

As I said earlier we were six children, but a seventh died at birth. I remember seeing my father very quietly working away making a box. I watched but he didn't speak to me. I later learned that he was making a coffin for our little sister.

At fourteen I left school and went to work on the farm, there being no other work available. You worked where you lived in the country, as there was no transport and we didn't have bicycles. Before this, my brother (two years my junior, but much bigger and stronger) and I, would work on the farm at harvest time. We would be 9 or 10 years old and work for 4 weeks in the summer holidays, from 7am until 8.30pm during the week, and on Saturday from 7am – 5.30pm. Our job would be to take the empty carts out to the fields and bring them back, loaded with sheaves. We would have 4 carts in use. Sometimes we would lead the horses from stook to stook, and sometimes even be loaders. On occasions we had horses run away with us, but luckily escaped injury, except to our pride.

I remember on one occasion I was considered man enough (12 years old) to take a horse 2½ miles to the blacksmith. My father put a sack on the shire's back and hoisted me on board. I set off proudly. After about a mile the horse, going ever more slowly, decided to have a feed on the grass verge. Down goes his head and over I go. If ever a horse grinned that one did. I then had to walk all the way as there was no way I could get back on that huge animal.

For this 4 weeks' work we received £4 each. We were handed 5s of this and had a really big spend-up in Woolworths at Cambridge. After all, nothing cost more than 6d.

When I started work full time it was January. I'll never forget that day. I had my bag with sandwiches and a bottle of tea wrapped in brown paper in a hopeless endeavour to keep it warm. I was sent 1½ miles across the fields with a grass-hook (a small scythe) to trim round the edge of the field. I was very cold, very lonely and extremely miserable. I did not tell anyone! My pay was 12s 6d per week ~ 3d per hour.

By the time I was 16, things were gradually getting mechanised and I had a tractor to drive. Rolling corn in March left one frozen to the very core. One would be forced to dismount and huddle by the exhaust manifold to try and keep warm. The tractor had a paraffin-fuelled engine, and one couldn't pause too long, as when it idled the paraffin would not vaporise, and then you were in trouble.

About this time, my oldest brother, who was stockman on the farm, decided to go bus-driving and I was given the task of tending the pigs and poultry and milking the 3 cows. The farmer sold all the good cows and only kept the troublesome ones. They didn't like me. I was kicked without mercy. For one in particular, a harness was made to prevent it kicking. It took quite a while to put this contraption on the cow. I would stand back and the cow would just topple over, and so on. It was not a happy time.

Come September 1939 and war. I was taken ill, and while in hospital, two RAF men were brought in. I held them in awe. One of them couldn't write, so I used to write to his sister for him. She asked what she could send me for being so kind. I didn't know what to say, but my RAF friend said 'cigarettes'. I said 'I don't smoke'. He said he would smoke them and he did!

There and then I decided it was the RAF for me. I wrote to the farmer from my bed, tendering my notice. He wrote back to say, in that case my grandmother would have to leave her cottage, as he would want it for my replacement.

I showed my letter to my mother, who was rather a fiery lady, and she went 'bonkers'. What she said to the farmer I never knew but the subject was never brought up again. We were a very patriotic family. Soon after the outbreak of war my father was called up in a Defence Regiment and went guarding aerodromes.

When the war ended I was kept in Germany with the Army of Occupation until May 1946 when I was demobbed.

I went to work on a building site, and in October I went to Bath to marry Chrissie, whom I met whilst stationed near there in 1943. We lived with my parents for a bit as we couldn't get a house. We were married on the last day of my demob leave. My gratuity pay as a corporal was quite good, so we able to get some second-hand furniture. I won't mention rationing or dockets etc, as their existence is well known.

I then made another big mistake. Being impatient for a home, I took a tied cottage and went to work on a farm. My wages were then £4 8d per week. I was soon made tractor foreman and then received £4 9s 6d. Now I was stuck. If I changed my job I lost my house. I couldn't get a council house because I already had a home, and the wages were not high enough to get a mortgage. This situation stayed with me for 37 years, more or less. I was able to celebrate the start of the second half of the 20th century with the birth of a daughter, in 1950.

Other memories
We had candles and paraffin lamps, heated housebricks in the oven and wrapped them in pieces of blanket to heat the bed. we used a tin bath by the fire and had a bucket lavatory in the garden. Drinking water was brought from the farm. We were self-supporting in vegetables (almost). A postman with a wooden leg would cycle a 7–8 miles round trip on a specially adapted bike, and always be on time, regardless of weather.

Whiting, Ron b.1931

In 1928 my parents bought what was then called Moor Farm, on the death of Johnny Newling. Because no one knew the name Moor Farm, only the name Newlings, they changed the name to Newlings Farm. The story was that Johnny Newling buried a pot of gold coins somewhere on the farm but extensive digging has never brought the pot to light.

I can remember the old house opposite Newlings Farm, occupied by the Misses Ellis, before their nephew, Sir Geoffrey Ellis, demolished it and built his own property. The old Moat House was a long, low building with long corridors and lots of small rooms.

Towards the end of the Second World War, US Mustang fighters were based at Fowlmere. I was taken for a ride around the airfield in one. The Mustang was a single-seater aircraft and so I sat on the pilot's lap!

One day, when I was shopping for my mother in the butcher's shop, a Mustang crashed in Rose Lane. Everyone ran out of the shop to see what had happened. As the plane caught fire the ammunition started to explode and the crowd had to seek shelter. The poor pilot died, of course.

The farms in the Melbourn area, mostly grew fruit or had pasture land for cows and other animals.

Band's, the grocers opposite the Vicarage, had a big barrel of dog biscuits inside the door. A well known dare for the young of the village was to go into the shop and ask for something on a high shelf, and whilst the assistant was away, take a dog biscuit without getting caught. They tasted very nice!

Mr Ogden, who taught at the school, taught piano at his house. Mr Impey in Little Lane repaired radios and delivered the Sunday papers. Mr Cranfield, at the Post Office, would greet all by raising his finger and saying 'Ning!' which the children found very amusing!

Winter, Norman *b.1920*

I was educated at the local school and left, at 14 years of age, to work as a boot boy at the house and surgery of Dr Gregor, the local doctor. The house is no longer in the High Street. The Gregor family consisted of Dr and Mrs Gregor, Master Binks and Miss Barbara. The staff were Mabel and Mary Day, a Miss Read, Bernard Webb's aunt Ron Green, (a lady who did the rough charring from 8am to 1pm), and me. Everyone was provided with a uniform.

My everyday duties were to get the water from the pump, clean fireplaces and start the fires, chop wood and keep the log basket in the hall filled, clean shoes, brass, and windows. I also looked after the kitchen garden and kept the Doctor's Daimler clean; it was serviced by Archie Hale the local mechanic. Once a week Mrs Gregor went to shop at John Buchan's in the High Street, which is now a private house. Later in the day I took the wheelbarrow to the shop to bring home the week's order.

Willmott, Roger *b.1876*

Roger Oswald Willmott was one of the characters of Melbourn during the 1920's, 30's and 40's. He was known for his shrewd property deals and his knowledge of the building industry. He was also believed, by some, to be careful as he would only give to the charities of his choice, which in his case were the British Legion, the Red Cross and the Association for the Blind.

Born in Ashwell into a large Victorian family, he was the youngest son. His father was a farmer and a builder. Young Roger was envious of his oldest brother, who did not have to work, but rode around all day on horseback, visiting the men working on the farm or building sites. Roger's first introduction to the building industry, at the age of twelve, was making clay bats for his father. This involved leading a cart horse round and round, attached to a mixer containing clay, chaff and water. The mix was then put into moulds to dry. Later he served an apprenticeship as a bricklayer.

One story from a local resident told of Roger walking with his sister one evening, when a local man said to him 'Mr Willmott you have holes in your gloves, I would have thought a man with your money could have afforded a new pair. You cannot take it with you when you go.' He replied. 'No, but I can afford to write a cheque when I get there.'

Roger was a keen racing cyclist and learnt to play the cornet, which gave him a lifelong interest in brass bands.

Around 1905 he met, and married, Ellen Muncey, who came from another large farming family. At first they lived at Moor Corner, later moving to Fieldgate Farm in Station Road, where their daughter Marjory was born.

In 1915 Roger bought a piece of land between the Pink Geranium and the Fire Engine House, and designed and built two houses. There was a large hole in the ground, the earth having been used to build up the churchyard, and at the outset this was a problem. It was resolved by putting cellars under each of the rooms.

Building commenced in 1916 but was interrupted when Roger had to report for service in the army. He was invalided out of the army in 1917, refusing to take a pension because he said he did not want to join up in the first place. He was advised, by the Army doctors, never to go on a building site or to go up a ladder again. However, work on the houses recommenced and was finished in 1918. Roger and his wife Ellen, moved into the house closest to the Pink Geranium and rented out the other. By 1926, he decided the garden was not big enough and so he bought the houses opposite the old Vicarage in the High Street, with about three acres of orchard.

He also rented the field next door to his property, in order to keep cows and pigs. Having rented out his house in Station Road, he moved into his new house in the High street and then rented out the house next door. Due to the Depression, Roger found himself unemployed, so with spare time on his hands, he designed and built a bungalow, which he named Grove Lodge, on land he owned in Orchard Road.

In the early thirties he noticed a GPO advertisement asking for property to rent in Melbourn in which to install the first telephone exchange. He offered to rent out one side of the houses in the High Street. It took the GPO six months to install the equipment. When the job of caretaker was advertised Roger applied and was successful. Ellen and their daughter Marjory were also employed to work the daytime switchboard. At that time he was still working in the building trade in Royston, but would return in the evening, feed the livestock and then run the night-time switchboard; not too arduous a task, as there were few calls after 10pm in those days. The telephone exchange became automated in 1938 and was moved to Station Road opposite Mill House.

In 1936 Roger became the Clerk of Works for South Cambridgeshire Council, which involved travelling around South Cambridgeshire supervising the building of council houses. Then in 1938, he bought a large house, once a private school known as The Beeches, belonging to Mr Campkin. The building was converted back to a house by Roger, who then gave it as a gift to his daughter Marjory and her husband. After the death of his wife, Roger remarried in 1942. He continued in full-time employment until he was seventy-eight. On his retirement he sold his car, but then, two years, later, at the age of eighty, he bought another and went back to work, this time for the South Cambridgeshire Council for three years as a water engineer. He finally retired in 1959.

The Old
Elm Tree

*...just after the procession
had passed underneath, the
bough snapped off, depositing
the boys in the road!*

The old Elm Tree, disappeared in the late 1930s, after several attempts to save it. However, it was at the centre of village life for many centuries as the following extracts from newspaper articles, books, paintings, engravings and photographs show. Its circumference was reported to be seventeen feet.

'On Wednesday two former vicars of Melbourn, Canon Selwyn and the Rev F.G. Jenyns, with the curate the Rev T.C. Gardner, planted three trees in the church yard, to take the place hereafter of 'the old elm tree', the oldest inhabitant showing signs of old age and decay.'

Cambridge Chronicle November 1874

The visit of Queen Victoria and Prince Albert in 1843

'The town of Royston had been decorated with flags and devices but a tremendous gale was blowing which destroyed these. The Earl of Hardwicke met the royal couple at the Cambridgeshire border with the Cambridgeshire militia, on horseback, but it is reported that the Hertfordshire militia failed to give way and there was a great deal of 'bumping and boring' between Royston and Melbourn, where the Royal carriage was to change horses. At Melbourn a considerable crowd had assembled around the old elm tree and such a crush of mounted men had never been seen before. Upon the gigantic branch of the elm tree the loyal Melbournites, short of brightly coloured flags, had spread a large piece of tarpaulin upon which was a loyal message of welcome. This attracted some attention, and some of the yeomanry were heard to remark 'a very coarse piece of loyalty' but evidently the young Queen and her Consort accepted it for what it meant and what was wanting in elegance was made up for by the sincerity and welcome of the people. It is fair to add that Melbourn had its triumphal arch!'

'Fragments of Two Centuries' 1893 Alfred Kingston

The Old Elm Tree in Melbourn has been reduced by storms and attempts to fill it in and support it by iron bars have proved useless.

Royston Crow October 1881

A horse being shod in Mr. J. Bullen's workshop (smith and wheelwright) took fright, and galloped the length of the High Street before colliding with the 'Old Bank Tree'. The cart was wrecked but the horse was uninjured.

Royston Crow October 1892

The Bank Tree at Melbourn

'As its name indicates, the great elm stood on a rising portion of the village green, hard by the churchyard wall. It is impossible now to say just how long it stood there, but someone recorded, long ago, that Queen Elizabeth the First passed under its shade as her coach rumbled along the main road to Cambridge in 1564. It was still there when the horses of Queen Victoria's coach were changed nearby in 1843. It eventually died, quite a number of years ago, but it was photographed in its latter days.

Quite a lot of Melbourn's sturdy, progressive history was – literally – fought out in the shadow of the old Bank Tree. For centuries too, the Tree stood silently by as all the roistering and clamour of Melbourn's annual Feast took place on the green. This ancient Fair, held – as it still is – in July, continued on the village green for many, many centuries.'

'Through all these turbulent years, the old Bank Tree stood serenely by – unmoved even by the voice of John Bunyan, who preached on the village green when the Dissenters were making themselves felt in the district.

It fell, like all very old elms, because of age. But really its story did not end. On the same spot, new shoots sprang up, and a few years ago the Parish Council, having taken expert advice, selected the best of seven saplings for future growth. So there may be yet a 'New Bank Tree' to keep traditional sentinel over the hub of Melbourn.'

F.S 1930s

In January 1939, Dutch Elm Disease had been reported in the area. It may be possible that the Old Elm Tree finally died due to this disease!

The Old Elm Tree

'Many are fortunate to possess an engraving of the old elm tree when it was at the height of its glory. No doubt it was there in 1640, as 200 years later it began to decay, and an elm tree will go on growing in favourable circumstances for 200 years. No one knows why it was planted, or whether it replaced another that had done duty as the village trysting place centuries before. But we know that it was a giant tree when Queen Victoria passed through the village on her way to Cambridge in 1843. A large branch of the tree, perhaps it would be correct to call it an arm, stretched right across the road. And it afforded a natural front seat for the more venturesome to witness the travels of Royalty. The Queen and her retainers were no sooner by, than crack went the tree and its living freight received warning to get down as quickly as possible from a perilous situation. The branch eventually broke clean away. A Melbourn man on horseback rode up, with the intention of proving his loyalty to her Majesty by shaking hands, his design was thwarted by a Lifeguard who rode up and said, 'approach another step and I will cut you down.'

Jubal Howard, Herts and Cambs Recorder August 1931

Bibliography

Archaeological dig at New Road, Melbourn. 1959; The East Anglian: or Notes and Queries Vol.6: Extract on earthworks in agricultural districts. W.M. Palmer, 1895

Archeology of Cambridgeshire Vol. 1, South West Cambridgeshire, Alison Taylor, C.C.C. 1997, ISBN 1-870724-84-4

Archaeology of South-West Cambridgeshire

Argentine's Manor, Melbourn, Cambs. 1317-18, W.M. Palmer M.D. F.S.A., 1924, CAS Comm. Vol XXVIII

Atlas of Cambridgeshire and Huntingdonshire History, An, ed. Tony Kirby and Susan Oosthuizen, Centre for Regional Studies Anglia Polytechnic University, 2000, ISBN 0-907262-19-8

Cambridge Independent Press, 1848-1869

Cambridge Chronicle, 1770-1880

Charm of the English Village, The, P.H. Ditchfield, Bracken Books, 1985

Chronicle of the World, Longman, ISBN 0-582-05884-8

Common Stream, The, Rowland Parker, Granada Publishing Ltd, 1976

Contrasting Communities: English Villagers in the Sixteenth and Seventeenth Centuries, Margaret Spufford, CUP, 1974, ISBN 0-7509-3

Convinced That These Were God's People, Rev. Reginald Rooke, to mark the Tercentenary of the Melbourn United Reformed Church, 1994

Cromwell, Our Chief of Men, Antonia Fraser, Weidenfeld & Nicholson, 1973

East Anglia at War 1939–1945, Derek E. Johnson, Jarrold Publishing, Norwich, 1992, ISBN 0-7117-0598-4

East Anglian Cottages, J. M. Proctor, Providence Press, 1979

English Emigration, Kinship and the Recruitment Process: Migration from Melbourn in Cambridgeshire to Melbourne in Victoria in the Mid-Nineteenth Century, Paul Hudson, Dennis Mills, Rural History 10, 1999

English Local History, An Introduction, Kate Tiller, Sutton Publishing Ltd, 1992, ISBN 0-7509-2714-3

English Social History, G.M. Trevelyan

Excavations in the Cambridgeshire Dykes VI Bran Ditch. Second Report: T. C. Lethbridge, F.S.A. and W.D. Palmer, M.D. F.D.A., 1929

Exploring Villages, Joscelyne Finberg,Alan Sutton Publishing,1958, Routledge & Kegan Paul ISBN 0-086299-346-6

Folklore and Customs of Rural England, Margaret Baker, David & Charles (Holdings) Ltd, 1974, ISBN 0-7153- 6579-7

Fragments of Two Centuries, Alfred Kingston, Royston, Warren Bros & Cooke Ltd, 1893

Herts and Cambs Recorder

History of Cambridgeshire, A: Armingford Hundred: Melbourn, compiled from a variety of sources

History of England, A. Keith Feiling, Book Club Associates, Redwood Press Ltd 1948

Illustrated Handbook of Vernacular Architecture, R.W. Brunskill, Faber and Faber, 1971, ISBN 0-571-13916-7

Illustrated History of the Countryside, The, Oliver Rackham, George Weidenfeld & Nicolson Ltd, 1994, ISBN 1-85799-953-3

Initial Excavation of an Anglo-Saxon Cemetery at Melbourn Cambs, The, D.M. Wilson BA 1956 Proc. Camb. Soc. Vol. XLIX

Investigating the Twentieth Century: Sources for Local Historians, Evelyn Lord, Tempus Publishing Ltd, 1999, ISBN 0-7524-1426-7

Late Migration/Final phase cemetery at Water Lane, Melbourn, A, Albion Archaeology, BCC, St. Mary's Church, St. Mary's Street, Bedford, 2000

Medicine in Wisbech and the Fens 1700-1920, ed. Jane Arthur, Wisbech and Fenland Museum, Seagull Enterprises, 1984, ISBN 0-948147-00-8

Melbourn Parochial Church Council & Parish Council Records 1719-1950

Melbourn School Story, The, Jeffrey Barham, 1996

Melbourn Village History, Nina I. Campkin, 1958

Monument in its Landscape, A, Sheepshead Row, Melbourn, Cambridge, Tina Rafft, 2001

Nonconformist Bi-centenary Memorial, A: Congregationalism at Melbourn 1694-1894, G. Porter Chapple. London, H.R. Allenson, 1895

Puritan in Melbourn, The, 1640- 1688, W.M. palmer M.R.C.S. Royston, Warren Bros, 1895

Quality of Life in Melbourn, Cambs, in the period 1800-50, The, Dennis R. Mills, International Review of Social History Vol. 23, 1978

Remember When, A nostalgic trip through the consumer area, Robert Opie, Mitchell Beazley 1999, ISBN 1-84000-129-1

Road transport and Economic Growth in the 18th Century. J. Chartres, 1989

Roman Cambridgeshire, David M. Browne, The Oleander Press 1977, ISBN 0-900891-09-2

Royston Crow, The, 1829-1950

Sites and Monument Record: from lists, records and schedule entry copies. County Archaeology Office, CCC, Castle Hill, Cambridge

Small sword: Sylvia P. Beamon, M.A., Archaeological report, 1981

Taste of History, A, English Heritage, British Museum Press, 1993, ISBN 0-7141-1732-3

The Peasant Culture, D.R. Mills, New Society, April 1977

Transport and Economy: the Turnpike Roads of Eighteenth Century Britain. E. Pawson, 1977

Truth about Cottages, The, John Woodforde, Routledge & Kegan Paul Ltd, 1969, ISBN 0-7100-0165

Victorian Melbourn, A Passing Glance, J. Mcneice, 1995

Wartime Women, A Mass Observation Anthology of Women's Writing 1937-1945, ed. Dorothy Sheridan, Phoenix Press, 2000

Watching brief at Melbourn Churchyard: Wendy Horton B.A. M.Phil., CCC Archaeological Field Unit, Fulbourn, 1989

Wedd, David article: Ref: 117/28/35. A 10 page hand written report Ref: P.117/28/35. County Archives, Shire Hall, Cambridge

Year 1000, The, Robert Lacey & Danny Danziger, Little, Brown and Co., 1999, ISBN 0-316-64376-0

Glossary

Accumulator Rechargeable lead-acid battery used in early battery wireless sets.

Almshouses Dwellings for the poor funded by charity.

Anabaptists Member of a Protestant sect (orig. from Germany 1521) who rejected infant baptism, believing only adults should be baptised.

Anglo-Saxon Germanic people who inhabited Britain from around the 5th Century AD comprising Angles and Saxons (*from Northern Germany and the Baltic region of Jutland*).

Artesian Well Well bored so that natural pressure produces a constant supply of water.

Aumbrey Recess or cupboard, where consecrated elements (bread and water) may be safely kept before being taken out to give communion to the sick. When In use, a candle is lit above the recess.

Bailliff's Roll Record made by Bailliff, official under Norman Kings.

Baptist Member of Protestant Christian denomination advocating the Baptism of only adult believers by total immersion.

Baulk A ridge of land left unploughed between the fields in common lands.

Beaker Type of pottery drinking vessel common in Europe from the third millenium BC onwards. Mainly associated with a people who spread across Europe of Iberian origin (*modern day Spain and*

Portugal) known as the *Beaker People*. "Beaker People" appear to have been the first builders of chambered tombs – particularly long barrows.

Black Death (Plague) A bacterial epidemic disease causing a high rate of mortality; transmitted to man by rats.

Bondsman Slave – a person who was in thrall to another.

Bordar A free peasant holding a cottage and a few acres.

Bowl barrows Funerary monuments dating from the late Neolithic period to the Late Bronze Age – constructed of earth or rubble, sometimes with a ditch and covered multiple burials.

Breeching Rite of passage when a male child would come out of dresses and wear his first breeches (short trousers).

Bronze age Period in cultural development between the Stone Age and the Iron Age, characterized by the use of weapons and implements made of bronze.

Buttery Room where ale was brewed and kept.

Calvinist Follower of the Genevan religious reformer Calvin 1509-1564.

Causewayed Enclosure Roughly circular or oval shaped area bounded by one or more lines of banks and ditches.

Chattel A slave or an article of movable personal property.

Churchwarden One of two elected lay representatives in an Anglican parish responsible for moveable church property and for keeping order in church.

Clerestory Upper row of windows in a church, above the level of the aisle roofs.

Clunch, **Melbourn rock** Very hard chalk found between layers of softer chalk in SE England.

Copyhold Land held by the lord, according to the custom of the manor. Abolished by Copyhold Act of 1894.

Corn Dolly 'dolly', derived from idol. Figure made from the last corn of the harvest, kept until following year, thought to contain the 'spirit of the harvest'.

Cottar A peasant occupying a small holding in return for services.

Cross dykes Linear earthwork possibly boundary markers or demarcation of land allotment within communities, other suggestions include track ways, cattle driveways or defensive earthworks.

Danelaw Law established by the Danish invaders and settlers in the ninth and tenth centuries.

Dark ages The years before 1066 esp 5th to 10th centuries.

Daub A mixture of mud and horse hair used to cover wattle.

Demesne That part of manor not held by tenants, but kept for use by lord of the manor.

Deodand Fine levied as a forfeit where goods or chattels caused death or injury.

Deverel-Rimbury Culture of southern England covering the 15th to 12th centuries BC. Distinctive traits are barrows, field systems and circular enclosures. Some examples date back as far as 1800 BC.

Dirge Funeral song or hymn.

Dissenter Non-conformist, separated from the established Church.

Dogcart Light horse-drawn 2-wheeled vehicle originally with boxed section for transporting gun-dogs.

Domain Landed property, held in own right.

Dredge Mixture of grains grown as a forage crop.

Easter Sepulchre Niche in the wall of the Church – at Easter time a representation of the crucifixion would be displayed.

Ergot A fungus found on grain. Cause of medieval mass poisonings and

hallucinations after eating bread made from infected grain. Used in medicine. Active principal - *lysergic acid*. LSD is a derivative of lysergic acid.

Feast Day A periodic religious festival.

Feudal system System flourishing in Europe from 9th to 15th. based upon the relation of lord to vassal.

Flint Hard variety of quartz, used for building, primitive tools and making fire when struck with steel.

Frankpledge System under which each male, 12 years and over, was responsible for the good conduct of the other members of his tithing (group).

G.I. American soldiers were known as G.I's after their uniform which was Government Issue.

Garderobe Upstairs closet with a chute into the moat.

Gleaners People who gather or pick up ears of corn which have been left by the reapers.

Glebe Land attached to a Parish Church, Glebe House – a Manse or Vicarage.

Grid bias battery Linked dry-cell batteries for applying voltage between the electrodes of valves in a wireless set.

Guilds Any of various medieval associations having social and semi-religious features.

Hautboy Ancient musical instrument, similar to the modern oboe.

Hayward Constable with special responsibilities for boundaries and encroachments.

Hearth Tax Tax levied on the number of fireplaces in a dwelling.

High tension battery Linked dry-cell batteries to produce power for early battery wirelesses (commonly 120 volts).

Horkey East Anglian word for the celebration after the last load of the harvest.

Indenture A contract binding one person to work for another for a given period of time (to a master craftsman).

Inhumation The ritual placing of a corpse in a grave.

Interred Place in a grave or tomb; bury.

Iron Age Period in cultural development characterized by the introduction of iron around the eighth century BC.

Lancet Tall, narrow, arched window.

Lauds Prayers immediately following matins.

Lengsthmen *Linesmen* – People employed by County Councils to ensure a length of road or rail is kept in good condition.

Little White Ribboners Junior branch of the Total Abstinence Society.

Madrigal A part song for several voices.

Magna Carta Charter of rights granted by King John on June 15th 1215.

Malt Grain steeped in water and allowed to germinate, then dried and used in brewing.

Mangle Manual contrivance with two cylinders through which wet washing was rolled to squeeze out water.

Manor Historical, land, with house etc, belonging to a lord.

Marsh Fever Fenland term for malaria.

Maslin (meslin) Mixture of grains, especially their flours.

Matins Morning prayer.

Maundy Thursday The day before Good Friday.

Mediaeval Pertaining to the Middle Ages (13th 14th and 15th centuries).

Mercian A *border people*. An early English kingdom that covered most of the central part of England in the 8th century.

Middle Stone Age *Mesolithic* The period from *c.*10,000–4000 BC.

Miracle Play Dramatic representation in the Middle Ages based on the life of Christ or the Saints.

Miracle, Mystery play Medieval type of dramatic representation showing a sequence of episodes from the life of a saint or Martyr.

Morris Dancing Moorish Dance, a grotesque dance performed in fancy costume.

Mummers Actors in old, masked play, often performing house to house.

New Stone Age *Neolithic c.*10,000 BC. The period between the Mesolithic and the Bronze Age (the early part was sometimes referred to as the Copper Age). The main defining feature of the Neolithic is the cultivation of plants – *i.e.* organised agriculture.

Obits Services or masses said for the dead, in perpetuity.

Old Stone Age *Palaeolithic c.*500,000–10,000 BC. This period was subdivided into three stages, Lower, Middle and Upper.

Open field system Common fields of a parish, strips, furloughs, (furrow lengt)hs of each being farmed by different people.

Overseer of the poor Appointed annually by the Parish and had to provide work or relief for those who were in need.

Paganism Worship of or belief in more than one god. Not a Christian, Muslim, or Jew.

Parvis room Room over a church porch

Patera Saucer-like vessel of earthenware or metal, used by the Greeks and Romans in libations and sacrifices.

Pattens Shoe or clog with a raised sole to keep the shoe out of the mud.

Pauper Person without means, a beggar, someone dependent upon Poor Relief.

Peplos Loose outer robe worn by women in ancient Greece. Also called a *peplum*.

Phonograph Early form of gramophone for reproducing sound from wax cylinders.

Pinder A constable with the special duty of impounding stray animals.

Piscina Small sink used for washing holy vessels like the Chalice, or for disposing of consecrated water.

Plague (Black Death) An epidemic bacterial disease causing a high rate of mortality; transmitted to man by rats.

Plough Monday The Monday after Epiphany, once celebrated as the first day of ploughing.

Poor rate A tax levied upon the village to pay for its paupers.

Porter Strong beer drink.

Potage Thick soup made from available vegetables and/or bones – peasant food.

Prehistory Time before history. In Britain prehistory is regarded as ending with the coming of the 'civilisation' by the Romans in AD 43.

Privy Toilet – usually outside.

Pugilist A boxer.

Purgatory The state, place or condition of spiritual purging, Holy Fire.

Quern A grinding stone for pounding grains of corn into flour.

Quill pen Pen cut from the shaft of a feather, usually goose. Every schoolchild had to learn to make these.

Reeve Anglo-Saxon term, supervisor of an estate, a bailiff.

Reformation Culmination of events and circumstances both here and abroad, which led to a seismic shift in the religious framework.

Rick Stack of corn in sheaves, before threshing.

Ridge-and-furrow The pattern developed on common fields by the use of a mold boarded plough and 8 oxen. The crops were planted on the ridges.

Romano British Term for people who lived in the Romanised parts of the British Isles from the 2nd century onwards.

Rood Screen Ornamental partition at the entrance of the chancel, separating the Nave from the choir. The rood is Christ's cross.

Round barrow Cemeteries comprising of single or multiple burials appearing as closely grouped mounds of up to 30 in number.

Salvation Army Militarist, Christian Evangelical movement known as the Christian Revival Association.

Samhain Festival held by the ancient Celts on 1st November, marking the beginning of winter.

Sanctuary The Church, particularly the Chancel, afforded immunity to arrest and was much used in Mediaeval times.

Scythe Long curved blade on long handle used for cutting hay and corn.

Shard or Sherds Pieces of broken pottery, especially those found in an archaeological dig; a potsherd.

Shrove Tuesday On which one confessed one's sins, and was shriven or cleansed, before Lent. Pancake Day.

Sick & dividing club Type of insurance by which you paid a small weekly sum and would be entitled to a pay-out if you became unable to work.

Sickle A hook shaped blade fitted on a short handle, used for cutting corn and hay.

Square barrows Funerary monuments from the Iron Age.

Statute Labour Duty Seventeenth century requirement to undertake highway repair or other public service.

Stews Fish ponds kept by Monasteries or Manors in which fish were farmed.

Surplice White linen vestment worn over the cassock.

Tallow Candles Candles made from rendered down animal fat, as opposed to the more expensive beeswax candles.

Tenement A building with sets of rooms such as a block of flats.

Tied cottage Cottage owned by farmer, inhabited by workers employed by him.

Tithe A tenth part

Tithe Barn Built to hold the church tithes, tenths, of the crops grown in the parish

Tithing A small administrative division consisting of ten men and their families, or of the tenth part of the hundred

Tumulus Term used to describe a burial mound or cairn.

Turnpike Road Road with a gate or barrier set across it to prevent passage until a toll had been paid.

Utility mark CC41 Civilian Clothing 1941 – Logo designed by Reginald Shipp had to appear on all clothing, furniture etc. to show it was made to economic wartime standards

Vassal A person who is under the protection of another as his feudal lord and is vowed to homage and fealty to him

Vestry meeting Forerunner of the Parish Council, held in the church by church official to handle village affairs.

Villein A free peasant of a rank higher than cottars and bordars

Warming pan Copper lidded pan on the end of a long pole in which the embers of the fire would be placed and then the pan would be put into the bed to warm it.

Wattle and Daub A wall of woven branches covered with a mixture of mud and horse hair

Waywarden Seventeenth century Surveyor of Highways.

Whitsun Pentecost, the custom of wearing white robes by the newly baptized, who were numerous at this season.

Yeoman Name given to farmers in 15th, 16th and 17th centuries

Currency

In ancient times gold, silver and precious stones were weight against dried grains of wheat taken from the middle of the ear. In the Middle Ages every town had it's own weight standards. A grain was the smallest unit of weight. On average one pound weighed 7,680 grains of wheat. A 'Troy' pound (from Troyes in France, an important trading centre) weighed 5,760 grains and was used for weighing gold, silver and precious stones.

The Pennyweight was 24 troy grains- the weight of an English penny. Currency was referred to as pounds, shillings and pence, £ s d, or L s d.

In terms of purchasing power in the twentieth century,
One penny in the 13th century was approximately one pound.
One penny in the 16th century was approximately 40p.
One penny in the mid-19th century was approximately 20p.
However, much would depend on the particular commodity.

Currency Values

Old currency	Value – *Other Names* (Symbols)	Decimal equivalent
One guinea	Twenty one shillings (£1 1s, 21/-)	£1.05
One pound	Twenty shillings *also known as a Quid* (£1, 20s/-)	£1
One sovereign	One pound (£1, 20s/-)	£1
Ten shillings	Ten shillings *also known as Ten bob* (10/-)	50p
Crown	Five shillings *also known as Five bob* (5/-)	25p
Half-crown	Two shillings and six pence *also known as Half-a-crown* (2/6d)	12.5p
Florin	Two shillings *also known as Two bob* (2/-)	10p
Shilling	Twelve pence *also known as a Bob* (1/-)	5p
Sixpence	Six pence (*also known as a Tanner* (6d)	2.5p
One groat	Four pence (4d)	1.7p
Three pence	Three pennies *also known as a Thrupenny bit* (3d)	1.25p
Penny	One twelfth of a shilling *from Latin denarius* (1d)	0.4p
Halfpenny	Half a penny or *Ha'penny pronounced 'haypny'* (½d)	0.2p
Farthing	Half a halfpenny (¼d)	0.1p

Weights

Avoirdupois

16 drams	= 1 ounce (28.34grams)
16oz	= 1 pound (0.45kg)
14 lbs	= 1 stone (6.35kg)
2 stones	= 1 quarter (12.7kg)
4 quarters	= 1 hundredweight (50.8kg)
20 hundredweight	= 1 ton (1.016 tonnes)

Apothecary's Dry

20 grains	= 1 scruple (1.3 grams)
3 scruples	= 1 drachm (3.89 grams)
8 drachms	= 1 ounce (31.10 grams)
12oz	= 1 pound (0.37 kg)

Dry Weight

2 pints	= 1 quart
4 quarts	= 1 gallon
2 gallons	= 1 peck
4 pecks	= 1 bushel
8 bushels	= 1 quarter
36 quarters	= 1 chaldron
5 quarters	= 1 wey
2 weys	= 1 last

Troy Weight

3.1683 grains	= 1 carat
24 grains	= 1 penny weight
20 penny weights	= 1 ounce
12 oz	= 1 pound

Hay and Straw

36 pounds of straw	= 1 truss
56 pounds old hay	= 1 truss
60 pounds new hay	= 1 truss
36 trusses	= 1 load

Wool Weight

7 pounds avoirdupois	= 1 clove
14 pounds	= 1 stone
28 pounds	= 1 tod
182 pounds	= 1 wey
364 pounds	= 1 sack
4,368 pounds	= 1 last

Measurement

Linear

1 inch (in)	2.54 cm (4 in = approx. 10 cm)	
1 link	7.92 in	0.201 m
1 foot (ft)	12 in	0.3048 m
1 yard (yd)	3 ft	0.9144 m
1 rod, pole or perch	5.5 yd	5.0292 m
1 chain	22 yd or 4 rods or 100 links	20.11678 m
1 furlong	10 chains or 220 yd	201.1678 m
1 mile	8 furlongs or 1760 yd	1.60934 km

Square measures

1 sq in	6.452 sq cm	
1 sq ft	144 sq in	0.0929 sq m
1 sq yd	9 sq ft	0.8361 sq m
1 sq rod, pole or perch	30.25 sq yd	25.29 sq m
1 rood	40 sq rods	0.101 hectare
1 acre	4 roods or 10 sq chains or 4840 sq yd	0.405 hectare
1 sq mile	640 acres	2.59 sq km

Index